How to B
Christian

BOOK 1 IN THE REAL CHRISTIANITY SERIES

SEAN KEHOE

realchristianity.com

PUBLISHING DETAILS AND ACKNOWLEDGEMENTS TO BIBLE PUBLISHERS

 Published 2015

How to Become a Christian – Book 1 in the Real Christianity series

Originally published online in May 2014 via our website. This first print edition of the book has been amended from that online version and is copyright 2015.

Published by realchristianity.com of Box Number 5262, 6 Slington House, Rankine Road, Basingstoke, RG24 8PH, United Kingdom

ISBN 978-1-910968-00-0

Scripture quotations in this book are from a variety of translations. The Bible version used is indicated by the relevant initials at the end of each reference, as follows and the following acknowledgements are made to each of the publishers:

NIV = New International Version

KJV = King James Version

RSV = Revised Standard Version

NKJV = New King James Version

ASV = American Standard Version

NASB = New American Standard Bible

ESV = English Standard Version

Image © iStockphoto

Cover design by Kev Jones (kevdesign@me.com)

www.realchristianity.com

DEDICATION

This book is dedicated to my parents, Michael and Bridget Kehoe. Without their example and inspiration I would never have been in a position to write it. I had the privilege to share the good news of Jesus Christ with each of them. I also know that at the end of their lives they both called on His name and were saved. My hope is that many readers will do likewise and genuinely come to know the Lord Jesus Christ for themselves and be saved:

[21]***And everyone who calls***
on the name of the Lord will be saved.
Acts 2:21 (NIV)

HOW TO BECOME A CHRISTIAN

BOOK 1 IN THE REAL CHRISTIANITY SERIES

CONTENTS

ACKNOWLEDGEMENTS

This book could never have been written without the help, influence and teaching of countless people whom God has brought into my life. Without my parents' example I would not have developed the love of the truth. That is what causes a person to prefer to speak the truth no matter how much more difficulty it may cause in comparison to compromise. My Dad in particular would tell the truth as an automatic reflex reaction to any situation. Few people do that, even in churches. I have tried to be completely honest in this book, no matter how many denominational traditions, practices or teachings are contradicted.

I was told the good news about Jesus Christ by an American missionary from Oklahoma called Dave Brown. I will be eternally grateful to him. Thereafter I was influenced at a distance by many Bible teachers. Their tapes and CDs nourished me while the quality of teaching in the churches I attended went down and down.

The most significant Bible teachers in my own life have been Derek Prince, David Pawson, Jacob Prasch, Arnold Fruchtenbaum, Chuck Missler, Dave Hunt and Martyn Lloyd-Jones. Each of them has had a major impact upon me, the value of which is beyond calculation. I am profoundly grateful to them all.

I also thank all of those people who have reviewed and checked the book for me while it was at draft stage. They offered valuable suggestions for how to improve it. Most of them have asked to remain anonymous. Very great help and support came from Chris Hill of CL Ministries. He urged me to complete and publish this book and was a Barnabas to me.

INTRODUCTION

"My people are destroyed for lack of knowledge....."
Hosea 4:6(a) (RSV)

The Bible says that what it has to say about Jesus is good news. The Greek word for that, in English, is 'Gospel'. I have written this book about the Gospel because I couldn't find a book that I could comfortably give to a non-Christian, or to a new or inexperienced Christian, which would tell them what Christianity really is.

There are countless books about specific aspects of Christianity. However, there are very few which tell you frankly what Christianity actually is, or how to become a real Christian. I searched for such a book for years but couldn't find exactly what I wanted. The nearest thing I can find are books written in the nineteenth century or earlier. But they are too old fashioned in their language. Most are out of print anyway.

Most books written since World War Two give only an incomplete account of what the Christian Gospel really is. They leave out or under emphasise many essential parts of the message, such as sin, judgment, Hell, the Lake of Fire, the return of the Lord Jesus Christ to the earth and the Kingdom of God. Most also give little or no emphasis to repentance. The Gospel they usually present has been watered down and reduced to something along the lines of: "*God loves you and wants you to love Him*".

That is very true, but it isn't the Gospel. It is only a fragment of it. There is far more that you need to know, believe and do if you want to become a real Christian. I want in this book to give you all the basics, without leaving anything out merely because it is controversial or worrying. If the Bible is true, then we need to be worried, until and unless we meet God's conditions. Those are that we must repent and believe and find salvation and eternal life through the Lord Jesus Christ.

The aim of this book is to show you how to do that. This book is aimed at a wide audience. I have tried hard to make it simple enough to be understood by complete beginners who know little or nothing about Christianity. But it is mainly aimed at people who have some church background. It is also intended for those who are already real Christians, but know they need to understand the Gospel more clearly and thoroughly, not least in order to be able to explain it to others.

That is frequently necessary because in so many churches the basics are not properly taught. A person can easily be an otherwise mature Christian and know many things, but have only a flimsy grasp of the Gospel itself. It is rather like someone who is doing 'A' level maths but has never been shown how to do long division. So, this book is also aimed at mature Christians.

I have been asked why I have chosen the somewhat controversial title, *'Real Christianity'*, for this series of books and for my website. It is to distinguish the authentic message of the Bible from the many unbiblical alternatives. Those inadequate or false gospels are liberal, sceptical, mystical, ecumenical or incomplete. Most have added in elements from false religions or man-made ideas, traditions and philosophies. In short, I want to focus on what the Bible actually says, as opposed to what men say, or even what churches say.

I also want to present the 'ingredients' of Christianity in the right proportions and with the right amount of emphasis, giving greater focus to the things that Jesus emphasised and less attention to those which He did not. Every false religious belief system tends to do the opposite. In this regard it is worth quoting the distinguished Bible teacher Martyn Lloyd-Jones who said:

"We have somehow got hold of the idea that error is only that which is outrageously wrong; and we do not seem to understand that the most dangerous person of all is the one who does not emphasise the right things".

So in this first book, and in the following books in this series, I aim to cover as much as I can of what the Bible has to say and to be as balanced as possible in doing so. One day I hope to rewrite Book 1 in three or more versions so that it can be made shorter and simpler, and aimed more precisely at each of the above levels of person.

Until then I would ask you to be patient if you feel at any particular point that I am being too detailed or too complex. Press on and read the whole of Book One. Then you will find out why the message of Jesus Christ is called "*the good news*" and how you can be saved by responding to it. That is my hope.

Sean Kehoe
17 August 2015

CHAPTER 1

SOME IMPORTANT POINTS AT THE OUTSET

In writing this first book and indeed, all the other books in this series, I have no desire to offend anyone. I have gone out of my way to try to avoid doing so. However, real Christianity, when understood correctly, is unavoidably offensive. It confronts you with the truth about yourself. Most people don't like that and it will offend them, no matter how politely it is said. That is why Jesus Himself said:

And blessed is he who takes no offense at me
Luke 7:23 (RSV)

Instead of taking offence, why not open-mindedly consider the astonishing claims that Jesus Christ makes about Himself? Try to ask yourself *"Is this true?"* rather than *"Does this suit me?"* Then you will be in the right frame of mind to come to a proper conclusion. Sadly, many people do approach Christianity by asking whether it suits them and is convenient to their lifestyle or ambitions.

If you do that you are unlikely ever to become a Christian, because real Christianity is difficult and challenging. In fact, it could cost you everything, even your life, and it's unlikely ever to be convenient. Jesus never claimed to be convenient.

He does not merely want you to "make some room" for Him on your existing agenda. He wants you to make Him the very center of your life and will not accept any less than that. He offers us a stark choice: to wholeheartedly accept Him as Lord and follow Him, or else to reject Him. There is no middle ground. You cannot be neutral about Jesus Christ.

You must either be totally for Him or against Him. Jesus will not accept us being half-hearted. He wants us to be radical and passionate about Him and His message. He hates it when we are spiritually lukewarm. Listen to what Jesus Himself said about this:

15 I know your deeds, that you are neither cold nor hot. I wish you were either one or the other! 16 So, because you are lukewarm—neither hot nor cold—I am about to spit you out of my mouth.

Revelation 3:15-16 (NIV)

Watered down Christianity

Nowadays, very many writers and speakers present a watered down version of Christianity. Much of the real message is edited out to make it inoffensive. It ends up as a confusing mixture of truth and error. So, I want to tell you about Christianity as it really is, even at the risk of offending you. But that is never my intention. Apostle Paul faced the same problem and he decided to tell people the whole truth, without leaving anything out:

For I did not shrink from declaring to you the whole purpose of God.
Acts 20:27 (NASB)

I want to try to write an accurate and complete explanation of the Christian Gospel (that's Greek for "good news"). I want it to be clear but not simplistic, detailed but not too lengthy, and accessible to people of any educational or religious background. I also want to cover some of the key mistakes people make and the reasons why so many people fail in their Christian life, or even fall away. I also want to give you helpful information on several related topics that I wish someone had told me about when I first became a Christian. Some of that is within this first book, but there is much more in the subsequent books in this series.

Most importantly of all, I have tried to be true to the Bible and to focus on what the Bible itself actually says, rather than on what men say about it, or the traditions of any denomination. I want to tell you the real truth to the best of my ability, without compromising or pulling my punches, and yet as courteously as I can.

I do not want to 'sell' Christianity to you like a used car. I won't use any kind of marketing techniques or try to hide anything from you. I want to just tell you the full truth and hope that you will be open minded enough to see it. That was apostle Paul's approach:

Rather, we have renounced secret and shameful ways; we do not use deception, nor do we distort the word of God. On the contrary, by setting forth the truth plainly we commend ourselves to every man's conscience in the sight of God.
2 Corinthians 4:2 (NIV)

However, it will not be easy. The Devil is real. So are the demons who serve Him. They will do everything they can to confuse you and to blind your eyes spiritually. They want to prevent you reading this book at all. If they can't prevent that, then they will try to stop you from understanding it.

[3]And even if our Gospel is veiled, it is veiled to those who are perishing. [4]The god of this age has blinded the minds of unbelievers, so that they cannot see the light of the Gospel of the glory of Christ, who is the image of God.
2 Corinthians 4:3-4 (NIV)

Also, our own human intellect by itself won't enable us to see the truth about God or spiritual things. Without God's help, the Gospel will seem like foolishness to you and will make no sense:

The man without the Spirit does not accept the things that come from the Spirit of God, for they are foolishness to him, and he cannot understand them, because they are spiritually discerned.

1 Corinthians 2:14 (NIV)

Ask God to help you to see the truth

Pause for a moment and ask God to help you to understand this book and to know whether it is true or not. Without God's help nobody can ever understand the Bible. He has to open your eyes first or you will be blind. Therefore ask Him right now to help you to understand this. That is the kind of prayer He loves to answer quickly:

If any of you lacks wisdom, you should ask God, who gives generously to all without finding fault, and it will be given to you.

James 1:5 (NIV)

So, why not pray broadly along these lines: "*LORD, please help me as I read this book, and especially the passages from the Bible, to know whether it is true. Please open my eyes and my mind to see the truth and to be able to see and abandon any wrong beliefs that I currently have.*"

I hope that after reading this first book, you will have enough relevant information to be able to make an informed choice about Jesus Christ and whether to believe in Him and follow Him. I hope you will then start to study the whole Bible for yourself. This book is written so as to be understandable by those who have never been in a church or heard anything of the Gospel.

However, it is also intended for people who are already involved in churches and who assume they are Christians, but perhaps aren't really saved. It's also for those who have no assurance of salvation. And it's for those who just feel they know less than they should.

Likewise, this book is also for those who are in lukewarm churches where the leaders do not preach the real Gospel but teach instead something watered down or even false. There are many such churches where wishy washy liberal ideas, political correctness, and dead religious rituals have replaced real Christianity.

If you are in such a church it is quite possible you may still be unsaved even if you have been going to church for 50 years. I would therefore invite you to examine yourself to see whether you are really a Christian in the biblical sense, rather than just a "churchgoer". Merely going to church doesn't make you into a real Christian, just as standing in your garage at home doesn't make you into a car.

Are you sure you are a Christian?

So, if you assume that you are a Christian already, I would urge you to think carefully as to whether you really are. Try the quiz type questions in chapter 19. They are designed to help you work out whether you are a real Christian or not. You may find that all you really have is something shallow and superficial.

It could be that what you have is merely "religion," rather than a genuine personal relationship with Jesus Christ. Real Christianity is a personal relationship with Him; not just to know *about* Him, but actually to know *Him.* Perhaps you have that already, or perhaps not. If not, the aim of this book is to try to convince you that you need to know Him and to show you how you can.

Examine yourselves to see whether you are in the faith; test yourselves. Do you not realise that Christ Jesus is in you—unless, of course, you fail the test?
2 Corinthians 13:5 (NIV)

Many who go to church would be offended if asked whether they are a real Christian and truly saved/born again/forgiven. In Britain many would consider it impolite even to ask such a question. Yet it needs to be asked, because throughout all the denominations there is now widespread biblical illiteracy and deep confusion.

Millions of people are misinformed, even those who go to church. Many believe they already know what Christianity is about because they have read books, heard sermons, prayed and even been in leadership positions. To suggest to such a person that what they have been taught is not true, and that they may not be saved, is unlikely to be welcomed.

Yet, there are millions of people worldwide, in all denominations, to whom that applies. They may think they are Christians, but many are mistaken. Instead, what they have believed is just a set of man-made ideas. These come from their own minds, or from tradition, or from misunderstanding the Bible, or from what they have been mistakenly taught by others, rather than from the Bible. Such a person can be sincere and yet still be very wrong. If so, then what they believe in, however sincerely, may not be genuine biblical Christianity.

If you believe yourself to be a Christian already, do try not to be offended. Please read on and weigh up as open-mindedly as you can whether your beliefs are in line with what the Bible actually says. You may be in for a surprise. A very high percentage of people describe themselves as "Christian" when filling in forms. They can't all be genuine Bible-believing Christians. But if not, then what are they?

The answer is that they are at many different levels. Some are genuine Christians. Some are on the way there, exploring and seeking. Some are misinformed but relaxed about it, because they don't realise they are misinformed. Others are completely uninformed. Yet, all these categories of people might put "Christian" on official forms without hesitating.

The 'good news' is primarily about the coming Kingdom of God and about us having the chance to be in it.

I shall try to make another thing clear throughout this book and the other books which follow. That is that the *Gospel* or *good news* of Jesus Christ is primarily about the fact that He has been appointed to be the King and that His Kingdom is coming. We are being offered the opportunity to be part of that Kingdom. If we could not be part of it, then the fact that Jesus is going to set up His Kingdom would not be good news, at least not for us. Conversely, if everybody is going to be part of His Kingdom, regardless of what they believe, then it would not even be news.

There would be nothing worth announcing or making a fuss about if we were all inevitably going to be part of God's Kingdom, without exception. If that was true then none of us would need to be or do anything. There would also be no need to tell us anything and certainly no need for us to respond.

The Kingdom of God is at the very heart of what the 'good news' is all about. When He spoke in shorthand of what His message was basically about, note how often Jesus used the phrase 'the Kingdom of God'. So did the gospel writers. These are just some examples. There are very many more.

As you look at these sample verses you will see that Jesus and the apostles regarded the Kingdom of God as being crucially important. By contrast, in most churches today the Kingdom of God is another of the many things that are rarely mentioned. Even where it is referred to in passing it is not explained or understood. However, the good news we are going to be hearing about needs to be understood in the context of Jesus being a King whose Kingdom is coming. That is why that Kingdom is referred to so often and given so much emphasis:

But he said to them, "I must preach the good news of the kingdom of God to the other towns as well; for I was sent for this purpose."

Luke 4:43 (ESV)

"I tell you, among those born of women none is greater than John. Yet the one who is least in the kingdom of God is greater than he."

Luke 7:28 (ESV)

[1]And he called the twelve together and gave them power and authority over all demons and to cure diseases, [2]and he sent them out to proclaim the kingdom of God and to heal.

Luke 9:1-2 (ESV)

When the crowds learned it, they followed him, and he welcomed them and spoke to them of the kingdom of God and cured those who had need of healing.

Luke 9:11 (ESV)

And Jesus said to him, "Leave the dead to bury their own dead. But as for you, go and proclaim the kingdom of God."

Luke 9:60 (ESV)

Even the prayer known as the *'Lord's prayer'*, or the *'Our Father,'* begins with a direct reference to the Kingdom:

[9]Pray then like this: Our Father who art in Heaven, Hallowed be thy name.
[10]Thy kingdom come. Thy will be done, On earth as it is in Heaven. [11]Give us
this day our daily bread; [12]And forgive us our debts, As we also have forgiven
our debtors; [13]And lead us not into temptation, But deliver us from evil.

Matthew 6:9-13 (RSV)

The writer of the letter to the Hebrews (probably Paul in my view) also referred to the Kingdom:

Therefore let us be grateful for receiving a kingdom that cannot be shaken, and thus let us offer to God acceptable worship, with reverence and awe,

Hebrews 12:28 (ESV)

Also, when the approach and emphasis of apostle Paul's ministry is summed up by Luke at the end of the book of Acts, the Kingdom of God is clearly central to it:

[30]He lived there two whole years at his own expense, and welcomed all who came
to him, [31]proclaiming the kingdom of God and teaching about the Lord Jesus
Christ with all boldness and without hindrance.

Acts 28:30-31 (ESV)

Likewise, apostle Peter emphasised the Kingdom:

For in this way there will be richly provided for you an entrance into the eternal kingdom of our Lord and Saviour Jesus Christ.

2 Peter 1:11(ESV)

That Kingdom which Jesus spoke of will be referred to several times in this book and in the other books in this series. We will try to explain its implications and also to look at the different levels of meaning about it. In one sense, the Kingdom of God has already come. Yet, in another sense, it is still to come. In fact, we can validly say all the following things about the Kingdom of God:

a) **It began in the past**

The Kingdom came nearly 2000 years ago and it includes the whole Earth, which Jesus has won back from the Devil through His death on the cross and His resurrection.

b) **The Kingdom is in operation now**

The Kingdom exists now wherever two or three genuine Christians are gathered together in Jesus' name as part of His body, the Church.

c) **The Kingdom is in the future and will last for 1000 years**

Although the Kingdom already exists, it is also yet to come. That is in the sense that it also includes the literal, physical return of Jesus Christ to this Earth in His resurrection body to rule as King over Israel. He will also reign as King over the whole Earth for 1000 years during what is known as the *'Millennium'*. By the end of that time Jesus will rule over a world which is made up of both Christians and non-Christians. The activity of Satan and his demons will be severely restricted during most of that 1000 year period and there will be perfect government. However, there will still be sin and death, albeit far less than we experience today.

d) **The Kingdom will change again after those 1000 years and become eternal and perfect**

After the Millennium is over the Kingdom will change again. It will then continue for eternity in a completely perfect condition. God Himself will come down to live on this physical Earth and will create what the Bible calls the *'New Jerusalem'*. There will then be perfection on Earth. Every person will be a believer and there will be no sin, death or pain and no demonic activity whatsoever. This is the ultimate and perfected form of the Kingdom. All of us can be part of it if we choose to follow Jesus.

This next passage speaks of the 1000 year period called the Millennium when Jesus will reign over the whole Earth as King:

1Then I saw an angel coming down from Heaven, holding in his hand the key
to the bottomless pit and a great chain. 2And he seized the dragon, that ancient
serpent, who is the devil and Satan, and bound him for a thousand years, 3and
threw him into the pit, and shut it and sealed it over him, so that he might not
deceive the nations any longer, until the thousand years were ended. After that
he must be released for a little while.4Then I saw thrones, and seated on them
were those to whom the authority to judge was committed. Also I saw the souls
of those who had been beheaded for the testimony of Jesus and for the word of
God, and those who had not worshiped the beast or its image and had not
received its mark on their foreheads or their hands. They came to life and
reigned with Christ for a thousand years. 5The rest of the dead did not come to
life until the thousand years were ended. This is the first resurrection. 6Blessed
and holy is the one who shares in the first resurrection! Over such the second
death has no power, but they will be priests of God and of Christ, and they will
reign with him for a thousand years.

Revelation 20:1-6 (ESV)

So, the Kingdom of God began in the past, and is in operation now, but even so, it has not yet fully come. Moreover, even when it does come in a much more dramatic and visible form, when Jesus reigns for 1000 years, it will still not be complete. The Kingdom of God has yet another stage to reach, when it becomes totally perfect, complete and eternal.

We shall examine more of the different aspects of the Kingdom's meaning and significance in the chapters that follow, because it is central to the whole message of the Gospel. Everything that we are going to say in terms of sin, judgment, Hell, the Lake of Fire, repentance, faith, salvation and so on needs to be seen and understood in the context of Jesus being a King. He has a Kingdom, into which we are being allowed to enter and remain for all eternity, provided we repent and put our faith and trust in Him.

If you come from some other non-Christian background such as Hinduism or Islam, or if you are totally secular, please accept my assurance that I have no desire to offend or attack you. I merely want to explain real Christianity as best I can, because you may never have heard any of this before.

One of the distinctive features of Christianity is that Jesus commands us to tell other people about Him. Therefore, I am not writing this just to get people to agree with me. It is to obey Jesus' solemn command that I tell everybody I can about Him, whatever their reaction may be:

18Then Jesus came to them and said, "All authority in Heaven and on earth has
been given to me. 19Therefore go and make disciples of all nations, baptising
them in the name of the Father and of the Son and of the Holy Spirit, 20and

teaching them to obey everything I have commanded you. And surely I am with you always, to the very end of the age."

Matthew 28:18-20 (NIV)

However, you should not believe or accept anything that I say at face value. Everything in this book needs to be checked against what the Bible says. My aim is to present you with an accurate and balanced account. But it is always your responsibility to check whether I have done so, by carefully reading the whole Bible for yourself and in a reliable translation. I would strongly urge you to do what the people of Berea did when the apostle Paul came to speak there:

Now the Bereans were of more noble character than the Thessalonians, for they received the message with great eagerness and examined the Scriptures every day to see if what Paul said was true.

Acts 17:11 (NIV)

CHAPTER 2

WHAT IS THE BIBLE? – HOW DID IT COME TO BE WRITTEN AND WHY SHOULD WE BELIEVE IT?

***16**All Scripture is God-breathed and is useful for teaching, rebuking, correcting and training in righteousness, **17**so that the man of God may be thoroughly equipped for every good work.*

2 Timothy 3:16-17 (NIV)

For the word of God is living and active and sharper than any two-edged sword, and piercing as far as the division of soul and spirit, of both joints and marrow, and able to judge the thoughts and intentions of the heart.

Hebrews 4:12 (NASB)

Throughout this book there will be frequent quotations from the Bible. I have included these to explain and justify the points I am making. However, that begs the question *"Why should we believe what the Bible says?"* In part it is a matter of faith, but only in part. We can prove that the Bible is true. It is an extraordinary and unique book which came into existence by a series of miracles.

Its contents are so amazing that they cannot be simply the words of men. The Bible was physically written by men. Each book or letter reflects the different styles and personalities of those men. But each writer was inspired by God so that they were saying what God wanted to say to us through them. The Bible is therefore, in effect, written by God Himself. It is His own Word to us.

That is why we must value it and devote our lives to learning it. It is infallible. Everything in it is true. It is not merely some men's opinions. It is the truth, told to us by God Himself. That puts it into a class of its own. By reading the Bible you can find out what God Himself wants to say to you. Once they realise that, how can any wise person not want to read it and reread it to find out what God wants to say?

Therefore, I urge you to read the whole Bible for yourself. Look how it is amazingly interwoven, even though it was written in stages over about 1,500 years by 40 different people. Even a modern computer would not be able to arrange all the countless interconnections. It is like a "relational database" in computing terms. It is all cross referenced with itself and inter-related. There is no other book like it, anywhere in the world.

Who wrote the Bible and when?

The Bible consists of 66 separate books or letters written by 40 different men, starting with Moses in about 1,500 BC. He wrote the first five books of the Bible: Genesis, Exodus, Leviticus, Numbers and Deuteronomy. These five books are, together, called "*The Law of Moses*" or "*The Torah*". In the book of Genesis, Moses gives the history of the world from the first moment of creation, right through to the formation of the Jewish nation, from the family line of Abraham, Isaac and Jacob.

Then, in the second book, Exodus, Moses tells of how the Israelites were set free by God from Egypt where they had been kept as slaves. These first five books are foundational to the whole Bible. Everything else builds on them. The sixth book is written by Joshua. He tells of how he took over the leadership of the nation of Israel after Moses died and then led the Israelites into the Promised Land, establishing the nation of Israel, which is at the very centre of God's plan for our salvation and also for Jesus' future Kingdom.

It then continues, book by book, until we come to the book of Malachi, which is the last book of what we call the "Old Testament". When we refer to the "*Old Testament*", we mean all those books from Genesis through to Malachi which are accepted as Scripture by the Jewish people. By "*Scripture*" we mean something which is effectively written by God, because the human author is inspired by God to write it. That is what happened with each of the men who wrote the books of the Old and New Testaments. I have mentioned Moses and Joshua. Each of them were leaders of Israel. However, many different kinds of men wrote the other books.

Most of them were what we call "*Prophets*". That means someone who was recognised by the Jewish people as having been sent by God to speak on God's behalf to the people. In a certain sense, we can all do that from time to time. We can speak to our neighbours or to the people at work. God can use anyone to speak for Him. However, a prophet in the biblical sense is someone who does this on a much larger scale. Many of the men who wrote the Bible were prophets, such as Isaiah or Jeremiah.

They told the Jewish people what God wanted to say and they wrote it down so that we can now all benefit from it. One amazing thing the Bible does is to tell us about the future. A very high percentage of the Bible consists of prophecy. God does this for a number of reasons. Firstly, he wants us to understand what lies ahead so that we can be equipped and prepared to face it. Secondly, He wants to prove the truth of the Bible.

He does this by giving hundreds of different prophecies about what will happen. Then, as those come to be fulfilled to the letter, it verifies the truth of the Bible generally. No other book in the history of the world has ever been able to do anything even remotely like this. Only the Bible can tell you what will happen in the future. About 80% of the prophecies in the Bible have already been fulfilled. A large number of them had to do with the birth, life and death of Jesus Christ Himself. That is because He is the central figure of the whole Bible. Almost everything in it, from beginning to end is, in some way, pointing to Him. However, prophecies are also made about many other things to do with the future of Israel and of the whole world.

Thus if 80% of the prophecies have been fulfilled exactly in every detail, then we ought to be interested in what the other 20% of the prophecies are about. We can expect them to be literally fulfilled as well. So, if you are wise, one of your purposes in reading the Bible will be to learn what it has to say about the future. Then you can know what history is leading towards.

The Bible is also about the whole history of God's past dealings with the human race, but especially with His chosen people, Israel. That is a central theme. However, it also covers a whole range of other different subjects and types of writing, i.e. history, law, poetry, letters, instruction, doctrine and teaching/explanation.

There is also "*wisdom literature*", such as the books of Proverbs and Ecclesiastes. These books contain a wealth of instruction on how to live successfully. They cover business, marriage, money, work, farming, education, commerce, military matters, civil government, village life, neighbourliness, health, and so on. The advice given will revolutionise your whole life if you follow it.

People are willing to take advice from all sorts of different people, many of whom may not even be qualified to give it. Yet the advice given in Proverbs and Ecclesiastes comes from God Himself. If you listen to it and put it into practice, it is life changing. No other book can offer you that.

How to find references in the Bible

Underneath each Bible quotation I put what is called a "reference". For example, at the beginning of this chapter there is a quotation, i.e. 2 Timothy 3:16-17. That means verses 16 and 17 from chapter three of apostle Paul's second letter to a man called Timothy. We will look now at how a Bible reference is broken down so you can see what it means. The first part of the reference gives you the name of the book or letter. For example, it might say "Genesis" or "Romans" or "Revelation".

Each of the 66 books of the Bible has got its own shorthand name like that which we use for convenience. So instead of saying "Apostle Paul's letter to the

Christians in Rome" we simply say "Romans", i.e. naming it after the recipients of the letter. Many of the books in the Old Testament are instead named after their human author, such as Isaiah, Jeremiah, Ezekiel, Daniel etc.

However if the author has written more than one book or letter, or if the recipient has been sent more than one letter, then you will find a number at the front. For example we say 1 Timothy and 2 Timothy. That number at the front tells you whether it is the first or second letter to Timothy. Likewise, where the letter is named after its author, but he has written more than one letter, then the number at the front tells you which letter it is.

For example apostle Peter wrote two letters so we say "1 Peter" and "2 Peter". The apostle John wrote three letters, so we call these "1 John", "2 John" and "3 John". However, John's gospel is just called "John". The next part of the reference is the chapter number. So, if we say "Daniel 3" then we mean the 3rd chapter of Daniel. If however we extend the reference to say Daniel 3:1 then we mean verse 1 within chapter 3 of Daniel.

When the Bible was first written each book or letter was just one continuous whole. They were not broken down into chapters or verses at all. Since then, for convenience, and so that we can quote more easily, men have artificially subdivided the Bible. It has been cut into large blocks which we call chapters and then into small chunks which are called verses.

That is how you can now find anything that you want to quote from. This has many advantages but it also has some disadvantages. The main problem of thinking in terms of quotations and references is that it encourages people just to read little snippets of the Bible in isolation. There is a danger in that. It is possible to take what is being said out of context and misunderstand it.

The safest policy is to read the Bible in whole books or letters. Then you get the context and background and understand what is said in its proper setting. Even the things we say in day to day life can only be properly understood if we hear the context and setting in which the statement was made. The same is true with the Bible.

Therefore it is wise to try to read an entire letter in one sitting so that you get the full flow of what is being said. Often each part of the letter or book is drawing upon and referring to other parts of that letter or book. They hold together as a whole document. Isn't that exactly how you would read a letter written to you today? You wouldn't normally expect to just look at single sentences on their own. If you did, you could easily misunderstand things.

How to interpret the Bible – adopting *"the golden rule"* as our starting point

We can get ourselves into an awful mess by not knowing how to interpret the Bible. However, we can avoid most of those problems by adopting the following approach as our starting point. This is often referred to as *"the golden rule"*. That is to simply **take everything that is said at its literal, ordinary, face value meaning unless the words used, or the context, clearly indicate that you are meant to do otherwise**.

Most of the time the Bible simply means exactly what it is saying in plain and literal terms. That, therefore, is how it should usually be taken. However, there are other times when the Bible is obviously using metaphors, analogies or other figures of speech. You need to recognise devices like that or you will miss part of the meaning. However, even when the Bible is using a figure of speech, the message being conveyed is still the truth.

Even in our own everyday language we instinctively know when to take a thing literally and when devices like metaphors or analogies are being used. For example, if someone said to you *"It is raining very heavily"* you would know that that is a literal, face value statement which means exactly what it says. There is no literary technique or device being used there. It is plain speech.

If however that person said *"It is raining cats and dogs"*, you would know instinctively that in the English language that is a figure of speech. It is obviously not to be taken literally, because there are no cats or dogs falling from the sky. However, that does not mean that the statement is untrue. It is still true that it is raining heavily. It is simply that the speaker has chosen to use a figure of speech to express that fact more vividly.

Thus, in both cases, it is literally true that it is raining heavily. Now let's look at some examples of different types of speech from the Bible: When Jesus said to a woman who was caught in adultery *"Neither do I condemn you. Go and sin no more"*, He was just using simple direct speech. He meant exactly what He said and there were no figures of speech involved.

However, when Jesus said *"I am the door"* or *"I am the vine and you are the branches"* He was using figures of speech. Yet the meaning that He is conveying in those phrases is still true. Therefore it is not literally true that Jesus is a door, but it is true that He is "*the*" door. He means that He is the only way that we can get to God or find salvation.

Likewise, He is not literally a vine, and we are not literally branches, but it is factually true that He is what that figure of speech meant. It means He is the one and only source from which we can obtain eternal life. Apart from Him we cannot have that life, just as a branch cannot live unless it is attached to the vine. If you apply the golden rule of interpretation as your starting point throughout the Bible, you will save yourself from a lot of mistakes and problems. Everything in the Bible is true. You simply need to use common sense and read everything in context in order to get the proper meaning.

The Bible is infallible

Beware of people who "explain away" the Bible or assume that it does not really mean what it says. The Bible always means what it says and is always true. There are no errors or contradictions in it. That is one of the reasons why we know that it is inspired by God, because it is 100% perfect.

By that I mean that it is perfect in its original Hebrew or Greek, i.e. the languages it was written in. The Bible is not necessarily free of errors when we go on to translate it into English. When we translate it we can go wrong, unless we have good scholarship and follow the golden rule, as above, as our starting point for interpreting it.

The Bible is factually true and is meant to be taken literally. However, we *also* need to recognise things such as types and prophetic patterns when they arise.

Most of the time we are meant to take the Bible literally. We are supposed to accept the plain, everyday meaning of the words on the page, unless a figure of speech is clearly being used. That approach should always be our *starting point.* However, we should not *stop* there. We need to be aware that the Bible was written by Jewish men, not by Westerners with a Greek way of thinking.

The prophets and apostles had a Hebraic mind set and they engaged in what is known in Hebrew as '*midrash*'. Therefore they were very comfortable about seeing additional layers of meaning, over and above, *but not instead of*, the plain, literal meaning.

This Jewish approach to interpreting the Bible is explained more fully in Book Three, which deals with how we are meant to study the Bible as a whole. However, for our present purposes, let it suffice to say that *as well as* taking the Bible literally and accepting that the plain, everyday meaning is factually true, we *also* need to be alert to see *types* and *prophetic patterns* wherever they genuinely arise.

A '*type'* is where a person or event is a shadow or forerunner of some later person or event. So, the type illustrates something that is also going to be true of the later person or event. A classic example of this would be the many parallels between the lives of Joseph, the son of Jacob, and Jesus Christ.

I will give a few examples of what I am referring to. Firstly, Joseph and Jesus were both betrayed for pieces of silver. Secondly, Joseph was greatly loved by his father, just as Jesus was greatly loved by His Father. But, Joseph and Jesus were both rejected by their brothers. In Joseph's case it was his natural brothers. In the case of Jesus, it was His brothers in a much wider sense, i.e. the Jewish people.

Thirdly, Joseph's brothers did not recognise him when they first saw him, just as most of Jesus' brothers, the Jewish people, did not recognise Him when He was first amongst them. Yet, the second time they saw him, Joseph made himself known to his brothers. He revealed his true identity to them in an instant and they all immediately realised who he really was. They also repented of how they had treated him. Prior to that they were completely unaware that the person standing right in front of them was their own brother, Joseph.

That is very similar to what Jesus will do in the future when He makes Himself known to His brothers, the Jewish people. They will all suddenly recognize Him as their own Messiah. Then every Jewish person who is alive at that time will turn to Him in sorrow and repentance and they will all believe in Him. They will repent and believe in Him collectively, as a whole nation. Fourthly, Joseph took a Gentile bride, called Asenath, just as Jesus takes a Gentile bride, namely the Church.

There are very many more of these similarities. When seen in their entirety they are startling and we realise that we are meant to see Joseph as a type, shadow or forerunner of Jesus. The events of his life help to explain and clarify many things about the life and ministry of Jesus. Having said that, it is important to emphasise that we cannot base any *doctrine* on such types or patterns. However, they can certainly help to *illustrate* doctrines that are already expressly stated elsewhere.

One of the problems we face in the churches is that some of us make the major mistake of refusing to take the Bible literally. Others make the smaller, but still important, error of *only ever* seeing the literal meaning and never accepting that it contains anything *in addition to* the literal facts. The correct position is that the underlying facts are literally true, unless they are clearly a figure of speech.

However, we can and should go further than that. We should be open minded to take note of these types and prophetic patterns, *over and above* accepting the plain, literal, factual meaning of the words used. When you come across unusual things in the Bible such as miracles, demons, or anything supernatural, then accept them as literally true. Do not try to explain them away or assume that they did not really happen. Millions of people think that way because they have been trained to do so.

For example, when Moses parted the Red sea, or Jesus fed 5000 men, (plus thousands of woman and children), using a boy's packed lunch of loaves and fishes, *that is exactly what happened.* The Bible means you to take that literally, as word for word what actually took place. There is no figure of speech involved, as you will see if you look at the plain text with common sense and honesty.

In this book, I have included a lot of quotations from the Bible. I often include a series of different passages all on the same issue or all proving the same point. If you have only got limited time it is possible in most cases to look at the first one or two passages in the list and skip over the rest. You will get the main meaning that way. However, if you do have enough time to do so then you will benefit from reading them all.

I frequently include multiple passages because I want to give you exposure to many parts of the Bible that you may never have come across. Sometimes I also just want to prove my point conclusively by showing several references to support it. However, it is also to get you to see how the Bible fits together and explains itself.

You will see that best by reading all the quotations, rather than just the first one or two. However, please do not feel obliged to do so. It is not essential. I also want to encourage you to begin to believe that it is realistic to think that you could read the whole Bible yourself. Many people never get to know the whole Bible. They assume that is for others to do.

I know a person whom I challenged about reading the Bible for himself. He only dips into it in places that he likes, and avoids the rest. His response was that other people, whom he trusts, have read those other books or letters and they can tell him what they are about. That is not the right way to approach the Bible. You must tackle it for yourself. No matter what your level of education is, your aim should be to study, and become familiar with, the whole Bible. God wants you to read it all, and many times over, until you really know it. You may think at the moment that that is too ambitious, but you can achieve it, if you set your mind to it.

The Bible -v- men's ideas and traditions

I am going to urge you throughout this book always to focus on what the Bible says, not on what men say and not on what your denomination says either. If you form a view or believe something, let it be solely because the Bible says it. Do not believe anything merely because it is customary, traditional or cultural, or even because it is what your church leader or denomination says. Jesus had this to say to those who ignore the Bible and, instead, follow man-made traditions:

[6]And He said to them, "Rightly did Isaiah prophesy of you hypocrites, as it is
written: 'This people honours me with their lips, but their heart is far away from
me.[7]'But in vain do they worship me, teaching as doctrines the precepts of men.'
[8]"Neglecting the commandment of God, you hold to the tradition of men." [9]He
was also saying to them, "You are experts at setting aside the commandment of
God in order to keep your tradition."

Mark 7:6-9 (NASB)

Many of us can easily see how the Pharisees of Jesus' day got things badly wrong by ignoring the Bible and instead focusing on men's ideas, customs and traditions. Yet, that is exactly what we do, even today. In fact, we probably do it more than the Pharisees did. Ask yourself in relation to any belief or opinion you hold, *"Where did I get this idea from? Was it from the Bible or from tradition?"*

The answers may surprise you. It is amazing how many things we say, do and think that we imagine to be biblical but which are, in fact, just man-made traditions adopted at various points in the history of the church. The most obvious example of that is the Roman Catholic Church. It has countless non-biblical traditions, such as penance, purgatory, saints, the Virgin Mary, confession, mass, priests, nuns, bishops, cardinals, popes, images, relics, rosary beads, holy days of obligation, sacraments, etc, etc.

None of those things are in the Bible. Yet, millions believe and practice them and are quite unaware that they actually contradict what the Bible says. In case anyone thinks that I am singling out the Roman Catholic Church for criticism, let me say that I have also found that same tendency to form non-biblical traditions and customs in every denomination I have ever come across, albeit on a lesser scale, and I have found it in myself too.

Every unbiblical idea or tradition has to be resisted and rejected. The best way to do that is to insist that every proposition be proved from the Bible, and not from any other authority, however eminent or famous. It doesn't matter what the church is or who the person is; if what is being said or done has no biblical basis, then reject it.

CHAPTER 3

GOD'S CHARACTER – WHO HE IS AND WHAT HE IS LIKE

Great is our LORD, and abundant in power;
his understanding is beyond measure.
Psalm 147:5 (RSV)

[3]***"For I proclaim the name of the LORD; Ascribe greatness to our God!*** [4]***"The***
Rock! His work is perfect, For all His ways are just; A God of faithfulness and without injustice, Righteous and upright is He.
Deuteronomy 32:3-4 (NIV)

The LORD is faithful in all his words,
and gracious in all his deeds.
Psalm 145: 13b (RSV)

The aim of this chapter is to prevent some misunderstandings that might arise in the chapters that follow. In the first part of this book I will say a lot about the severity of God's judgment. He is going to punish our sin and send the majority of the human race to Hell and then from there to the Lake of Fire for eternity. I have had to devote a large proportion of this book to explaining those awful things.

We therefore need this chapter at the start of the book to provide some balance, so that people do not misunderstand God's character. Let me say, right at the start, that God is infinitely loving. Love is so important a part of God's nature that apostle John goes so far as to say that He is love:

Whoever does not love does not know God, because God is love.
1 John 4:8 (NIV)

What's more, God is good and is full of loving kindness and compassion which never end:

Give thanks to the LORD, for He is good,
For His loving kindness is everlasting.
Psalm 136:1 (NASB)

The LORD is just in all his ways, and kind in all his doings.
Psalm 145:17 (RSV)

He is also gracious, merciful, just, gracious and slow to anger:

[8]The LORD is merciful and gracious,
slow to anger and abounding in steadfast love.
Psalm 103:8 (RSV)

So, we have seen that God is loving, good, gracious, merciful, patient, compassionate and kind. However, I have no option but to talk as well about God's perfect holiness and, therefore, the severity of His judgment on sin. Those things are also real. But, there is a danger that if the reader has to focus for several chapters on such things he may lose heart and stop reading.

If so, he may be left with a false impression about God's character. He might see Him only as a judge and not see any of the other aspects of what and who God is, such as a compassionate Father and a friend. Please try to look at God in a rounded and balanced way. Take note of all of His many characteristics, not only His holiness and severity, but His love and kindness as well.

Consider therefore the kindness and sternness of God: sternness to those who fell, but kindness to you, provided that you continue in his kindness. Otherwise, you also will be cut off.

Romans 11:22 (NIV)

Despite the statement by apostle John about God's love, which I have quoted earlier, the way the Bible *introduces* us to God is never to emphasise His love. Instead the Bible focuses, first of all, on His holiness and the fact that He will judge us. That is how Jesus and the apostles spoke to unbelievers. They spoke in that way even to the Jewish people, who believed in God, but had not yet realised that Jesus was their Messiah.

We have to meet God first at the level of His holiness, and to realise how we have wronged Him. Only then can we go on to know Him as a Father and a friend. So, I have tried to take that approach in this book and to look at things in that order. Remember that when apostle John was writing those words about God's love, he was writing to Christians who had already repented, believed, been baptised, received the Holy Spirit, and come to know God for themselves.

He was not writing to unbelievers or even to Jews who had not yet accepted Jesus as Messiah. So, with such a mature, believing, Christian audience John felt able to say a good deal about God's love. He knew that his audience already understood about God's holiness. I cannot make that assumption in writing this book. Neither could Jesus when He spoke to the crowds during His earthly ministry. Those crowds contained at least some people who did not understand the truth or realise the seriousness of their situation. That is why Jesus always began by speaking of sin, judgment and Hell first. That has to be the starting point.

We must approach God first with respect, not familiarity

God loves you and wants an intimate and personal relationship with you. But before you can have that you must first respect Him for what He really is and honour Him as the Lord, King and Judge of the universe. In the Western world today, the holiness and severity of God are not emphasised. They are not even mentioned at all in many churches. But they need to be, because if we want to get to know God we must begin by respecting and fearing Him. It won't work properly any other way.

It is like meeting a very important man for the first time. Imagine you went to work for Winston Churchill, the war-time Prime Minister, and were about to meet him on your first day at work. You would not approach him with familiarity or address him on first name terms at that stage. There would be a formality to the relationship to begin with. Your main feelings would be respect, and also some fear. You would, in the beginning, have to relate to him in his capacity as Prime Minister and as your boss, not as a friend.

There is no other way for it to happen. However, as time passes, you would begin to form a personal relationship and get to really know him in a more rounded sense, as he truly is. You would see other aspects of his personality and find out about other areas of his life, besides being Prime Minister. The people who worked for Churchill always began by fearing him, but ended up devoted to him.

Maintain a balanced view of God

The example of Winston Churchill is also appropriate to illustrate the fact that God is multi-faceted and has many different aspects to His character. Although Churchill was a hugely powerful man, feared by many, making decisions that affected the whole world, he was also a merciful, kind, literary, artistic, generous, amusing and playful person. He loved to make jokes and play tricks on those he knew and worked with. He was loved and admired as well as feared and respected.

If you saw Churchill as one-dimensional you would be badly misunderstanding Him. That is even more true of God. If you wanted to, you could write books about Churchill, each one of which could focus on just one aspect of his life, his interests and his achievements. He lived to be 90 and in that time he was all of the following things, and much more besides:

He was a son, schoolboy, soldier, journalist, prisoner of war, politician, husband, father, Trade Secretary, Home Secretary, First Lord of the Admiralty, a soldier again, unemployed, Colonial Secretary, Chancellor of the Exchequer, a back bench MP, a voice crying in the wilderness, then at the Admiralty again, then Prime Minister in war time, then Leader of the Opposition, then Prime Minister in peace time, then a back bench MP again. During all of that time he was also a writer, a historian, a pilot, a wit, a traveller, a painter, a bricklayer, and a keeper of cats, fish and pigs!

So, if you focused, on just one or other of those roles or aspects of his life, then whatever you wrote would be true up to a point but it wouldn't be the whole truth. For example, if you were to say *"Churchill was an artist"* it would be a true statement. However, it would be very far from being the whole truth. Therefore, to say it as if it was the whole truth would be seriously misleading.

People have actually written books solely on what he achieved as an artist, examining the many watercolours that he painted. There's nothing wrong with that. Yet it would obviously be very wrong to think of him *only* as an artist. It would be equally invalid to think of him only as a politician or only as a writer or only as a soldier or only as a husband/father/grandfather etc.

Don't make the mistake of focusing on just one aspect of God's nature

Many of us make the same mistake with God. We tend to think of him solely in terms of one favourite aspect. Usually people like to dwell upon God's love, or His mercy, or his forgiveness. Of course all of that is true. But it is even more misleading than in Churchill's case if we focus only on one aspect of God. We need to see Him in the round, in every possible aspect and appreciate every feature. Then we will have a much truer picture of Him.

Like God, Churchill related to different people in different ways. When he was dealing with cabinet ministers and generals he could be stern and rigorous. Yet, if he was dealing with ordinary humble people then he would reveal a much softer and gentler side of his nature. For example, Churchill was very easily moved to tears.

On one occasion he was out inspecting bomb damage during the 'blitz'. He saw some houses, newly destroyed, and their occupants standing in the road, homeless. As he stood looking at the scene he began to weep. The public standing nearby were surprised, having heard his defiant and resolute speeches on the radio. His display of emotion and tenderness did not fit their image of him.

Yet, there was no contradiction in any of that, because he was all of those things. During World War One Churchill fought for a time at the rank of Lieutenant Colonel. One night he caught a man who had fallen asleep on sentry duty. He could have had him shot for that, but he had mercy on him and spared the soldier's life, because he felt pity for him. Yet, this is the same man who later ordered the daily bombing of German cities.

On another occasion Churchill was having a meeting at 10 Downing Street involving various ministers including the Foreign Secretary Sir Anthony Eden. His grandson aged 5 was visiting at the time and Churchill allowed him into the room. It was a small group meeting in a sitting room. His grandson hid behind an armchair and rolled up some pieces of paper and threw them at Churchill's head. He knew what was happening, but pretended that he thought it was the Foreign Secretary doing it.

He began to rebuke Sir Anthony Eden saying *"Foreign Secretary, will you stop throwing those pieces of paper!"* This delighted his grandson who then threw more pieces of paper, resulting in more protests to the Foreign Secretary, to the amusement of all those present. Yet, this was the same man who spoke in the gravest and most serious tone about life and death issues for national defence.

Therefore we see that even whilst operating as Prime Minister, there were intimate aspects of Churchill's character that he displayed to those who knew him. But you could not approach him on your first meeting with him in the same way his grandson did, or as his staff did, who knew him well. You could not be familiar or jocular with Churchill on your first day at work and hope to get away with it.

You first had to approach him in his capacity as Prime Minister and start to get to know him. Then you could gradually discover all of the many other aspects of his character. It is rather like that with God. He is holy and righteous. He hates sin. He will be our judge one day. Most people will be condemned by Him and sent to the Lake of Fire, because that is how seriously He views sin. Therefore when we approach God for the first time it must be with reverence and respect.

There must also be sorrow and repentance for our many sins against Him and other people. We can't approach Him in a casual or presumptuous manner. Neither can we be familiar with God, or take liberties. Yet, for those who do know Him and have repented, they can start, from that point onwards, to get to know Him in a much wider way. They can learn about the many other aspects of God's character and personality, in addition to His holiness and awesome power.

God is a Trinity - three Persons who, together, form One God

Although the Bible speaks of God as being One, it also makes clear that there are three distinct and separate Persons. Together they make up what we call the "*Trinity*". They are God the Father, The Son of God and the Holy Spirit. The word "Trinity" is not used in the Bible, but it is a good word to summarise what the Bible does say about God. He is three Persons, but One God.

The word Trinity means "*tri-unity*" or "*three-in-oneness*". The New Testament gives us a much clearer understanding of the Trinity than the Old Testament. But even in the Old Testament there are many passages which clearly suggest that God exists as more than one person. Let's look at a few examples where God is referred to in plural terms. Note in each case the use of the words "*Us*" or "*Our*":

Then God said, "Let Us make man in Our image, according to Our likeness; ...."

Genesis 1:26(a) (NASB)

Then the LORD God said, "Behold, the man has become like one of Us, knowing good and evil;..."

Genesis 3:22(a) (NASB)

Come, let Us go down and there confuse their language, so that they will not understand one another's speech.

Genesis 11:7 (NASB)

In each of these verses God is speaking in terms which make clear that He is more than one person. It is not simply the so called "Royal we" that the Queen uses. That is something our own British royalty have used, but it is not found anywhere in the Old Testament in relation to the Kings of Israel or Judah. So it can't be explained away in those terms. God is clearly speaking to, and of, Himself in plural terms. Also, there are many passages where God is speaking but He is clearly speaking to another Person who is also God. Let's look at some examples, though there are many more:

6 Your throne, O God, is forever and ever;
A scepter of uprightness is the scepter of Your kingdom.
7 You have loved righteousness and hated wickedness;
Therefore God, Your God, has anointed You
With the oil of joy above Your fellows.

Psalm 45:6-7 (NASB)

In the passage above it initially refers to the Son of God (Jesus). We are told that God (i.e. the Father) has anointed Him. This passage cannot make sense any other way. Two Persons, both of whom are God, are being spoken of. However, they are distinct from each other. Let's look at two more passages from the Old Testament where the Holy Spirit is also referred to as God. But He is, likewise, differentiated from the other Person being referred to as God:

Yet they rebelled
and grieved his Holy Spirit.
So he turned and became their enemy
and he himself fought against them.

Isaiah 63:10 (NIV)

In the verse above the Holy Spirit is referred to but a distinction is made between Him and God. See also this next verse, where a distinction is drawn between "*The Spirit of the Lord God*" (which is the Holy Spirit), "*the LORD*" (which is the Father) and the person speaking, which is Jesus Himself. So, all three Persons of the Trinity are involved in this verse. Jesus is speaking and He is referring to the Holy Spirit and the Father:

The Spirit of the Lord GOD is upon me,
Because the LORD has anointed me
To bring good news to the afflicted;
He has sent me to bind up the brokenhearted,
To proclaim liberty to captives
And freedom to prisoners;

Isaiah 61:1 (NASB)

Then, when we get to the New Testament, more is revealed. The fact that God is three Persons is made very clear:

The grace of the Lord Jesus Christ, and the love of God, and the fellowship of the Holy Spirit, be with you all.

2 Corinthians 13:14 (NASB)

In this verse all three Persons of the Trinity are named separately and all three are clearly presented as being divine. It cannot be read any other way. The same is true in this next passage from Ephesians:

4There is one body and one Spirit, just as also you were called in one hope of
your calling; 5one Lord, one faith, one baptism, 6one God and Father of all who
is over all and through all and in all.

Ephesians 4:4-6 (NASB)

There are many more such passages. Please refer to chapter 15 for more examples of verses which prove and help to explain the Trinity.

Summarising what we mean by the Trinity

In short, what we mean is that:

a) God is three Persons

b) Each Person is fully God

c) Nevertheless, there is only One God.

To understand the Trinity we must accept all three of the above points. Each one is essential. So, it would not be correct to say that the members of the Trinity form one Person, because there are three Persons. But it is true to say that those three Persons together are one God. Therefore, it is appropriate to refer to God as "He".

Why does it matter that God is three Persons but still One God?

The doctrine of the Trinity is vitally important for many reasons. Thus, when cults such as the Jehovah's Witnesses reject these facts, they are rejecting something which is essential to the genuine Christian faith. Let's look at a few reasons why this matters so much:

a) If Jesus was merely a created being like we are, and not fully God, then how could He save us? How could He ever have lived a sinless life and how could His death on the cross have paid the price for our sins if He was only a man? (See chapters 10 and 11 for more details).

b) If Jesus was not fully God in His own right, then how could we ever pray to Him or worship Him? We would be praying to, or worshipping, a mere man, which we must never do.

c) If there is no Trinity then it would mean that before He created the angels and mankind, God would have had nobody else with whom to relate. Yet we know that God did have personal relationships before He created any of us. He did so within the Trinity. Each of the three Persons related perfectly to each other. And, they always have done, for all eternity past.

What are the distinctions or differences between each of the three Persons of the Trinity or 'Godhead'?

In terms of their nature, character, attributes and power, each of the three Persons of the Trinity are equal. They are each divine and are all knowing and all powerful. That is why Jesus, said: "*If you have seen me you have seen the Father.*" So, the Father, the Son and the Holy Spirit do not differ in their essence. But they do differ in the roles they play and the functions they have as they relate to the world and to us as believers.

We see in the Bible that God the Father spoke the words which brought the universe into existence. However, God the Son was also active in the process of creation. He brought the Father's words to completion. We also see that the Holy Spirit played a different role in the creation of the world. He was "moving" or "hovering" over the face of the waters and taking part in what was occurring.

Then, when it comes to the salvation of mankind, all three Persons of the Trinity played different roles. The Father planned the redemption and sent the Son into the world. Jesus, the Son of God, carried out that plan. He became a man and died on the cross while the Father and the Holy Spirit watched. Imagine how firmly they must have held back their natural desire to intervene and stop the crucifixion. Even in their restraint they played their part.

The current role of the Holy Spirit is mainly to bring to completion the salvation of individuals and the development of the Church. He is fulfilling what was planned by the Father and carried out by the Son. Until we die and meet God face to face, we will never be able to properly understand this mystery of God being three Persons in One. It is beyond our minds to grasp it. Even so, the Bible tells us that it is true.

God is formed from the perfect union and co-operation of three distinct Persons. Each of them is fully divine and eternal. They relate so closely together and are so perfectly united, that it is right to say that they are One. We cannot really understand that. We must just accept it because the Bible says it is true. Perhaps we could see marriage as a partial analogy here.

The Bible presents marriage as a bond or union which is so solemn and profound that although the husband and wife are two people they are, in a certain sense, viewed as being one. Therefore as we seek to form a correct and biblical understanding of who and what God is and how He operates, let us always remember that He is three Persons. Sometimes when we see different aspects of God's character being emphasised it may be because one of the Persons of the Trinity is being focused upon at that moment.

God's character

God is not just a disembodied "force" or electrical power, as some people imagine Him to be. He has personality, and emotions. He feels love and anger. He can also be hurt and grieved and made to feel sad, just like you, even though He is the God who created the whole universe. He also displays every virtue to an infinite degree. He is more kind than you could ever imagine. Likewise He is utterly generous, good, gentle, patient, loving, and faithful.

If you imagine the best person you have ever met, they are only a pale reflection of what God is like. God's kindness is infinitely greater than any kindness that you have ever come across from a human being. His love is infinitely greater that any love that you have ever known. Therefore, as well as being our King and our Judge, God is also our Father. Jesus sometimes even addressed God as "*Abba*". That means "Daddy", as a child would say. We can do the same.

This amazing God, who created everything, is also our Father

To be allowed to be so intimate as to call God "Father" is a great privilege. Consider how much it means. The very God who created the whole universe is inviting you and me to relate to Him as a child relates to their father. He wants to have a one to one relationship with you which is close, tender and personal. There are even ways and times when God plays and jokes with us and deals with us softly.

Yet, at the same time, He still remains the awesome, all-powerful King of the universe. God is far from being one-dimensional. He is the most brilliant person in the world. He created everything that we know. If you have ever studied science, you will realise how complex it is. Yet God did not simply learn about science. He created all the rules of science. Can you imagine how indescribably intelligent He must be?

Not only did He create the universe in scientific terms, but He also designed it in artistic terms. Look at how beautiful everything is. It is obvious that God is an artist. There is nothing that He has made that is not beautiful. That is true of the stars and planets, the sun, moon and sky and of all the plants, mountains, lakes, animals, birds, fish and insects on this earth. Every one of these is a work of art in itself.

Taken together, they are an astonishing masterpiece of design. God is a complex mixture of every virtue and quality. He is a genius of a kind that we cannot begin to imagine. He is in charge of the entire universe and yet is able at the same time to relate individually to everybody on the earth. He knows about everything that is happening throughout the whole of creation.

At this moment He knows exactly what is happening on every planet and where each one is on its orbit around the sun. At the same time, He also knows what a particular insect is doing that is sitting on a leaf somewhere in the Amazon rain forest. He is watching it, and He is watching every other creature too. He knows what every atom is doing and what every electron is doing as it orbits around each proton. He is observing it all happening simultaneously, because He is fascinated by His entire creation and enjoys its beauty. What does that tell you about the capacity of His mind? It is beyond calculation.

The kindness of God and the interest He takes in our lives

At the same time He knows you personally. He knows everything that you have ever done, and every thought you have ever had. He knows your needs and what is best for you. There have been times where I have been astonished at how much

God cares for me as an individual. He finds time, amongst everything else He has to think about, to consider all the little things that I need.

For example, when I was a student I was working one summer as a gardener. I had no car at the time and used to walk a few miles each day to my customers. One day I was intending to go knocking on doors to ask if people wanted any gardening work doing. I set off in the morning and realised, after walking about two miles, that I had forgotten to bring a pen. That bothered me, because I needed one to write down phone numbers etc. As I was thinking over this little problem, I prayed and asked God to help me to sort it out.

Then, to my amazement, I walked on just 10 yards or so and I found, lying on the pavement, a biro pen that someone had dropped! It was just a cheap one, but it solved my problem. You may say that was just a coincidence. But I knew immediately that God had been concerned for my little problem and wanted to help me.

He treated me as a parent might treat a small child. He saw my need and He met it and looked after me. Isn't that how we are with our own children? What's more, I felt God was chuckling about it. The incident amused Him and I felt He was laughing to Himself with anticipation as he watched me find the pen, saying *"Was that answer quick enough for you?"*

That is exactly how God can be at times, when you get to know Him, but not before. That, therefore, is the amazing God that we are privileged to serve and worship. He is Almighty and is a King and a Judge, but He is also a Father and a friend. He cares about us and looks after even the most trivial details of our lives.

If you choose to believe in Him and to follow Him, then He will not disappoint you. He has never, ever, let me down, in my whole life. He has never been faithless or unreliable. Can you say that of any friend, or even of your own parents?

Therefore, I will try to present God to you in this book in an accurate way, telling you honestly about His judgment and His severity. However, I do not want you to misunderstand Him by failing to remember as well all the other aspects of His nature, such as His love, grace and mercy. We need to hold them all in balance at the same time.

Perhaps above all we need to realise that God takes no pleasure from judging or punishing any of us. His holy nature means that He has to do it or He would not be true to Himself. However, He actually wants all of us to avoid His judgment by turning to Him in faith and repentance:

"For I have no pleasure in the death of anyone who dies," declares the Lord GOD. "Therefore, repent and live."

Ezekiel 18:32 (NASB)

We are now going to embark upon several serious and worrying chapters. As I do that, please continue to bear in mind the fuller picture of God's character that I have begun to describe in this chapter. We shall expand upon all of that once we get past chapter nine.

CHAPTER 4

HOW THE CHURCH GOT INTO ITS CURRENT CONDITION

[3]For the time will come when they will not endure sound doctrine; but wanting to have their ears tickled, they will accumulate for themselves teachers in accordance to their own desires, [4]and will turn away their ears from the truth and will turn aside to myths.

2 Timothy 4:3-4 (NASB)

Anyone looking at the state of Christianity today would have good reason to be confused by the wide range of opinions and denominations. By 'denomination' we mean a group of people who have a particular tradition, structure or form of organisation. These denominations have each been started, one after the other, particularly since the sixteenth century, as men have tried to reform Christianity, or to emphasise a different approach, or doctrinal stance.

It is too complicated within the scope of this book to try to go into these, but it is generally true to say, for many denominations, that they began well. Many have been used by God to correct some error or clean up some problem or to bring the church back closer to where it should be.

Sadly, history tends to repeat itself. Therefore within a generation or two, each new denomination has usually begun to degenerate and to reintroduce errors and man-made traditions of their own. The net effect of all this is that there is a baffling range of different opinions and styles. A person may wonder how they could possibly choose between all these alternatives, or how they can know who is right and who is wrong about various controversial issues.

I want therefore to recommend an approach which will enable you to arrive at a clear understanding of Christianity, without confusion. It is that you should be confident and ambitious enough to read the whole Bible for yourself. Also take it at face value and believe what it says.

In other words, instead of relying on other people, or on the traditions of any particular denomination that you may have been born into, just take the Bible on its own as your guide. If you read all the way through it, taking seriously everything that is said and believing it, then the Bible will gradually make more and more sense to you.

Also, what you read in one book or letter will help you to understand something written somewhere else. The Bible refers to itself a lot and many quotes or references are made which assume you have read the earlier book being referred to. So, you will find parts of the Bible difficult to begin with, but if you persist, things will steadily become clearer.

We must get our beliefs solely from the Bible, not from men's ideas or traditions

Our confusion comes from focusing, instead, on what church leaders or denominations say. When what they say differs from what the Bible says, too many of us opt to go along with what our leaders say and ignore the Bible. My strong advice is always to put the Bible at the centre. Then decide that you will base all your beliefs and practices on what the Bible says, not on what you're used to, or what you've always been told, regardless of who told you.

That is the way I have put this book together. I want to introduce you to all the main ingredients of Christianity and explain them as the Bible explains them, emphasising whatever the Bible emphasises. I want to stick only to what the Bible says and not add anything to it or take anything from it. I would invite you to check carefully for yourself whether I achieve that.

It is very possible to go to church but not be a real Christian

I have been a Christian since 1981. I can point to the very date and time when I became a Christian and had my sins forgiven. It was 2.30pm in the afternoon on the 8 June 1981 when I made a clear and firm decision to repent and put my trust in Jesus Christ. At 2:29pm I was not a Christian, but a few moments later I was. I had begun my journey and stepped on to the path which the Bible calls "*the Way*".

That is how decisively it happened for me. It is not always the same for everyone. Some people cannot point to an exact moment when they first became a Christian. However, there is a stark choice to be made between continuing as you are, or becoming a Christian. If you are properly instructed, you will come to a distinct crossroads where that definite choice has to be made.

In my case I made it after nine months of Bible study and discussion with a Christian missionary called Dave Brown from Oklahoma. He took the time to explain things from the Bible until I had a clear knowledge and understanding. I could no longer deny that Christianity was true and that Jesus Christ was who He said He was. I realised that I had to make a clear choice, either to follow Him or reject Him.

I also knew that if I was to follow Him it had to be with my whole heart, mind and soul and that there could be no half measures. That was not just some strange notion that I took. That is the way that Jesus presents it in the Bible. He does not want people merely to 'approve' of Him or even to agree with Him. He wants us to believe and trust in Him with all our hearts and also to turn away from our sins.

He then wants us to follow Him and acknowledge Him as the Lord and King of our life who occupies first place at all times. It is a big challenge that He makes to us. But, He offers us no alternatives. It is either Him, and only Him, or nothing. Also, it is on His terms, or not at all. I came to realise all of that after nine months of Bible study.

I can say now, with many years of hindsight, that I made the right choice. I handed my life over completely to Jesus Christ. I accepted that from then on He was in charge, not me and that I had to do whatever He wanted, not what I wanted. When I made that decision, aged 19, I had only a limited understanding of what lay ahead and no idea of how many difficulties it would bring me into.

Yet, Jesus Christ has always been utterly faithful to me. He has never left me or forsaken me, even when life has been very hard. Living as a Christian in an increasingly secular and pagan Britain has not been easy. It is getting more difficult and more hostile every year. Yet, I would never go back to what I had before.

Despite any hardships I have had to face, which are far less than many Christians elsewhere in the world have to face, I know that I made the right decision. Let me say a little more about my own personal background and the life that I lived until I was 19. I was brought up in Roman Catholicism. I was born into an Irish family living in Britain and went to a Catholic school until I was 11. I continued going to the Catholic church quite faithfully until I was 19.

For most of that time, never having known anything else, and never having even looked at the Bible, I did not know that there was anything missing or wrong. It was all I knew. I was very sincere, as many Catholics are. I genuinely believed the little I knew of Roman Catholic teaching. In those years growing up in the Catholic Church I received some good things. I was taught a number of Bible stories and some parts of the Bible.

However, many things were left out and a lot of false things were added in. That is because the Roman Catholic Church is a mixture. It does contain some real Christianity taken from the Bible. But it also adds to that many other beliefs, traditions and practices which are not from the Bible. Some of these directly contradict what the Bible says.

The origins of the Roman Catholic Church

The Roman Catholic Church is not the *"original"* or *"true"* church. It does not date back to the first century, or to the apostle Peter, as it claims to do. In fact it really began to develop properly from AD 312, when the Roman Emperor, Constantine, alleged that he had become a Christian. He did so because he said that he had seen a vision of a cross in the sky and when he was successful in a subsequent battle he attributed it to this.

As a result, this Roman Emperor, who had known nothing other than paganism all his life, suddenly "joined" the early fourth century church in Rome. He effectively took it over. Thus, overnight, the real church, which had existed for three centuries, and which had had to be underground for some of that time due to persecution, was suddenly legal. The persecution was over and the Emperor was now supposedly a Christian. Multitudes of practising pagans flooded into the church.

They joined the church, not because they believed in the Bible or had repented. Many of them did so because they now calculated that it would be socially and financially advantageous to join this institution called the "church", which the Emperor had taken over. Thus, the church changed from being a persecuted group, whose biblical values and beliefs were the opposite of those around them, to a group with official state backing. A massive influx of insincere, unrepentant pagans, who had no genuine Christian beliefs, took over the church.

It was an invasion by the pagan world into the church as it then was. The pagans brought with them into the church all of their own occult beliefs and practices. Instead of abandoning these and taking up Christianity in their place, they kept their pagan beliefs and practices. They simply added some bits of Christianity alongside, to create a mixture.

So, many of the traditions which still exist in the Roman Catholic church come directly from paganism, not from the Bible. It dates back to the fourth century and does not reflect the pure church of the first century which the apostles set up. Many of the genuine believers within the fourth century church felt they had no option but to leave. They had to go outside of the newly institutionalised church which was now meeting in former pagan temples.

They carried on meeting in homes as they had done for three centuries. Those genuine Christians who left were the real church, not the semi-pagan/semi-Christian church that Emperor Constantine was now leading. That real church carried on separately, and has always carried on, to this day. Meanwhile, from the fourth century onwards, this huge institution that we now know as the Roman Catholic church, developed steadily.

It added more and more unbiblical features that came from paganism or just from men's imagination and blended them with Christian beliefs and practices. The mixing of different beliefs and practices is known as '*syncretism*'. It continues in the church today. Many even view this mixture as a good thing. They think it brings together all the best aspects of different religious beliefs.

However, the Bible condemns this kind of mixture. It sets out clearly what the truth is and forbids us from adding anything to it, taking anything from it, or mixing it with anything else. Jesus condemns this very clearly in Matthew's gospel. He is referring to the way Jewish leaders of the first century ignored God's Word, as set out in the Bible. Instead they focused on their own ideas and traditions which they or their predecessors had invented:

1Then some Pharisees and scribes came to Jesus from Jerusalem and said,
2"Why do Your disciples break the tradition of the elders? For they do not wash their hands when they eat bread." 3And He answered and said to them, "Why do you yourselves transgress the commandment of God for the sake of your tradition.

7"You hypocrites, rightly did Isaiah prophesy of you:
8'This people honours Me with their lips,
but their heart is far away from Me.
9'But in vain do they worship Me,
teaching as doctrines the precepts of men.'"

Matthew 15:1-3 and 7-9 (NASB)

What Jesus said to the Jewish leaders back then is equally applicable to us today. We have allowed all sorts of humanly invented ideas and traditions to replace what the Bible says. The net effect of this unhealthy mixture of Christianity and paganism, that we now know as the Roman Catholic Church, is that I was able to remain in it for 19 years but never find salvation or become a genuine Christian.

To make matters worse, I had no idea that I was lacking anything, or that I was believing in a mixture of truth and error. If someone had asked me at that time what would happen to me if I was to die, I would have had no idea. If someone had asked me what "salvation" is, or how it is obtained, I would have been unable to answer.

Error, confusion and apathy have crept in to most churches, not only the Catholic Church

That vagueness was not unique to me. It is the position of most Catholics. But, I must emphasise, it is by no means confined only to the Catholic church. It is widespread in the modern Western church, throughout the denominations. Much of the Church of England is also deeply confused and mixed up. The same applies to the Methodist church, the Baptist church, the Lutheran church and so on. It alarms me to see how many people, even in what used to be solid, Bible believing, evangelical churches, are drifting along with no clear faith or repentance.

I fear that millions of people, even in Reformed Protestant and nonconformist denominations, may be unsaved, due to the shallow and compromised teaching they are receiving. A lot of what goes on in all kinds of churches is just dead tradition and things being done by rote, without sincerity or passion. Isaiah spoke of this condition long ago, but it still applies:

Then the Lord said,
"Because this people draw near with their words
And honour Me with their lip service,
But they remove their hearts far from Me,
And their reverence for Me consists of tradition learned by rote,
Isaiah 29:13 (NASB)

So, I was an unsaved, unrepentant "churchgoer" in the Catholic Church, together with countless others. But there are also millions of unsaved churchgoers in other denominations too. We each need to ask ourselves whether that applies to us personally. Having said that, I should also add, for the sake of accuracy and balance, that there are also, within such denominations, some people who are saved and who are genuine believers.

People are at all sorts of different levels and stages. That means we can't make blanket statements about them as groups. Each person's circumstances are unique to them. The key point, though, is that we also cannot assume that people are saved, or that they are real Christians, just because they go to church. That is the case whatever denomination they belong to.

In case anyone imagines that I am picking on the Catholic Church, I should emphasise again, and more clearly, that even within what are known as the 'Protestant' denominations, such as the Lutheran Church or the Church of England, and also in the nonconformist denominations such as the Baptists, Methodists and Pentecostals, there is today a large and growing amount of error, ignorance, deception and apostasy. 'Apostasy' is where someone has known the truth but they subsequently turn away from it.

There are many problems and errors in Protestant churches too

The Protestant denominations arose in the *"Reformation"* of the sixteenth century. They are called that because they protested against many of the false teachings and practices of Roman Catholicism. The nonconformists went even further in the seventeenth and eighteenth centuries and were in some ways even more biblical in their approach. Yet, it is sadly true to say that in the Western world today, even the Protestant and nonconformist denominations have declined alarmingly.

They have degenerated in the quality of their teaching and preaching and in the nature of the message that they give. I am speaking of denominations such as the Church of England, the Lutheran churches, the Baptists, Methodists, Pentecostals and also the Charismatic churches. The problem is basically across the board.

Many churches in these denominations have watered down their teaching. They have also mixed it with ideas and teaching that come from the New Age, humanism, liberalism, scepticism and higher criticism. "Higher criticism" involves sitting in judgment on the Bible and criticising it as if it was an ordinary work of literature, rather than honouring it as God's Word.

Many churches focus on what is called *"the social gospel."* By that they mean that Christians should bring the good news to our societies, especially to the poor, by doing good works. That means seeking to relieve poverty or deal with disease, hunger, homelessness etc, rather than just speaking about personal salvation from our sins and from God's judgment.

There is more than a grain of truth in that approach. God does want us to have a heart for the poor and needy and to seek to make a practical difference in our world. That is beyond doubt. (See Book Four for more detail.)Where the problem arises is when people begin to focus solely or excessively upon such social issues and forget about, or cease even to believe in, the very heart of the Gospel.

That is that Jesus came to commence His Kingdom and to save us from our sins and from being sent to Hell and the Lake of Fire after we die. Those facts must always remain in the central place as the most crucial points that we emphasise. If not, we will end up, eventually, with an unbalanced and even a false gospel.

The "apparent church"

In the Western world therefore we see, by and large, a spineless, and biblically illiterate church. It is too weak to be a witness to our world and too unimpressive to be able to teach or preach effectively. One could call it the *'apparent church'*. It appears to outsiders and non-believers to be the church, but very many of the people in it have no true faith or accurate understanding of what the Bible teaches.

This ignorance and error applies even to church leaders. Thus, what they do not know, they cannot teach, but, any wrong ideas they have will be passed on to others. Tragically, countless people have rejected real Christianity solely on the basis that they are not impressed by what they have seen and experienced within what I call the "apparent church." They mistakenly assume, when they reject all of this, that they are rejecting the real church.

They have seen a lot of hypocrisy, falseness, confusion, compromise and shallowness in the apparent church and have been appalled by it. On that basis, they have then rejected real Christianity. It is almost as if they have been "vaccinated" against real Christianity. They have had a small dose of something which is not the real thing, but which sufficiently resembles it to put them off Christianity for life. It prevents many from ever looking into it any further, so they never find the real thing.

Therefore, people can reject real Christianity solely because of what they imagine it is, based on what they have seen in the apparent church, without ever finding the real church or the real Gospel. However, if Christianity really was what they wrongly imagine it to be, then I would reject it myself, as would any sensible person. Who would want to be part of a church which is about self-righteousness, religious smugness, empty tradition and superstition?

Who would want a church which is spectator-orientated, with a large group of people depending on one man to do everything for them, rather than actively participating, serving, forming relationships, studying and learning for themselves? Unbelievers can see that the apparent church is largely an irrelevance. It has little to offer in their lives or to society.

Non-Christians are astute and can see that lukewarm Christianity is empty and false. But, they do not realise that elsewhere the real thing does exist, because most have never come across it. The media certainly doesn't report it. What I experienced growing up in Roman Catholicism, and what many other people experience, even in the Protestant and nonconformist denominations, is a lifeless, superficial church. It does not bring them to a place of salvation.

That was my position for 19 years. Then I discovered that Jesus is offering us eternal life, forgiveness of our sins and a complete set of blessings that we call 'salvation'. Yet, I had entirely missed it in all my years in institutionalised religion.

What is *"religion"*?

I have just used the word *"religion"*. It is a much misunderstood word. Real Christianity is not a religion. Christianity is God's one and only way of reaching out to lost people who need His mercy and forgiveness as a free gift. "Religion" is the many different futile ways in which men attempt to find their own way to God. It is usually done through seeking to improve their behaviour so as to impress God. They hope to earn a place in Heaven through living a good life, or at least a life that is more good than bad.

That viewpoint is so widespread that to challenge it shocks people. Yet, I can say, quite clearly, that real Christianity is not about trying to impress God or being a good person. Neither is it anything to do with trying to earn salvation through a good life or good works. That is what every type of religion is about. But it is the opposite of what real Christianity is about.

The need to check everything for yourself in the Bible

I urge you to read what I say with caution. Do not just casually assume that what I say, or what anybody else says, must be true because it's in a book. Check it carefully for yourself in the Bible. Be like the people of Berea that we referred to earlier. Take the responsibility upon yourself to find out from the Bible whether what I say, or what anybody else says, is true or not.

I have come across many people over the years who are highly suspicious of any idea or book which comes from someone outside of their own denomination or church tradition. They imagine they will be safe provided they only listen to people of their "own kind". However, you are just as likely, if not more likely, to be misinformed and led astray by a teacher from within your own denomination as you are from one outside it.

Safety and truth are not to be found simply by staying true to your denomination, but by staying true to the Bible. The people you know are just as likely to get things wrong and have gaps in their knowledge as the people you don't know. In fact, there is danger in only ever listening to or reading the teaching of people you are used to. It will tend to accentuate and entrench any error that you and your teachers already have. That is why there is value in looking at a wide selection of good and genuine teachers from other backgrounds.

See the Real Christianity website for more information on this, www.realchristianity.com. Go to the section called 'Approved Ministries' and listen to the teachers listed there. They are all of the highest quality. That said, even though genuine Bible teachers are very important, the real key is to study the whole Bible for yourself. Weigh up everything and everybody by what the Bible says, not the other way around. Don't weigh up the Bible according to what men say. Resolve now that that you will approach the Bible correctly from now on and that you will abandon any belief or practice which is shown to contradict the Bible.

CHAPTER 5

WHY SHOULD WE BOTHER TO BECOME A CHRISTIAN?

Before looking at valid reasons why we should become a Christian, let's look at some common reasons people put forward which are **not** valid, or at least which the Bible never puts forward:

Invalid reason 1 - It is not to do God a favour.

God does not need any favours from any of us. You or me finding out about Him and learning what the Bible says, is not going to benefit God. The good news about Jesus Christ is something that God has put in place for our benefit, not His. In other words, we need Him, but He does not need us.

Invalid reason 2 - It is not because He loves you.

It is absolutely true to say that God is love, and that His perfect love is the model for us all to follow. However, that is never put forward in the Bible as the *reason* why an unbeliever should seek to find Him. That may sound surprising. Most people have heard churches telling the public how much God loves them and giving that as the reason for them, in return, wanting to come to Him. The point is that although God is love, He generally only speaks about His love to those who have already repented and believed in Him. With those who do not yet know or love Him, the Bible focuses on His holiness and His impending judgment, not on His love:

The LORD watches over all who love him,
but all the wicked he will destroy.
Psalm 145:20 (NIV)

God knows our hearts and how we operate. If He was to present Himself to us on the basis of His love and ask us to come to Him simply because He loves us, then it would not cause us to respect Him. On the contrary, it would only create contempt for Him in the hearts of most of us. That is not just a theoretical statement. It is the practical experience of many unbelievers. They are actually turned off by a message that God loves them. They see it as a kind of weakness in God. Imagine how we would react to a human being who went around telling complete strangers that he loves them and wants them to come to him and be his friend in response to that love.

At best we would pity such a person. More likely, we would despise them and consider them socially inadequate and pathetic. This idea that the Gospel should be presented in wholly positive terms, without making any mention of sin, judgment, death or Hell and, instead, just emphasising God's love, is relatively new. It is a false and unbalanced way of presenting Christianity that has only really arisen in the twentieth century and in the West. Before that no such man-centred message was ever given as the basis for turning to God and accepting Jesus Christ.

The inappropriate overemphasis on God's love since the middle of the twentieth century also has the effect of misleading many people into thinking that God would never judge or punish us. We are told that He is too "loving" to do so. That is another false idea which has caused great harm. So, I will not present God to you in that manner, nor appeal to you to believe in Him on the basis of His love for us. That is not how the Bible presents God to unbelievers. Instead, I will begin, as the Bible does, by focusing on God's holiness and how He feels about our sin.

Invalid reason 3 - It is not to improve your life or to achieve happiness.

This again is a misleading basis upon which to urge people to come to Jesus Christ and believe in Him. Firstly it is not the way that Jesus presents Himself in the Bible, nor the way the apostles presented Him. Secondly it is only partially true. The reality is that by becoming a Christian we will not solve all our problems. In fact we will create some extra problems. Neither will it always produce happiness for us. This rose-tinted presentation of Christianity has been put forward by well-meaning people. They have wanted to make Christianity seem more appealing, so as to get people to accept it.

Those presenting it this way may be too scared to tell you the real reasons why you should become a Christian. They fear that if they did tell you the complete truth then you may feel offended, or be put off. It is very possible that you would be offended or put off. But that is still no reason to mislead you about the true nature of the Christian message and what suffering and trouble the Christian life can involve. Look at how hard life was for apostle Paul:

24Five times I received from the Jews the forty lashes minus one. 25Three times I was beaten with rods, once I was stoned, three times I was shipwrecked, I spent a night and a day in the open sea, 26I have been constantly on the move. I have been in danger from rivers, in danger from bandits, in danger from my own countrymen, in danger from Gentiles; in danger in the city, in danger in the country, in danger at sea; and in danger from false brothers. 27I have laboured and toiled and have often gone without sleep; I have known hunger and thirst and have often gone without food; I have been cold and naked. 28Besides everything else, I face daily the pressure of my concern for all the churches.

2 Corinthians 11:24-28 (NIV)

These two passages give us a glimpse of the terrible hardship that apostle Paul had to endure. It may not be so extreme for you, though it could be, and you need to realise that from the outset. If you become a real Christian it will lead to persecution and trouble and it could even be severe. Yet, too often, a falsely positive message is presented, as if becoming a Christian will solve all our problems and make life easy. It won't.

For all these reasons, much of the Western church has presented Christianity in an artificial and misleading way, making promises which Jesus does not make and which are not supported by the Bible. I do not want to do that. I want to present Christianity to you honestly, as Jesus presented it, and as the Bible presents it, without trying to improve it or make it more marketable. To do so would not only be dishonest, but also very ineffective.

Most people are too astute to be misled by such tactics. Even if people are naïve enough to believe such a message, it is not the true Gospel and they will end up being disappointed and disillusioned and, quite probably, falling away. Most of the public can see through such falseness and hype and they reject it instinctively.

That is one reason why so many millions of people have rejected what now passes for Christianity in the Western world. They can see through it and realise that much of it is empty, false and irrelevant to their lives. Sadly, they are arriving at those conclusions not because that is what *real* Christianity is about, but because that is what *apparent* Christianity is about, i.e. the false and compromised message they have been given.

Valid reasons why a non-Christian should believe in Christianity:

Valid Reason 1: Because it is true.

This is actually the only valid reason for believing in or accepting any idea. The reality is that biblical Christianity, (i.e. the real thing, not the various false alternatives), is either true or it is not. If it is true then you should accept it, simply because it is true. But if it is false, then you should reject it simply because it is false, without needing any other reason. That may sound like an unnecessary statement of the obvious, but that is not how most of us think today.

Our society no longer thinks in terms of something as being simply true or false. Instead they think in terms of it being attractive or unattractive, realistic or unrealistic, likely to appeal or unlikely to appeal, practical or impractical etc. In other words, many of us do not accept or reject an idea on the basis of whether it is true in itself.

Instead we do so according to whether it would be convenient or inconvenient to believe in it and/or whether we like the implications it might have for our lives if we did believe it. Previous generations did not think that way.I am reminded of a colleague at work with whom I spoke about Christianity. This colleague said to me that she believed in Jesus but that *"I just don't want to change my life"*. What she was referring to was the fact that she had a non-Christian boyfriend. She was in a sexual relationship with him and was actively going out to night clubs, drinking very heavily and engaging in a generally sinful life style.

What she meant was that, although she could now see clearly that Christianity was true, she was still not going to accept it, because she knew that Jesus would want her to change her lifestyle. She decided that the inconvenience of changing her life was more than she was willing to accept. Therefore she decided to ignore a message which she already knew to be true. If a person is honest, then they will surely see that that is an absurd way to think.

Yet, it is how the majority of people do think in my own experience of telling people about Christianity. No matter how inconvenient Christianity might be to you, that has no bearing on whether Christianity itself is actually true. If Jesus is the Son of God then He is the Son of God. If He rose from the dead then he rose from the dead. If He is coming again to this world to judge the world then that is what He is going to do.

Those things are true no matter what we think about them and no matter whether we find those facts attractive, inconvenient or otherwise. So, I would invite you throughout this book, and indeed in all aspects of life, to test every comment solely on the basis of whether it is true, without any regard to whether or not you want it to be true. **If a thing is true, believe in it. If it is not true reject it, regardless of whether you like it**.

It seems strange that I should even need to say that, let alone emphasise it so much, but in the Western world today, our thinking has become so superficial, and we are so dumbed-down, that it does need to be said.

Valid Reason 2: Because when we die we will face God's judgment, and there will be catastrophic results if we did not believe in and follow Jesus Christ.

This is an unpopular and unfashionable thing for me to say and, sadly, it will offend some people. However, it is an inescapable fact that the Bible tells us that if we do not repent, and believe in Jesus Christ, then we will incur God's wrath and be punished for our sins forever. By that I mean that after we die we will be judged at the Great White Throne judgment. Jesus Himself will be the judge.

Instead of being allowed to be part of the Kingdom of God and to spend eternity living a life of happiness and perfection we will then be cast into the Lake of Fire, which is an eternal punishment. It was created for the Devil and for his fallen angels. But it will also be used for all those people who do not accept Jesus Christ and follow Him. God is not simply recommending that we should repent and believe in Jesus Christ. He is *commanding* us to do so:

"...God commands all men everywhere to repent."
Acts 17:30 (NIV)

The good news about Jesus Christ is not something which is simply being passively suggested or offered to us, which we are free to accept or reject without any consequence. It is true to say that we are free to reject Jesus and to refuse to repent. But it is not true to say that there is no consequence. Though I do not wish to offend anybody, I have no alternative but to say that a dreadful eternal fate awaits all who reject Jesus Christ.

They will not be admitted into the Kingdom of God. Instead they will spend eternity in the Lake of Fire and in a fully conscious condition. I really wish that that was not true and that God would forgive and accept all people whether they repent and believe in Jesus Christ or not.

I wish that that was the message that I could present to you now. Not only would it be a much more attractive message, but it would also make me more acceptable for saying it. Yet, what can I do? I can only present the genuine message that the Bible presents. I have no authority to change it in any way.

Many would view it as politically incorrect and undemocratic of God to presume to "command" us to do anything, rather than merely suggest it to us politely. However, you and I both need to remember who God is. He is not merely a man. He is not on the same level as us. He is the Creator of the entire universe. He created us and he owns us. We are His property and He has every right to instruct us and judge us:

10for every animal of the forest is mine,
and the cattle on a thousand hills.
11I know every bird in the mountains,
and the creatures of the field are mine.
12If I were hungry I would not tell you,
for the world is mine, and all that is in it.
Psalm 50:10-12 (NIV)

Know that the LORD Himself is God;
It is He who has made us, and not we ourselves;
We are His people and the sheep of His pasture.
Psalm 100:3 (NASB)

Every one of our lives is also sustained by Him. The very atoms of which we are made are held together in their various orbits and movements by God. For that reason too, He has the authority, as the God of the whole universe, to tell us anything He wants to tell us. He equally has the authority, the right and the power to punish us if we disobey or ignore Him:

"Behold, all souls are Mine; the soul of the father as well as the soul of the son is Mine. The soul who sins will die."

Ezekiel 18:4 (NASB)

Thus, if He tells us that ignoring and rejecting Him in this life will result in eternal separation from Him in the Lake of Fire, then we need to take that seriously. It needs to be a real inducement to us to repent and get right with God. Some would say that it is wrong to present God in this "unattractive" way, i.e. as someone who is capable of judging us and punishing us.

They argue that it would be better, instead, to present Him as someone *"nicer"*. That is exactly what much of the modern Western church has done and is still doing. It has edited out anything about God which it does not find attractive in marketing terms and replaced it with more acceptable characteristics.

The Bible presents to us a God who is perfectly holy, righteous and just. He has pledged that He will judge and punish sin. However, most of the churches in the West are presenting a God who is "*tolerant*", and "*accepts us unconditionally*". It may, perhaps, appeal to some of us if God was like that, but there is no biblical basis for saying that He is. On the contrary, the Bible tells us clearly that God is going to judge sin eternally. God has enemies and He openly states that He will punish them.

Some criticise God for that and reject Him on the basis that He ought to act differently. They say He should accept us all, regardless of how we respond to Him. But it would be most unwise to think like that. We must humbly accept that He is God, and that we are not, and then take these things seriously. If we do, then we will be in the right frame of mind to flee from God's wrath, which is most certainly coming.

More detail about God's Judgment

Please consider all the following passages which make clear that sin, judgment and the need to repent are major recurring themes throughout the Bible. I want to demonstrate that I am not exaggerating or basing what I say on just one or two verses, taken out of context. This theme of judgment is stated over and over again to ensure we do not miss it. In fact I could have listed dozens of other passages too:

For God will bring every act to judgment, everything which is hidden, whether it is good or evil.

Ecclesiastes 12:14 (NASB)

12 For the LORD of hosts will have a day of reckoning
Against everyone who is proud and lofty
And against everyone who is lifted up,
That he may be abased.

Isaiah 2:11 (NASB)

30 "Therefore, O house of Israel, I will judge you, each one according to his ways, declares the Sovereign LORD. Repent! Turn away from all your offenses; then sin will not be your downfall.

Ezekiel 18:30 (NIV)

See, the Lord is coming out of his dwelling
to punish the people of the earth for their sins.
The earth will disclose the blood shed on it;
the earth will conceal its slain no longer.

Isaiah 26:21 (NIV)

"The day of the Lord is near
for all nations.
As you have done, it will be done to you;
your deeds will return upon your own head.

Obadiah 15(NIV)

49 "This is how it will be at the end of the age. The angels will come and separate the wicked from the righteous 50 and throw them into the fiery furnace, where there will be weeping and gnashing of teeth."

Matthew 13:49-50 (NIV)

It surely makes sense for any rational person, having been given such a clear warning to take note of it and get into line. The warning God gives is not just clear, it is repeated over and over again. The only way you can miss it in the Bible is if you decide you don't want to hear it. Sadly, that is a common response. When an unsaved, unforgiven person faces God's judgment, everything he has ever said, done or thought will be judged. Then his sins will be punished.

If you knew that you were going to be put on trial in front of a very senior criminal judge, who was going to evaluate you closely and punish you, would that not affect you? Would it not influence the way you act, think and speak? It certainly ought to. Yet, that is precisely the position that every non-Christian is in. We simply need to recognise the reality of that.

Later in this book we shall see in clearer detail each of the different ways that that judgment will operate. There is not just one single judgment. There are many different stages to the overall judgment and it operates very differently for Christians and non-Christians. Non-Christians will be judged and punished for their sins.

Christians will not be, because their sins are forgiven and forgotten. However, they will still be judged, albeit in a very different way, at the Judgment Seat of Christ. At that judgment every Christian will be judged on the basis of what he did with his life and how he used his talents and his time from the point of his conversion onwards.

Everything before then is forgiven and forgotten, provided we are a genuine Christian. Jesus will then reward, or rebuke, each Christian on the basis of how well he does in that assessment of his life as a disciple. (See Book Four for much more detail on how Christians will be judged, what the criteria for the judgment will be, and what the rewards may be.)In simple terms, therefore, each of us will be judged, whether we are Christians or non-Christians.

That fact ought to have a major bearing on the way we live if we are rational people. That would be true even if it was a merely human judge before whom we were awaiting trial. It ought to be much more true if the one judging us has perfect information, perfect evidence, perfect wisdom and where it is absolutely impossible to deceive Him or hide anything from Him.

So, the fact that we all face God's judgment should profoundly influence us. It is also a major reason why we should accept Jesus Christ and deal with our sin now and seek to be forgiven for it now. The alternative is to leave it too late and go to the judgment with our sins unforgiven and undealt with. You cannot repent after you die. It will be too late then. Once we die it is all over. We then face God's judgment and there is no opportunity to change our minds or to repent belatedly:

And just as it is appointed for men to die once, and after that comes judgment,
Hebrews 9:27 (RSV)

You have no way of knowing when your life will end. It could be that you will die tonight or in five years' time or 50 years' time. Or it may be that you are only 10 seconds away from a Boeing 747 jet flying in to the side of your office building and bringing your life to an end in an instant, totally unexpectedly. Our lives and our bodies do not belong to us. God can take our lives away from us at any time. We belong to God, who made us:

Who has a claim against me that I must pay? Everything under Heaven belongs to me.

Job 41:11 (NIV)

"All these things my hand has made and so all these things are mine," says the Lord.

Isaiah 66:2 (a) (RSV)

God therefore has every right to bring our lives to an end whenever He wishes. He does nothing wrong by ending our lives. You have no valid basis to complain about anything God does, because He made you and He owns you. Thus, you need to seize your chance to get right with God. Do it now and don't leave it till later. If you do it now then you will be forgiven. Then, when you face God's judgment, instead of being at the Great White Throne judgment, it will be at the "Judgment Seat of Christ".

That judgment is solely for believers who have been forgiven. They face no condemnation. It is for reckoning up what rewards (if any) are due to them, or alternatively, what rebuke is due to them for what they did, or failed to do, after their conversion, while they were meant to be operating as Jesus' disciples.

If however we do not repent, believe and follow Him, then we go instead to the Great White Throne judgment. This is for unsaved people. No rewards will be given out, but only eternal wrath and punishment. You have the chance to make a decision now and have your trial transferred from the Great White Throne to the Judgment Seat of Christ. You would then be judged as a believer, rather than as an unbeliever. Then it would be on the basis of what reward you should receive, rather than what punishment you should get.

The choice is yours now, but it will not always be your choice. The chance can be lost, and lost forever and you have no way of knowing how much time is left to you. I appeal to you therefore to take this warning seriously and to respond. Apostle Paul did the same when he wrote to the Corinthians and begged them to be reconciled to God:

We are therefore Christ's ambassadors, as though God were making his appeal through us. We implore you on Christ's behalf: Be reconciled to God.

2 Corinthians 5:20 (NIV)

Eternal life

You and I, and everybody else, are eternal. That is the case whether we want to be or not. The Bible says that we are made in the image of God. That has many implications, but one of them is that we are eternal. This is where we differ from the animals. Their lives come to an end and are not eternal, because they have no spirit. However, each of us is eternal, whether we want to be or not, and whether we believe it or not.

The irony is that even the most hardened atheist will one day die and discover, to his surprise and horror, that he has an eternal conscious existence. He will also realise that there is a God, whose anger and judgment he must now face. We are eternal because, uniquely amongst all God's creation, we have been given a spirit. We are made up of:

a) our body,

b) our soul (which is a collective term for our mind, emotions and will) and

c) our spirit.

Whereas our physical body dies, our soul and our spirit are eternal. They will live on forever and ever. We shall all do so either in Heaven or in Hell (temporarily) and then in the Lake of Fire (permanently).

Resurrection bodies

Moreover, all of us, whether we are Christians or not, are going to be physically resurrected one day, as Jesus was. We will all be given resurrection bodies which will be physical but also eternal. Christians will be given resurrection bodies and will live with Jesus Christ forever. Unrepentant unbelievers who have rejected Jesus Christ will also be given resurrection bodies which will be equally eternal. But they will then be cast into the Lake of Fire where they will suffer punishment forever.

That is a terrible prospect. The eternal and indestructible nature of the resurrection body is shown by the fact that even in the Lake of Fire that body will not be burnt up or damaged in any way. As unpleasant and as unfashionable as it is, we need to reflect upon this dreadful prospect. It is valid that it should motivate us to respond to God.

This horrifying prospect of judgment is a crucial truth that the Bible clearly teaches. However, it has been covered up and ignored by much of the Western church, because it is not politically correct. They also feel that it will put people off. Yet, regardless of those things, the fact remains that it is true. I can see no alternative but to speak about it. How can I hide it when Jesus spoke openly about it?

There are various ways in which many people in the apparent church have tried to do away with or at least tone down judgment, Hell and the Lake of Fire. One way is the idea of '*annihilation*'. The people who believe in that suggest that God is too nice or too good to punish anyone eternally. They say that what He does instead is to simply end their existence, or annihilate them completely. If so, then they no longer have any conscious existence.

That would be a comfort if it was true, but there is no basis whatsoever for believing in it. It is the direct opposite of what the Bible actually teaches. Others teach an even more misguided idea, namely *"universalism"*. They go further and argue that God is so nice that He won't even annihilate people. Their idea is that He will simply save and forgive everybody, no matter what they believe or do.

It is remarkable how many people within the apparent church think like this. It implies that they do not need to have any concern about eternity or about the fate of unbelievers, because on this basis everybody will be saved anyway. So, nobody has anything to worry about. Again, it would be wonderful if it was true, but it is not true. It directly contradicts what Jesus has said to us out of His own mouth, let alone what the prophets and apostles have said.

Although this has been a lengthy section, I feel it has been necessary to really drive home this point about judgment. We face a terrible end if we do not repent, accept Jesus Christ and believe in Him. Thus in choosing whether to do so, we need to be very aware of the consequences of choosing not to. That prospect needs to influence us to make the right decision, and to make it now, while there is still time.

How does God resurrect people?

I would also just mention, in passing, that in my experience people often get confused as to how exactly God can manage to resurrect people whose bodies have decayed away centuries ago. Some people's bodies have even been cremated and so are totally obliterated. Many have asked me how it can be possible for God to raise them to life again. Some have asked me if God uses the very same physical remains and even whether He has to retrieve all the atoms of carbon and hydrogen and so on that were in our bodies when we were alive.

The answer, in my view, is probably best explained by saying that all God needs is the information that was used to form our bodies in the first place. That is all contained within the DNA in our genes. That is really just a complex code which arranges every part of our physical make up. So, I expect God will just recreate us in accordance with our DNA. It doesn't matter what physical material God uses and whether they are the same atoms or different ones.

Indeed, even as we live now, the atoms of which we are made are continually changing and being replaced. We are not the same person physically today that we were a few years ago. Most, or all, of the atoms in our bodies will have been replaced over that time. So, it's a non-issue. As for where the information about our DNA is now, it is simply stored in God's memory. He knows the DNA codes for every person He has ever created. So, when He recreates them, i.e. resurrects them, He will just speak their bodies back into existence.

He spoke everything into existence in the first place in Genesis chapters one and two when He tackled the far larger job of creating the entire universe. That said, when God resurrects us He will not make us exactly as we are now. We will be entirely recognisable as ourselves, but we will be perfect. Any faults, defects or imperfections will be gone. So, any handicapped person will no longer be handicapped. They will be whole and perfect.

We have to focus on the bad news first

My objective in the rest of this book is to set out for you as clearly as I can what the Christian message is, so that you can make an informed choice. However, before I can tell you the good news that Jesus Christ came to bring, I must first tell you a lot more about what the bad news is. It is only by knowing all about the bad news that we can ever begin to understand the good news and realise just how good it is.

I hope that you will bear with me therefore as I spend some further time clarifying exactly what the Bible means when it talks about sin, judgment, Hell and the Lake of Fire. That is necessary before I start to look at what Jesus did to save us from it all. For now, I must continue focusing on the bad news because it is essential to understand that before we can begin to understand or appreciate the good news.

Moreover, you are unlikely to have heard much, if any, of this before because the true Christian message has been so suppressed and 'toned down' within the apparent church. Therefore, even if you have gone to church all your life, you may not have been told these things. Some readers may be discouraged as they read the chapters that follow.

They may be thinking that the bad news just seems to go on and on and that we never seem to be getting to the good news or seeing any benefit from believing in Jesus Christ. But hang on in there and keep going. It will all make sense by the time you get to the end. Then you will be equipped to make a fully informed decision to follow Jesus Christ and to receive the amazing benefits and blessings that that leads to.

The benefits of being a Christian

We have already seen some of the bad news, and there is more to look at. However, there are also many very positive advantages which come from being a Christian. Though I'm determined to tell you all the bad news and to leave none of it out, there are certainly many blessings and advantages that will come to you if you become a real Christian.

You will experience peace of mind in a new way and you will always have God to turn to in any times of difficulty or grief. In addition you will become a part of the wider family of the church and will make many genuine friends, probably far more than you would have as an unbeliever.

The greatest advantage of all though, is that if you become a Christian, not only will you be saved from God's judgment and from Hell and the Lake of Fire. You can also look forward to spending all of eternity in glory, being in God's presence within the Kingdom of God and enjoying all the immense blessings and joys that that will involve.

The world that awaits us is going to be indescribably wonderful. Why would any sane person choose not to go there? Moreover, how tragic it would be to miss it all simply because you did not choose to make the effort to find out about it.

CHAPTER 6

WHAT IS THE CHRISTIAN MESSAGE? THE BAD NEWS FIRST – SIN AND ITS CONSEQUENCES.

for all have sinned and fall short of the glory of God.
Romans 3:23 (NIV)

For the wages of sin is death, but the gift of God is eternal life in Christ Jesus our Lord.
Romans 6:23 (NIV)

To explain the Gospel message properly we have to go back to the beginning of time and look at the creation of the world and of the human race. When we understand why God created us in the first place it helps us understand why Jesus had to come to save the human race. The main details of the creation of the world are set out in the early chapters of the book of Genesis. That is the first book of the Bible. At some point in the past, God decided to create planet earth, the universe and the human race.

He did this in six literal 24 hour days, simply by speaking everything into existence. He created the earth and then the stars and then all of the creatures that live on the earth. Finally He created man on the sixth day. He did so by creating one single man called Adam, which is just the Hebrew word for 'man'. He then created a woman, called Eve, to be Adam's wife.

When Adam and Eve were created they were perfect in every way. They came into existence as adults from the very beginning, with ready-made knowledge, and understanding. They also had the ability to relate to God and to speak to Him face to face. Adam was no caveman. Far from being primitive, he was probably much more intelligent and capable than we are. He may well have been cleverer than Einstein.

He was created with knowledge already programmed into him. His mind operated perfectly, as did his body. There was no sickness, death or sin in the world. All was perfect and in harmony with everything else. That was the way God designed the world and the human race. He intended that Adam and Eve should have children and populate the whole world with people who would have an equally perfect and sinless relationship with God.

The origin of sin in the human race – *the fall*

However, Adam and Eve then spoiled everything by disobeying God. They did so through eating fruit from a particular tree in the Garden of Eden, from which God had told them not to eat. This was the first occasion when a human being had ever sinned against God and it had massive consequences. It is known as *"the fall"*. From that moment, when they first disobeyed God, they lost their innocence and they died spiritually.

Their eyes were opened so that they became aware for the first time of good and evil. They also became aware for the first time that they were naked and tried to cover up their nakedness. Previously they had been entirely relaxed and comfortable about it, due to their complete innocence. More importantly, a physical death sentence was passed on Adam and Eve, such that they lost their immortality. That meant that they and all their descendants must one day die physically:

Therefore, just as sin entered the world through one man, and death through sin, and in this way death came to all men, because all sinned.

Romans 5:12 (NIV)

From that moment their bodies began the aging process, with which we are familiar. They also became susceptible to illness, accidents and decay. Previously they had been immune to all of these things. The way that Adam and Eve lived on the Earth originally was very similar to how Heaven will be. Suddenly, however, Adam and Eve found that the Earth itself, that God had created for them, had also dramatically changed.

It became for them as we know it today, full of death, sickness, sin, crime and violence. The whole world came under God's curse and has been so ever since. The very forces of nature now work against us at times and can be lethal, with earthquakes, floods, tornadoes, droughts and famines. Adam and Eve's sin affected not only themselves but the whole of nature. Plus, the soil began to produce thistles, weeds and thorns instead of being a beautiful garden. Therefore gardening and farming became very hard work, instead of being easy:

17 To Adam he said, "Because you listened to your wife and ate from the tree about which I commanded you, 'You must not eat of it,' "Cursed is the ground because of you; through painful toil you will eat of it all the days of your life. 18 It will produce thorns and thistles for you, and you will eat the plants of the field. 19 By the sweat of your brow you will eat your food until you return to the ground, since from it you were taken; for dust you are and to dust you will return."

Genesis 3:17-19(NIV)

All of the chaos and misery, that we still experience today, came from that one first act of disobedience by Adam and Eve. Their very nature also changed, such that they were now inherently sinful rather than innocent. From that point on Adam and Eve continued to sin and every child born to them did the same. This is because every human being from that point on, including you and me, has inherited a *'sin nature'*.

That means that we will inevitably sin. We sin because we are sinful by our very nature. The only question is how much we will sin and in what ways. We will shortly look in closer detail at our sin and its consequences. Before we do, we need to look at God's holiness, because it is the fact of God's perfect holiness that makes our sinfulness such a huge problem.

God's holiness

Why should God be so concerned about our sin and why should it make such a difference? The answer is that He is perfectly holy. We will never be able to understand God, or the Gospel, unless we grasp this concept of His holiness. It is largely forgotten or ignored in the modern Western church. Therefore, even within churches, holiness is either not understood at all, or it is seriously misunderstood. It tends to bring to mind images of someone who is stuffy and pompous.

Yet that has nothing to do with it. Holiness is a quality that only God has. It is His utter sinless perfection and His absolute cleanness and righteousness. It means that in every way and at all times He is perfect. There is no evil in Him or any deception or selfishness or cruelty or any other form of wickedness. He is completely good and virtuous, to a degree that we cannot imagine.

Because of God's infinite holiness, it means that He cannot, and will not, allow any person to be in His presence unless they are equally holy. Thus, even one sin in your life will wreck the relationship between God and you. God has to be true to His nature and above all to His own holiness. He cannot compromise on that by ignoring or overlooking sin of any kind. Let's look closer at God's holiness and why it is so important:

"Holy, holy, holy, is the Lord God Almighty."
Revelation 4:8(b) (NIV)

15But just as he who called you is holy, so be holy in all you do; 16for it is written: "Be holy, because I am holy."
1 Peter 1:15-16 (NIV)

"It is the LORD of hosts whom you should regard as holy. And He shall be your fear, And He shall be your dread.

Isaiah 8:13 (NASB)

God's attitude towards our sin

We see from the above verses that God takes His own holiness and sinlessness extremely seriously. There is no alternative for Him but to do so, because He must remain true to His own nature. Now consider by contrast the following passages. These show what our sin is like and how seriously God takes it:

5The LORD saw how great man's wickedness on the earth had become, and that every inclination of the thoughts of his heart was only evil all the time. 6The LORD was grieved that he had made man on the earth, and his heart was filled with pain.

Genesis 6:5-6 (NIV)

11Now the earth was corrupt in God's sight and was full of violence. 12God saw how corrupt the earth had become, for all the people on earth had corrupted their ways.

Genesis 6:11-12(NIV)

3Everyone has turned away,
they have together become corrupt;
there is no one who does good, not even one.
Psalm 53:1-3 (NIV)

These verses describe all of mankind. We are all like that, including you and me. This was not what God had intended. He had planned for the world to be perfect and for Adam and Eve, and all their descendants, to have a perfect relationship with Him, and each other, in a sinless way. In short, it was meant to be like Heaven will be.

Why did God allow Adam and Eve to sin?

One might ask why God allowed Adam and Eve to sin, given the terrible consequences it had for them and everyone since, including us. However, there was no alternative. Remember that God wants human beings to relate to Him freely and to voluntarily love, honour, obey and worship Him. He created us in order to do those things freely, not automatically, or by compulsion. The big problem that God had was that, above all, He wanted us to be completely free, with genuine freedom of choice and free will.

That has major implications. If men and women are to be truly free to choose to obey God, then that can only mean anything if they are equally free to choose not to. If God had created us with no option but to obey Him, then we would be reduced to mere toys for God to play with. Our love and worship towards Him would mean nothing.

You can ponder on that for as long as you wish, but you will not be able to find a way round it. If God cannot do so, then you cannot. It was of paramount importance to God that we be genuinely free. He therefore had to accept the consequence. That was that Adam and Eve, and all of us, would fail that test and would deliberately choose to disobey Him.

Our sin separates us from God

The moment when Adam and Eve first sinned was when the whole human race fell from its level of perfection to the dismal level where it is now. Consider these verses which refer to the separation that resulted between God and man. That separation arose because God could not allow sinful people like you and me to be in His presence:

"But your iniquities have separated you from your God; your sins have hidden his face from you, so that he will not hear."

Isaiah 59:2 (NIV)

[33] ***The LORD replied to Moses, "Whoever has sinned against me I will blot out of my book.***

Exodus 32:33 (NIV)

Now look at the passages below from apostle Paul's letter to the Romans. Chapter 1 of Romans is filled with important insights about the way people really are. Paul explains what a person's heart and mind are like and how wicked we can be when we don't repent or believe in God. He also deals with the difficult question of what happens to people who have never heard of Jesus Christ or the Bible Can they be considered guilty even if they have never had a chance to know what the Bible says?

The answer Paul gives is that nobody has any excuse for not believing in God. That is because the evidence of God's existence is plain for all to see. It is obvious because of His creation, i.e. the world and all the plants, animals, birds, fish, stars, and people that God has made. Even if we do not have the Bible, we can see all these things. They are enough in themselves to prove God's existence. So all men know deep down, that there is a God. They deny and ignore God because they don't want to obey Him. It is a deliberate choice to reject God.

Likewise, no person anywhere in the world, has any excuse for the sins they commit, even if they have never heard of Jesus. We all know, deep down, what is right and wrong. We all do evil things because we choose to do so, even if we have never heard of the Bible. So, a man isn't guilty because he doesn't know about Jesus Christ. He is guilty from the very beginning, because He chooses to reject God, whose existence is obvious. And he is guilty because he chooses to do sinful things, the wrongness of which is also obvious.

We all know all of that instinctively because of the conscience that God has put within us. It is like a form of 'software' which enables all of us to tell right from wrong. We all have that conscience programmed into us and we all deliberately choose to ignore it. So, we are all without any excuse. We are all guilty and deserve God's punishment, whether or not we know the Bible or have heard of Jesus Christ:

18The wrath of God is being revealed from Heaven against all the godlessness
and wickedness of men who suppress the truth by their wickedness, 19since what
may be known about God is plain to them, because God has made it plain to
them. 20For since the creation of the world God's invisible qualities—his eternal
power and divine nature—have been clearly seen, being understood from what
has been made, so that men are without excuse.21For although they knew God,
they neither glorified him as God nor gave thanks to him, but their thinking
became futile and their foolish hearts were darkened. 22Although they claimed
to be wise, they became fools 23and exchanged the glory of the immortal God for
images made to look like mortal man and birds and animals and reptiles.

Romans 1:18-23 (NIV)

Paul goes on in the same chapter to explain that people choose to reject God even though His existence is obvious. They worship false gods instead and thus become fools. Therefore, God eventually leaves them to get on with it. What it means is that because people decided to reject and ignore Him He *"gave them over"* or let them go, so that they could be free to behave as badly and as foolishly as they wanted to.

In other words, if we show God that we are determined to reject Him and to sin, He will, eventually, wash His hands of us. He then leaves us to take our sin and our stupidity to their limits. Look at verses 24-32 below to see the kinds of things people go on to do when they are left to behave as they wish:

24Therefore God gave them over in the sinful desires of their hearts to sexual
impurity for the degrading of their bodies with one another. 25They exchanged
the truth of God for a lie, and worshiped and served created things rather than
the Creator who is forever praised. Amen. 26Because of this, God gave them over
to shameful lusts. Even their women exchanged natural relations for unnatural
ones. 27In the same way the men also abandoned natural relations with women

and were inflamed with lust for one another. Men committed indecent acts with other men, and received in themselves the due penalty for their perversion.[28]Furthermore, since they did not think it worthwhile to retain the knowledge of God, he gave them over to a depraved mind, to do what ought not to be done. [29]They have become filled with every kind of wickedness, evil, greed and depravity. They are full of envy, murder, strife, deceit and malice. They are gossips, [30]slanderers, God-haters, insolent, arrogant and boastful; they invent ways of doing evil; they disobey their parents; [31]they are senseless, faithless, heartless, ruthless. [32]Although they know God's righteous decree that those who do such things deserve death, they not only continue to do these very things but also approve of those who practice them.

Romans 1:24-32(NIV)

The letter to the Romans was written over 19 centuries ago but is as up to date as if it was written yesterday. Paul says that God's existence is obvious simply by looking at the natural world which He created. Thus, if we decide not to believe in God we are sinning because, deep in our hearts, we all know that He is real. Yet, we still choose to deny His existence and ignore Him. As a result we degenerate and our lives become ever more corrupt and depraved. God therefore has no alternative but to separate Himself from us.

None of us have any excuse

We have no excuse for not believing in God, or for our sins, even if we have never heard of the Bible or Christianity. Verses 19 and 20 above from Romans chapter one show that God has made the truth about Himself completely obvious. Nature itself, i.e. the beauty and order of God's creation, show us plainly that God exists and is real.

Yet, we choose to ignore Him and do whatever we please rather than obey our conscience. We are born knowing that God exists. It is self-evident anyway. But it does not suit us, so we blank Him out of our minds. If we do that we are guilty, no matter who we are, or how little we know. Therefore there is no unfairness on God's part. We all deserve His judgment.

The three main definitions of sin

In the verses above, three main words are used to define the different types of sin:

a) **"Sin"** – This is the widest term and means falling short of God's perfect standard. It is like an arrow which is fired at a target but which falls several yards short of it. We are sinners because we simply do not match up to God's standard of holiness. Every failure to reach His standard is sin.

b) **"Transgression"** – This means breaking some known law or rule. Thus, because Adam and Eve were told not to eat from that particular tree, it was a transgression when they did so. It was a specific rule that they broke. Thus, transgression is a particular category of sin. It is one of the ways that we 'fall short'.

c) **"Iniquity"** – This means our tendency towards rebellion or lawlessness. Rebellion is the root of our sin problem. Every one of us, deep down, is a rebel against God. We defy Him and reject His authority in our lives. We refuse to obey, honour or serve Him in the way that we should. We go about it in different ways and it takes different forms, but it is all based on rebellion. Thus, rebellion is a particular form of sin, but it is also a cause of sin.

Everybody is a sinner. There are no exceptions.

Every one of us is guilty of all three of these different aspects of sinfulness. We all fall short of God's standards. We all break God's laws. We are all rebels. There are no exceptions. The Bible makes that unmistakably clear:

8If we claim to be without sin, we deceive ourselves and the truth is not in us. 9If we confess our sins, he is faithful and just and will forgive us our sins and purify us from all unrighteousness. 10If we claim we have not sinned, we make him out to be a liar and his word has no place in our lives.

1 John 1:8-10 (NIV)

And do not enter into judgment with Your servant,
For in Your sight no man living is righteous.
Psalm 143:2 (NASB)

9What then? Are we Jews any better off? No, not at all; for I have already charged that all men, both Jews and Greeks, are under the power of sin, 10as it is written: "None is righteous, no, not one; 11no one understands, no one seeks for God. 12All have turned aside, together they have gone wrong; no one does good, not even one."

Romans 3:9-12 (RSV)

The consequences of our sin – God's judgment

God's judgment is going to come upon the whole Earth and upon every person. None of us are exempt and nobody will escape it. Moreover it will be Jesus Christ Himself who will be our Judge:

And He ordered us to preach to the people, and solemnly to testify that this is the One who has been appointed by God as Judge of the living and the dead.
Acts 10:42 (NASB)

I said in my heart, " God shall judge the righteous and the wicked, For there is a time there for every purpose and for every work."

Ecclesiastes 3:17 (NKJV)

***Against everyone who is proud and lofty
And against everyone who is lifted up,
That he may be abased.***

Isaiah 2:12 (NASB)

***[9]Before the LORD, for He is coming to judge the earth;
He will judge the world with righteousness
And the peoples with equity.***

Psalm 98:9 (NASB)

***[11]Thus I will punish the world for its evil
And the wicked for their iniquity;
I will also put an end to the arrogance of the proud
And abase the haughtiness of the ruthless.***

Isaiah 13:11 (NASB)

"Just as man is destined to die once and after that face judgment."

Hebrews 9:27 (NIV)

The above verse from Hebrews also shows that the idea of "reincarnation" is totally false. We only ever die once. After that, we are judged. There are no second chances. We do not come back to this Earth as another person or animal, as Hindus believe. That is a false hope (if indeed that prospect can even be called a hope).

We must face the fact that this life, whether long or short, is our one and only chance to repent, believe and follow Jesus. If we don't do it in this life, we never will. When we die physically we then face God's ultimate and final judgment.

See below how apostle Paul shows that the level of knowledge we each have will affect how we are judged. However, even those who have little or no knowledge of God or His law will still be answerable for what they do know about what is right and wrong:

[1] All who sin apart from the law will also perish apart from the law, and all who
sin under the law will be judged by the law. [13]For it is not those who hear the
law who are righteous in God's sight, but it is those who obey the law who will
be declared righteous. [14](Indeed, when Gentiles, who do not have the law, do by
nature things required by the law, they are a law for themselves, even though
they do not have the law, [15]since they show that the requirements of the law are
written on their hearts, their consciences also bearing witness, and their

thoughts now accusing, now even defending them.) 16This will take place on the
day when God will judge men's secrets through Jesus Christ, as my gospel
declares.

Romans 2:12-16 (NIV)

Note how fair and just God is. He will judge each of us at different levels, according to what we know. The more we know, the stricter the judgment will be. But if you imagine that the answer therefore is to deliberately avoid knowing anything, you would be wrong. **As we have seen, even a man who has never heard of Christianity or the Bible is still guilty, because God has written His law into all our hearts in the form of conscience.**

Even the most uneducated and simple person knows right from wrong. God writes it into our software. We are born with that knowledge. Thus nobody can ever say that they "did not know" they were sinning, because we all know. Our conscience tells us.

Even if there are some specific laws that you don't know about, there are plenty of others that you do know. You know the difference between right and wrong, whoever you are, and whatever country or group you come from. So, unless God intervenes to do something about it (and we shall see later that He did do something), then we are all doomed. There is no way that we can avoid God's judgment and the eternal consequences of our sinfulness.

The judgment for unbelievers, i.e. non-Christians, is spoken about further in the last book of the Bible, called Revelation. It makes frightening reading, but it is vitally important to face head on what the Bible says will happen to any person who rejects Jesus Christ and who therefore remains unforgiven. They will have to go to the judgment for unbelievers.

The judgment for non-Christians– the Great White Throne

11Then I saw a great white throne and him who was seated on it. The earth and
the Heavens fled from his presence, and there was no place for them. 12And I
saw the dead, great and small, standing before the throne, and books were
opened. Another book was opened, which is the book of life. The dead were
judged according to what they had done as recorded in the books. 13The sea gave
up the dead that were in it, and death and Hades gave up the dead that were in
them, and each person was judged according to what they had done. 14Then
death and Hades were thrown into the lake of fire. The lake of fire is the second
death. 15Anyone whose name was not found written in the book of life was
thrown into the lake of fire.

Revelation: 20: 11-15 (NIV)

That is a grim passage, but there are many others like it in the Bible where Jesus Himself speaks about the Lake of Fire and tells us what it will be. He warns us of it very clearly and directly, because it is a terrible place and He doesn't want us to ignore or underestimate it.

Verses where Jesus Himself speaks about the judgment for non-Christians and the Lake of Fire:

Please read all the following verses carefully and remember that all of these were spoken by Jesus personally. I have included a lot of examples because many people have a mental blockage about this. They are unable or unwilling to see Jesus as a person who will judge or punish us, or send anybody to Hell or to the Lake of Fire. But He will do all these things, as these passages show:

***4** I say to you, My friends, do not be afraid of those who kill the body and after*
*that have no more that they can do. **5** But I will warn you whom to fear: fear the*
One who, after He has killed, has authority to cast into Hell; yes, I tell you, fear
Him!

Luke 12:4-5 (NASB)

***40** As the weeds are pulled up and burned in the fire, so it will be at the end of the*
*age. **41** The Son of Man will send out his angels, and they will weed out of his*
*kingdom everything that causes sin and all who do evil. **42** They will throw them*
*into the fiery furnace, where there will be weeping and gnashing of teeth. **43** Then*
the righteous will shine like the sun in the kingdom of their Father. He who has
ears, let him hear.

Matthew 13:40-43 (NIV)

***49** This is how it will be at the end of the age. The angels will come and separate*
*the wicked from the righteous **50** and throw them into the fiery furnace, where*
there will be weeping and gnashing of teeth.

Matthew 13:49-50(NIV)

***31** When the Son of Man comes in his glory, and all the angels with him, he will*
*sit on his throne in Heavenly glory. **32** All the nations will be gathered before*
him, and he will separate the people one from another as a shepherd separates
*the sheep from the goats. **33** He will put the sheep on his right and the goats on*
*his left. **34** Then the King will say to those on his right, Come, you who are*
blessed by my Father; take your inheritance, the kingdom prepared for you
since the creation of the world

Matthew 25:31-34 (NIV)

Then they will go away to eternal punishment, but the righteous to eternal life.
Matthew 25:46 (NIV)

Please note that the phrase '*Son of Man*' in the above passages means Jesus Himself. It is one of His many titles. Many people are surprised when they realise that Jesus Himself said all these things (and more). It doesn't fit in with the public's image of Jesus. Yet, He really did say these things. Perhaps you need to change your view of Jesus and who He really is, the future Judge of all mankind. We need to consider very seriously what to do about that.

Verses where the apostles Peter or Paul refer to the drastic nature of God's judgment

If that series of verses spoken by Jesus Himself doesn't convince you that judgment is coming, look at some more verses from the writings of Paul and Peter. These prove that they too preached about judgment and the Lake of Fire, and very clearly. These passages also show that what Jesus had said earlier was not just for the Jewish people or for the time of the Old Testament. In these passages which follow, Peter and Paul are speaking in the New Testament. They are speaking to us:

[8]He will punish those who do not know God and do not obey the gospel of our Lord Jesus. [9]They will be punished with everlasting destruction and shut out from the presence of the Lord and from the majesty of his power

2 Thessalonians 1:8-9 (NIV)

[4]For if God did not spare angels when they sinned, but sent them to Hell, putting them into gloomy dungeons to be held for judgment; [5]if he did not spare the ancient world when he brought the flood on its ungodly people, but protected Noah, a preacher of righteousness, and seven others; [6]if he condemned the cities of Sodom and Gomorrah by burning them to ashes, and made them an example of what is going to happen to the ungodly; [7]and if he rescued Lot, a righteous man, who was distressed by the filthy lives of lawless men [8](for that righteous man, living among them day after day, was tormented in his righteous soul by the lawless deeds he saw and heard)— [9]if this is so, then the Lord knows how to rescue godly men from trials and to hold the unrighteous for the day of judgment, while continuing their punishment.

2 Peter 2:4-9 (NIV)

[7]By the same word the present Heavens and earth are reserved for fire, being kept for the day of judgment and destruction of ungodly men.

2 Peter 3:7 (NIV)

I have not included every reference to Hell and the Lake of Fire, as there are very many more. But I have included several, to show that Hell and the Lake of Fire are consistent and major themes. Moreover, they show that the references to the Lake of Fire are mainly in the New Testament, rather than the Old Testament.

I have lost count of how many people have misguidedly said to me comments like: *"The God of the Old Testament was all about judgment, but Jesus and the New Testament are all about God's love."* In fact, God is exactly the same in the Old and New Testaments. He does not change at all. We must therefore abandon any idea that judgment, Hell and the Lake of Fire no longer apply.

What kind of people will go to the Lake of Fire?

Many people say they can understand that other people are sinners, such as Adolf Hitler. They will accept that people like him might be worthy of the Lake of Fire, but not themselves. They say that they themselves are not really bad people, because they *"try to live a good life"* and do quite well, *"compared to other people"*. I have heard countless people say such things in one way or another. In their opinion they themselves would never be condemned by God or sent to Hell and the Lake of Fire when they die.

That's because they look upon themselves as being *"basically good",* but they are totally mistaken. Before we can even begin to understand the good news of the Gospel of Jesus Christ, we have got to grasp that you and I are both sinners. So is everybody in your family, everybody on your street, everybody in your town and everybody in the whole world. There are no exceptions whatsoever. Consider what King Solomon said on this point:

When they sin against You (for there is no man who does not sin)……
2 Chronicles 6:36(a) (NASB)

You might argue back that although you can accept that you are sometimes a sinner in small ways, you are not a 'bad' sinner. Perhaps you can only imagine God punishing a particularly bad sinner who commits dramatic crimes such as murder, but not someone like yourself. It would be nice if that was true, but that is not what the Bible says. Therefore if you believe that, then you are basing it simply upon your own wishful thinking and speculation. You would also be contradicting what God says directly about it.

The key to understanding Christianity is to realise that you really are a sinner and that your sin is not trivial, but grievous. Therefore unless you become a Christian and have your sins forgiven, you are facing God's wrath, just the same as all the other people whom you, perhaps, imagine to be "worse" than you. God finds all of us guilty and unworthy be in His presence.

I am not exaggerating, as I will seek to demonstrate. Let me explain it with an illustration: Imagine that you had in front of you 10 glasses of water into which cyanide poison has been placed. In the first glass there are ten teaspoons of cyanide and in the second glass there are nine and then eight, and so on, down to the tenth glass, which only has one teaspoon of cyanide in it. Which of the ten glasses of water would you be willing to drink?

The answer is that you would not drink any of them. That is exactly how God sees sin in us. The exact amount of sin in you, compared to someone else, is not the point. Any sin at all is like cyanide to God. That's how He sees it. That's why He must reject even the very "best" people.

The point is that it might be that I am a far worse sinner than you. Perhaps your life (as you imagine it to be) is represented by the glass of water with only one teaspoon of cyanide in it? Even if I was to agree with you about that and accept your assumption, what good would it do you?

The point is that God has declared that He will not accept any sin in His presence, not even a single sin on a single day in the middle of a life that is otherwise sinless. Even that one sin would separate you from God because it would be an abomination that He could not accept.

We have to realise what God is really like. Many people have been misled through false ideas that have been put around about God being a kindly old gentleman, slightly senile, who would not harm anyone or get angry about anything. Likewise with Jesus, He is often portrayed as a soppy weakling who goes around patting children on the head and being nice. That is very far from the truth.

The fear of the Lord

The reality is that the Bible tells us that *"our God is a consuming fire"* and that we are to fear and respect Him. Consider the following passages. I will underline each of the references to the *"fear of God"* or the *"fear of the Lord"* to illustrate how clearly the concept is emphasised in the Bible. There are many other verses too, which I could have added:

Let all the earth fear the LORD;
Let all the inhabitants of the world stand in awe of Him.
Psalm 33:8 (NASB)

The LORD Almighty is the one you are to regard as holy, he is the one you are to fear, he is the one you are to dread,

Isaiah 8:13 (NIV)

[28]Therefore, since we are receiving a kingdom that cannot be shaken, let us be thankful, and so worship God acceptably with reverence and awe, [29]for our "God is a consuming fire."

Hebrews 12:28-29 (NIV)

Behold, the eye of the LORD is on those who fear Him,
On those who hope for His lovingkindness,
Psalm 33:18 (NASB)

Yet the reality is that most of mankind does not fear God. On the contrary, it ignores and despises Him:

There is no fear of God before their eyes
Romans 3:18 (NIV)

To get a picture of God's Holiness and the awe and reverence we need to feel towards Him, imagine the Niagara Falls. If you were to go too close to the edge, then the immense power of that waterfall would sweep you away to your death.

Yet if that happened, it would not be the fault of the waterfall. It is in the very nature of the Niagara Falls that it has colossal power. You therefore treat it with respect and fear. You would be a fool not to fear the Niagara Falls.

That is partly what is meant when the Bible repeatedly tells us that we need to fear God. It is a consistent theme emphasised throughout the whole Bible. Here are some more verses to prove that fact and to prove that I am not over stating any of this or taking it out of context:

Oh, that their hearts would be inclined to fear me and keep all my commands always, so that it might go well with them and their children forever!
Deuteronomy 5:29 (NIV)

13Now all has been heard;
here is the conclusion of the matter:
Fear God and keep his commandments,
for this is the whole duty of man.
14For God will bring every deed into judgment,
including every hidden thing,
whether it is good or evil.
Ecclesiastes 12:13-14 (NIV)

26If we deliberately keep on sinning after we have received the knowledge of the
truth, no sacrifice for sins is left, 27but only a fearful expectation of judgment
and of raging fire that will consume the enemies of God. 28Anyone who rejected
the law of Moses died without mercy on the testimony of two or three witnesses.
29How much more severely do you think a man deserves to be punished who has
trampled the Son of God under foot, who has treated as an unholy thing the
blood of the covenant that sanctified him, and who has insulted the Spirit of
grace? 30For we know him who said, "It is mine to avenge; I will repay," and

again, "The Lord will judge his people." [31]***It is a dreadful thing to fall into the hands of the living God.***

Hebrews 10:26-31 (NIV)

What does the fear of God really mean?

There are various aspects to fearing God. In part it means that we are to literally fear Him. You should be in awe of Him, because of His colossal power and the dreadful consequences of being on the wrong side of Him. In fact, you would be a fool not to fear Him. Yet there is more to it than just fear. There is also awe, respect and reverence. We need to feel all of those things, and intensely. Indeed, when we consider God it should cause us to tremble:

Tremble, O earth, before the Lord,
Before the God of Jacob,
Psalm 114:7 (NASB)

My flesh trembles for fear of You,
And I am afraid of Your judgments.
Psalm 119:120 (NASB)

Many years ago, the Queen came to visit the town where I lived. I was standing by a path next to the Queen as she walked along slowly. There was a certain moment when the Queen stopped right next to me and stood for a little while only perhaps 3 feet from me. I could have reached out and touched her. Yet, I was in awe that I was standing right next to the Queen. It seemed unthinkable to do anything to draw attention to myself, or to speak, or move.

I felt rooted to the spot. I was in the presence of someone great, at least in comparison to me. That placed boundaries on what I could say or do. That experience has often come back to me when I have thought about the reverence and fear that we need to feel towards the Lord God Almighty. However much respect we might properly show towards the Queen, the fact is that she is still only a human being like the rest of us. She is a sinner who is mortal and fallible, with limited knowledge and strength. But God is infinitely greater.

The fear of the Lord also involves being overwhelmed by how extraordinarily brilliant God is. He is the only person who is all-knowing, all-powerful and who is present everywhere. He is perfect, holy, righteous, wise, magnificent, creative, imaginative, artistic and musical. He possesses every virtue to an infinite degree. Given that He is all those things and has all those immense qualities, how much more should we be in awe of Him? He is indescribably impressive.

If you were to imagine a person who combined all the qualities of the Queen, Shakespeare, Isaac Newton, Winston Churchill, Abraham Lincoln, Albert Einstein, Mozart, Michelangelo, Leonardo Da Vinci and a host of other brilliant scholars, artists, scientists, musicians, mathematicians, politicians and monarchs, then that might give you a fragment of a picture of how awesome God is. Yet He is infinitely more than such an imaginary composite person could be.

Remember that God created the entire universe. Even within our own galaxy, the Milky Way, there are billions of stars. Yet there are billions of other such galaxies in the universe. He created all of them in a single day, simply by speaking them into existence. He did it through the power of His own words and His creative imagination. Reflect on that for a moment. That is how powerful He is.

At the same time, He created all of what we know as the arts and every other form of beauty. Every person who creates any piece of music, art or poetry is just reflecting a little glimpse of what God naturally is. He is an artist, as you will immediately see by just looking at the beauty of the world that He created. You only have to see a sunset to know that it was intentionally created by a brilliant artist. It cannot have come about by chance.

It's obvious, likewise, that each of the creatures that He has made, and especially the human race, have a beauty and complexity that make clear that they were designed by someone of the utmost brilliance. None of it is accidental and none of it 'evolved' by itself. For all these reasons, we must respect, honour and fear God. We must do so because of who and what He is and because of what He can do with us and to us.

That may not be a fashionable way to talk about God, but as we have seen in the verses quoted earlier, He repeatedly describes Himself in the Bible as someone who is to be feared. He does not merely suggest that. He commands it. It is up to us to choose whether to listen to Him or obey Him. But we must recognise the terrible consequences of failing to do so.

30For we know him who said, "It is mine to avenge; I will repay," and again, "The Lord will judge his people." 31It is a dreadful thing to fall into the hands of the living God.

Hebrews 10:30-31 (NIV)

Therefore, let me come back to my earlier point. Do not be so misguided as to imagine that you are not a sinner or that you are not such a bad sinner as to be in any danger of God's wrath and separation from him in the Lake of Fire. I have no desire to offend or insult you, or anybody, or to be impolite about any of this. But we may as well face facts. No matter who you are, you are a sinner. Therefore you are in the same position as me and everybody else. The only question is what are you going to do about it?

The disadvantage of being a *"respectable"* person

The people who find it hardest to realise the extent and seriousness of their own sin are the so called *"respectable"* people. If you have a job, own a house, and have never been to prison or convicted of a crime, then beware. The chances are very high that you will miss the point and assume that sin is what 'other people' do.

Please be willing to abandon any self-righteous ideas about yourself. Accept that when the Bible speaks of sin and sinners, it means you and me. It does not mean *"them"*, or *"others"*, or "*that group over there*". We are all sinners:

There is not a righteous man on earth who does what is right and never sins.
Ecclesiastes 7:20 (NIV)

Finally, remember that if we don't fear the Lord and put Him first then there will be dire consequences:

24 But be sure to fear the LORD and serve him faithfully with all your heart; consider what great things he has done for you. 25 Yet if you persist in doing evil, both you and your king will be swept away."
1 Samuel 12:24-25 (NIV)

CHAPTER 7

THE TEN COMMANDMENTS - PROOF THAT YOU AND I ARE SINNERS, NOT JUST OTHER PEOPLE

I have included this chapter to address the problem many people have. When 'sin' or 'sinners' are referred to, they assume somebody else is being spoken about, not themselves. Most of the people I have ever spoken to have believed that they are good. But they aren't. We are all sinners, including me and you. If any further proof is needed, that you and I are sinners, let us look at the Ten Commandments as an exercise.

The Law of Moses actually contains 613 commandments from God to the Jewish people. But among those there are the ten main ones which Moses was given by God on Mount Sinai. You could say that these ten sum up all of the others. Let us look at them, just as examples, and work out whether or not you have broken them and if so, how often.

However, please note that the Jewish Law of Moses, of which the Ten Commandments are a part, does not apply any longer. That is because Jesus has fulfilled the Law of Moses and we are not now subject to it. However, nine of the ten commandments were specifically *restated* in the New Testament. That means that they do apply to us today. The only one not restated was the fourth commandment about the Sabbath day. We are therefore still bound to obey the other nine, not as part of the Law of Moses, but because they are restated in the New Testament.

The Ten Commandments which God gave to Israel:

1) *7"You shall have no other gods before me.*

2) *8"You shall not make for yourself an idol in the form of anything in Heaven above or on the earth beneath or in the waters below. 9 You shall not bow down to them or worship them; for I, the LORD your God, am a jealous God, punishing the children for the sin of the fathers to the third and fourth generation of those who hate me, 10 but showing love to a thousand generations of those who love me and keep my commandments.*

3) *11"You shall not misuse the name of the LORD your God, for the LORD will not hold anyone guiltless who misuses his name.*

4) *12"Observe the Sabbath day by keeping it holy, as the LORD your God has commanded you. 13Six days you shall labour and do all your work, 14but the seventh day is a Sabbath to the LORD your God. On it you shall not do any work, neither you, nor your son or daughter, nor your manservant or maidservant, nor your ox, your donkey or any of your animals, nor the alien within your gates, so that your manservant and maidservant may rest, as you do.* [15]*Remember that you were slaves in Egypt and that the LORD your God brought you out of there with a mighty hand and an outstretched arm. Therefore the LORD your God has commanded you to observe the Sabbath day.*

(NB Remember, this fourth commandment about the Sabbath was not restated in the New Testament so it does not apply to us today).

5) [16] *"Honour your father and your mother, as the LORD your God has commanded you, so that you may live long and that it may go well with you in the land the LORD your God is giving you.*

6) [17] *"You shall not murder.*

7) [18] *"You shall not commit adultery.*

8) [19] *"You shall not steal.*

9) [20] *"You shall not give false testimony against your neighbour.*

10) [21] *"You shall not covet your neighbour's wife. You shall not set your desire on your neighbour's house or land, his manservant or maidservant, his ox or donkey, or anything that belongs to your neighbour."*

Deuteronomy 5:7-21 (NIV)

Are you guilty of breaking these commandments?

Possibly you feel you are not guilty of breaking any of them? Or perhaps you assume that you have only broken them to a slight extent and therefore that you are doing relatively well. However, let's look at each of the nine commandments that still apply to us and consider whether you are innocent or guilty. I am doing this because, in my experience, so many people just cannot see, or will not admit, that they are sinners.

I hope that by the time we get to the end of this chapter there will no longer be any argument about this and that you will accept that you have sinned in more ways than you have realised, and that you are just as guilty as I am. By the way, I am not saying that these are the only sins that you and I are guilty of. There are many more besides these, such as pride, selfishness, cruelty, callousness, rebellion, lack of love etc etc. These nine commandments are just examples to prove the general point. The true extent of our sinfulness is far wider than this.

1. Do you put other gods before God?

The first commandment - "*You shall have no other gods before me.*"
Deuteronomy 5:7 (NIV)

The word "*gods,*" spelled with a small "g", refers to a number of things. Firstly it means the worship of gods in polytheistic religions such as Hinduism, where they have a multitude of gods. Likewise in the religions of ancient Greece, Rome and Scandinavia, they had very many gods such as Diana, Jupiter, Thor, Woden, etc. The Bible tells us that in reality, behind all such false gods or idols, there are demons. For most of us who are from the West, the idea of worshiping false gods such as this, whether demons or otherwise, is alien.

You might imagine therefore that you are innocent of this sin and that you do not worship any gods ahead of God Himself. However, you can make anything into a god. Your own god could be yourself, your career, family, money, comfort, a house, pleasure, car, hobby, pop star or a football team.

It is anything that you value more highly than God Himself and to which you give greater emphasis and importance than to Him. When you put it that way, you will quickly realise that you have probably got several 'gods' in your life that you actively worship. Take money for example. How much time to do you spend thinking about money as compared to thinking about God Himself? Do you love God as much as you love money? You may have never even considered such a question.

Alternatively, ask yourself about your career or some other ambition. If you are honest with yourself you will admit that you have, on countless occasions, and in many different ways, elevated something or someone to a higher place than God. I certainly have.

The point of the first commandment is that God alone is to be worshiped. Nothing else and nobody else is ever to be worshiped. This commandment does not sound very serious to our Western ears. Yet God sees it as crucial. He will not accept anything other than first place in your life. Therefore to give anything else first place is to make that thing a god instead of, or ahead of, Him. He refuses to share His place as the God of the universe and as your God.

It is therefore a dreadful insult to put any god before Him. This is worth reflecting upon at length until you can see where you have been committing this sin. It may not be obvious to you at first. But once you dwell upon it you will see that you have done it all your life and are probably still doing it now.

2. Are you guilty of idolatry?

The Second Commandment - ***[8]"You shall not make for yourself an idol in the form of anything in Heaven above or on the earth beneath or in the waters below. [9]You shall not bow down to them or worship them; for I, the LORD your God, am a jealous God, punishing the children for the sin of the fathers to the third and fourth generation of those who hate me, [10]but showing love to a thousand generations of those who love me and keep my commandments.***

Deuteronomy 5:8-10 (NIV)

The first commandment, forbids us to have any gods in place of God Himself. The second forbids us to have any idols. An idol is any statue, object, thing, person or institution that we idolise. We are not to idolise or worship any created thing. We are only to worship God Himself. You may protest that you do not do this, but perhaps you do.

If you come from a Roman Catholic background or from the Greek or Russian Orthodox churches, you will have almost certainly done so. Those churches all have statues or icons which people venerate and even pray to. For example, in the Catholic Church, Mary, the mother of Jesus, is elevated and prayed to in ways which are unbiblical and inappropriate. Likewise a host of different "saints" are prayed to.

By saints they mean dead people who are alleged to have been especially holy. Many of them are made into statues, ornaments or pictures and are prayed to. Those who do this usually protest that they are not praying *to* Mary or the saints, but merely asking them to pray *for* us. That is the basis on which they usually seek to justify it. However, even if that was true, it is still not valid. In presenting our prayer to or through Mary or a 'saint', and/or in venerating a statue or image, we are making an idol of them. The second commandment forbids that.

However, even the explanation that people give for it is not true. Very few people limit themselves to asking Mary or some other saint to pray for them. I know from my own experience and from many people I have known, that people do, in fact, pray directly *to* Mary and the saints. That is certainly what I was taught to do when I was young. Here are some examples of the kind of prayers that are made. Just look at the words.

How can anybody deny that these prayers are to Mary or the saints, not mere requests for them to pray for us. Let's look first at a short prayer to Saint Anthony, supposedly the "patron saint of lost things". People pray directly to him in these words when they need to find a lost item of property:

"Saint Anthony, Saint Anthony, please come around. There's something that's lost that's got to be found."

Now consider this description *of* Mary:

"Mary, the Mother of God, to whom all the faithful fly for protection in all their dangers and needs."

These words could only be validly spoken of God, not of a mere human being. It indicates that Mary is being viewed as if she was on the same level as God. But, even more alarmingly, look at this prayer *to* Mary. It was written by Pope John Paul II:

"Comfort, guide, strengthen the whole of humanity. Sustain us O Virgin Mary on our journey of faith and obtain for us the grace of eternal salvation."

That prayer cannot mean anything unless one assumes that Mary has powers that only God has. If not, then how could she possibly answer a prayer like that? Lastly, and worst of all, consider this prayer. It comes from the Catholic book *'Devotions in honour of our Mother of Perpetual Help'*:

"Come then to my aid, dearest Mother for I recommend myself to thee. In thy hands I place my eternal salvation and to thee do I entrust my soul. For if thou protect me, dear Mother, I fear nothing; not for my sins because thou wilt obtain for me the pardon of them; nor from the devils because thou art more powerful than all Hell together; nor even from Jesus my Judge himself because by one prayer from thee, he will be appeased. But one thing I fear, that in the hour of temptation I may neglect to call on thee and thus perish miserably. Obtain for me then the pardon of my sins".

How can we describe that as anything other than a prayer *to* Mary? Again, it obviously elevates her to the level of God. Even more seriously, it misrepresents Jesus. It portrays Him as our accuser, when in fact He is our advocate and Saviour. It gives to Mary Jesus' role as our advocate and implies that Jesus is reluctant to save us and would not do so without Mary's intervention. That is all blasphemy.

However, it goes further. Within Roman Catholicism, the Pope is also widely idolised. There is no other word for it. He is elevated to a place which only God can be in. He even takes to himself titles reserved only for God, which the Bible never authorises any man to use of himself. Some examples of this are as follows:

a) *"Holy Father"* - this is a phrase Jesus used in the Bible, but only of God the Father – (John 17:11). The Pope has no right to use that title for himself and we must never call any pope by that title.

b) *"Vicar of Christ"* – *"vicar"* means *"in place of"* Christ i.e. that the Pope is the bodily representative of Jesus on this earth. How can he presume to take such a title to himself? There is nothing in the Bible to support such a title for any man, whether he is a pope or not.

c) In 1894 Pope Leo XIII said that as Pope he held on Earth the place of God Almighty!

d) Pope Pius X (1903-1914) said that when the Pope speaks it is Jesus Christ Himself speaking and that the Pope is the one hope for the world!

e) Pope Pius XI (1922 – 1939) said that because he was Vicar of Christ, he was *"God on Earth"*.

f) Pope Boniface VIII said that unless people submit to the Pope they cannot be saved.

There are many other such examples. However, one only has to see the way in which the recent Polish Pope, John Paul II, was venerated by huge crowds to see that he was an idol to them. It is blasphemous for those popes, who are just ordinary, sinful men, to take such titles or to make such claims for themselves. That is something they will have to answer for personally. However, your responsibility is not to join in. You must not idolise them, even if you have been taught to do so.

You must choose either to obey the traditions of the Catholic church or to obey the Bible. You can't do both. **Before I go on, let me emphasise again that I am not picking on or singling out the Catholic Church. It is just that I happen to know it well, due to my background. Thus I find it easier to think of examples from Catholicism.**

Idolatry is by no means limited to the Catholic church. It exists all over the world, for example in Hinduism, Buddhism, Sikhism and Islam. For many people it could even be the national flag of their country. There is no sin in being patriotic. In fact it is a virtue, because it was God who created each nation and He wants us to love our own country and to be loyal to it. However, there are people whose devotion to their country and its flag reaches the level of worship, or comes close to it. Whatever form the god or idol takes, God is appalled by it:

They will be turned back and be utterly put to shame,
Who trust in idols,
Who say to molten images,
"You are our gods."
Isaiah 42:17 (NASB)

So, I am by no means picking on Catholicism alone. Even so, it affects around one billion people, and it happens to be my own personal background so, let me give another example of where idolatry arises there.

Transubstantiation

Let us turn now to the belief within the Roman Catholic Church that the communion bread and the wine are the actual, real body and blood of Jesus. This is called "*transubstantiation*". Roman Catholics are taught to worship the host or wafer, i.e. the physical piece of bread, as being Jesus' literal and actual body. Instead of just *representing* Him, they believe it *actually is* Him.

They mean well by it, and are sincere, but that belief is plainly wrong. That is not what Jesus meant when He took the bread and wine and gave it to the apostles at the last supper, on the night before His crucifixion. Apostle Paul explains this very well:

23 For I received from the Lord what I also passed on to you: The Lord Jesus, on
the night he was betrayed, took bread, 24 and when he had given thanks, he broke
it and said, "This is my body, which is for you; do this in remembrance of me."
25 In the same way, after supper he took the cup, saying, "This cup is the new
covenant in my blood; do this, whenever you drink it, in remembrance of me."
26 For whenever you eat this bread and drink this cup, you proclaim the Lord's
death until he comes.

1 Corinthians 11:23-26 (NIV)

When Jesus said *"This is my body ....."* He was saying that the bread and wine represented His body and blood and that when we eat and drink them we are to remember Him. He did not want us to worship or make an idol of the physical bread and wine themselves. They were only symbols, just as Jesus used symbolic speech when He said *"I am the door"* or *"I am the vine and you are the branches"*. Indeed, how can He have meant that the bread He was holding was His real body, when He Himself was there holding it? It makes no sense at all and is obviously not what Jesus meant.

Yet, within Roman Catholicism and amongst some "High Anglicans," the bread and wine have ended up being made into idols. The physical bread and wine are literally worshiped on the basis that they *are* Jesus, not that they are a symbol to remind us of Him. That is precisely the kind of thing that God wanted us to avoid doing, which is the very reason for the second commandment.

I could give many more such examples but let it suffice to say that we are forbidden to make any idols or images of Mary, or saints, or the Pope, or the bread and wine, or of any other thing or person. When we do those things we are dishonouring and disobeying God, even if we genuinely mean well by it. Consider what the apostles Paul and John said about this:

Therefore, my dear friends, flee from idolatry
1 Corinthians 10:14 (NIV)

Dear children, keep yourselves from idols.
1 John 5:21 (NIV)

But look how the prophet Ezekiel is even more emphatic about how God views idolatry:

"Therefore say to the house of Israel, 'Thus says the Lord GOD, "Repent and turn away from your idols and turn your faces away from all your abominations.
Ezekiel 14:6 (NASB)

3. Do you misuse (or take in vain) the name of the Lord?

The Third Commandment - ***"You shall not misuse the name of the LORD your God, for the LORD will not hold anyone guiltless who misuses his name"***
Deuteronomy 5:11 (NIV)

In the King James Bible this commandment reads slightly differently saying **"You shall not take the name of the Lord your God in vain…"** It mainly relates to disrespecting or abusing God's name by what we say. It also means living in any way that brings Him and His name into reproach or dishonour. That is a sobering thought, because many more of us are guilty of that than of directly insulting God's name in our speech. There are many ways in which we can break this third commandment. It is common to hear people openly using God's name as a swear word and to say the most blasphemous things.

Blasphemy means disrespecting God or His name or to mock Him in any way. How many times have you said or heard people say *"Christ!"* as a way of expressing surprise or concern? Equally, people say *"God!"* or *"Oh my God!"* or *"OMG"*. The one that grieves me the most is when people exclaim *"Jesus Christ!"* Yet, consider what it means. It is taking God's precious and Holy name and using it as an expletive to express surprise or anger. That is profoundly disrespectful and there will be a consequence for all who do it:

Do not be deceived: God cannot be mocked. A man reaps what he sows.
Galatians 6:7 (NIV)

If you cannot see why this matters so much, imagine your work colleagues deciding that from now on, when they wish to swear or express abuse, they will use the names of your family. Imagine someone who has just dropped a hammer on their foot using your mother's name as an expletive, or even your own name. How would you feel? We are also forbidden from using God's name flippantly, or joking about Him.

It's no coincidence that God's name, and in particular the name of Jesus, are routinely blasphemed. It is a deliberate satanic strategy to undermine God's name. It's almost certain that you've never heard anybody insulting the name of Buddha, Mohammed, Allah or any of the Hindu gods. It's never done, because Satan doesn't want it done. He therefore doesn't cause it to be done. He only encourages people to mock God's name. He leaves every false religious figure alone.

The very fact that the attack is exclusively against the names of God and Jesus demonstrates that they are true and that the others are not. Satan will never attack any false religion. He wants them all to prosper and to attract people. It is solely Christianity, and especially the name of Jesus Christ, that he hates. What the third commandment can also mean, even for believers, is to presumptuously express a view, presenting it as God's view when it isn't.

So if you have an opinion, then don't use God's name to justify your view and to make out that He agrees with you. You must not attribute views to God which He does not hold, or misuse His glorious name as an authority for things which He has not said. You will be held equally accountable for every word you say about God or on His behalf. That ought to make every church leader or preacher tremble.

We all need to be so careful what we say about God. In the book of Job, God rebukes the three friends of Job who misrepresented God in the things they said. They told Job, a righteous man, that his afflictions and sufferings were a punishment from God because of some sin in Job's life. That was not true. You might not consider that to be the worst falsehood that you have ever heard being said about God. However, look how seriously God takes it. He is very angry at having His actions and motives wrongly portrayed:

It came about after the LORD had spoken these words to Job, that the LORD said to Eliphaz the Temanite, "My wrath is kindled against you and against your two friends, because you have not spoken of Me what is right as My servant Job has.

Job 42:7 (NASB)

Therefore, be very careful what you say about God, or about His actions, motives or views. Even if you mean well you could misrepresent Him, which is a very serious matter indeed. Lastly, taking God's Name in vain can mean that in the way we live we are a 'poor witness' or a poor advert for God. Our sin or hypocrisy can easily discredit God's name. That possibility worries me. I do not want my sin ever to bring God's name into disrepute.

In short, we need to be very careful as to when and how we use His Name at all. It should only be spoken with great respect and reverence, never with flippancy or casualness. We need to live as ambassadors, knowing that if we claim to be a believer then we will be taken to represent Him. If so, then we will be answerable for the impression we give, whether intentionally or unintentionally. We should reflect on that sobering responsibility. Therefore examine yourself now as to whether you have ever broken this commandment in any of the ways described above. Almost inevitably, the answer will be yes, and on countless occasions.

4. Observing the Sabbath day

This is the only one of the Ten Commandments which no longer applies to us. We are no longer under an obligation to observe a particular day of rest. However, it's still a very good thing to have a day of rest. The Jewish people were commanded to refrain from working on the Sabbath, i.e. Friday sunset to Saturday sunset. That commandment was not restated in the New Testament, whereas the other nine were.

Thus the other nine commandments still apply, even to Christians, but the commandment about the Sabbath does not, because we are not bound by the law of Moses. We are only bound by those parts of it that were restated in the New Testament, or which our own consciences tell us to obey. However, in that case, it is your conscience you would be obeying, not the Law of Moses itself. So, I will now move on to the Fifth Commandment.

5. Do you honour your Father and Mother?

The Fifth Commandment - ***"Honour your father and your mother, as the LORD your God has commanded you, so that you may live long and that it may go well with you in the land the LORD your God is giving you.***

Deuteronomy 5:16 (NIV)

Few people even know about this commandment, let alone take it seriously. Respect for parents is not a widespread feature of British society. This commandment is not only for young children. It is equally about how adults treat their middle aged or elderly parents. God has created the very concept of parenthood to teach us something about Him. We would have no way of knowing what the word "Father" means if He had not created human fatherhood as a model.

That is one reason why it is so tragic when children are abused or mistreated by their parents. It can give them a warped view of what a human father is. That then creates a negative image of what God the Father must be. God's ideal is for every parent to reflect to their children something of what He is. Then every child can later look upon God the Father in a positive light and grasp the concept of God's Fatherhood.

God wants us to learn respect for our human father and mother so that we can develop the ability to respect our Heavenly Father. If we do not have respect for our human parents, then we will never have a proper respect for God the Father either. You have both or you have neither. So, the way we treat our human parents is a training ground. It is where we begin to learn how to have a right relationship with God the Father.

Moreover, if we dishonour our human parents we also dishonour God Himself. He created the family unit as the building block of human society. The family is of great importance. It must work vertically, between parents and children, but also horizontally, between siblings, and members of the wider family too. If family life is not honoured and valued then society will disintegrate. That is what we are seeing happening in the Western world now.

There has probably never been so much crime, degradation and chaos as we see now. It principally flows from two things: the abandonment of Christianity and the breakdown of family life. Where there is no respect for parents, then family life as a whole will also break down. Once that goes beyond a certain point, then society in general breaks down. That is what we are seeing now, with promiscuity, divorce, abortion and dysfunctional families.

For all these reasons God wants us all to honour our parents, not only when we are very young but throughout our lives. Even if we are in our seventies, we are still under a solemn duty to honour our elderly parents, to the very end of their lives. The final years of frailty and dependency, when elderly parents need your help most, can be a time of great blessing. Yet it is increasingly resented as an unwelcome burden, which should be avoided, even by euthanasia.

The final years of an elderly parent can be your God-given opportunity to serve them and honour them in ways you may have neglected to do when they were younger and fitter. Take that chance gladly. Make the most of it. Cherish those final years. God will bless you for everything you do to honour your parents. The question therefore is do you do this? Do you honour your parents now, and have you honoured them in the past?

It is not just a question of buying them cards on Mothers' Day or Fathers' Day or visiting them from time to time. It is much deeper than that. We are to actively honour our parents in practical ways, and to make it a priority to do so. We are to go out of our way to respect and care for our parents. Do you do that? Moreover, it is not only our own parents, but all elderly people who should be honoured:

"'Stand up in the presence of the aged, show respect for the elderly and revere your God. I am the LORD

Leviticus 19:32 (NIV)

However in Britain today there are huge numbers of elderly people who live alone and who never receive a visit from anybody for months on end. Many more are in nursing homes and rarely, if ever, receive visitors. Obviously, there are many families where things are done well, and great care is taken of elderly parents. But in some families elderly parents and relatives are not well cared for.

That is one reason why there is a growing movement to legalise euthanasia. If we do, and it seems inevitable, then it will be disastrous for our society. In many families children, both as teenagers and adults, show contempt, disrespect and disregard for their parents. They take them for granted, receive without giving back, and fail to show gratitude for all that their parents have done for them.

One of the most painful things we ever have to experience is ingratitude. The pain of that is multiplied according to the closeness of the relationship. The ingratitude of an acquaintance hurts far less than that of a close work colleague. Even that hurts far less than the ingratitude of a family member. However, the ingratitude of one's own child is the ultimate.

It may be that even looking into this subject is painful, because your family background may not have been a happy one. Alternatively, maybe it was happy but you now know, as you look back, that you have not honoured your parents as you should? Have you thanked your parents meaningfully and adequately? Do you repay them? Do you care for them now and put yourself out financially, and in terms of time and effort, to look after them?

It is common to see people focusing upon their expected inheritance from their parents rather than on what they can give to their parents, especially in their old age. In fact, caring for them ought to be the emphasis. The 'social security' system throughout history has always been based on the family. It is the job of all children, when they grow into adulthood, to care for their parents and to make sure that all their material needs are fully met. Our society, in the West at least, has delegated that duty to the state so that we have now lost the habit. It does not even occur to many of us to care for our elderly parents.

In fact, a peculiar thing happened to me some time ago. It serves as a useful illustration of this point about who is primarily responsible for our parents. A man rang my law firm when I was in practice and was put through to me as he wanted to speak to a Christian Solicitor. He said that his parents were elderly and were retired missionaries. His father had started to develop dementia and he wanted his parents to be given advice and help with drafting powers of attorney and generally arranging their affairs.

He then said, very revealingly: *"But my parents don't have any money. That's why I'm looking for a Christian firm to act for them"*. He explained that he wanted it to be done free of charge. It seemed to me that he was making two inaccurate assumptions:

a) that a Christian Solicitor should feel an obligation to act for someone else's parents without charging anything.

b) that *he himself* had no duty even to consider paying the legal fees of his own parents and could validly offload that burden onto me.

It's only when you pause and press the replay button that the full significance of that second assumption hits you. That man saw nothing wrong or unusual in what he'd said to me. His mind had never formed the thought that his parents' welfare was primarily *his own* obligation, rather than mine. But see how Apostle Paul speaks about this:

But if anyone does not provide for his own, and especially for those of his household, he has denied the faith and is worse than an unbeliever.

1 Timothy 5:8 (NASB)

When I was in practice as a lawyer, I was always very willing to donate the time of myself and of my staff in a good cause. But that is not the issue here. The point is that he did not want to give his own money to provide what his own parents needed. In fact, such an idea was so unthinkable that he had never thought of it. He wanted me to be generous to them instead of him being so. I wish I could say that men like him were rare, but they are not. His was a very typical view.

There are multitudes of people, even amongst Christians, who think the same way. They have never even considered whether there could be anything wrong in that. I have focused on our duties to our parents at some length because it is not a well-known commandment. Even those who are aware of it find it difficult to believe they have broken it. Yet, you may now realise that you have, perhaps, broken it many times?

By the way, have you noticed that this is the only one of the Ten Commandments that also carries a promise: " *...so that you may live long and that it may go well with you in the land..."* So, those who do what God requires and honour their parents were promised long life and success/security. Although we are no longer operating under the Law of Moses, I believe God still honours that principle today. That should give you all the more reason to take it seriously.

6. Are you a murderer?

The sixth commandment – ***"You shall not murder"***
Deuteronomy 5:17 (NIV)

You are, perhaps, seeing a pattern here such that, so far, you are guilty of breaking all of the commandments. But, when it comes to murder perhaps you will protest and say that at least on that count you are innocent. However, Jesus has clarified the meaning of murder and has broadened its definition. Jesus said that even where we feel hatred or sinful rage towards another person then it is as if we have committed murder:

21 "You have heard that it was said to the people long ago, 'Do not murder, and anyone who murders will be subject to judgment.' 22 But I tell you that anyone who is angry with his brother will be subject to judgment. Again, anyone who says to his brother, 'Raca,' is answerable to the Sanhedrin. But anyone who says, 'You fool!' will be in danger of the fire of Hell.

Matthew 5:21-22 (NIV)

Apostle John went further in his first letter, saying that if we hate our brother, we are a murderer. By 'brother' he meant fellow believers, not just our natural brothers:

14 We know that we have passed from death to life, because we love our brothers. Anyone who does not love remains in death. 15 Anyone who hates his brother is a murderer, and you know that no murderer has eternal life in him. 16 This is how we know what love is: Jesus Christ laid down his life for us. And we ought to lay down our lives for our brothers.

1 John 3:14-16(NIV)

If we use Jesus' definition of murder, or apostle John's, then we are all murderers. We need to take that as seriously as they do and repent of hate and rage and confess them to be sins. That said, for many people, the murder they have been involved with is real and literal, not just figurative. Let us consider the tragic situation in the Western world with regard to abortion.

Every year in Britain 200,000 unborn children are killed deliberately. Almost always, this is done for purely social or economic reasons and has nothing to do with anybody's medical condition, (not that that would make it right even if medical factors were involved). In the vast majority of cases the mother simply does not want to have the child due to her career, education, lifestyle or finances being at stake.

Our society has convinced itself that there is nothing wrong in this. We go out of our way to use euphemisms like *"termination of pregnancy"* instead of *"killing the baby"* or *"foetus"* instead of *"child"*. Yet, if we reflect on this, we must conclude that Britain is guilty of systematic mass murder on an industrial scale.

In Great Britain alone, about 7,000,000 babies have been killed so far since it was legalised in 1967. That represents more than 50 Hiroshima atom bombs. It is bigger in number than the holocaust, when 6,000,000 Jews were killed by the Germans. And that is just in Britain alone. Imagine the number of abortions if you were to calculate it worldwide!

Consider how God views that. He sees the unborn baby as a child. He is not fooled or deflected by our politically correct language. Abortion is murder, not *"termination of pregnancy"*. That means that 200,000 murders of unborn children are happening every year in Britain alone. There are about five times as many in America. They legalised it in 1973. God will not just stand by and let all of that happen. His judgment will come.

Indeed, it is already coming. Moreover, bear in mind that any mother, father, boyfriend, husband, doctor, nurse, counsellor, sister, grandparent, friend or relative who advises someone to have an abortion, or assists in it, is guilty too. All of them are accomplices in it and stand guilty before God, just like the woman who has the abortion. Indeed, they could perhaps be even more guilty if they persuade or pressurize her into agreeing to it.

I realise that those are strong statements. Some may view them as condemning. However, I personally am not condemning anybody, either for this sin or any other. I have no authority to do that. I merely state the obvious and express what the Bible says about what we are doing in our society. Abortion will inevitably bring God's judgment upon every nation that practises it. Indeed His judgment has already begun, and it will continue. Look at how God viewed the practice of child sacrifice in the days of the prophet Jeremiah. Note the severity of the judgment that God said was coming on them:

4Because the people have forsaken me, and have profaned this place by burning incense in it to other gods whom neither they nor their fathers nor the kings of Judah have known; and because they have filled this place with the blood of innocents, 5and have built the high places of Ba'al to burn their sons in the fire

as burnt offerings to Ba'al, which I did not command or decree, nor did it come into my mind; [6]therefore, behold, days are coming, says the LORD, when this place shall no more be called Topheth, or the valley of the son of Hinnom, but the valley of Slaughter. [7]And in this place I will make void the plans of Judah and Jerusalem, and will cause their people to fall by the sword before their enemies, and by the hand of those who seek their life. I will give their dead bodies for food to the birds of the air and to the beasts of the earth. [8]And I will make this city a horror, a thing to be hissed at; everyone who passes by it will be horrified and will hiss because of all its disasters.

Jeremiah 19:4-8(RSV)

When you add up all the people who have been involved in abortion, directly or indirectly, then there could be perhaps 30 million people in Britain who have played a part in it in some way at some time. Even an indirect involvement makes a person guilty. It is just as it would be if you were indirectly involved in an armed robbery where a guard is shot dead.

If you were a lookout, or drove the van, or provided the gun, or hid the proceeds, then you would be part of it. The same is true with abortion. That means it may possibly involve half of the British population. Yet, we tend to blank it out of our minds and deny our own guilt. We need to stop deluding ourselves and openly confess to God where we have done things, or assisted in things, which have caused abortion to happen.

If you have been involved in abortion, either now or long ago, whether directly or indirectly, you need to repent and seek God's forgiveness, just as with any other sin. Until you do, you will never be free from the burden of guilt and pain that abortion causes. People know in their hearts that it is wrong but they suppress the voice of their own conscience. Therefore, if this applies to you, confess it now and you can receive God's cleansing and forgiveness. It is fully available to you.

God is ready and willing to forgive the mother, the father, the husband, the boyfriend, the doctor, the nurse, the anaesthetist and all the relatives and friends who assist and co-operate. He also wants to heal and restore them all. But He first requires us to admit to ourselves, and to Him, that abortion is murder, and to stop calling it by any other name.

Until we do, we cannot get free of the guilt and the pain that abortion causes. The pain of abortion goes very deep and does not go away. I remember once speaking in an Anglican Church where I was a guest speaker. I referred to abortion, sensitively but openly. An old lady in her seventies got up in the aisle and literally waved her walking stick at me, and shouted abuse. She was letting out her pain and grief over something in her life. I spoke to her later but never got to the heart of what was troubling her. So, I do not condemn her, or anyone else, but I must tell the truth. We are all sinners and we do not help ourselves by denying it, whether in regard to this sin, or any other sin.

7. Are you an adulterer?

The seventh commandment - *"You shall not commit adultery".*
Deuteronomy 5:18 (NIV)

It could be that you have literally committed adultery. Alternatively, you might think that on this one you are in a strong position because you have never physically done this. If so, you need to think again, because Jesus also clarified and broadened this commandment for us:

27 "You have heard that it was said, 'Do not commit adultery.' 28 But I tell you that anyone who looks at a woman lustfully has already committed adultery with her in his heart.
Matthew 5:27-28 (NIV)

What Jesus meant was that it is not enough simply to avoid literal physical adultery. He said that merely to look upon a woman lustfully is adultery. In other words, even to look upon a woman (or a man) lustfully is regarded by God as being adultery, even if it does not go as far as anything physical. I do not suppose that there is a person anywhere who has never *'committed adultery in their heart'* by looking lustfully upon a member of the opposite sex.

It is widespread, which is precisely why businesses base so much of their advertising on using sexual imagery. They know very well that every customer is prone to committing adultery in their heart and that this powerful motivation can be used to sell products. I hope that you will accept that you, like me, are guilty of this.

I should add that this also involves fornication (i.e. pre-marital heterosexual sex), pornography and homosexuality. The sin of adultery is a broad one and is not restricted solely to married people. Any sex, or even lustful thought, is sinful unless it is within heterosexual marriage and is with or towards one's own spouse. God, fully approves of sex within marriage. Remember, it was He who invented sex.

Thus we must not get the wrong idea and think that God disapproves of sex. He just reserves it for heterosexual married couples. Our society has largely abandoned that view over the last 40 years, and especially in the last 20 years. But it remains true and it is how God sees it. Consider what apostle Paul says about any misuse of our bodies for sexual sin, whether outside marriage or before marriage:

[15]Do you not know that your bodies are members of Christ himself? Shall I then take the members of Christ and unite them with a prostitute? Never! [16]Do you not know that he who unites himself with a prostitute is one with her in body? For it is said, "The two will become one flesh." [17]But he who unites himself with the Lord is one with him in spirit. [18]Flee from sexual immorality. All other sins a man commits are outside his body, but he who sins sexually sins against his own body. [19]Do you not know that your body is a temple of the Holy Spirit, who is in you, whom you have received from God? You are not your own; [20]you were bought at a price. Therefore honor God with your body.

1 Corinthians 6:15-20 (NIV)

Look too at what the writer of the letter to the Hebrews says:

Marriage should be honoured by all, and the marriage bed kept pure, for God will judge the adulterer and all the sexually immoral.

Hebrews 13:4 (NIV)

That is how seriously God views it. Our society has grown so used to adultery, fornication, vulgar speech, pornography, sexual promiscuity, and now homosexuality, that it is no longer able or willing to see that there is a problem. But there is. What we do with our bodies and our minds does matter. God will judge us for it. We are not free to do as we wish with our own bodies. That is because they do not actually belong to us. They belong to God, because He made us. Therefore He owns us and is fully entitled to tell us what we can and cannot do.

8. Are you a thief?

The eighth commandment - ***"You shall not steal."***
Deuteronomy 5:19 (NIV)

Go back throughout your life and ask yourself honestly whether you have ever stolen anything, however small, from a shop or a person, or fiddled a tax return or expenses claim. Alternatively have you ever received wages for work that was not actually done or not properly done? Or have you ever spent time in your working day doing things for yourself on the internet, or texting, or on the telephone, or shopping when you should have been working for your employer? If you have then, at the very least, you have stolen time and wages from that employer, not to mention his phone bill. That alone makes you a thief and a lawbreaker, even if you have only ever done it once:

For whoever keeps the whole law and yet stumbles at just one point is guilty of breaking all of it.

James 2:10 (NIV)

James' point is that to do a thing even once means that you have broken the law. If so, then you are a *'lawbreaker'* overall. In God's eyes it is as if you have broken the whole law. In case you are still insisting that you have never stolen, what about failing to give your money or possessions to God, or to a person whom He wants you to help? To fail to give away what God wants you to give is equal to theft, because you would be robbing God. The book of Malachi shows this principle:

[8]"Will a man rob God? Yet you rob me. "But you ask, 'How do we rob you?'
"In tithes and offerings. [9] You are under a curse—the whole nation of you—
because you are robbing me. [10] Bring the whole tithe into the storehouse, that
there may be food in my house. Test me in this," says the LORD Almighty, "and see if I will not throw open the floodgates of Heaven and pour out so much blessing that you will not have room enough for it.

Malachi 3:8-10 (NIV)

See also what God says about giving to the poor and the attitude we are commanded to have towards those in need:

[7] If there is a poor man among your brothers in any of the towns of the land that the LORD your God is giving you, do not be hardhearted or tightfisted toward
your poor brother. [8] Rather be openhanded and freely lend him whatever he
needs. [9] Be careful not to harbour this wicked thought: "The seventh year, the year for cancelling debts, is near," so that you do not show ill will toward your needy brother and give him nothing. He may then appeal to the LORD against
you, and you will be found guilty of sin. [10] Give generously to him and do so without a grudging heart; then because of this the LORD your God will bless
you in all your work and in everything you put your hand to. [11] There will always
be poor people in the land. Therefore I command you to be openhanded toward your brothers and toward the poor and needy in your land.

Deuteronomy 15:7-11 (NIV)

You might argue that these verses are from the Old Testament and that they perhaps do not apply to us now if we are Christians That would be a mistake. The New Testament still teaches the need to give, and to give generously. All that has altered is the way in which the level of our giving is to be calculated. If anything, the duty to give is even higher now. In the Old Testament the Jewish people had to give *"tithes and offerings"*. (A tithe means a tenth of your income.) The duty to tithe no longer applies to us, but the duty to be generous still applies. Indeed, whatever it meant to be *"generous"* back then, I would think that God expects more of us now than He expected of the people of the Old Testament.

So, the mere fact that we do not have to tithe does not necessarily mean that we should give any less. Many of us ought in fact to give more. Even more importantly, God wants us to be cheerful as we do it. That's a tall order and, so far as I can tell, not many people seem to manage it. Giving should be something we enjoy and look forward to with relish. Instead of finding out the minimum that we are obliged to do, we should be volunteering cheerfully to give more. Look at what apostle Paul has to say on this:

6Now this I say, he who sows sparingly will also reap sparingly, and he who sows bountifully will also reap bountifully. 7Each one must do just as he has purposed in his heart, not grudgingly or under compulsion, for God loves a cheerful giver.

2 Corinthians 9:6-7 (NASB)

Are you generous to the poor? Do you give sacrificially, to the point where it really costs you something and you have to go without? Or, are you hard-hearted and tight-fisted? Be honest with yourself. Many people are mean and stingy. Otherwise why would the Bible have to correct us on this point so frequently? Even if you imagine yourself to be innocent concerning this commandment, or any of the others, you probably aren't. You are probably just blind to your own sin if you think that. Look at what the Psalmist says about people who can't see their own sin:

1 An oracle is within my heart
concerning the sinfulness of the wicked:
There is no fear of God
before his eyes.
2 For in his own eyes he flatters himself
too much to detect or hate his sin.
Psalm 36:1-2 (NIV)

9. Are you a liar?

Ninth commandment - ***"You shall not give false testimony against your neighbour"***

Deuteronomy 5: 20 (NIV)

Translated in more simple terms, this means '*you shall not lie'*. But have you ever told a lie? If you look at it frankly and try not to kid yourself, then you will accept that you have lied on many occasions. Human beings lie to each other daily at work, in their marriages, in their families and everywhere else. We do it both directly and indirectly. Lying and deception are endemic in all societies.

But, if you have ever told a lie, even once, then you are 'a liar'. Remember that according to the book of James, that makes you a lawbreaker across the board. However, the reality is that you have not lied just once, but countless times. I have too. You even lie to yourself. Our very hearts are crooked. Look how the prophet Jeremiah puts it:

The heart is deceitful above all things
and beyond cure.
Who can understand it?
Jeremiah 17:9 (NIV)

10. Do you covet?

Tenth Commandment - ***"You shall not covet your neighbour's wife. You shall not set your desire on your neighbour's house or land, his manservant or maidservant, his ox or donkey, or anything that belongs to your neighbour."***
Deuteronomy 5:21 (NIV)

This is a commandment about something which few people consider even to be a sin. Yet it catches everyone. It even caught the apostle Paul. He spoke in his letter to the Romans about how, before he became a Christian, he was trying with all his might to obey the commandments. Yet he eventually realised that he was covetous. He was doing quite well, or so he thought, in obeying the other commandments. But he discovered that he was definitely guilty of this one:

7 What shall we say, then? Is the law sin? Certainly not! Indeed I would not have known what sin was except through the law. For I would not have known what coveting really was if the law had not said, "Do not covet." 8 But sin, seizing the opportunity afforded by the commandment, produced in me every kind of covetous desire. For apart from law, sin is dead.
Romans 7: 7- 8 (NIV)

Covetousness means inappropriately and unhealthily desiring those things that are not ours. We do this about money, property, houses, cars, jobs or even other people's wives. It means to crave for that which is not yours and not meant to be yours. It is not wrong to desire something in a healthy and proper way. Thus, it is alright for you to desire to get a promotion or to buy a new house. What is wrong however is to crave for it in an unwholesome, unbalanced and excessive way. The essence of covetousness is that you are allowing your fleshly, carnal cravings to direct your life. Then you long for possessions, or positions, and are not content with what God has given you. Look at what Jesus says about this when speaking to a young man who came asking Him to make his brother divide an inheritance with him:

13 Someone in the crowd said to him, "Teacher, tell my brother to divide the inheritance with me." 14 Jesus replied, "Man, who appointed me a judge or an arbiter between you?" 15 Then he said to them, "Watch out! Be on your guard

against all kinds of greed; a man's life does not consist in the abundance of his possessions." [16]***And he told them this parable: "The ground of a certain rich man produced a good crop.*** [17]***He thought to himself, 'What shall I do? I have no place to store my crops.'*** [18]***"Then he said, 'This is what I'll do. I will tear down my barns and build bigger ones, and there I will store all my grain and my goods.*** [19]***And I'll say to myself, "You have plenty of good things laid up for many years. Take life easy; eat, drink and be merry."*** [20]***"But God said to him, 'You fool! This very night your life will be demanded from you. Then who will get what you have prepared for yourself?'*** [21]***"This is how it will be with anyone who stores up things for himself but is not rich toward God."***

Luke 12:13-21 (NIV)

Look closely at what Jesus says in verse 15 above: "*Watch out! Be on your guard against all kinds of greed; a man's life does not consist in the abundance of his possessions*". All of us are, in one way or another, guilty of this sin. We all yearn for things which are not meant to be ours. And we are not content with what God has given to us. But contrast this with apostle Paul's attitude, as shown, in his letter to the Philippians:

[11]***I am not saying this because I am in need, for I have learned to be content whatever the circumstances.*** [12]***I know what it is to be in need, and I know what it is to have plenty. I have learned the secret of being content in any and every situation, whether well fed or hungry, whether living in plenty or in want.*** [13]***I can do everything through him who gives me strength.***

Philippians 4:11-13 (NIV)

The right attitude for each of us to have is simple and sincere contentment with whatever we have, in our job, home, savings, car, and so forth. It is right for us to work hard and to ask God to bless us with good things and, if we get good things, then to enjoy them. Yet, if we do not have those things, or if the things we have are not as good as we would like them to be, we are to practice the art of contentment.

We must not be consumed with striving to acquire more, or better, things. All of us know that we are, or have been, guilty of this. That is especially so in our materialist European and American societies. The debt crisis which engulfed the world in 2008 illustrates how damaging and corrosive the sin of coveting really is. The world would not be in this financial mess if it was not for covetousness.

I have covered nine of the commandments, but there are so many other things that we do wrong as well, besides breaking the Ten Commandments. What about ingratitude? None of us fully appreciate or thank God for all that He has done for us. Also what about pride? And what about selfishness? Which of us would even attempt to deny that we are proud and selfish? How could we? We know it's true.

Remember that it was pride which caused Satan to fall from his position as God's most senior angel.

Pride is the most dangerous and corrosive sin because it leads us into every other sin. It also prevents us from repenting. Likewise, selfishness is what we are at the core of our character. It also causes an infinite number of other sins and enables us to justify more or less anything to ourselves.

Self-interest has become our main guiding principle, instead of conscience. Thus let's admit to pride and selfishness and many other sins too. Let's also recognise that our sinfulness extends far beyond breaking the Ten Commandments, which we have looked at only as a starter.

Conclusion

I hope you will by now accept that you have, like me, broken all nine of the commandments we looked at, and are also guilty of pride, selfishness and a host of other sins too. Perhaps you will argue, however, that you have not done so very often, and that you are not guilty of "many" sins. However, imagine that you have only sinned once per day, which is totally unrealistic. Over say 60 years, that would be 365 sins x 60 years = 21,900 sins!

When viewed as a whole, you could hardly call that combined total trivial, or deny that that makes you well and truly a sinner. But, think how many times you must really have sinned each day of your life. You could probably multiply the above figure ten-fold, or a hundred-fold, in order to be more realistic. That gives a better picture of the true scale of your sin and mine. Hopefully it will persuade you to abandon any lingering hope that you can justify or excuse yourself.

Most Christians find that as they grow in maturity and understanding, their ability to see their own sin increases. That is still the case even if they are actually less sinful in their behaviour. God causes us to get more and more sensitive to sin as we mature. That means that the battle against our sinful nature is lifelong. It will not go away, even in a real believer, until the day he dies.

I have dwelt at length on the question of sin and the sinful nature of man. I have also tried to prove that it includes you. I have done so to prove to you beyond all doubt that you, just like me, have got a real problem. There is no way that you will ever accept God's solution, (which is found through the death and resurrection of Jesus Christ) unless you first recognise that you truly do have a major problem.

If you don't accept you have a sin problem, and that there is no other way out of it, why would you want, or need, Jesus to save you? But if you can admit that you are a sinner then it follows that the inevitable consequences of judgment, Hell and then the Lake of Fire lie in store for you.

That is everyone's position until and unless they find salvation in Jesus Christ. We shall come to that wonderful process of salvation shortly. But for now, let us look at judgment, Hell and the Lake of Fire in closer detail. Then we can see even more clearly how desperate our problem is.

CHAPTER 8

MORE BAD NEWS - JUDGMENT, HELL AND THE LAKE OF FIRE IN CLOSER DETAIL

because He has fixed a day in which He will judge the world in righteousness through a Man whom He has appointed, having furnished proof to all men by raising Him from the dead."

Acts 17:31 (NASB)

But because of your stubbornness and unrepentant heart you are storing up wrath for yourself in the day of wrath and revelation of the righteous judgment of God,

Romans 2:5 (NASB)

He who believes in the Son has eternal life; he who does not obey the Son shall not see life, but the wrath of God rests upon him.

John 3:36 (RSV)

[26]"For just as the Father has life in Himself, even so He gave to the Son also to have life in Himself; [27]and He gave Him authority to execute judgment, because He is the Son of Man.

John 5:26-27 (NASB)

Many people have heard the phrase *'the Day of Judgment'*. It is not surprising that most people view it as just one single event. It is actually much more complicated than that. There are a number of separate judgments which take place at different times, for different reasons and for different groups of people.

We need to work briefly through each of these judgments and distinguish them from each other. In particular we need to remember that Christians will be judged separately from non-Christians, and on a different basis. So, firstly, God will separate out the Christians from the non-Christians.

[40] Just as the weeds are gathered and burned with fire, so will it be at the close of the age. [41] The Son of man will send his angels, and they will gather out of his kingdom all causes of sin and all evildoers, [42] and throw them into the furnace of fire; there men will weep and gnash their teeth. [43] Then the righteous will shine like the sun in the kingdom of their Father. He who has ears, let him hear.

Matthew 13:40-43 (RSV)

[49] ***So it will be at the close of the age. The angels will come out and separate the evil from the righteous,*** [50] ***and throw them into the furnace of fire; there men will weep and gnash their teeth.***

Matthew 13:49-50 (RSV)

The last two verses illustrate the difference between the judgment for believers (wheat) and the final judgment for unbelievers (chaff) at the end of time. However, there are other aspects and stages of God's judgment as well, which occur much earlier. The first type of judgment God brings has already been experienced. Because of the sin of Adam and Eve, and the sins of all of us since then, the natural world itself has been cursed by God:

[17]***To Adam he said, "Because you listened to your wife and ate from the tree about which I commanded you, 'You must not eat of it,'***

"Cursed is the ground because of you;
through painful toil you will eat of it
all the days of your life.
[18]***It will produce thorns and thistles for you,***
and you will eat the plants of the field.
[19]***By the sweat of your brow***
you will eat your food
until you return to the ground,
since from it you were taken;
for dust you are and to dust you will return."

Genesis 3:17-19 (NIV)

Instead of being the paradise that was originally created for the human race, the world is now a place of pain, suffering, death and injustice. All of this is because of sin. That curse is, in itself, a form of immediate judgment here and now. The difficulties we experience in the natural world are the direct and indirect consequences of our sin, which are rebounding on us.

We are already experiencing this judgment or curse right now, during our mortal lives. However, there will also be a number of other future judgments. These will be covered in greater detail in subsequent books in this series but the major one, for non-Christians, is the *"Great White Throne Judgment."*

The Great White Throne Judgment – the judgment for all non-Christians

This is the largest and the final judgment which comes at the very end. It is the main judgment that affects all people who are not genuine Christians. In other words, it is for all people who have not been born again because they have not genuinely repented and believed in Jesus Christ. We need to be clear about that.

It does not only relate to people who do not believe that Jesus *exists* or those who do not believe that He is the Son of God. There are many people who believe Jesus exists and that He is the Son of God, but they are still not born again and they are not saved. The Bible tells us that even demons believe in who Jesus is. They know very well who He is. In fact, they tremble when they think of Him. However, demons are not *"believers"* in the sense that we mean here. Thus, tragically, many people will go to the Great White Throne Judgment, and then to the Lake of Fire, even though they were *'churchgoers'* or even church leaders.

That is because, despite all appearances, they were never real Christians. That is a frightening thought, but it is the truth. When I use the word *"churchgoer",* I don't mean it as a compliment. It usually suggests (to me) someone who has no genuine personal relationship with God, but who merely has the outward form of religion, rather than anything real and sincere. Churchgoers are not necessarily saved, because they may never have truly repented or believed. I have never heard a real Christian refer to himself as a *"churchgoer."*

It is usually a word used by or about nominal Christians. They attend churches and observe all sorts of man-made traditions, rituals and liturgies, but they have never truly repented. Neither have they sincerely believed in Jesus in the biblical sense, by putting all their trust in Him to save them. See Jesus' words in Matthew:

7You hypocrites! Isaiah was right when he prophesied about you:
8"These people honour me with their lips,
but their hearts are far from me.
9They worship me in vain;
their teachings are but rules taught by men."
Matthew 15:7-9 (NIV)

Jesus is talking about people who appear to be believers. They attend church meetings and they seem to say and do all the right religious sounding things. But, they aren't real. They are, in some way, phoney, shallow and superficial. I was one of those people myself for the first 19 years of my life when I was in the Roman Catholic Church. Many people would have said I was *"religious"*, but I now know that I was unsaved and unforgiven.

Mere "*churchgoers*", whatever denomination they belong to, may well receive a terrible shock when they die. They may discover that all their years attending church were of no use, because Jesus might say *"I never knew you"*. Those are terrible and frightening words. We must therefore assess ourselves soberly and test whether we really are genuinely in the faith or just shallow and false. We must also ask ourselves whether we are willing to be openly identified with Jesus Christ. If so He will accept us and endorse us in front of God the Father. But if we deny Him now, He will deny us then:

[32] "Therefore everyone who confesses Me before men, I will also confess him before My Father who is in Heaven. [33] "But whoever denies Me before men, I will also deny him before My Father who is in Heaven.

Matthew 10:32-33 (NASB)

So, the Great White Throne Judgment will be conducted by the Lord Jesus Christ Himself. It involves a far larger number of people than the Judgment Seat of Christ. It will involve all people throughout history who have not put their trust in Jesus by repenting, and truly believing in Him in order to be forgiven. In other words, it will involve everyone who is not judged at the earlier, and quite separate, Judgment Seat of Christ. That is solely for genuine believers.

Those two judgments are mutually exclusive. You can't be at both. We do not know how many people will be at each of these two separate judgments. The numbers will be vast at both. What we can say, however, is that most people will go to the Great White Throne judgment, for non-Christians. There are many reasons for saying that. The simplest would be to refer to the words of Jesus Christ Himself, who said:

"Enter by the narrow gate, for the gate is wide and the way is easy that leads to destruction and those who enter by it are many. For the gate is narrow and the way is hard that leads to life, and those who find it are few".

Matthew 7: 13-14 (NIV)

At the very least, we know that there will be a majority who go to the Great White Throne Judgment and on from there into the Lake of Fire. We do not know how large a majority that is. We are not told. But the clear implication of that passage, and of other passages, is that it is a large majority. That is real Christians are in a small minority. It is not just a situation of 49:51, but perhaps 1:10 or 1:20 or even 1:100. It varies from country to country and from one time in history to another.

Nobody knows how many real Christians there are, as opposed to apparent believers or mere churchgoers. Only God knows which of us are genuine and which of us are not. There is no way for us to count and no way of judging. That is because we are not competent to know the real nature of another man's heart and motives, even if he is sitting next to us in church. You cannot know for sure whether he is saved. We can only know what we ourselves are.

There are going to be many surprises in both directions when we discover, in the end, who was genuine and who was false, who really was a Christian and who only seemed to be. It is a dreadful prospect to think that most of the people who have ever lived on the earth will end up standing before the Lord Jesus Christ at the Great White Throne Judgment for unbelievers. They will have to give an account of all the sins they have committed in their lives.

This will not be to decide whether or not to allocate rewards to them, as at the Judgment Seat of Christ, which is for real Christians. On the contrary, it will be in order to assess and publicly expose the precise level of sin in a non-Christian's life and the intensity of punishment that will be given to each of them. I do not want to be at it. Consider the following passages:

***11**Then I saw a Great White Throne and him who was seated on it. Earth and sky fled from his presence, and there was no place for them. **12**And I saw the dead, great and small, standing before the throne, and books were opened. Another book was opened, which is the book of life. The dead were judged according to what they had done as recorded in the books. **13**The sea gave up the dead that were in it, and death and Hades gave up the dead that were in them, and each person was judged according to what he had done. **14**Then death and Hades were thrown into the Lake of Fire. The Lake of Fire is the second death. **15**If anyone's name was not found written in the book of life, he was thrown into the Lake of Fire.*

Revelation 20:11-15 (NIV)

Note that in the passage above, *Hades*, which is the Greek word for Hell, is itself thrown into the Lake of Fire in its entirety. That shows the vastness of the Lake of Fire. It also proves that Hell is not the same thing as the Lake of Fire. Hell is only temporary. It is where non-Christians are held until they are finally judged at the Great White Throne, whereas the Lake of Fire is eternal. Let us look at a description of some of the people who will go to the Lake of Fire at the end:

But the cowardly, the unbelieving, the vile, the murderers, the sexually immoral, those who practice magic arts, the idolaters and all liars—their place will be in the fiery lake of burning sulphur. This is the second death."

Revelation 21:8 (NIV)

Jesus will judge each of the unbelieving dead (non-Christians) at the Great White Throne Judgment. He will do so according to what particular sins they have committed in their lives. Note that in the passage above the first type of person listed is the *cowardly*. That is perhaps more significant than you may realise. Many would not even consider cowardice to be a sin.

In fact it is a major one, because it causes us to fail to do our duty across the board and to persistently avoid pressure or conflict. We often choose to sin rather than do what is right, purely because of our cowardice. It is a form of selfishness. No action, word or thought, however small, will be forgotten or ignored at the Judgment. Everything will be dealt with:

[36]But I tell you that men will have to give account on the day of judgment for every careless word they have spoken. [37]For by your words you will be acquitted, and by your words you will be condemned.

Matthew 12:36-37 (NIV)

And, what's more, it will all be made public. That is very significant. Each person's own judgment will not be a private or confidential matter. Things will be revealed publicly. Every spiteful, selfish, cowardly, dishonest, corrupt or manipulative thing that a non-Christian has ever said or done will be publicly revealed. Everyone, or at least everyone who needs to hear it, will do so. That is a very sobering thought.

It may be that through carefulness and deception you have managed to conceal something you have done. There may be crimes or sins that nobody knows about. If so, you can only cover them up during this life. After your death, if you go to the Great White Throne Judgment, they will be made known to everyone who was ever affected by your actions or words. Nobody who goes to that judgment will ever get away with anything. Neither will they be able to keep anything hidden any longer:

[2]There is nothing concealed that will not be disclosed, or hidden that will not be made known. [3]What you have said in the dark will be heard in the daylight, and what you have whispered in the ear in the inner rooms will be proclaimed from the roofs.

Luke 12:2-3 (NIV)

So, anything an unsaved, non-Christian person does, even in secret, and even if it was when they were on their own with nobody watching, will all come out at the Great White Throne Judgment. Everything an unsaved person has ever done will be revealed. Even the things that have been whispered in private rooms will be made known to everyone.

Thus, even the most secret murder, lie, adultery or theft, that no one has ever detected, will be revealed publicly and punished at the Great White Throne Judgment. But, note that this public exposure of *sin* does not apply in the same way at the Judgment Seat of Christ, i.e. for genuine Christian believers. Their sins have been forgiven and will not be exposed, publicly, or at all. It is vital to keep that distinction in mind.

However, the only way we can avoid this public disclosure of our sins is to seek God's forgiveness now and become a real Christian. (See Book Four for a much more detailed discussion of the types of things which will, and will not, be publicly revealed about the lives of real Christians at the Judgment Seat of Christ.)No unsaved person will ever truly get away with anything. If a man's crimes have gone undetected in his earthly life, he is no better off. They will all be revealed publicly at the Great White Throne Judgment. It will be a day of terrible shame and humiliation. Punishment will then be given that will match the crimes exactly. Therefore we can trust God to correct all the injustices of this present life.

We know that in this world most crimes are never detected. Even those that are detected are not properly punished. Therefore, most people get away with most things. However it is only for a time. In the end, every crime and every sin will be punished. The wrongdoer will not get away with anything at all. It will all be straightened out and fully dealt with at the Great White Throne Judgment.

Complete justice will be done and every record will be set straight. Every person who was ever falsely accused will be vindicated. Moreover, every false accuser will be exposed. That is why the Bible says that we must not, and don't need to, take personal vengeance for any injustice. God will do it all for us:

***30**For we know him who said, "It is mine to avenge; I will repay," and again, "The Lord will judge his people."* ***31**It is a dreadful thing to fall into the hands of the living God.*

Hebrews 10:30-31 (NIV)

Do not take revenge, my friends, but leave room for God's wrath, for it is written: "It is mine to avenge; I will repay," says the Lord.

Romans 12:19 (NIV)

We do not need to take any vengeance ourselves in this life. God will take vengeance upon all those who commit acts of wickedness or injustice. It is His responsibility, not ours, and He will not overlook it. God puts in place governments, whose job it is to punish crime here and now. That is valid. It is part of God's overall judgment. What is not valid is for us personally to seek vengeance against others individually.

We are to let God do it, either through the police and courts now, or at the Great White Throne Judgment later. (See Book Two for a fuller discussion of what forgiveness really involves and why we are commanded to forgive others who have wronged us and not seek for any vengeance ourselves.)

It is impossible for us to imagine exactly what the punishment will consist of and how it will be different for one person than for another. The Bible does not tell us in detail. In one sense the question of the degrees of punishment between one unbeliever and another is not so important. The real point is that every single person who goes to the Great White Throne Judgment will be sent on from there to the Lake of Fire.

Thus, it is not only the destination for famous people like Adolf Hitler, but also for every ordinary sinner who does not repent and believe in Jesus Christ. It is not just for extreme cases, as many complacently assume. The Great White Throne Judgment is for *every* sinner who does not put their trust in Jesus Christ. Yet the fact is that in the Western church today judgment, Hell and the Lake of Fire are barely ever spoken about. If they are, then it is usually only to dismiss them as old fashioned imagery, mythology or metaphor. They are not metaphors. Be assured, they are real and literal.

Yet, even if we were somehow to say that the Great White Throne Judgment and the Lake of Fire were metaphors, we would still have to ask, *"metaphors for what?"* In other words, even if they were metaphors, which they clearly aren't, it can still only mean that they represent something indescribably awful which is the fate awaiting all unbelievers.

Thus it would not be much of a comfort to think that the Lake of Fire was not literal if, instead, it simply 'represented' something equally terrible. So, even those who interpret the Lake of Fire as a metaphor or symbol should still be just as concerned as I am. Remember that, of all the references in the Bible to Hell and the Lake of Fire, most of them come out of the mouth of Jesus Christ Himself.

You are, of course, free to reject Him and disbelieve Him if you wish. But you need to be very clear that if you are rejecting the concepts of Hell and the Lake of Fire and treating them as a myth, then you are directly contradicting Jesus Christ Himself. He spoke of them not just once, but many times and in very plain and clear terms. Some people have also tried to reduce the significance of the Lake of Fire by suggesting that those who enter it are simply destroyed in its flames and cease to exist.

This is called "*annihilationism*". However there is no biblical basis for it. On the contrary, the Bible is clear that the opposite is the case. Those who enter the Lake of Fire do so for eternity and remain in a fully conscious state. Though they are in the flames, they are never consumed by them. That is because their resurrection bodies are indestructible, just as a Christian's resurrection body will be eternal and indestructible. Therefore, for the unsaved, their punishment will go on forever and ever and will never cease:

And the devil, who deceived them, was thrown into the lake of burning sulphur, where the beast and the false prophet had been thrown. They will be tormented day and night for ever and ever.

Revelation 20:10 (NIV)

The punishment that takes place in the Lake of Fire is eternal and it is also conscious. If those who go there were not conscious, they could not experience torment at all. Also, if their lives were simply ended then it would not make sense to refer to their torment as going on forever and ever. It would obviously stop at the point when they ceased to exist. Therefore annihilationism is not true. The

Lake of Fire goes on forever and those who go into it remain fully conscious forever.

This is undoubtedly true of Satan, the antichrist and the false prophet. Logically, it must be equally true of all those human beings who are sent to the same place. There can be no doubt that the Lake of Fire is presented by Jesus as real, literal and eternal. The words used are absolutely clear. It is only doubted by those who do not *want* to believe in it.

People do not want to believe in the Lake of Fire, or judgment, or even sin, because these things offend them. They just do not like these ideas. Yet we have already made the point that a thing does not become untrue simply because we do not like it. It is either true or false as a matter of fact, irrespective of whether we are for it or against it. Judgment and the Lake of Fire are classic examples of this.

For completeness I should add that there are some other aspects to the concept of judgment, apart from the Judgment Seat of Christ and the Great White Throne Judgment. There will also be some other smaller scale judgments. However, I will explain those in later books in this series, in particular in Book Four, so as to avoid too much complexity at this stage. Those other judgments also require us to have some understanding of the return of Jesus to the earth.

The distinction between "Hell" and the "Lake of Fire"

There is a difference between 'Hell' and the 'Lake of Fire'. They are not the same place. In most people's minds these are blended into one, but that is not biblically accurate. We therefore need to distinguish these places from each other and define them clearly.

Hell

Hell is not the Lake of Fire. At this moment, as you read this, nobody is yet in the Lake of Fire. The first person to go into the Lake of Fire will be the antichrist, followed by the false prophet and then, 1000 years later, by Satan himself. This will occur in the future, after Jesus has returned to the Earth. It is not until after these enter it that the great mass of unbelievers will be thrown into the Lake of Fire. Thus, nobody is in the Lake of Fire at the moment. Yet, there are countless people currently in Hell.

What then is Hell? The simplest way to describe Hell is to refer to some of the words that are used in the Hebrew and the Greek of the Old and the New Testaments. The Old Testament uses a Hebrew word *"Sheol"* and the New Testament uses a Greek word, *"Hades"*. These both refer to the same thing.

Until the time of Jesus, Sheol or Hades, was divided into two sections. One of those is what we now call Hell. This was for unsaved unbelievers. The other section was for genuine believers who lived in Old Testament times, i.e. up until the time of the resurrection of Jesus Christ. Until then, any genuine believing Jew would go to the good part of Sheol or Hades which was set apart for them. This was given another name, i.e. *"paradise"* or *"Abraham's bosom"*.

It was not Heaven, but it was a place where those people were sent by God to wait until the time of the crucifixion and resurrection of Jesus Christ. After Jesus came and paid for their sins on the cross, those believing Jews and also faithful believers in God before the time of Abraham such as Adam, Abel, Seth, Noah, Job, etc, were then taken to Heaven. That is where they are now.

We are now required to put our faith in Jesus Christ and in the sacrifice that he made (in the past) on the cross at Calvary. However, the Jewish people and other believers in the Old Testament did not know that that was going to happen. Therefore, they had to put their faith in God to forgive and save them. That is what God eventually did do when Jesus, their Messiah, finally came. The Jewish People did not have a full understanding of what exactly the Messiah would do.

They had no expectation of the cross, or the death of their Messiah on their behalf. But they knew that their Messiah would one day come. Thus, when He did actually come, it was possible for those who had already died prior to then to receive their complete salvation and to have it more fully explained to them. They were then taken up from that temporary paradise, or "Abraham's bosom", to Heaven itself. That is where they have been since that time.

Therefore, from then on, since the time of the resurrection, when Jesus removed the Old Testament believers from it, Sheol/Hades has been populated only by unsaved people. Thus only the 'bad' section remains in operation. This is now where a person goes when they die, if they are an **un**believer and are unsaved. Our word for it is 'Hell'.

They go there to wait for the judgment at the Great White Throne which is to come in the future. They have at least 1000 years to wait for the Great White Throne Judgment, even if they were to die today. The millennial reign of Jesus Christ on Earth will itself last for 1000 years and that period has not yet begun.

Some people have been in Sheol or Hades, or what we now call Hell, for thousands of years already. We know from the Bible that the people in Hell are fully conscious and waiting for what lies ahead of them. They are therefore in a dreadful condition of torment, fear and anxiety, combined with extreme regret and bitterness. It is difficult to imagine what a harrowing place Hell must be.

Consider how it must be waiting for a judgment, from which you know that you will inevitably go on to the Lake of Fire. The only question is the precise degree of punishment that you will have to receive there. It is a terrible prospect. It should motivate us to give our lives now to tell others about Jesus while we, and they, still have the chance. Consider this important passage from Luke chapter 16. In it Jesus speaks about a man who was already in Hell:

[19]"There was a rich man who was dressed in purple and fine linen and lived in luxury every day. [20]At his gate was laid a beggar named Lazarus, covered with sores [21]and longing to eat what fell from the rich man's table. Even the dogs came and licked his sores. [22]"The time came when the beggar died and the angels carried him to Abraham's side. The rich man also died and was buried. [23]In Hell, where he was in torment, he looked up and saw Abraham far away, with Lazarus by his side.

[24]So he called to him, 'Father Abraham, have pity on me and send Lazarus to dip the tip of his finger in water and cool my tongue, because I am in agony in this fire.' [25]"But Abraham replied, 'Son, remember that in your lifetime you received your good things, while Lazarus received bad things, but now he is comforted here and you are in agony. [26]And besides all this, between us and you a great chasm has been fixed, so that those who want to go from here to you cannot, nor can anyone cross over from there to us.'

[27]"He answered, 'Then I beg you, father, send Lazarus to my father's house, [28]for I have five brothers. Let him warn them, so that they will not also come to this place of torment.' [29]"Abraham replied, 'They have Moses and the Prophets; let them listen to them.' [30]" 'No, father Abraham,' he said, 'but if someone from the dead goes to them, they will repent.' [31]"He said to him, 'If they do not listen to Moses and the Prophets, they will not be convinced even if someone rises from the dead."

Luke 16:19-31 (NIV)

Many people assume that Jesus is teaching a parable here when He speaks about the rich man and Lazarus. A parable is a story which is not literally true, but which illustrates a point or a message. Jesus told many of these, such as the parable of the sower, or the wheat and the tares, or the grain of mustard seed and so on. However the account of the rich man and Lazarus is not actually a parable, even though some people wrongly assume that it is.

Here Jesus is giving a true account which involves the real facts of two real men who had died. The people in parables were never given names. So, we learn from this literal account that Jesus gives in Luke 16 what Sheol/Hades was like at the time prior to Jesus' resurrection, when it was divided into two parts. It is Hell that is being referred to in the next passage from Psalm 49. We are warned not to trust in or focus on financial wealth, because we cannot take any of it with us when we die:

16Do not be overawed when a man grows rich,
when the splendour of his house increases;
17for he will take nothing with him when he dies,
his splendour will not descend with him.
18Though while he lived he counted himself blessed
and men praise you when you prosper-
19he will join the generation of his fathers,
who will never see the light of life.
20A man who has riches without understanding
is like the beasts that perish.

Psalm 49:16-20 (NIV)

The rich man described in this psalm is pictured here in Hell (without his money) awaiting the final Great White Throne Judgment. That thought is meant to sober us.

The Lake of Fire

Just to clarify again, the Lake of Fire does not at present, have anybody in it. But in the end, there will be thrown into it not only the antichrist, the false prophet and Satan, but also all of the fallen angels that we know as demons. They fell with Satan out of Heaven when he rebelled against God. This took place before the world was created. At that time, Satan had the name '*Lucifer*' and was the most senior angel in Heaven.

He was, in effect, God's Prime Minister. But his pride swelled up and he decided that he wanted to be like the Son of God, the Second Person of the Trinity. He envied the Son of God and wanted His place and started to look upon himself as equal to Him. There began in him at that time a hatred for, and a rivalry with, the Son of God that has continued ever since.

God exposed Satan's rebellion, and threw him out of Heaven. But He did not do so until approximately one third of the angels in Heaven at that time had joined with Satan to rebel against God. Because of this, they too were thrown out of Heaven.

They now operate as demons, causing havoc on this earth. They do so through opposing and sabotaging the work that God wishes to do in our lives, particularly the preaching of the Gospel and the saving of human beings from their sins.

Satan and his demons have pledged themselves to oppose God in all of this and especially to resist people's salvation. They are filled with hatred and do all that they can to attack, undermine, deceive, demoralise and discourage God's people. (See later books in this series for more details of what Satan and his demons are and how they operate in your life day by day). [1]

The demons will, one day, go into the Lake of Fire for eternity. Indeed the Lake of Fire was originally created for them, not for us. It was intended for Satan and his fallen angels before any human being was ever created. Therefore those human beings who end up in the Lake of Fire are going to a place that was never originally intended for them.

I regret the fact that I have had to dwell so long upon these very unpleasant and terrifying things. But, without doing so you cannot understand what the good news is, because Jesus Christ came to save us from these very things.

Without realising how terrible they are, we cannot fully appreciate what a magnificent thing Jesus has done for us. He died on the cross to suffer all that punishment in our place. That enables us to be saved and to avoid Hell, the Great White Throne judgment and the Lake of Fire. Please remember that God does not want anybody to go to Hell or the Lake of Fire. He takes no pleasure in condemning any of us:

"Say to them, 'As I live!' declares the Lord GOD, 'I take no pleasure in the death of the wicked, but rather that the wicked turn from his way and live. Turn back, turn back from your evil ways! Why then will you die, O house of Israel?'
Ezekiel 33:11 (NASB)

What about when children die?

I feel that I ought to add a brief explanation about children, and what happens when they die. Strictly speaking, the Bible does not directly address this question. Nor does it define what a 'child' is exactly, i.e. what age childhood goes up to. Presumably the age of responsibility for one's own sin varies from child to child,

---

[1] Note - for a brief summary of Satan's background and personal history, read Isaiah 14:12-17 and Ezekiel 28:11-19. These passages show what he once was and how pride caused his downfall

depending on their level of knowledge and circumstances. We are not told. We can however look at 2 Samuel chapter 12, which refers to the death of King David's baby son:

***21**His servants asked him, "Why are you acting this way? While the child was alive, you fasted and wept, but now that the child is dead, you get up and eat!"*
***22**He answered, "While the child was still alive, I fasted and wept. I thought, 'Who knows? The LORD may be gracious to me and let the child live.' **23**But now that he is dead, why should I fast? Can I bring him back again? I will go to him, but he will not return to me."*

2 Samuel 12:21-23 (NASB)

Note that King David says *"I will go to him, but he will not return to me"*. That is a very important indicator of what had happened to that baby. We know, because the Bible makes it clear elsewhere, that King David was saved and has now gone to Heaven. King David himself knew that he was going to go to Heaven.

So, when he said *"I will go to him"* he meant he would see his dead child again in Heaven, i.e. after his own death. That seems very clear. So, if anybody reading this has lost a young child, you have a valid basis to be comforted by King David's words. The above passage strongly suggests that the child is safe and has eternal life.

The reason why a young child is not condemned is, presumably, because they are not yet at the age of accountability i.e. where they become responsible for their own sins. Prior to that they are, evidently, deemed to be innocent. That is my understanding. But what is the exact age of accountability or responsibility? The Bible does not tell us.

However, Jewish tradition, which may be an indication, is that it is at the age of 12 or 13. That is when a Jewish child has its Bar Mitzvah and becomes legally an adult. At that point they are said to become responsible for their own sins. Whether that is the actual age or not, I do not know. Only God knows that. I expect it varies from child to child, according to their knowledge and maturity.

What about baptism for babies?

Should babies be baptised? The answer is no, because baptism is something that each believer must choose to do when they have repented and believed in Jesus for themselves. Baptism is not something that we can do to, or for, our infant children. They must choose for themselves later, when they are old enough. Our task is to bring them up to know and fear the Lord and to encourage them to believe and be baptised. But they must, in the end, do it for themselves.

That said, they can make that decision while still children, even if they are quite young. All that is required is that they know and understand the Gospel and are genuinely able to realise what they are doing. The age at which they become ready for that varies from child to child.

What we can say clearly is that the Bible does not support "*infant baptism*". That is where people baptise their children while they are young babies. That practice is an invention of men, brought into the church after the first century. It is not biblical.

Ironically, one generally sees nominal Christians baptising their babies, whereas Bible believing Christians do not. That apparent contradiction confuses some people, but the thinking behind it is as I have set out above. (See chapter 16 for more detail on baptism in water).

CHAPTER 9

SETTING THE SCENE FOR THE FIRST COMING OF JESUS

In about the year 2000 BC, God began the process of forming a unique nation called Israel into which His Son, the Second Person of The Trinity, could be born as a human being. This was not done overnight. God spent many centuries developing the nation of Israel. It began with a man called Abraham. He came from a place called Ur of the Chaldees, in what we now call Iraq.

God searched for a man with the right heart attitude and He found Abraham. He saw that he was a man who was *"a friend of God"*. God prepared Abraham over many years and gave him a promise which is described in the book of Genesis at Chapter 12 and restated again later at various times:

[1]"The LORD had said to Abram, "Leave your country, your people and your father's household and go to the land I will show you.[2]"I will make you into a great nation and I will bless you; I will make your name great, and you will be a blessing.[3]I will bless those who bless you, and whoever curses you I will curse; and all peoples on earth will be blessed through you."

Genesis 12:1-3 (NIV)

The promises God made about making Abraham's descendants into a great nation were eventually fulfilled, but it took a long time. Abraham had a son called Isaac and he, in turn, had a son called Jacob. God repeated to each of them the promises He had made to Abraham. Jacob had twelve sons, and due to a famine throughout all the world at that time, they went into Egypt, where one of Jacob's sons, Joseph, had become the Prime Minister. They were all therefore preserved from famine.

The whole extended family amounted to 70 people when they went into Egypt. They stayed there 430 years. By the time they came out of Egypt, those 70 descendants of Abraham, Isaac and Jacob had grown into a nation of over two million people. It was that nation that God miraculously allowed to walk between the vertical walls of water of the divided Red Sea to escape from Egypt where they had suffered hardship under Pharaoh.

The nation of Israel then spent just under forty years living in the desert wilderness before entering into what was then known as the land of Canaan. It is now the land of Israel. This was the land God gave to them to fulfil His promise. The Israelites then spent many hundreds of years living in the land of Israel preparing for the arrival of the unique person that God had promised to them called the "*Messiah*". That is the Hebrew word for the equivalent Greek word, *"Christ,"* which means *"anointed one."*

So, when we say Jesus Christ, the second word is a title rather than a name, i.e. Jesus the Christ, or Jesus the Messiah. God promised that this person, the Messiah, or the Christ, would be King of Israel. He also promised that He would rule the whole world and that through Him the whole world would be blessed. Hundreds of different prophecies are made in the Old Testament about this unique person called the Messiah. In order for these to be fulfilled many things had to take place first within the nation of Israel.

Jesus is a direct descendent of King David

About 1000 years BC, which is about 1000 years after Abraham's days, God took a shepherd boy called David and raised him up to be King of Israel. God also promised that one of David's descendants would sit on David's throne forever as King of Israel.

Jesus, who is the Messiah, is the heir of King David. Therefore He is legally entitled to rule over the nation of Israel as its King. In the future He will do exactly that. Jesus descends physically from King David and derives His right to sit on the throne of King David through his mother, Mary.

Her lineage is shown in the gospel of Luke at Chapter 3. He also descended from King David through his adoptive father, Joseph. This is shown in the gospel of Matthew at Chapter 1. However, He inherited His right to the throne through His mother, Mary, not His step-father, Joseph. Through the prophet Nathan, God had promised King David that one day he would have an heir who would rule on the throne of Israel forever:

12 When your days are over and you rest with your ancestors, I will raise up your offspring to succeed you, your own flesh and blood, and I will establish his kingdom. 13 He is the one who will build a house for my Name, and I will establish the throne of his kingdom forever.

2 Samuel 7:12-13 (NIV)

Your house and your kingdom will endure forever before me; your throne will be established forever

2 Samuel 7:16 (NIV)

God also made a covenant (a binding agreement) with King David that God would establish David's Kingdom forever and give David an heir (Jesus Christ) who would rule forever:

3 I have made a covenant with My chosen;
I have sworn to David My servant,
4 I will establish your seed forever

And build up your throne to all generations.
Psalm 89:3-4 (NASB)

Two centuries later the prophet Isaiah enlarged the details of that prophecy about the coming King and Messiah:

[6]For to us a child is born,
to us a son is given,
and the government will be on his shoulders.
And he will be called
Wonderful Counselor, Mighty God,
Everlasting Father, Prince of Peace.
[7]Of the increase of his government and peace
there will be no end.
He will reign on David's throne
and over his kingdom,
establishing and upholding it
with justice and righteousness
from that time on and forever.
The zeal of the LORD Almighty
will accomplish this.
Isaiah 9:6-7 (NIV)

That prophecy has not yet had a complete fulfilment through David's ordinary human lineage, because David's line lost the kingship several generations later under a king called Zedekiah. They have never regained it since. Thus, for over two thousand five hundred years since then, there has been no Jewish King of Israel.

Note that the Kings in Jesus' day i.e. King Herod and his sons, were not Jewish. They were Edomites. They were put in place by the Romans and were nothing to do with the royal line of King David.

But there is a day coming when Jesus Christ, the Jewish Messiah, and the rightful King of Israel, will physically return to this earth. He will then sit on David's throne and become King of Israel. This is not just poetic language. It will all literally happen. So, Jesus is not only the Saviour; He is also the King of Israel and of the whole world. Moreover, He is going to judge the whole world:

[31] "But when the Son of Man comes in His glory, and all the angels with Him,
then He will sit on His glorious throne. [32] All the nations will be gathered before
Him; and He will separate them from one another, as the shepherd separates
the sheep from the goats; [33] and He will put the sheep on His right, and the goats
on the left. [34] "Then the King will say to those on His right, 'Come, you who

are blessed of My Father, inherit the kingdom prepared for you from the foundation of the world.

Matthew 25:31-34 (NASB)

The setting up of the temple system of animal sacrifice - to illustrate how Jesus would one day die as a sacrifice on our behalf

Another important background fact to show the way that God established the nation of Israel to prepare for the coming of His Messiah is that He set up the Temple system of worship and sacrifices. King David had a son called Solomon who built the first Temple, within which goats, lambs and bulls were sacrificed. This carried on the practice that was seen centuries before at the time of Abraham, and which Moses developed, even before the Temple was built.

When God gave the Law to Israel through Moses, God set up a complicated system of sacrifices which had to be given to *'cover'* for the sins of the people. Every day animals were sacrificed. A priest would put his hand on the head of the animal such that the sins of himself, and also the sins of the people of Israel, would be symbolically passed on to that animal. This enabled the people to be made right with God, at least temporarily.

1The LORD called to Moses and spoke to him from the Tent of Meeting. He said, 2"Speak to the Israelites and say to them: 'When any of you brings an offering to the LORD, bring as your offering an animal from either the herd or the flock. 3"'If the offering is a burnt offering from the herd, he is to offer a male without defect. He must present it at the entrance to the Tent of Meeting so that it will be acceptable to the LORD. 4He is to lay his hand on the head of the burnt offering, and it will be accepted on his behalf to make atonement for him. 5He is to slaughter the young bull before the LORD, and then Aaron's sons the priests shall bring the blood and sprinkle it against the altar on all sides at the entrance to the Tent of Meeting.

Leviticus 1:1-5 (NIV)

The animals that were sacrificed also symbolised the way in which Jesus Christ would later lay down His own life on the cross and shed His own blood as a sacrifice for our sins. They were a *"type"* or illustration of the greater sacrifice which Jesus was to make later. That would finally deal with our sin once and for all.

The Scapegoat - another practical illustration of Jesus taking our sins away

Another type, or illustration, of Jesus was the *'scapegoat'*. Each year one goat was taken and the High Priest would lay his hands on its head to transfer the sins of the people onto the goat. Then it was released into the wilderness, where it symbolically carried away the sins of the people.

[20] "When Aaron has finished making atonement for the Most Holy Place, the Tent of Meeting and the altar, he shall bring forward the live goat. [21] He is to lay both hands on the head of the live goat and confess over it all the wickedness and rebellion of the Israelites—all their sins—and put them on the goat's head. He shall send the goat away into the desert in the care of a man appointed for the task. [22] The goat will carry on itself all their sins to a solitary place; and the man shall release it in the desert.

Leviticus 16:20-22 (NIV)

In the same way, all the sin of the world was later put on the head of Jesus, the ultimate scapegoat. He bore it all upon Himself and took it away from us. We use the word scapegoat today to refer to a person who is blamed in place of others who are actually guilty. That is exactly what happened to Jesus.

The temple sacrifices and the scapegoat are a 'type' (an illustration) of God the Father's ultimate sacrifice of Jesus to take away the guilt of our sin

So, prior to the first coming of Jesus, the people's sins were placed on to the animal that was being sacrificed. It could be a lamb or a goat or a bull. This system was pointing forward symbolically to the coming of Jesus the Messiah. He was to be the ultimate and perfect sacrifice for sin.

That is why John the Baptist referred to Him, at the beginning of Jesus' public ministry, as the *"Lamb of God"*. Even as he said it, John the Baptist did not fully understand all the implications of his own words:

[28] These things took place in Bethany beyond the Jordan, where John was baptizing. [29] The next day he saw Jesus coming to him and said, "Behold, the Lamb of God who takes away the sin of the world!

John 1:28-29 (NASB)

What it meant was that one day Jesus was going to become the ultimate substitutionary sacrifice, to die in our place as a sacrificial lamb. He would take our sins on His own shoulders and be punished for our sins instead of us. The whole Temple system and the animal sacrifices point us to Jesus and help us to understand why He had to die and what His death would achieve in paying for our sins. The animals that died were a 'type' of Jesus. They help us to see the pattern and principle and therefore to understand what Jesus would later do in dying in our place:

[12]He did not enter by means of the blood of goats and calves; but he entered the Most Holy Place once for all by his own blood, having obtained eternal redemption. [13]The blood of goats and bulls and the ashes of a heifer sprinkled on those who are ceremonially unclean sanctify them so that they are outwardly clean. [14]How much more, then, will the blood of Christ, who through the eternal Spirit offered himself unblemished to God, cleanse our consciences from acts that lead to death, so that we may serve the living God!

Hebrews 9:12-14 (NIV)

In fact, the law requires that nearly everything be cleansed with blood, and without the shedding of blood there is no forgiveness.

Hebrews 9:22 (NIV)

[12]And so Jesus also suffered outside the city gate to make the people holy through his own blood. [13]Let us, then, go to him outside the camp, bearing the disgrace he bore.

Hebrews 13:12-13 (NIV)

Long before the Temple was ever built God provided an even more dramatic illustration of the sacrifice that God the Father would one day make of His Son, Jesus.

God commanded Abraham to sacrifice his *adult* son, Isaac, as a type of what God would do to Jesus

We saw above how God promised to form a nation (Israel) through Abraham. God told him that that promise would be fulfilled through his *adult* son Isaac and through no other son. However, when Isaac was about 33 years of age God told Abraham to go to Mount Moriah (known to us now as Mount Calvary) and to kill his son Isaac and offer him to God as a sacrifice. Abraham went to Mount Moriah (Calvary) with a heavy heart, dreading what he had to do. But he was willing to do it because God had commanded him to do so.

God allowed this test to go on until almost the last minute, when Isaac was placed on an altar. He fully cooperated, even though he was a grown man and could have resisted Abraham. However, at the last moment God told Abraham not to do it. It had been a test of Abraham's faith and obedience and he (and Isaac) had passed that test. Abraham went into that test fully believing that if Isaac was killed on the altar as a sacrifice then God would, inevitably, raise him from the dead.

He knew that because God had promised that His chosen nation (Israel) would come through Isaac. Thus he believed that resurrection would be the way for that promise to be fulfilled, i.e. that God would raise Isaac from the dead. In the end, however, God did not make Abraham, or Isaac, go through with it. He intervened and stopped them. I will set out the account of this from Genesis 22 because it is a very important drama. It perfectly acts out for us what God the Father was willing to go through 2000 years later when He sacrificed His own Son, Jesus:

[1]Now it came about after these things, that God tested Abraham, and said to him, "Abraham!" And he said, "Here I am." [2]He said, "Take now your son, your only son, whom you love, Isaac, and go to the land of Moriah, and offer him there as a burnt offering on one of the mountains of which I will tell you." [3]So Abraham rose early in the morning and saddled his donkey, and took two of his young men with him and Isaac his son; and he split wood for the burnt offering, and arose and went to the place of which God had told him.

Genesis 22:1-3 (NASB)

[9]Then they came to the place of which God had told him; and Abraham built the altar there and arranged the wood, and bound his son Isaac and laid him on the altar, on top of the wood. [10]Abraham stretched out his hand and took the knife to slay his son. [11]But the angel of the LORD called to him from Heaven and said, "Abraham, Abraham!" And he said, "Here I am." [12]He said, "Do not stretch out your hand against the lad, and do nothing to him; for now I know that you fear God, since you have not withheld your son, your only son, from Me." [13]Then Abraham raised his eyes and looked, and behold, behind him a ram caught in the thicket by his horns; and Abraham went and took the ram and offered him up for a burnt offering in the place of his son. [14]Abraham called the name of that place The LORD Will Provide, as it is said to this day, "In the mount of the LORD it will be provided."

Genesis 22:9-14 (NASB)

Not only did God do the very same thing with His Son, Jesus. He actually did it in the very same place, i.e. Mount Calvary, which is also called Mount Moriah. What is more, Isaac and Jesus were about the same age, 33. Although in our traditions Isaac is portrayed as a boy, he was in fact a man. That is how he is portrayed in Jewish circles. In their children's books, when the account of Abraham and Isaac is told, Isaac is correctly pictured as a fully grown man.

The main reason God put Abraham through that ordeal was to test his faith. It was also to provide us with a vivid and dramatic illustration of what Jesus our Messiah and Saviour would one day do for us. See how much emphasis is placed in both the Old Testament and in the New Testament, especially in the letter to the Hebrews, on the shedding of blood.

God is making clear that only the shedding of Jesus' blood, i.e. His death in our place, could pay the price for our sins and enable us to be forgiven. (See chapter 10 for more detail on the importance of the blood of Jesus being shed for us). Another reason why God had to go to such enormous trouble to establish the nation of Israel as His chosen nation, was that there had to be a place where it would be possible for Jesus, the Messiah, to be born and brought up without sinning.

In any other nation, if Jesus had obeyed his parents, He would have had to engage in idolatry and worship false gods. Yet, to disobey His parents would have been sin in itself. So there had to be a nation which worshiped the one true God. Then Jesus could obey His parents without dishonouring God. This was vital, because Jesus had to live a perfectly sinless life.

What about the Gentiles?

You will note that so far in this chapter we have looked solely at what God was doing for Israel, His chosen people. However, if you are a Gentile (non-Jew) like me, then be reassured. This whole plan that God made foresaw you and me and provides a place for us. Until Jesus died and rose again God operated only through Israel. However, now even we Gentiles have access to God's blessings and forgiveness.

Previously, unless we became Jews (which many people did), we were excluded from the benefits of the promises made to Abraham, Isaac and Jacob. But now we can join in and participate alongside God's chosen people the Jews. Please carefully read this passage which sets out what a difference Jesus has made for all those who believe in Him, even if we are not Jewish:

11 Therefore, remember that formerly you who are Gentiles by birth and called
"uncircumcised" by those who call themselves "the circumcision" (that done
in the body by the hands of men)— 12 remember that at that time you were
separate from Christ, excluded from citizenship in Israel and foreigners to the
covenants of the promise, without hope and without God in the world. 13 But now
in Christ Jesus you who once were far away have been brought near through
the blood of Christ.
14 For he himself is our peace, who has made the two one and has destroyed the
barrier, the dividing wall of hostility, 15 by abolishing in his flesh the law with its
commandments and regulations. His purpose was to create in himself one new
man out of the two, thus making peace, 16 and in this one body to reconcile both
of them to God through the cross, by which he put to death their hostility. 17 He
came and preached peace to you who were far away and peace to those who
were near. 18 For through him we both have access to the Father by one Spirit.
19 Consequently, you are no longer foreigners and aliens, but fellow citizens with
God's people and members of God's household, 20 built on the foundation of the
apostles and prophets, with Christ Jesus himself as the chief cornerstone. 21 In
him the whole building is joined together and rises to become a holy temple in
the Lord.

Ephesians 2:11-21 (NIV)

Setting the scene for the coming of the Kingdom of God

Everything that God did during the time of the Old Testament was directed towards the coming of His Son to be the Messiah and to establish a Kingdom. This would make all the other kingdoms in this world seem small and insignificant by comparison. In fact, God's intention all along was to tear down those other kingdoms and put them all under the authority of His Son, Jesus Christ:

***20**The word of the LORD came a second time to Haggai on the twenty-fourth day of the month, **21**"Speak to Zerubbabel, governor of Judah, saying, I am about to shake the Heavens and the earth, **22**and to overthrow the throne of kingdoms. I am about to destroy the strength of the kingdoms of the nations, and overthrow the chariots and their riders. And the horses and their riders shall go down, everyone by the sword of his brother.*

Haggai 2:20-22 (ESV)

Everything that Jesus did and also everything He is going to do needs to be seen in the context of Him being a King who has a Kingdom. In fact, He is the *King of Kings* and His Kingdom is going to be perfect and eternal. We cannot say that of any other King or Kingdom that this world has ever known:

Thy kingdom is an everlasting kingdom,
and thy dominion endures throughout all generations
Psalm 145:13 (RSV)

So, even the things that God did long ago when He established the nation of Israel, and later the royal line of David, were all being done to set the scene for the first coming of the King of Kings and for the establishing of His Kingdom. At His first coming, Jesus died for us. At His second coming He will return to the earth to take up His position as King. He is going to overturn the ungodly kingdoms of this world and to replace them with His own Kingdom.

Isaiah prophesied that a virgin would conceive and give birth to a son who would be Immanuel - "God with us".

In the eighth century BC Isaiah spoke of how a virgin would conceive and give birth to a son and how that son born to her would be God. The word that the prophet Isaiah uses is *'Immanuel'*, which means *'God with us'*. So, even centuries before it happened, the Bible indicated that the Messiah would actually be both God and a man:

Therefore the Lord himself shall give you a sign;
Behold, a virgin shall conceive, and bear a son,

and shall call his name Immanuel.
Isaiah 7:14 (KJV)

Then, in or around the year that we call 4 BC, Jesus Christ was finally born, centuries after the prophecies had been given. He was born in a little village called Bethlehem in southern Israel. Even the place of His birth had been prophesied by the prophet Micah about 700 years earlier:

But you, O Bethlehem Ephrathah,
who are too little to be among the clans of Judah,
from you shall come forth for me
one who is to be ruler in Israel,
whose coming forth is from of old,
from ancient days
Micah 5:2 (ESV)

Jesus was born to a virgin called Mary who was a descendant of King David, and it was through her that Jesus inherited the right to be King of Israel and to sit on David's throne. Jesus was conceived within Mary while she was unmarried. This was done by the power of the Holy Spirit:

26 In the sixth month the angel Gabriel was sent from God to a city of Galilee
named Nazareth, 27 to a virgin betrothed to a man whose name was Joseph, of
the house of David. And the virgin's name was Mary. 28 And he came to her and
said, "Greetings, O favoured one, the Lord is with you!" 29 But she was greatly
troubled at the saying, and tried to discern what sort of greeting this might
be. 30 And the angel said to her, "Do not be afraid, Mary, for you have found
favour with God. 31 And behold, you will conceive in your womb and bear a son,
and you shall call his name Jesus. 32 He will be great and will be called the Son
of the Most High. And the Lord God will give to him the throne of his father
David, 33 and he will reign over the house of Jacob for ever, and of his kingdom
there will be no end." 34 And Mary said to the angel, "How will this be, since I
am a virgin?" 35 And the angel answered her, "The Holy Spirit will come upon
you, and the power of the Most High will overshadow you; therefore the child
to be born will be called holy—the Son of God.

Luke 1:26-35 (ESV)

Mary had been betrothed (engaged) to marry a man called Joseph. When he learned that she was pregnant he intended to divorce her quietly because he knew he was not the father. However, God sent an angel to reveal to Joseph what was happening and why. Joseph therefore married Mary and brought Jesus up as if he was his own son:

18 Now the birth of Jesus Christ took place in this way. When his mother Mary
had been betrothed to Joseph, before they came together she was found to be

with child from the Holy Spirit. 19 And her husband Joseph, being a just man
and unwilling to put her to shame, resolved to divorce her quietly. 20 But as he
considered these things, behold, an angel of the Lord appeared to him in a
dream, saying, "Joseph, son of David, do not fear to take Mary as your wife, for
that which is conceived in her is from the Holy Spirit. 21 She will bear a son, and
you shall call his name Jesus, for he will save his people from their sins." 22 All
this took place to fulfil what the Lord had spoken by the prophet:
23 "Behold, the virgin shall conceive and bear a son,
and they shall call his name Immanuel"
(which means, God with us). 24 When Joseph woke from sleep, he did as the
angel of the Lord commanded him: he took his wife, 25 but knew her not until
she had given birth to a son. And he called his name Jesus.

Matthew 1:18-25 (ESV)

When the time came for Jesus to be born, God engineered the circumstances so that the birth would take place in Bethlehem, as Micah had prophesied. It took place there because Joseph and Mary had to travel back to Bethlehem, which was the town that Joseph was from, in order to take part in a population census which the Roman Emperor had ordered:

In those days a decree went out from Caesar Augustus that all the world should
be registered. 2 This was the first registration when Quirinius was governor of
Syria. 3 And all went to be registered, each to his own town. 4 And Joseph also
went up from Galilee, from the town of Nazareth, to Judea, to the city of David,
which is called Bethlehem, because he was of the house and lineage of
David, 5 to be registered with Mary, his betrothed, who was with
child. 6 And while they were there, the time came for her to give birth. 7 And she
gave birth to her firstborn son and wrapped him in swaddling cloths and laid
him in a manger, because there was no place for them in the inn

. 8 And in the same region there were shepherds out in the field, keeping watch
over their flock by night. 9 And an angel of the Lord appeared to them, and the
glory of the Lord shone around them, and they were filled with fear. 10 And the
angel said to them, "Fear not, for behold, I bring you good news of great joy
that will be for all the people. 11 For unto you is born this day in the city of
David a Saviour, who is Christ the Lord. 12 And this will be a sign for you: you
will find a baby wrapped in swaddling cloths and lying in a manger." 13 And
suddenly there was with the angel a multitude of the heavenly host praising God
and saying,

14 "Glory to God in the highest,
and on earth peace among those with whom he is pleased!"

15 When the angels went away from them into heaven, the shepherds said to one
another, "Let us go over to Bethlehem and see this thing that has happened,

which the Lord has made known to us." [16] And they went with haste and found Mary and Joseph, and the baby lying in a manger. [17] And when they saw it, they made known the saying that had been told them concerning this child. [18] And all who heard it wondered at what the shepherds told them. [19] But Mary treasured up all these things, pondering them in her heart. [20] And the shepherds returned, glorifying and praising God for all they had heard and seen, as it had been told them. [21] And at the end of eight days, when he was circumcised, he was called Jesus, the name given by the angel before he was conceived in the womb.

Luke 2:1-21 (ESV)

The name Jesus was given was actually *Yeshua* in Hebrew. It is the same name as *Joshua* and means *"Saviour"*. Jesus is the Greek version of His Hebrew name. He then grew up in Nazareth and was apprenticed to His human step-father, Joseph, and became a carpenter/builder. That is what He did until the time came, at about the age of 30, for Him to begin His public ministry.

He then travelled in and around Israel teaching the people and announcing that the Kingdom of God had begun. His public ministry lasted for three and a half years and then ended with Him being crucified in Jerusalem and with Him rising from the dead three days later and ascending into Heaven 40 days after that.

So, in this ninth chapter we have looked at 2000 years of Jewish history which set the scene for the coming of the Messiah. Now, in the next chapter, we shall look at exactly how Jesus' death solved the problem of our sin. He made it possible for us to be forgiven, made righteous, and reconciled with God the Father. Thus we are now capable of entering the Kingdom of God and escaping from God's punishment.

CHAPTER 10

HOW JESUS' DEATH ON THE CROSS MADE IT POSSIBLE FOR OUR SINS TO BE FORGIVEN AND FOR US TO BE MADE RIGHTEOUS IN GOD'S EYES

For God so loved the world that He gave His only begotten Son, that whoever believes in Him should not perish but have everlasting life.

John 3:16 (NKJV)

*5Have this mind among yourselves, which is yours in Christ Jesus, 6who, though
he was in the form of God, did not count equality with God a thing to be grasped,
7but emptied himself, taking the form of a servant, being born in the likeness of
men. 8And being found in human form he humbled himself and became
obedient unto death, even death on a cross.*

Philippians 2:5-8 (RSV)

*30"The God of our fathers raised up Jesus, whom you had put to death by
hanging Him on a cross. 31"He is the one whom God exalted to His right hand
as a Prince and a Saviour, to grant repentance to Israel, and forgiveness of sins.*

Acts 5:30-31 (NASB)

*6While we were still weak, at the right time Christ died for the ungodly. 7Why,
one will hardly die for a righteous man--though perhaps for a good man one
will dare even to die. 8But God shows his love for us in that while we were yet
sinners Christ died for us.*

Romans 5:6-8 (RSV)

*22To this day I have had the help that comes from God, and so I stand here
testifying both to small and great, saying nothing but what the prophets and
Moses said would come to pass: 23that the Christ must suffer, and that, by being
the first to rise from the dead, he would proclaim light both to the people and to
the Gentiles."*

Acts 26:22-23 (RSV)

*21 And you, who once were estranged and hostile in mind, doing evil deeds, 22 he
has now reconciled in his body of flesh by his death, in order to present you holy
and blameless and irreproachable before him,*

Colossians 1:21-22 (RSV)

We now come to the crux of the matter. That is how Jesus' death on the cross solved the problem of sin and made it possible for us to avoid Hell, judgment and the Lake of Fire. In this chapter we shall give a brief overview of what the cross was about and what Jesus achieved for us by His death.

Jesus was 'qualified' to be our Saviour because He is God and because He was sinless

Jesus Christ, the Son of God, lived on the earth as a man for about 33-34 years. He was probably born in the year 4 BC - our calendar is slightly out of line. During His life He never committed any sin whatsoever. He was entirely innocent. This was because He had a sinless nature. He had been conceived within Mary through the power of the Holy Spirit.

Therefore He had not inherited the sinful nature that you and I have inherited from our first ancestor, Adam. Because Jesus had no sinful nature, and because He was also the Son of God, (at the same time as being a man), He was able to live His whole life entirely without sin. At the end of His time on this earth, He went to Jerusalem on the very day that the prophet Daniel had prophesied.

There, on what we now call Palm Sunday, He formally and publicly presented Himself to the Jewish people as Israel's long awaited Messiah. But, tragically for them, the majority of the Jewish people rejected Him. Many of them did so even though they already knew perfectly well that He really was their Messiah.

The Jewish High Priest and those around him were especially well aware that Jesus was the Messiah. They had followed Him around for three and a half years to investigate His miracles and had seen them happen right in front of them.

They rejected Jesus because He criticised them and the way they put their man-made traditions ahead of what the Bible says. It was not because they thought He was a fake. They knew He was genuine. Then, as a result of a conspiracy by some of the leading Jewish officials, working together with the Roman authorities, men contrived to have Jesus falsely accused. He was put on trial and falsely convicted.

He was then unjustly sentenced by the Romans to crucifixion. This was the Roman method of execution for those who were not Roman citizens. It was a slow and very cruel way to kill somebody. The word crucifixion is where we get the word *'excruciating'* from because it was so painful.

A brief overview of the crucifixion - what it was and how it worked in simple terms

Jesus was nailed onto a wooden cross with long nails through His wrists and heel bones. This was done after He had been flogged with a whip and had a 'crown' of long sharp thorns pressed into His head. This was done to cause pain, but also to mock Him for claiming to be the King of Israel.

He died on the cross in the most appalling and drawn out agony. But it was all part of God the Father's own plan. Therefore the crucifixion and death of Jesus was not a failure or a diversion from God's plan. It *was* the plan. Everything happened exactly as God had intended so that we could be saved by Jesus' death:

25And He said to them, "O foolish men and slow of heart to believe in all that the prophets have spoken! 26"Was it not necessary for the Christ to suffer these things and to enter into His glory?"

Luke 24:25-26 (NASB)

this Man, delivered over by the predetermined plan and foreknowledge of God, you nailed to a cross by the hands of godless men and put Him to death.

Acts 2:23 (NASB)

The key to understanding what happened on the cross is to realise that as Jesus suffered and died He was voluntarily taking upon Himself the punishment that was rightfully due to you, me, and everybody else as a result of our sin. God the Father viewed Him, while He was on the cross, as carrying on His own shoulders the guilt and blame of all the sin of the world. It was put on Him so that it did not have to be laid on us. In fact, our sin was *transferred* to Jesus. Thus, one man, Jesus Christ, was able to take upon Himself the punishment for the sin of the whole world:

For Christ also died for sins once for all, the righteous for the unrighteous, that he might bring us to God, being put to death in the flesh but made alive in the spirit;

1 Peter 3:18 (RSV)

For I delivered to you as of first importance what I also received, that Christ died for our sins in accordance with the scriptures,

1 Corinthians 15:3 (RSV)

The reason it was possible for Jesus to take our sins upon Himself and be punished for them instead of us was that He Himself was entirely sinless. He had no sins of His own to be punished for. If Jesus had been a sinner Himself, even to the slightest extent, then His death on the cross would have been what He deserved for His own sin. It would have been the rightful result of a sinful life. Yet, because He was entirely perfect and sinless, His death could not validly be a punishment for His own sin, because He had none. It was possible, therefore, for God to treat His suffering and death on the cross as being endured on behalf of us, i.e. in our place. It was a *'substitutionary'* punishment, just like the animals that were sacrificed in the Temple, as we saw in chapter nine.

He himself bore our sins in his body on the tree, that we might die to sin and live to righteousness. By his wounds you have been healed.

1 Peter 2:24 (RSV)

A technical word for this transfer of blame to Jesus is that He was punished *'vicariously'.* This comes from a Latin word which means *'in place of'.* So, Jesus was punished in our place. It is a little bit like the legal concept of *'vicarious liability'*, where an employer is considered to be to blame for the negligence of his employees.

So, if an employee injures someone in the course of their employment, then his employer is considered to be to blame for it in the eyes of the law, even where he had nothing to do with it. The employer then has to pay the damages, even if he himself did nothing wrong.

The bravery Jesus showed in going to the cross

In enduring what He went through, Jesus was extraordinarily heroic. He is the bravest man who ever lived. We tend to overlook the outstanding courage and endurance that He showed. It was at a level far higher than that shown even by those who win medals like the Victoria Cross. For such people their act of bravery is usually very quick. It is all over in seconds or minutes. However what Jesus had to face up to and endure was slow and sustained.

Moreover, He had always known, throughout all eternity, that one day He had to face this cruel and humiliating death. The knowledge of what lay ahead must have weighed on Him through all of eternity past. Can you imagine how it must have been for Jesus for all those long ages of time to know that, one day, He was going to have to suffer and die for us and have all our sin transferred onto Him? That thought must have appalled Him.

It must have been like an eternal "*Garden of Gethsemane*" experience as He anticipated what lay ahead of Him. Remember also that Jesus was infinitely more powerful than His executioners. He could have stopped the crucifixion at any moment simply by using His own power. Or He could have commanded the angels to remove Him from the cross. Therefore He could have ended His own ordeal at any time, but He resisted the temptation to do so.

Instead He bravely endured it all to the bitter end. Many people have endured terrible ordeals that they were powerless to stop. However, what made Jesus' suffering unique was that He had the power all along to stop it, but never chose to do so. Who else but Him could show such restraint? He endured it all because He knew it had to be done that way. There was no other way to save us:

53 "Or do you think that I cannot appeal to My Father, and He will at once put at My disposal more than twelve legions of angels? 54 "How then will the Scriptures be fulfilled, which say that it must happen this way?"

Matthew 26:53-54 (NASB)

The events leading up to the crucifixion

Jesus was very afraid and full of dread on the night before His arrest and trial, as He faced what lay ahead of Him the next day. But He bravely carried on with it. Reflect on the passage below and try to imagine the intensity of His emotional anguish on that final lonely night before His crucifixion, as the long awaited time of suffering drew near. None of the apostles were sensitive enough to realise how alone and afraid He felt.

He wanted them to sit up with Him and keep Him company as He waited for His ordeal to begin. He was in such turmoil He could not sleep. In fact His stress was so intense that the Bible says He actually sweat blood. That would have been due to small blood vessels under His skin bursting due to the pressure and fear He was experiencing:

And being in an agony he prayed more earnestly; and his sweat became like great drops of blood falling down upon the ground.

Luke 22:44 (RSV)

However, the disciples were insensitive and did not realise how He felt. Therefore they all just went to sleep. Therefore Jesus had to sit up on His own, waiting for His arrest, with nobody to comfort or encourage Him:

36Then Jesus went with his disciples to a place called Gethsemane, and he said
to them, "Sit here while I go over there and pray." 37He took Peter and the two
sons of Zebedee along with him, and he began to be sorrowful and troubled.
38Then he said to them, "My soul is overwhelmed with sorrow to the point of
death. Stay here and keep watch with me." 39Going a little farther, he fell with
his face to the ground and prayed, "My Father, if it is possible, may this cup be taken from me. Yet not as I will, but as you will."

40Then he returned to his disciples and found them sleeping. "Could you men
not keep watch with me for one hour?" he asked Peter. 41"Watch and pray so
that you will not fall into temptation. The spirit is willing, but the body is weak."

Matthew 26:36-41 (NIV)

Jesus felt horrified by what lay ahead of Him, on the cross, and especially at the prospect of having all the sin of the world transferred on to Him. He therefore prayed three times to God the Father. In fact, He was so desperate He was pleading with God the Father to find some other way to save us, which would not involve Him dying on the cross. But each time the Father said no and Jesus accepted that answer. He knew that there was no alternative. Jesus then went ahead with it all for our sake:

42 He went away a second time and prayed, "My Father, if it is not possible for
this cup to be taken away unless I drink it, may your will be done." 43 When he
came back, he again found them sleeping, because their eyes were heavy. 44 So
he left them and went away once more and prayed the third time, saying the
same thing.

Matthew 26:42-44 (NIV)

Consider, how it must also have broken God the Father's heart to have to say no three times when Jesus was praying in such a distraught manner. We will never fully realise how much it cost God the Father to refuse Jesus' prayer repeatedly in this way. God the Father did all of that to Jesus, and to Himself, for our sake. We need to be truly grateful for the Father's part in the crucifixion, because what He suffered must have been terrible. Finally the time came for Jesus to be arrested. Even in that He had to experience the pain of being betrayed by Judas, one of His own followers:

45 Then he returned to the disciples and said to them, "Are you still sleeping and
resting? Look, the hour is near, and the Son of Man is betrayed into the hands
of sinners. 46 Rise, let us go! Here comes my betrayer!" 47 While he was still
speaking, Judas, one of the Twelve, arrived. With him was a large crowd armed
with swords and clubs, sent from the chief priests and the elders of the people.
48 Now the betrayer had arranged a signal with them: "The one I kiss is the man;
arrest him."

Matthew 26:45-48 (NIV)

On top of that betrayal, Jesus also suffered the pain of having Peter, one of His three closest friends, deny that he even knew Him. Jesus told Peter in advance that this would happen:

31 "Simon, Simon, behold, Satan demanded to have you, that he might sift you
like wheat, 32 but I have prayed for you that your faith may not fail; and when
you have turned again, strengthen your brethren." 33 And he said to him, "Lord,
I am ready to go with you to prison and to death." 34 He said, "I tell you, Peter,
the cock will not crow this day, until you three times deny that you know me."

Luke 22:31-34 (RSV)

This was fulfilled within a matter of hours:

54 Then they seized him and led him away, bringing him into the high priest's
house. Peter followed at a distance; 55 and when they had kindled a fire in the
middle of the courtyard and sat down together, Peter sat among them. 56 Then a
maid, seeing him as he sat in the light and gazing at him, said, "This man also
was with him." 57 But he denied it, saying, "Woman, I do not know him." 58 And
a little later someone else saw him and said, "You also are one of them." But
Peter said, "Man, I am not."

*[59]And after an interval of about an hour still another insisted, saying,
"Certainly this man also was with him; for he is a Galilean." [60]But Peter said,
"Man, I do not know what you are saying." And immediately, while he was still
speaking, the cock crowed. [61]And the Lord turned and looked at Peter. And Peter
remembered the word of the Lord, how he had said to him, "Before the cock
crows today, you will deny me three times." [62]And he went out and wept bitterly.*

Luke 22:54-62 (RSV)

The extent of the suffering Jesus endured for us

Consider now this lengthy passage from Mark's gospel, together with some short extracts from the other gospels. These show the sequence of events from Jesus' trial before Pontius Pilate which led to Him being sentenced to death and then to the execution being carried out. See how cruelly He was treated, especially by the Romans, and how many different things were done to him:

*[11]Now Jesus stood before the governor; and the governor asked him, "Are you
the King of the Jews?" Jesus said, "You have said so." [12]But when he was
accused by the chief priests and elders, he made no answer. [13]Then Pilate said
to him, "Do you not hear how many things they testify against you?" [14]But he
gave him no answer, not even to a single charge; so that the governor wondered
greatly.*

Matthew 27:11-14 (RSV)

*[26]And as they led him away, they seized one Simon of Cyre'ne, who was coming
in from the country, and laid on him the cross, to carry it behind Jesus. [27]And
there followed him a great multitude of the people, and of women who bewailed
and lamented him. [28]But Jesus turning to them said, "Daughters of Jerusalem,
do not weep for me, but weep for yourselves and for your children.*

Luke 23:26-28 (RSV)

*[12]"What shall I do, then, with the one you call the king of the Jews?" Pilate
asked them.*
[13]"Crucify him!" they shouted.
[14]"Why? What crime has he committed?" asked Pilate.
But they shouted all the louder, "Crucify him!"
*[15]Wanting to satisfy the crowd, Pilate released Barabbas to them. He had Jesus
flogged, and handed him over to be crucified.*

*[16]The soldiers led Jesus away into the palace (that is, the Praetorium) and called
together the whole company of soldiers. [17]They put a purple robe on him, then
twisted together a crown of thorns and set it on him. [18]And they began to call
out to him, "Hail, king of the Jews!" [19]Again and again they struck him on the*

head with a staff and spit on him. Falling on their knees, they paid homage to him.

20 And when they had mocked him, they took off the purple robe and put his own clothes on him. Then they led him out to crucify him. 21 A certain man from Cyrene, Simon, the father of Alexander and Rufus, was passing by on his way in from the country, and they forced him to carry the cross. 22 They brought Jesus to the place called Golgotha (which means The Place of the Skull). 23 Then they offered him wine mixed with myrrh, but he did not take it. 24 And they crucified him. Dividing up his clothes, they cast lots to see what each would get.

25 It was the third hour when they crucified him. 26 The written notice of the charge against him read: THE KING OF THE JEWS. 27 They crucified two robbers with him, one on his right and one on his left. 29 Those who passed by hurled insults at him, shaking their heads and saying, "So! You who are going to destroy the temple and build it in three days, 30 come down from the cross and save yourself!"

31 In the same way the chief priests and the teachers of the law mocked him among themselves. "He saved others," they said, "but he can't save himself! 32 Let this Christ, this King of Israel, come down now from the cross, that we may see and believe." Those crucified with him also heaped insults on him. 33 At the sixth hour darkness came over the whole land until the ninth hour. 34 And at the ninth hour Jesus cried out in a loud voice, "Eloi, Eloi, lama sabachthani?"—which means, "My God, my God, why have you forsaken me?"

35 When some of those standing near heard this, they said, "Listen, he's calling Elijah." 36 One man ran, filled a sponge with wine vinegar, put it on a stick, and offered it to Jesus to drink. "Now leave him alone. Let's see if Elijah comes to take him down," he said. 37 With a loud cry, Jesus breathed his last. 38 The curtain of the temple was torn in two from top to bottom. 39 And when the centurion, who stood there in front of Jesus, heard his cry and saw how he died, he said, "Surely this man was the Son of God!"

Mark 15:12-39 (NIV)

23 When the soldiers had crucified Jesus they took his garments and made four parts, one for each soldier; also his tunic. But the tunic was without seam, woven from top to bottom; 24 so they said to one another, "Let us not tear it, but cast lots for it to see whose it shall be." This was to fulfil the scripture, "They parted my garments among them, and for my clothing they cast lots."

John 19:23-24 (RSV)

Try to reflect on how much Jesus suffered and in so many different ways in the passages above. It would also be helpful for you to look up the full parallel accounts of the crucifixion in Matthew chapters 26-27, Luke chapters 22-23 and

John chapters 18-20. Jesus suffered many different forms of pain and anguish. It included mental, emotional, physical and spiritual agony. These various sufferings were deliberately directed towards Jesus by God the Father.

The wrath, or anger, of God was being poured out on Him so that He could suffer in our place, instead of us. He took the full blast of God's anger at the sin of the world so that it did not have to be directed at us. The pain and injury He endured also left Him so physically mutilated that He was unrecognisable, just as the prophet Isaiah had prophesied. In fact He no longer even looked human, because He had been so butchered by His executioners. His whole body was a mass of wounds:

Just as there were many who were appalled at him his appearance was so disfigured beyond that of any man and his form marred beyond human likeness
Isaiah 52:14 (NIV)

The shame and humiliation that Jesus also endured

Moreover, Jesus' humiliation was added to by the fact that the Roman Soldiers took away all of His clothes. Few people realise that when Jesus was upon the cross He was entirely naked. Passers-by were jeering and laughing at Him. Imagine the shame and degradation that that must have caused Him. He even had to suffer the brutality and indignity of having His beard pulled out of His face. That would have caused great mutilation and disfigurement in itself.

In addition, great damage was done to His back and legs by being scourged or flogged with a whip made of many cords tied together. Each of those cords had sharp pieces of metal or bone attached to them to tear open the flesh. In addition to all of that, the passers-by actually spat on Him, directly into His face:

I gave My back to those who strike Me, And My cheeks to those who pluck out the beard; I did not cover My face from humiliation and spitting.
Isaiah 50:6 (NASB)

Then they spat in his face, and struck him; and some slapped him,
Matthew 26:67 (RSV)

The Prophet Isaiah's amazing prophecy which sets out many of the details of Jesus' crucifixion

One of the most extraordinary things in the Bible is the fact that what Jesus did on the cross was prophesied in fine detail by Isaiah eight centuries before it happened. We have just seen two such prophecies above. Isaiah carries on and gives a long description of the further things which the Messiah must suffer on behalf of His people. It is amazingly accurate and detailed.

That is because God put the words into Isaiah's mind. Please read these further passages, written about 800 years BC. Note the many other specific things Isaiah foretold, all of which happened, exactly as was prophesied. All of these verses are speaking about Jesus. See how many details you can identify:

***13** See, my servant will act wisely;*
he will be raised and lifted up and highly exalted.
***14** Just as there were many who were appalled at him –*
his appearance was so disfigured beyond that of any human being
and his form marred beyond human likeness –
***15** so he will sprinkle many nations,*
and kings will shut their mouths because of him.
For what they were not told, they will see,
and what they have not heard, they will understand.

***1** Who has believed our message?*
And to whom has the arm of the LORD been revealed?
***2** For He grew up before Him like a tender shoot,*
And like a root out of parched ground;
He has no stately form or majesty
That we should look upon Him,
Nor appearance that we should be attracted to Him.

***3** He was despised and rejected by men,*
a man of sorrows, and familiar with suffering.
Like one from whom men hide their faces
he was despised, and we esteemed him not.

***4** Surely he took up our infirmities*
and carried our sorrows,
yet we considered him stricken by God,
smitten by him, and afflicted.

***5** But he was pierced for our transgressions,*
he was crushed for our iniquities;
the punishment that brought us peace was upon him,
and by his wounds we are healed.

***6** We all, like sheep, have gone astray,*
each of us has turned to his own way;
and the LORD has laid on him
the iniquity of us all.

7He was oppressed and afflicted,
yet he did not open his mouth;
he was led like a lamb to the slaughter,
and as a sheep before her shearers is silent,
so he did not open his mouth.

8By oppression and judgment he was taken away.
And who can speak of his descendants?
For he was cut off from the land of the living;
for the transgression of my people he was stricken.

9He was assigned a grave with the wicked,
and with the rich in his death,
though he had done no violence,
nor was any deceit in his mouth.

10Yet it was the LORD's will to crush him and cause him to suffer,
and though the LORD makes his life a guilt offering,
he will see his offspring and prolong his days,
and the will of the LORD will prosper in his hand.

11After the suffering of his soul,
he will see the light of life and be satisfied;
by his knowledge my righteous servant will justify many,
and he will bear their iniquities.

12Therefore I will give him a portion among the great,
and he will divide the spoils with the strong,
because he poured out his life unto death,
and was numbered with the transgressors.
For he bore the sin of many,
and made intercession for the transgressors.

Isaiah 52:13 – 53:12 (NIV)

When Jewish people hear Isaiah 53 read out, they often imagine it is from the New Testament. They know it is talking about Jesus, but they often do not realise it is actually from their own Hebrew Scriptures, which we call the Old Testament. It is speaking about their own Messiah, but most of them have not yet recognised Him. One day all of Israel will recognise Jesus and accept Him as their Messiah:

King David's *'Messianic psalms'* which give further details (1000 years beforehand) about what Jesus would experience on the cross

Just as we have seen with the long prophecy by Isaiah, much of the information we have about what Jesus had to suffer on the cross is actually set out in the Old Testament rather than the New Testament. For example, consider Psalm 22. This was written by King David (a physical ancestor of Jesus). In this psalm, although David is speaking, for most of the time he is actually speaking on behalf of Jesus, the future Messiah.

David is setting out what Jesus would think and feel while on the cross. It is a long psalm so we will not look at all of it, but here are some of the most relevant parts. They reveal a lot of useful and poignant facts about what Jesus experienced during his crucifixion:

Psalm 22 (NIV)

1My God, my God, why have you forsaken me?
Why are you so far from saving me,
so far from my cries of anguish?
2My God, I cry out by day, but you do not answer,
by night, but I find no rest.

In verses 1-2 King David reveals the anguish Jesus felt on the cross about being abandoned by God. This occurred when God the Father and the Holy Spirit withdrew from Him and rejected Him while He was carrying the guilt of the sin of the whole world. Then in verses 6-8 David goes on to express the pain Jesus felt at being despised, mocked and insulted by those around Him as He hung on the cross. They jeered at Him, telling Him to get God to rescue Him, even as He was dying to save them:

6But I am a worm and not a man,
scorned by everyone, despised by the people.
7All who see me mock me;
they hurl insults, shaking their heads.
8"He trusts in the LORD," they say,
"let the LORD rescue him.
Let him deliver him,
since he delights in him."

In verses 12-13, David expresses what Jesus experienced as He was surrounded by jeering, snarling enemies. This refers to both human beings and demons, i.e. all of those who were gnashing their teeth at Him in hatred and contempt. Note that the *"bulls of Bashan"* referred to here are demons. While Jesus was dying on the cross, demons were surrounding Him.

The demons believed they had defeated Him and prevented Him from becoming the Messiah, Saviour and King of Israel. That is why they were rejoicing, jeering and roaring at Him. But in fact, He was outwitting them and triumphing over them. Even though Jesus knew the truth, the hatred and mockery of His enemies, especially that of the demons, must have been intensely degrading for Him. He could see them clearly, all around Him:

12Many bulls surround me;
strong bulls of Bashan encircle me.
13Roaring lions that tear their prey
open their mouths wide against me.

Then, in verses 14-15 David refers to Jesus' physical suffering and to the agonising movements He had to endure. He had to struggle to lift Himself up to be able to breathe, because His hands and feet had been nailed to the cross. He was also twisted and contorted. It also refers to the extreme thirst He felt. He had lost vast amounts of blood and had had nothing to drink, despite the hot sun.

14I am poured out like water,
and all my bones are out of joint.
My heart has turned to wax;
it has melted within me.
15My mouth is dried up like a potsherd,
and my tongue sticks to the roof of my mouth;
you lay me in the dust of death.

Finally, verses 16-18, deal with two of the most well-known features of Jesus' crucifixion. They refer to how His hands and feet were pierced by nails and also how the Roman Soldiers divided His clothes among them and cast lots to decide who should have his robe. Isn't it astonishing that facts as accurate and specific as these were written about Jesus 1000 years before His crucifixion?

16Dogs surround me,
a pack of villains encircles me;
they pierce my hands and my feet.
17All my bones are on display;
people stare and gloat over me.
18They divide my clothes among them
and cast lots for my garment.

Now let us also consider Psalm 69. This is another 'Messianic psalm' in which King David reveals more of the thoughts and experiences that Jesus was going to have on the cross:

Psalm 69 (NIV)

Verses 1-4 refer to Jesus feeling overwhelmed on the cross by the sheer hatred and contempt of those surrounding Him. As we know from Psalm 22, those were both humans and demons.

1Save me, O God,
for the waters have come up to my neck.

2I sink in the miry depths,
where there is no foothold.
I have come into the deep waters;
the floods engulf me.

3I am worn out calling for help;
my throat is parched.
My eyes fail,
looking for my God.

4Those who hate me without reason
outnumber the hairs of my head;
many are my enemies without cause,
those who seek to destroy me.
I am forced to restore
what I did not steal.

Next, in verses 7-9, we get a glimpse at how Jesus felt at enduring scorn for our sake and at His feeling of shame. He was rejected and misunderstood even by His own immediate family. We know from the gospels that even His own brothers did not (at that point) believe in Him or understand Him:

7For I endure scorn for your sake,
and shame covers my face.

8I am a foreigner to my own family,
a stranger to my own mother's children;

9for zeal for your house consumes me,
and the insults of those who insult you fall on me.

Verses 19-21 reveal more about the scorn, disgrace and shame Jesus experienced, which broke His heart. Finally it even specifies that He would be given vinegar to drink. This detail was literally and exactly fulfilled on the cross. He was handed a sponge soaked in vinegar by those who had heard Him saying *"I thirst":*

19You know how I am scorned, disgraced and shamed;
all my enemies are before you.

20Scorn has broken my heart
and has left me helpless;
I looked for sympathy, but there was none,
for comforters, but I found none.

21They put gall in my food
and gave me vinegar for my thirst.

It is impossible to include all the facts and details of the crucifixion in this book. But it is helpful to look at the prophecies about Jesus from the Old Testament and to cross reference them with the accounts of the crucifixion in the four gospels. The exactness of the literal fulfilment of each of these prophecies is amazing.

The burden and guilt of our sin was placed on Jesus

In addition to having to suffer physical pain on the cross, Jesus also had to suffer something far worse. All the sin of the world was, for a time, heaped on to Him. While that was happening, God the Father and The Holy Spirit withdrew from Him. He was required to bear the burden of the sin of the world entirely alone. While all of that sin was upon Him, God the Father and The Holy Spirit needed to show their utter unwillingness to be associated with our sin or to be tainted by it.

Jesus had never sinned or been guilty of anything throughout His eternal existence. Therefore it must have felt horrific to be directly associated with sin and to have the sin, transgression and iniquity of all the world heaped on to Him and treated as if it was His own. In fact, as He hung on the cross and the guilt of all of it was put upon Him, God the Father and the Holy Spirit viewed Jesus as if He actually *was* sin. We are told that he was made *"to be sin":*

He made Him who knew no sin to be sin on our behalf, so that we might become the righteousness of God in Him.

2 Corinthians 5:21 (NASB)

God the Father and the Holy Spirit regarded Jesus as being so closely identified with our sin, and so covered by it, that they actually viewed Him as though He *was sin itself* in bodily form. In the eyes of God, He became sin personified and was defined by sin. He was also polluted and desecrated by it in a way that appalled Him.

It was also necessary for Jesus to be rejected and abandoned by God the Father and the Holy Spirit

For a time, while the sin of the whole world was pressing down upon Him, God the Father and the Holy Spirit had to separate themselves from Jesus. He was therefore left entirely on His own, just like the scapegoat that we referred to in Chapter 9. Even His Father and the Holy Spirit rejected Him during those hours.

This was the time when Jesus reached the very lowest depths of His degradation, rejection and shame. He was, by this stage, totally forsaken, even by God. Notice what Jesus says from the cross about this feeling of abandonment. He says the words from Psalm 22 which King David had prophesied that He would say:

***33**At the sixth hour darkness came over the whole land until the ninth hour.*
34**And at the ninth hour Jesus cried out in a loud voice, "Eloi, Eloi, lama sabachthani?"—which means, "My God, my God, why have you forsaken me?"
Mark 15:33-34 (NIV)

It is impossible for us to overstate the significance of this abandonment. Jesus suffered indescribably through being rejected by and separated from His Father and The Holy Spirit. It had never happened before. He had been together with them in perfect harmony for all eternity past. The emotional pain of this sudden rejection and isolation, combined with the disgust and revulsion He felt at the sin of the world pressing down upon Him, probably caused Jesus more suffering than the crucifixion itself.

As well as His physical, mental and spiritual suffering, Jesus also had to die for us

When all these forms of suffering had been completed, it was time for Jesus to die. His death was essential. It had to go that far. He had to die, as well as suffer, in order to pay the full penalty for our sin. We are told this many times, but perhaps the verses which express the point most directly are in John's gospel. God caused Caiaphas, the wicked High Priest, who hated Jesus, to prophesy, (without realising it), that Jesus had to die for the nation (of Israel) and also for all of us:

***45**Therefore many of the Jews who had come to visit Mary, and had seen what Jesus did, put their faith in him.* ***46**But some of them went to the Pharisees and told them what Jesus had done.* ***47**Then the chief priests and the Pharisees called a meeting of the Sanhedrin. "What are we accomplishing?" they asked. "Here is this man performing many miraculous signs.* ***48**If we let him go on like this,*

everyone will believe in him, and then the Romans will come and take away both our place and our nation."
[49]Then one of them, named Caiaphas, who was high priest that year, spoke up, "You know nothing at all! [50]You do not realize that it is better for you that one man die for the people than that the whole nation perish." [51]He did not say this on his own, but as high priest that year he prophesied that Jesus would die for the Jewish nation, [52]and not only for that nation but also for the scattered children of God, to bring them together and make them one. [53]So from that day on they plotted to take his life.

John 11:45-53 (NIV)

Who actually killed Jesus?

Many blame the Jewish people for putting Jesus to death. That is unfair and inaccurate. The Jews did not do it. The Romans were more to blame, but even they weren't really responsible for it and did not bring it about. They were not even capable of doing so. As for who it was who put Jesus to death, it was primarily God the Father, not the Romans or the Jewish authorities.

It was He who punished Jesus in our place to pay for our sins. God the Father deliberately offered Him up for our sake, just as Abraham was told to offer up his son, Isaac. That said, Jesus' death came, in the end, when He gave up His own spirit. He did so because His mission was complete. He had finished the job that His Father had asked Him to do. He had paid the full penalty for the sin of the world.

[28]Later, knowing that all was now completed, and so that the Scripture would be fulfilled, Jesus said, "I am thirsty." [29]A jar of wine vinegar was there, so they soaked a sponge in it, put the sponge on a stalk of the hyssop plant, and lifted it to Jesus' lips. [30]When he had received the drink, Jesus said, "It is finished." With that, he bowed his head and gave up his spirit.

John 19:28-30 (NIV)

Jesus decided the moment of His own death

It was Jesus Himself who decided the moment of His own death. No human being killed Him. Indeed, nobody was capable of killing Jesus. Nobody could take His life from Him by force. He laid it down freely, of His own choice, just as Isaac had been willing to do:

"I am the good shepherd; the good shepherd lays down His life for the sheep.

John 10:11 (NASB)

[17]"For this reason the Father loves Me, because I lay down My life so that I may take it again. [18]"No one has taken it away from Me, but I lay it down on My own initiative. I have authority to lay it down, and I have authority to take it up again. This commandment I received from My Father."

John 10:17-18 (NASB)

The punishment of Jesus in our place makes it possible for God to forgive our sin

We have seen in chapter 9 how the repeated sacrifices of animals in the Temple provided a temporary cover for the sins of the people. However, Jesus' death made it possible for our sin to be fully and permanently forgiven. It could therefore be completely cancelled, removed and disposed of. This solution was achieved once and for all:

[24]For Christ did not enter a man-made sanctuary that was only a copy of the true one; he entered Heaven itself, now to appear for us in God's presence.
[25]Nor did he enter Heaven to offer himself again and again, the way the high priest enters the Most Holy Place every year with blood that is not his own.
[26]Then Christ would have had to suffer many times since the creation of the world. But now he has appeared once for all at the end of the ages to do away with sin by the sacrifice of himself.

Hebrews 9:24-26 (NIV)

The death of Jesus on our behalf paid our debt to God. That enabled God the Father to cancel the *"certificate of debt"* because all of our sins had been dealt with by Jesus on the cross:

[13]When you were dead in your transgressions and the uncircumcision of your flesh, He made you alive together with Him, having forgiven us all our transgressions, [14]having cancelled out the certificate of debt consisting of decrees against us, which was hostile to us; and He has taken it out of the way, having nailed it to the cross.

Colossians 2:13-14 (NASB)

Note that last phrase, *"having nailed it to the cross"*. This is a reference to the practice in those days when a man was crucified. The executioner would write on a piece of wood the crime or unpaid debt for which the man was being put to death. This served to warn all those passing by about what might happen to them if they were to get involved in the same crime or debt.

The point is that on the cross of Jesus no such note was nailed, because He had no crime or debt. The Roman Governor, Pontius Pilate, was well aware of that fact.

Therefore he gave orders for the soldiers to nail a sign above Jesus' head which simply said *"Jesus of Nazareth, the King of the Jews"*. No crime was referred to.

So, what apostle Paul means in the above passage from Colossians, is that it is as if God the Father had nailed *our* certificate of debt to the cross. It was the debt we owed to Him because of our sin. That is the debt that is nailed to Jesus' cross.

That would correspond exactly to how executions were done in those days. It illustrates very clearly how God saw Jesus as paying our debt for us, thus enabling us to be forgiven. The way the prophet Isaiah puts it is that our sins are washed away and we are made as white as snow:

"Come now, and let us reason together,"
Says the LORD,
"Though your sins are as scarlet,
They will be as white as snow;
Though they are red like crimson,
They will be like wool.
Isaiah 1:18 (NASB)

This washing away or cancelling out and forgiving of our sin is possible solely because the guilt of it was placed on Jesus' shoulders. He received all our punishment. Therefore, if we repent and believe, God no longer needs to punish us, because Jesus has taken that punishment in our place, as our substitute:

Therefore there is now no condemnation for those who are in Christ Jesus.
Romans 8:1 (NASB)

How can Jesus pay our penalty by dying in our place? How does it work, legally and practically?

Perhaps it will help to give an analogy to try and show the way Jesus paid our penalty. Think of an extremely wealthy man, such as Bill Gates. Imagine he was to stand outside a court with a cheque book or debit card and offer to pay the fines of any person fined in that court, provided they wanted him to do so and asked him to do it.

Thus, as people came out with fines of one amount or another, Bill Gates could write out a cheque to pay each fine, whether it be high or low. His bank account would be more than big enough to pay for the fines of all the people who asked him to do so. It was a little bit like that when Jesus paid the penalty for our sin. He was infinitely holy and sinless and yet He died a brutal death.

That created an infinite capacity for Him to pay for your sin and mine. It is almost as if Jesus, through His infinitely unjust death, acquired an infinite 'bank account'. He can then use that to pay the 'fines' of people like you and me.

Mathematically that would be correct. One man with an infinite bank account could pay the fines owed by any number of people. Another way to understand the idea of Jesus dying in our place is to think of a Judge. One day there appears before him a man whom he knows, someone he went to school with, who is now facing a criminal prosecution.

Imagine the dilemma that the Judge faces. He has his own professional duty, or code of conduct, which requires him to fully carry out the due process of the law. He has to make sure that the prosecution is conducted properly and that it arrives at a proper verdict. Then, if guilt is found, it is his duty to impose an appropriate sentence. If he failed to do so, he would be doing wrong and acting improperly, which he would never be willing to do.

Imagine though that the Judge does not want to pass sentence on his old friend but would rather show mercy towards him. You see then the conflict between his sense of justice and the need to do his duty professionally, but on the other hand his heart's desire is to show mercy. He wishes to spare his friend from the full blast of the law, but he is not willing to break the law in doing so.

What could the Judge do to get around this dilemma? He could resolve it by finding his friend guilty and sentencing him to the full penalty. But then, having done so, he could take out his own cheque book and write out a cheque himself for the full amount of the fine that he has just imposed on his friend.

By doing that, he has fully honoured his duty to his office and to the law. He has not compromised himself or broken the law in any way. Yet, the judge has found a way to redirect the severity of the criminal law away from his friend and towards himself. He takes its full penalty upon himself. Then his friend can be spared from its impact.

Likewise, Jesus found a way to ensure that the full penalty for the breaking of God's Law came to be paid by Himself. Thus there was no compromise or breaking of the Law. But at the same time, God's mercy could fully come into operation, because Jesus redirected all of the severity of the Law towards Himself, rather than letting it fall on us.

What Jesus did on the cross looks like foolishness to proud and worldly people. It only makes sense to the humble and lowly

To proud, selfish and worldly people who do not believe in Jesus, what happened on the cross seems foolish. God has deliberately made it that way so that Christianity can only make any sense to humble and lowly people. Proud or worldly people who are *"wise in their own eyes"* will never be able to understand what Jesus did on the cross and why it was essential. Yet a child can understand it easily:

***[18]For the message of the cross is foolishness to those who are perishing, but to
us who are being saved it is the power of God. [19]For it is written: I will destroy
the wisdom of the wise; the intelligence of the intelligent I will
frustrate.'[20]Where is the wise man? Where is the scholar? Where is the
philosopher of this age? Has not God made foolish the wisdom of the
world?[21]For since in the wisdom of God the world through its wisdom did not
know him, God was pleased through the foolishness of what was preached to
save those who believe. [22]Jews demand miraculous signs and Greeks look for
wisdom, [23]but we preach Christ crucified: a stumbling block to Jews and
foolishness to Gentiles, [24]but to those whom God has called, both Jews and
Greeks, Christ the power of God and the wisdom of God. [25]For the foolishness
of God is wiser than man's wisdom, and the weakness of God is stronger than
man's strength.***

Corinthians 1:18-25 (NIV)

No single word can adequately sum up all that Jesus achieved on the cross. But '*atonement*' is the word which probably comes closest to it. The suffering and death of Jesus involved a complicated series of transfers and transactions, during which many things were happening. We shall now begin to examine this process of the atonement in closer detail and break it down into its component parts. Then we will see more clearly what was happening and the many different ways in which Jesus' death benefited us.

The 'atonement'

And not only so, but we also joy in God through our Lord Jesus Christ, by whom we have now received the atonement.

Romans 5:11 (KJV)

We could define this word, *'atonement',* as the overall process by which Jesus Christ, through His sinless life and His unjust sacrificial death on our behalf, made our entire salvation possible. The word 'atonement' therefore includes many shades of meaning and different aspects of what Jesus did for us. Before we go into closer detail about the atonement, let's look at some passages from the writings of Moses which refer to this concept.

We will look at how, in the Old Testament, the priests used to sacrifice lambs, bulls and goats to 'cover for' the sins of the people. The death of the animal that was sacrificed, and the shedding of its blood in particular, made it possible for God to overlook the sins of the people for the time being.

The blood of these animals did not, in itself, have the power to save those people and take away their sins. But, when accompanied by repentance and faith in God, it was effective to cover the sins of the people temporarily, pending the coming of Jesus. It was His death on our behalf which really did deal with sin.

For it is impossible for the blood of bulls and goats to take away sins.
Hebrews 10:4 (NASB)

The shedding of these animals' blood was also an illustration. It set the pattern for what Jesus would later do. Let's look at what Moses told the priests to do in sacrificing animals to 'atone' for the sins of the people:

36"Each day you shall offer a bull as a sin offering for atonement, and you shall purify the altar when you make atonement for it, and you shall anoint it to consecrate it. 37"For seven days you shall make atonement for the altar and consecrate it; then the altar shall be most holy, and whatever touches the altar shall be holy.
Exodus 29:36-37 (NASB)

15'Then the elders of the congregation shall lay their hands on the head of the bull before the LORD, and the bull shall be slain before the LORD. 16'Then the anointed priest is to bring some of the blood of the bull to the tent of meeting; 17and the priest shall dip his finger in the blood and sprinkle it seven times before the LORD, in front of the veil. 18'He shall put some of the blood on the horns of the altar which is before the LORD in the tent of meeting; and all the blood he shall pour out at the base of the altar of burnt offering which is at the doorway of the tent of meeting.
Leviticus 4:15-18 (NASB)

20'He shall also do with the bull just as he did with the bull of the sin offering; thus he shall do with it So the priest shall make atonement for them, and they will be forgiven.
Leviticus 4:20 (NASB)

Why is blood so significant?

When apostle Paul is speaking to the church leaders in Ephesus he refers to how God 'obtained' the church, i.e. saved it and brought it into existence, *"with the blood of His own Son"*. Paul puts emphasis on the blood:

Take heed to yourselves and to all the flock, in which the Holy Spirit has made you overseers, to care for the church of God which he obtained with the blood of his own Son.

Acts 20:28 (RSV)

But why does blood matter? Why does God ask us to focus on the blood of Jesus and why was the blood of the sacrificed animals so important? The answer is that to God, blood represents life. Indeed, the Bible says that the life of every creature is contained within its blood:

For the life of the flesh is in the blood; and I have given it for you upon the altar to make atonement for your souls; for it is the blood that makes atonement, by reason of the life.

Leviticus 17:11 (RSV)

For us to be forgiven and to avoid God's punishment for our sin, somebody has to lay down their lives in our place. The laying down of that life is represented by the shedding of blood. So, Jesus' death is essential for us to be saved. That death also had to involve the shedding of His own blood for us. The blood of Jesus has real power to save us. If He had not shed His blood for us, there could be no forgiveness:

And according to the Law, one may almost say, all things are cleansed with blood, and without shedding of blood there is no forgiveness.

Hebrews 9:22 (NASB)

In the Old Testament, there could be no forgiveness unless the sacrificed animals shed their blood. But they were really only a temporary symbol or illustration which pointed towards the blood that really counts. That is the blood of Jesus, without which none of us can be saved.

The laying down of Jesus' life on our behalf was essential for our salvation. Moreover, His death had to involve the shedding of His blood. His execution could not have been done by some other means, such as hanging, which would not have involved the shedding of His blood.

These passages above from Exodus and Leviticus tell the Jewish people how to get their sins temporarily dealt with or 'covered for', by the death of lambs, goats and bulls. They also point forward to the completely effective and permanent sacrifice of Jesus.

That was how our sin problem was to be dealt with once and for all. The passages above relate to the daily sacrifices in the part of the Temple known as 'the Holy Place'. However, the most well-known reference to the word atonement is within the phrase *'the Day of Atonement'* or *'Yom Kippur'*. This is the most important day of all the Jewish feast days.

Yom Kippur - the Day of Atonement

This feast, 'the Day of Atonement', came only once a year. On this special day, and only on this day, the Jewish High Priest was allowed to go into the very most holy part of the Temple, the Holy of Holies. Once in there he would take some of the blood of a lamb which had been sacrificed and sprinkle it on what was called the 'mercy seat'.

This was to 'cover for' the sins of the Jewish people for another year. The actions of the High Priest on the day of atonement were yet another illustration or 'type' or what Jesus would later do for us. However, even this could not fully take sins away; it could only temporarily cover them, for one year, not permanently:

"Aaron shall make atonement on its horns once a year; he shall make atonement on it with the blood of the sin offering of atonement once a year throughout your generations. It is most holy to the LORD."

Exodus 30:10 (NASB)

The writer of the letter to the Hebrews in the New Testament refers to this very important concept of the Day of Atonement and the sacrifice made by the Jewish High Priest. It illustrates and explains what Jesus Christ did on our behalf:

24For Christ did not enter a man-made sanctuary that was only a copy of the true one; he entered Heaven itself, now to appear for us in God's presence.
25Nor did he enter Heaven to offer himself again and again, the way the high priest enters the Most Holy Place every year with blood that is not his own.
26Then Christ would have had to suffer many times since the creation of the world. But now he has appeared once for all at the end of the ages to do away with sin by the sacrifice of himself.

Hebrews 9:24-26 (NIV)

This is quite a complex passage but, basically, it explains that what Jesus did when He died for us on the cross was similar to what the Jewish High Priest did each year in sacrificing animals to cover for the sins of the people. The crucial difference was that Jesus' sacrifice of Himself and the shedding of His own blood was a perfect and permanent sacrifice.

What had gone on before in the Temple was only a shadow or forerunner of what He would later do. Whereas the sacrifice of the animals in the Jewish Temple had to be done over and over again, the perfect sacrifice of Jesus, the sinless Lamb of God, only had to be done once. That was enough to save all people, however many, and wherever and whenever they live:

10By this will we have been sanctified through the offering of the body of Jesus Christ once for all. 11Every priest stands daily ministering and offering time after time the same sacrifices, which can never take away sins; 12but He, having offered one sacrifice for sins for all time, sat down at the right hand of God,

Hebrews 10:10-12 (NASB)

In doing what He did, Jesus was playing the part of both the High Priest and the sacrificed lamb. He was the one making the offering and He was also the offering itself. Whereas the High Priest made an offering of a lamb and sacrificed it, Jesus offered Himself. So, having offered the perfect sacrifice of Himself, and having been raised from the dead, Jesus' task was done. He will never need to die for us again. Instead, He was able to sit down in the place of honour at the right hand of God the Father, because His task of paying for our sins was complete.

Justification – this means being deemed to be as righteous as Jesus and having all his righteousness transferred to us or imputed to us

All the aspects of the atonement that we have looked at so far have been to do with forgiving our sins, taking guilt *away from us* and *preventing* God's judgment happening to us. Justification, is different. It relates to *receiving* righteousness from Jesus and having it *added to us*. This aspect of what Jesus achieved for us on the cross means that it became possible for God the Father to see us as having all the righteousness of Jesus added to us or given to us as a free gift. This has a very positive dimension to it. It raises our status, and adds something to us that we had not got:

For our sake he made him to be sin who knew no sin, so that in him we might become the righteousness of God.

2 Corinthians 5:21 (RSV)

In other words, we have seen earlier that Jesus' death on our behalf made it possible for our sins to be taken from us and placed on Him so that we could be forgiven. That was essential, but it still wasn't enough. It merely cancels out our sin but does not, in itself, make us righteous. It would be like taking away all the wrong answers from an examination script, but there are still no correct answers on it.

Thus it prevents marks being lost, but no marks have been gained. The key to understanding the concept of justification is to realise that God wants to achieve far more than simply to forgive us and make us sinless. Being declared not guilty, or made sinless, is not quite enough. God also wants us to be *made as righteous as Jesus.*

That cannot be achieved solely by us having our sins taken away and forgiven. That by itself would make us innocent and sinless, but it would not make us righteous. We therefore need to have righteousness added to us as well as having our sins taken way. So, the process of being justified means being *'made just'.*

That has exactly the same meaning as being *'made righteous'.* It means that all of Jesus' righteousness, which He earned by His perfect life and His complete obedience to the Law of Moses, is credited to us. It is as if we had earned it for ourselves. It is as if we had perfectly obeyed the Law of Moses ourselves. We gain this justification or transfer of righteousness by having faith in Jesus and putting our trust in Him:

1Therefore, since we are justified by faith, we have peace with God through our Lord Jesus Christ. 2Through him we have obtained access to this grace in which we stand, and we rejoice in our hope of sharing the glory of God.

Romans 5:1-2 (RSV)

Here is an analogy to help explain the difference between having our sins washed away and being made righteous or justified. Imagine a man owes ten million pounds to another man and that the second man then forgives him the entire debt. Now the first man is no longer in debt. Previously he was hopelessly bankrupt and unable to pay his debts. But now he has no debts at all. However, he is still not rich. He merely has no debts. But if the second man was to then give him ten million pounds and add that to his bank account, he would now be wealthy as well as having no debts.

So, cancelling the debt corresponds to God forgiving our sins and washing them away, but adding ten million pounds to the bank account corresponds to being made righteous by having Jesus' righteousness transferred to us. The only flaw in the analogy is that Jesus' righteousness is *infinite* rather than limited to a particular figure like ten million pounds.

Let us consider another analogy which may be helpful in showing the distinction between having our sins forgiven and being made righteous. Imagine yourself dressed in filthy, torn, worn-out clothes. If a wealthy man was to offer to give to you his own expensive, brand-new clothes and to take away from you your filthy rags, then it would operate as follows:

a) the *taking away*, or taking off, of your filthy old clothes would correspond to forgiveness. It is the *remova*l of what is horrible, ugly and dirty. It means that you no longer have the sin and guilt that you had.

b) the *putting on* of the rich man's new, expensive, clean clothes would correspond to justification. It is righteousness being *added to you* so that you have something which you did not previously have.

So, merely to remove your filthy old garments would mean you were no longer dirtily dressed, but you would not yet be well dressed. You would merely be naked, with no garments at all, either good or bad. But the adding or putting on of the expensive new clothing represents receiving Jesus' righteousness. The Bible speaks of this as putting on the *'robe of righteousness'*:

I will greatly rejoice in the LORD, my soul shall exult in my God; for he has clothed me with the garments of salvation, he has covered me with the robe of righteousness, as a bridegroom decks himself with a garland, and as a bride adorns herself with her jewels

Isaiah 61:10 (RSV)

That is a picture or illustration of what Jesus does when He makes us righteous. He gives us His own 'robe of righteousness' and allows us to wear His clothes as if we were Him. Therefore, justification, (being made righteous) is perhaps the most positive and glorious part of the whole atonement. It means that we are not only forgiven and made clean, but also made righteous and perfect, just as Jesus was perfect. We are allowed to share in His perfection, as if we were equally perfect:

and being made perfect he became the source of eternal salvation to all who obey him,

Hebrews 5:9 (RSV)

We are therefore able to be raised up to a vastly higher level and made to *be* righteous by having all the righteousness of Jesus legally *transferred* to us, or '*imputed*' to us. So, whereas the sin of one man, Adam, caused the whole world to inherit his sin nature, the righteous actions of Jesus made it possible for us all to be made righteous. That enables us to inherit all the blessings that come from His perfectly righteous life:

17 For if, by the trespass of the one man, death reigned through that one man, how much more will those who receive God's abundant provision of grace and of the gift of righteousness reign in life through the one man, Jesus Christ.

[18]Consequently, just as the result of one trespass was condemnation for all men, so also the result of one act of righteousness was justification that brings life for all men. [19]For just as through the disobedience of the one man the many were made sinners, so also through the obedience of the one man the many will be made righteous.

Romans 5:17-19 (NIV)

To use yet another analogy, in a legal context, the transfer of Jesus' righteousness to us is similar to the concept in land law, or conveyancing, of having jointly owned freehold property. Usually, when a husband and wife buy a house they choose to be registered at the Land Registry as *'joint tenants'*. That means that each of them owns the whole of the property simultaneously.

So, if a man owns a house and, on marriage, wishes to make his wife a joint owner, he could transfer to her a joint interest in the house. That would not reduce his own ownership. He would still own all of it while, at the same time, she also owns all of it. It is a little like that with Jesus' righteousness. It is infinite and fully belongs to Him, but, at the same time, He chooses to share it all with us.

So, He transfers to us the *'joint ownership'* of all His righteousness, not just some of it. Therefore God is legitimately able to view us as if we were just as righteous as Jesus. That transferred righteousness is given as a gift to anybody who becomes a genuine Christian.

That imputed or transferred righteousness isn't *earned* by us. It is given to us as a *free gift* because of our faith in Jesus. In the same way, God chose to regard Abraham as being righteous because of the genuineness of his faith, not his good deeds. God 'credited' Abraham with righteousness simply because he believed and trusted God:

[6]Even so Abraham believed God, and it was reckoned to him as righteousness.
[7]Therefore, be sure that it is those who are of faith who are sons of Abraham.

Galatians 3:6-7 (NASB)

[20]yet, with respect to the promise of God, he did not waver in unbelief but grew strong in faith, giving glory to God, [21]and being fully assured that what God had promised, He was able also to perform.

Romans 4:20-21 (NASB)

Therefore, in the same way, righteousness is 'reckoned to' or 'credited to' all those who believe in Jesus and put their faith in Him:

[22]Therefore it was also credited to him as righteousness. [23]Now not for his sake only was it written that it was credited to him, [24]but for our sake also, to whom it will be credited, as those who believe in Him who raised Jesus our Lord from

the dead, [25]He who was delivered over because of our transgressions, and was raised because of our justification.

Romans 4:22-25 (NASB)

So, we can say that our sins are forgiven on the basis of faith. But we can also say that it is equally by faith that we are credited with all of Jesus' righteousness:

Therefore, having been justified by faith, we have peace with God through our Lord Jesus Christ,

Romans 5:1 (NASB)

Please refer to chapter 12 for a fuller explanation of the fact that we are saved by God's grace in response to our faith in Jesus, not as a result of doing good deeds. Because we are justified we are saved from the wrath of God:

Much more then, having now been justified by His blood, we shall be saved from the wrath of God through Him.

Romans 5:9 (NASB)

So, having had our sins fully forgiven, and having had all of Jesus' righteousness transferred to us, we are viewed by God as if we were the same as Jesus in terms of both innocence and righteousness. That means that nobody can charge us with any crime or convict us of anything. We are made both fully innocent and fully righteous:

[33]Who will bring a charge against God's elect? God is the one who justifies;
[34]who is the one who condemns? Christ Jesus is He who died, yes, rather who was raised, who is at the right hand of God, who also intercedes for us.

Romans 8:33-34 (NASB)

A brief summary of six of the main aspects of what Jesus achieved for us through His atoning death on the cross

It is right and proper to refer to Jesus as having 'died for us' or 'saved us'. Those are valid short-hand phases which sum up what He did for us. However, it is also right to say that when Jesus died on the cross many different things were also being achieved, all at the same time.

He saved us in many different senses and there are various different ways of viewing it and explaining it. These overlap to some degree, but they are also distinct and separate points. Therefore it would be helpful for us to differentiate them and understand each of them more fully.

There are so many benefits that come from Jesus' death for us that we cannot look at them all in Book One. However, as a foretaste of the extra things that we shall begin to explore in later books in this series, we could say that what Jesus achieved for us on the cross can be broken down into six key areas or aspects.

Taken together, we tend to refer to these six aspects combined as *'the atonement'*. Let's list them and briefly define them:

1) **Jesus dying in our place as a substitute** - (vicariously) This means that Jesus takes our place and receives our punishment so that our sins can be forgiven and the penalty avoided (The technical expression for this is *'penal substitution'*). This is the main thing we have focused on in chapter ten.

2) **The turning away of God's wrath by the offering Jesus made** - The offering of Jesus as a sacrifice appeased God and turned His anger away from us. Therefore God no longer needed to pour out His anger on us. (The technical word for this is *'propitiation'*).

3) **Redemption** - This means being bought back, rescued, or liberated by the payment Jesus made. He paid the necessary 'purchase price' to obtain our freedom from slavery to various things. This is a vast subject and we will look into it in a lot of depth in later books in this series. But, in very brief terms, we could break *'redemption'* down into the following achievements:

a) Jesus sets us free from slavery to sin

We inherited our sinful nature from our first ancestor, Adam. It causes us to sin continually. But Jesus gives us a new nature which does not have to sin. Then those two natures, the old and the new, live within us, alongside each other and they are at war with each other. We then gradually have to learn to obey the wishes of our new nature, rather than our old sinful nature. That takes time, but it is possible for our new nature to steadily gain the upper hand, more and more of the time.

b) Jesus sets us free from slavery to Satan, who is the ruler of this world

Adam used to be the ruler of this world, but when he sinned he handed his authority and rulership over to Satan. Thus, every non-Christian is under the rulership and authority of Satan. However, when Jesus died and rose again, all authority was transferred back to Him and away from Satan. That is one of the ways that Jesus defeated and disarmed Satan for us.

It means that when we become a Christian we are transferred out from under Satan's authority and put under Jesus' authority instead. We move from Satan's kingdom of darkness into Jesus' Kingdom. This has all sorts of important implications, which we will examine in later books in this series.

4) **Jesus' operating as our 'Passover Lamb'** - This is as in the book of Exodus, when the Israelites were in Egypt. So God's judgment can *'pass over'* us and not affect us. It is just as the Israelite families avoided God's judgment when the angel of death passed over their homes and killed every first-born in Egypt.

5) **Justification** - This is the mirror image of point one, where Jesus took our place and had our sin put onto Him as our substitute. *Justification* means we, likewise, take Jesus' place. That then allows us to be deemed to be righteous, or credited with His righteousness. We receive this justification by having Jesus' own perfect righteousness transferred to us, as if it was our own. It is as if we stand in His shoes and share His status.

6) **Reconciliation** - This means being reconciled with God the Father so that we no longer have to be alienated, estranged or separated from Him, due to our sinfulness. Because our sin can now be removed and forgiven, and because we can receive Jesus' righteousness instead, God no longer needs to separate Himself from us. That then means that we can be reconciled with God and, spend eternity with Him, instead of being sent to the Lake of Fire.

It may sound surprising that what was achieved by Jesus' death on the cross is capable of being looked at in so many different ways and that so many different benefits come from it. It is, perhaps, a little like studying a huge building such as Buckingham Palace. It is one overall structure and can be spoken of as one building. Yet, it can also be looked at from many different angles, so that all sorts of different aspects come into view.

Thus when you look at Buckingham Palace from the front it is correct to say that you are seeing the Palace. However, if you look at it from the left-hand side, or right-hand side, or from the rear, you will see different or additional features, but it's still Buckingham Palace. Then if you looked at it from a helicopter hovering above the roof you would see other features and make even more discoveries about it. Yet, all the time, it is the same Palace that you are examining, albeit from different angles.

Likewise, with Jesus' death on the cross we shall see in later books in this series that we can focus on and emphasise, one by one, a series of different achievements and blessings. All of them flow from the death and resurrection of Jesus. They are all closely connected and they overlap to some degree. Yet they are also distinct and separate points and they benefit us in different ways.

The anguish that God the Father and the Holy Spirit also endured as they had to watch Jesus suffer and die without intervening to stop it.

It would be wrong to finish this chapter on what Jesus suffered on our behalf on the cross without referring in more detail to what God the Father and the Holy Spirit also suffered for our sake. We rightly focus on the heroic feat of endurance, courage and unselfishness that Jesus displayed when He died on the cross for us.

However, consider for a moment what torment God the Father and the Holy Spirit were also going through as they watched Jesus suffering and being tortured, abused, and ridiculed. Try to imagine yourself for a moment as a parent, wife or sibling of a person you love very deeply who is being put to death. Imagine however, that you knew that it was necessary for them to give up their life, to save the lives of a much larger group of people.

Picture yourself, therefore, looking on as your own son, brother or husband is dying on behalf of the people of your town or nation. Perhaps it could be in Nazi occupied France in World War Two and he is being tortured to death by the Gestapo. They could be trying to get him to reveal vital information and/or the names of his fellow agents in the French Resistance. However, he is refusing to do so, for the sake of his comrades, and for the sake of the wider war-effort.

Let's imagine that if he reveals what the Gestapo want to know then his own life will be spared, but possibly hundreds of his comrades will die. They too have families. Moreover, perhaps the very success or failure of the Allied invasion of Normandy is at stake.

If you were that young man's father, brother or wife can you imagine the mental and emotional anguish you would be going through? What if the torture was being done nearby, so that you could hear his screams? It would be indescribably harrowing for you. But let's take it further. What if you yourself also had the secret information or knew the names of the people that the Gestapo wanted? What if you knew that you could go forward yourself, in private, and hand over the very facts or names that he is withholding? By doing so you could, by your own actions, prevent his death and end his suffering.

Would you go to the Gestapo and hand over the secret information? Or, would you be capable of restraining yourself and doing nothing? Would you stand aside and allow your own son, brother or husband to die in order to save the lives of the others and to safeguard the Normandy invasion? Isn't that similar in some ways to the agonising dilemma which God the Father and the Holy Spirit faced? They both knew that there was no other way for us to be saved except through Jesus giving His life on the cross.

However, they both also knew that, just like Jesus, they had the power to stop the crucifixion. Like Him, they could have sent 12 legions of angels to deal with the Roman soldiers. They could have stopped the torment at any moment, both for Jesus and for themselves. But they didn't. They exercised infinite self-control and endured the slow ordeal of watching Jesus die without ever intervening.

We rightly praise and thank Jesus for His courage and restraint in not putting a stop to His own suffering by removing Himself from the cross. But how many of us have ever even considered what God the Father and the Holy Spirit also did for us and the equivalent restraint they showed as they watched and suffered in silence as He was being crucified? Moreover, we have seen how Jesus cried out on the cross when God the Father and the Holy Spirit separated themselves from Him and forsook Him while our sin was upon Him.

That abandonment and separation was what, in the end, broke Jesus' heart, probably more than any other thing He suffered. But doesn't it follow that it must have felt very similar for God the Father and the Holy Spirit? They too had to endure being separated from the Son of God, just as He had to endure being separated from them. None of us can really grasp how terrible that was for each of them too, and how grieved they must have felt about it.

Even so, it was Jesus alone who saved us

The suffering and anguish of God the Father and the Holy Spirit were harrowing, but it was not redemptive as Jesus' suffering was. What they endured did not save us. Jesus was the only One being sacrificed to pay for our sin. It was Jesus alone who paid our penalty, not the Father or the Holy Spirit. But, even so, we still owe them a huge debt of gratitude, not for saving us as such, but for co-operating and holding themselves back from intervening while Jesus was suffering for us. So, it is very right and proper that we should also give heartfelt thanks to God the Father, and to the Holy Spirit, for what they endured, as well as thanking Jesus for dying for us.

Moreover, in case you ever doubt God's love and concern for you, as multitudes of people do, remember what God the Father personally was willing to go through when He allowed the crucifixion to continue in order to bring about your salvation. Then realise that if He was willing to do all that, He can certainly also be trusted to care for all your other needs:

He who did not spare his own Son but gave him up for us all, will he not also give us all things with him?

Romans 8:32 (RSV)

CHAPTER 11

PROOF THAT THE RESURRECTION REALLY HAPPENED

We have seen in the last two chapters that Jesus Christ died on the cross, in our place, and how important that is for our salvation. However, we must now turn to the question of His bodily resurrection. Although Jesus died, He did not remain dead. After three days He physically rose to life again.

Everything in Christianity hinges upon this one central event, namely the resurrection of Jesus Christ. If He did not rise again from the dead, then Christianity would not be true and Jesus' death on the cross would mean nothing. We would remain unforgiven and lost in our sins, awaiting God's judgment. The resurrection is therefore central. The apostle Paul put it well when he said:

***12** But if it is preached that Christ has been raised from the dead, how can some of you say that there is no resurrection of the dead? **13** If there is no resurrection of the dead, then not even Christ has been raised. **14** And if Christ has not been raised, our preaching is useless and so is your faith. **15** More than that, we are then found to be false witnesses about God, for we have testified about God that he raised Christ from the dead. But he did not raise him if in fact the dead are not raised. **16** For if the dead are not raised, then Christ has not been raised either. **17** And if Christ has not been raised, your faith is futile; you are still in your sins. **18** Then those also who have fallen asleep in Christ are lost. **19** If only for this life we have hope in Christ, we are to be pitied more than all men.*

***20** But Christ has indeed been raised from the dead, the first fruits of those who have fallen asleep. **21** For since death came through a man, the resurrection of the dead comes also through a man. **22** For as in Adam all die, so in Christ all will be made alive. **23** But each in his own turn: Christ, the first fruits; then, when he comes, those who belong to him.*

1 Corinthians 15:12-23 (NIV)

Given the vital importance of the resurrection, it is essential that we believe that it happened. Possibly you have never been taught about the resurrection or considered the evidence for it? Therefore, I propose in this chapter to set out some of the facts which prove conclusively that the resurrection really happened. Some people are surprised by that. They assume that after all these years it cannot be possible to prove that the resurrection really took place.

Yet we can prove it. In fact we can prove it beyond all reasonable doubt. The facts are so overwhelming that no other explanation is possible. In the 1920s a man called Frank Morrison set out to write a book to prove that there was no resurrection. He began to carefully assemble the evidence and the facts in order to write his book, but in the process of doing so he came to some surprising conclusions.

He discovered that in fact the evidence proved the exact opposite of what He had set out to prove. He therefore did write a book, but it was to prove the resurrection rather than disprove it. It is a very famous Christian classic called *'Who Moved the Stone?'* It is still in print and well worth getting. I have used some of Frank Morrison's ideas in this chapter.

I have also borrowed from another book, '*Know Why You Believe*' by Paul Little, to whom I am also indebted. Before we begin to look at the arguments and the evidence, it would be a good idea to read the following lengthy passage from Luke chapter 24, followed by some other shorter passages from Matthew, Mark and John. These will give you an understanding of the main facts which we will then consider:

Extract from Luke's gospel:

1On the first day of the week, very early in the morning, the women took the spices they had prepared and went to the tomb. 2They found the stone rolled away from the tomb, 3but when they entered, they did not find the body of the Lord Jesus. 4While they were wondering about this, suddenly two men in clothes that gleamed like lightning stood beside them. 5In their fright the women bowed down with their faces to the ground, but the men said to them, "Why do you look for the living among the dead? 6He is not here; he has risen! Remember how he told you, while he was still with you in Galilee: 7'The Son of Man must be delivered into the hands of sinful men, be crucified and on the third day be raised again.' "

8Then they remembered his words. 9When they came back from the tomb, they told all these things to the Eleven and to all the others. 10It was Mary Magdalene, Joanna, Mary the mother of James, and the others with them who told this to the apostles. 11But they did not believe the women, because their words seemed to them like nonsense. 12Peter, however, got up and ran to the tomb. Bending over, he saw the strips of linen lying by themselves, and he went away, wondering to himself what had happened. 13Now that same day two of them were going to a village called Emmaus, about seven miles from Jerusalem. 14They were talking with each other about everything that had happened.

15As they talked and discussed these things with each other, Jesus himself came up and walked along with them; 16but they were kept from recognizing him. 17He asked them, "What are you discussing together as you walk along?" They stood still, their faces downcast. 18One of them, named Cleopas, asked him, "Are you

only a visitor to Jerusalem and do not know the things that have happened there
in these days?"

19 "What things?" he asked. "About Jesus of Nazareth," they replied. "He was
a prophet, powerful in word and deed before God and all the people. 20 The chief
priests and our rulers handed him over to be sentenced to death, and they
crucified him; 21 but we had hoped that he was the one who was going to redeem
Israel. And what is more, it is the third day since all this took place. 22 In addition,
some of our women amazed us. They went to the tomb early this morning 23 but
didn't find his body. They came and told us that they had seen a vision of angels,
who said he was alive. 24 Then some of our companions went to the tomb and
found it just as the women had said, but him they did not see."

25 He said to them, "How foolish you are, and how slow of heart to believe all
that the prophets have spoken! 26 Did not the Christ have to suffer these things
and then enter his glory?" 27 And beginning with Moses and all the Prophets, he
explained to them what was said in all the Scriptures concerning himself. 28 As
they approached the village to which they were going, Jesus acted as if he were
going farther. 29 But they urged him strongly, "Stay with us, for it is nearly
evening; the day is almost over." So he went in to stay with them. 30 When he
was at the table with them, he took bread, gave thanks, broke it and began to
give it to them. 31 Then their eyes were opened and they recognized him, and he
disappeared from their sight. 32 They asked each other, "Were not our hearts
burning within us while he talked with us on the road and opened the Scriptures
to us?"

33 They got up and returned at once to Jerusalem. There they found the Eleven
and those with them, assembled together 34 and saying, "It is true! The Lord has
risen and has appeared to Simon." 35 Then the two told what had happened on
the way, and how Jesus was recognized by them when he broke the bread.
36 While they were still talking about this, Jesus himself stood among them and
said to them, "Peace be with you." 37 They were startled and frightened, thinking
they saw a ghost. 38 He said to them, "Why are you troubled, and why do doubts
rise in your minds? 39 Look at my hands and my feet. It is I myself! Touch me
and see; a ghost does not have flesh and bones, as you see I have." 40 When he
had said this, he showed them his hands and feet.

41 And while they still did not believe it because of joy and amazement, he asked
them, "Do you have anything here to eat?" 42 They gave him a piece of broiled
fish, 43 and he took it and ate it in their presence. 44 He said to them, "This is what
I told you while I was still with you: Everything must be fulfilled that is written
about me in the Law of Moses, the Prophets and the Psalms." 45 Then he opened
their minds so they could understand the Scriptures. 46 He told them, "This is
what is written: The Christ will suffer and rise from the dead on the third day,

*47and repentance and forgiveness of sins will be preached in his name to all
nations, beginning at Jerusalem. 48You are witnesses of these things.*

Luke 24:1-48(NIV)

Extract from Matthew's gospel:

*8So the women hurried away from the tomb, afraid yet filled with joy, and ran
to tell his disciples. 9Suddenly Jesus met them. "Greetings," he said. They came
to him, clasped his feet and worshiped him. 10Then Jesus said to them, "Do not
be afraid. Go and tell my brothers to go to Galilee; there they will see me."
11While the women were on their way, some of the guards went into the city and
reported to the chief priests everything that had happened.*

*12When the chief priests had met with the elders and devised a plan, they gave
the soldiers a large sum of money, 13telling them, "You are to say, 'His disciples
came during the night and stole him away while we were asleep.' 14If this report
gets to the governor, we will satisfy him and keep you out of trouble." 15So the
soldiers took the money and did as they were instructed. And this story has been
widely circulated among the Jews to this very day.*

Matthew 28: 8-15 (NIV)

Extract from Mark's gospel

*9When Jesus rose early on the first day of the week, he appeared first to Mary
Magdalene, out of whom he had driven seven demons. 10She went and told those
who had been with him and who were mourning and weeping. 11When they
heard that Jesus was alive and that she had seen him, they did not believe it.
12Afterward Jesus appeared in a different form to two of them while they were
walking in the country. 13These returned and reported it to the rest; but they did
not believe them either.*

*14Later Jesus appeared to the Eleven as they were eating; he rebuked them for
their lack of faith and their stubborn refusal to believe those who had seen him
after he had risen. 15He said to them, "Go into all the world and preach the good
news to all creation. 16Whoever believes and is baptized will be saved, but
whoever does not believe will be condemned.*

Mark 16:9-16 (NIV)

Extract from John's gospel

*19On the evening of that first day of the week, when the disciples were together,
with the doors locked for fear of the Jews, Jesus came and stood among them
and said, "Peace be with you!" 20After he said this, he showed them his hands*

and side. The disciples were overjoyed when they saw the Lord. [21]Again Jesus said, "Peace be with you! As the Father has sent me, I am sending you." [22]And with that he breathed on them and said, "Receive the Holy Spirit. [23]If you forgive anyone his sins, they are forgiven; if you do not forgive them, they are not forgiven."

[24]Now Thomas (called Didymus), one of the Twelve, was not with the disciples when Jesus came. [25]So the other disciples told him, "We have seen the Lord!" But he said to them, "Unless I see the nail marks in his hands and put my finger where the nails were, and put my hand into his side, I will not believe it."

[26]A week later his disciples were in the house again, and Thomas was with them. Though the doors were locked, Jesus came and stood among them and said, "Peace be with you!" [27]Then he said to Thomas, "Put your finger here; see my hands. Reach out your hand and put it into my side. Stop doubting and believe."

[28]Thomas said to him, "My Lord and my God!" [29]Then Jesus told him, "Because you have seen me, you have believed; blessed are those who have not seen and yet have believed." [30]Jesus did many other miraculous signs in the presence of his disciples, which are not recorded in this book. [31]But these are written that you may believe that Jesus is the Christ, the Son of God, and that by believing you may have life in his name.

John 20:19-31 (NIV)

The arguments for and against the resurrection:

Perhaps the simplest way to approach the resurrection is first of all to consider the alternative explanations that men have put forward over the years to try to disprove it. We can then examine whether they hold any water in comparison to what the Bible says happened.

So, we shall look in turn at each of the arguments/explanations of those who *don't* believe in the resurrection:

Alternative Explanation 1 – Did Jesus' disciples steal His body from the tomb and invent the whole story of the resurrection?

This false allegation dates back to the very beginning. It is what the Jewish officials spread around as a rumour to try to explain away what had happened. Yet they themselves knew it to be a lie. We can prove it to be false in many different ways:

a) How could the disciples have got past the guards?

Jesus was a very important public figure, famous throughout all Israel. His death was extremely controversial and both the Jewish authorities and the Roman Governor feared that trouble would come from it. Therefore a large group of guards was told to watch his tomb. It was not just a couple of men. There were probably 60-100 men guarding the tomb.

Therefore if the disciples were to steal Jesus' body they would have to get past that entire group. That would clearly be impossible. Moreover, even if they had somehow got there and overpowered the guards, those guards would have seen the disciples. Even if unable to prevent them taking the body, which is hard to imagine, they would at least be able to say *"We saw the disciples coming and they overpowered us and took Jesus' body by force"*.

However that was not said. Instead, a very strange story was put about. The Jewish authorities told the guards to say that the disciples had come and stolen the body *while they were sleeping*. But it was unheard of for even one Roman soldier to fall asleep on duty, let alone 60-100, and all at the same time. That is impossible. But there is another reason why that explanation is absurd. If the guards were all sleeping then how would they know who it was that had come and stolen the body?

Clearly, it did not happen that way and although that rumour was put about, it obviously could not be true. It is the type of lie that a small child tells. Yet the fact that the authorities needed to make up such an obviously false explanation shows the tight corner they were in. But, why would that be so, unless Jesus *had* risen?

b) If the resurrection was invented as a false story then it would mean that all the apostles were liars. But what about their subsequent ministries?

If we are to believe that the disciples stole the body and made up the story of the resurrection, then that makes them deliberate liars. Yet we see that each of the 11 surviving apostles embarked upon life-long ministries of preaching the Gospel about Jesus Christ. They were all proclaiming to the world that He had risen from the dead. All of them suffered persecution for saying this. In fact 10 of them were executed for insisting on it. The only one to survive and die of old age was the apostle John, but even he experienced great persecution and suffering for preaching about Jesus.

Why would any of these men be willing to suffer and die for something that they all knew to be a lie? One could imagine one person telling a lie, and even continuing to tell it, so long as it gained them something, whether financially or otherwise. But why would they all persistently tell a lie which brought them nothing but suffering, difficulty and death? Look at these passages which illustrate how much the apostles suffered for what they believed:

***27**Having brought the apostles, they made them appear before the Sanhedrin to be questioned by the high priest. **28**"We gave you strict orders not to teach in this name," he said. "Yet you have filled Jerusalem with your teaching and are determined to make us guilty of this man's blood." **29**Peter and the other apostles replied: "We must obey God rather than men! **30**The God of our fathers raised Jesus from the dead—whom you had killed by hanging him on a tree. **31**God exalted him to his own right hand as Prince and Savior that he might give repentance and forgiveness of sins to Israel. **32**We are witnesses of these things, and so is the Holy Spirit, whom God has given to those who obey him." **33**When they heard this, they were furious and wanted to put them to death.*

Acts 5:27-33(NIV)

***40**His speech persuaded them. They called the apostles in and had them flogged. Then they ordered them not to speak in the name of Jesus, and let them go. **41**The apostles left the Sanhedrin, rejoicing because they had been counted worthy of suffering disgrace for the Name. **42**Day after day, in the temple courts and from house to house, they never stopped teaching and proclaiming the good news that Jesus is the Christ.*

Acts 5:40-42 (NIV)

Even if we can imagine that the disciples were all capable of dishonestly inventing the resurrection, we have to assume that at least one or two of them would, at some point, have broken down under torture and persecution. Some of them would have said *"Alright, we made it all up – don't execute me"*. Yet, they never did. None of them ever denied the resurrection. All of them continued to proclaim it, even as they were executed, one by one, for doing so.

c) What about their subsequent writings?

One only has to read the letters that they wrote to see that the apostles were men of wisdom, love, truth, sincerity and maturity. If they were somehow willing to arrange a deceitful hoax, and to persist in it, that would mean they were men of bad character. They would have to be dishonest and devious. Yet we see the exact opposite of that shining out from every page of the New Testament as we read the things they wrote over the decades. Whatever you might say about the writers of the New Testament, it is plain that they were godly and honest men. They themselves obviously believed with all their hearts that the resurrection had truly happened.

d) What about the subsequent physical appearances of Jesus to many different people? They would all have to be liars too.

Jesus did not only physically appear to His apostles. He also appeared to many other people as well. For completeness I will go through all of the passages in the New Testament which refer to Jesus physically appearing to people. These incidents took place during a 40 day period following the resurrection whilst He remained physically present on the earth and travelled to various parts of Israel. He was openly seen by people and was touched and spoken to.

There are many instances where He appeared to more than one person at a time. On some occasions He appeared and spoke to large groups. On at least one occasion, in 1 Corinthians 15:5, we are told that He appeared to more than 500 people at the same time. That is highly significant. It means that the idea of it all being a fraud or a hoax is even more impossible.

Even if one can imagine a small group of people colluding together to deceive others, it is impossible to imagine such vast numbers of people all agreeing to carry out a deception in that way. It is equally impossible to imagine them *all* being mistaken, deluded or hallucinating. One person might hallucinate, but not a group, and certainly not 500 people all at the same time and all in the same way.

People who saw Jesus alive:

I will now set out all the physical appearances of Jesus after His resurrection. These are the ones that are recorded in the Bible, though there must have been many more. I will refer to each of the people who saw Him after His resurrection and then set out the Bible verses which record it:

1. Two women outside of Jerusalem, probably Mary Magdalene and another Mary:

9Suddenly Jesus met them. "Greetings," he said. They came to him, clasped his feet and worshiped him. 10Then Jesus said to them, "Do not be afraid. Go and tell my brothers to go to Galilee; there they will see me."

Matthew 28:9-10 (NIV)

2. Mary Magdalene:

15"Woman," he said, "why are you crying? Who is it you are looking for?" Thinking he was the gardener, she said, "Sir, if you have carried him away, tell me where you have put him, and I will get him." 16Jesus said to her, "Mary." She turned toward him and cried out in Aramaic, Rabboni!" which means Teacher).

17 Jesus said, "Do not hold on to me, for I have not yet returned to the father.
Go instead to my brothers and tell them, 'I am returning to my Father and your
Father, to my God and your God.' " 18 Mary Magdalene went to the disciples
with the news: "I have seen the Lord!" And she told them that he had said these
things to her.

John 20:15-18 (NIV)

3. Two travellers on the road to Emmaus

(see the earlier passage from Luke 24 verses 13-22)

4. Peter (Simon) in Jerusalem:

and saying, "It is true! The Lord has risen and has appeared to Simon."

Luke 24:34 (NIV)

5. Ten disciples in the upper room:

19 On the evening of that first day of the week, when the disciples were together,
with the doors locked for fear of the Jews, Jesus came and stood among them
and said, "Peace be with you!" 20 After he said this, he showed them his hands
and side. The disciples were overjoyed when they saw the Lord.

21 Again Jesus said, "Peace be with you! As the Father has sent me, I am
sending you." 22 And with that he breathed on them and said, "Receive the Holy
Spirit. 23 If you forgive anyone his sins, they are forgiven; if you do not forgive
them, they are not forgiven."

24 Now Thomas (called Didymus), one of the Twelve, was not with the disciples
when Jesus came. 25 So the other disciples told him, "We have seen the Lord!"
But he said to them, "Unless I see the nail marks in his hands and put my finger
where the nails were, and put my hand into his side, I will not believe it."

John 20: 19-25 (NIV)

6. Eleven disciples in the upper room:

26 A week later his disciples were in the house again, and Thomas was with them.
Though the doors were locked, Jesus came and stood among them and said,
"Peace be with you!" 27 Then he said to Thomas, "Put your finger here; see my
hands. Reach out your hand and put it into my side. Stop doubting and believe."
28 Thomas said to him, "My Lord and my God!"

29 Then Jesus told him, "Because you have seen me, you have believed; blessed
are those who have not seen and yet have believed." 30 Jesus did many other

***miraculous signs in the presence of his disciples, which are not recorded in this
book. [31]But these are written that you may believe that Jesus is the Christ, the
Son of God, and that by believing you may have life in his name.***

John 20:26-31 (NIV)

7. Seven disciples fishing:

***[1]Afterward Jesus appeared again to his disciples, by the Sea of Tiberias. It
happened this way: Simon Peter, Thomas (called Didymus), Nathanael from
Cana in Galilee, the sons of Zebedee, and two other disciples were together.
[3]"I'm going out to fish," Simon Peter told them, and they said, "We'll go with
you." So they went out and got into the boat, but that night they caught nothing.
[4]Early in the morning, Jesus stood on the shore, but the disciples did not realize
that it was Jesus. [5]He called out to them, "Friends, haven't you any fish?"
"No," they answered.***

***[6]He said, "Throw your net on the right side of the boat and you will find some."
When they did, they were unable to haul the net in because of the large number
of fish. [7]Then the disciple whom Jesus loved said to Peter, "It is the Lord!" As
soon as Simon Peter heard him say, "It is the Lord," he wrapped his outer
garment around him (for he had taken it off) and jumped into the water. [8]The
other disciples followed in the boat, towing the net full of fish, for they were not
far from shore, about a hundred yards. [9]When they landed, they saw a fire of
burning coals there with fish on it, and some bread.***

***[10]Jesus said to them, "Bring some of the fish you have just caught." [11]Simon
Peter climbed aboard and dragged the net ashore. It was full of large fish, 153,
but even with so many the net was not torn. [12]Jesus said to them, "Come and
have breakfast." None of the disciples dared ask him, "Who are you?" They
knew it was the Lord. [13]Jesus came, took the bread and gave it to them, and did
the same with the fish. [14]This was now the third time Jesus appeared to his
disciples after he was raised from the dead.***

John 21: 1-14 (NIV)

8. Eleven disciples on the mountain in Galilee:

***[16]Then the eleven disciples went to Galilee, to the mountain where Jesus had
told them to go. [17]When they saw him, they worshiped him; but some doubted.
[18]Then Jesus came to them and said, "All authority in Heaven and on earth has
been given to me. [19]Therefore go and make disciples of all nations, baptizing
them in the name of the Father and of the Son and of the Holy Spirit, [20]and
teaching them to obey everything I have commanded you. And surely I am with
you always, to the very end of the age."***

Matthew 28:16-20 (NIV)

9. To more than five hundred people, to James and (some years later) to the apostle Paul:

[3]For I delivered to you as of first importance what I also received, that Christ died for our sins according to the Scriptures, [4]and that He was buried, and that He was raised on the third day according to the Scriptures, [5]and that He appeared to Cephas, then to the twelve. [6]After that He appeared to more than five hundred brethren at one time, most of whom remain until now, but some have fallen asleep; [7]then He appeared to James, then to all the apostles; [8]and last of all, as to one untimely born, He appeared to me also.

1 Corinthians 15:3-8 (NASB)

(NB - Note that when apostle Paul refers to Jesus appearing to him, he does not mean the incident on the road to Damascus when Jesus spoke to Paul. Paul means a separate, later occasion when Jesus visibly appeared to him.)

10. Disciples who watched Jesus ascending into Heaven:

[44]He said to them, "This is what I told you while I was still with you: Everything must be fulfilled that is written about me in the Law of Moses, the Prophets and the Psalms." [45]Then he opened their minds so they could understand the Scriptures. [46]He told them, "This is what is written: The Christ will suffer and rise from the dead on the third day, [47]and repentance and forgiveness of sins will be preached in his name to all nations, beginning at Jerusalem. [48]You are witnesses of these things. [49]I am going to send you what my Father has promised; but stay in the city until you have been clothed with power from on high."

Luke 24:44-49 (NIV)

[3]After his suffering, he showed himself to these men and gave many convincing proofs that he was alive. He appeared to them over a period of forty days and spoke about the kingdom of God. [4]On one occasion, while he was eating with them, he gave them this command: "Do not leave Jerusalem, but wait for the gift my Father promised, which you have heard me speak about. [5]For John baptized with water, but in a few days you will be baptized with the Holy Spirit." [6]So when they met together, they asked him, "Lord, are you at this time going to restore the kingdom to Israel?" [7]He said to them: "It is not for you to know the times or dates the Father has set by his own authority. [8]But you will receive power when the Holy Spirit comes on you; and you will be my witnesses in Jerusalem, and in all Judea and Samaria, and to the ends of the earth."

Acts 1:3-8 (NIV)

In addition to all these recorded appearances, there must have been many others which aren't referred to in the Bible. Moreover, remember that Jesus also appeared to Paul and later to John in the book of Revelation. Those appearances were equally real and physical. Both Paul and John literally met Jesus. These meetings took place years after the resurrection, long after Jesus had ascended into Heaven. I will now set out the relevant Bible verses which refer to these:

11. Apostle Paul's first encounter with the risen Jesus, a few years after the resurrection when Jesus spoke to him on the road to Damascus:

1Meanwhile, Saul was still breathing out murderous threats against the Lord's disciples. He went to the high priest 2and asked him for letters to the synagogues in Damascus, so that if he found any there who belonged to the Way, whether men or women, he might take them as prisoners to Jerusalem. 3As he neared Damascus on his journey, suddenly a light from Heaven flashed around him. 4He fell to the ground and heard a voice say to him, "Saul, Saul, why do you persecute me?" 5"Who are you, Lord?" Saul asked. "I am Jesus, whom you are persecuting," he replied. 6"Now get up and go into the city, and you will be told what you must do." 7The men travelling with Saul stood there speechless; they heard the sound but did not see anyone. 8Saul got up from the ground, but when he opened his eyes he could see nothing. So they led him by the hand into Damascus.

Acts 9:1-8 (NIV)

12. Apostle Paul's face to face meeting with Jesus Christ. Paul received the gospel as a direct revelation from Jesus, not through any man:

Am I not free? Am I not an apostle? Have I not seen Jesus our Lord? Are you not my work in the Lord?

1 Corinthians 9:1 (NASB)

11For I would have you know, brethren, that the gospel which was preached by me is not according to man. 12For I neither received it from man, nor was I taught it, but I received it through a revelation of Jesus Christ.

Galatians 1:11-12 (NASB)

13. Apostle Paul seeing and speaking with the Lord Jesus while in a trance in Acts 22:

17"It happened when I returned to Jerusalem and was praying in the temple, that I fell into a trance, 18and I saw Him saying to me, 'Make haste, and get out of Jerusalem quickly, because they will not accept your testimony about Me.' 19"And I said, 'Lord, they themselves understand that in one synagogue after another I used to imprison and beat those who believed in You. 20'And when the blood of Your witness Stephen was being shed, I also was standing by approving, and watching out for the coats of those who were slaying him.' 21"And He said to me, 'Go! For I will send you far away to the Gentiles.'"

Acts 22:17-21 (NASB)

14. Apostle Paul being caught up into Heaven where he was given a direct revelation and was told many things:

***1** Boasting is necessary, though it is not profitable; but I will go on to visions and*
*revelations of the Lord. **2** I know a man in Christ who fourteen years ago--*
whether in the body I do not know, or out of the body I do not know, God knows-
*-such a man was caught up to the third Heaven. **3** And I know how such a man-*
*-whether in the body or apart from the body I do not know, God knows-- **4** was*
caught up into Paradise and heard inexpressible words, which a man is not
*permitted to speak. **5** On behalf of such a man I will boast; but on my own behalf*
*I will not boast, except in regard to my weaknesses. **6** For if I do wish to boast I*
will not be foolish, for I will be speaking the truth; but I refrain from this, so
that no one will credit me with more than he sees in me or hears from me.
***7** Because of the surpassing greatness of the revelations, for this reason, to keep*
me from exalting myself, there was given me a thorn in the flesh, a messenger
*of Satan to torment me--to keep me from exalting myself! **8** Concerning this I*
*implored the Lord three times that it might leave me. **9** And He has said to me,*
"My grace is sufficient for you, for power is perfected in weakness " Most
gladly, therefore, I will rather boast about my weaknesses, so that the power of
Christ may dwell in me.

2 Corinthians 12:1-9 (NASB)

15. Apostle John's meeting with Jesus about 60 years after the resurrection:

***12** I turned around to see the voice that was speaking to me. And when I turned*
*I saw seven golden lampstands, **13** and among the lampstands was someone "like*
a son of man," dressed in a robe reaching down to his feet and with a golden
*sash around his chest. **14** His head and hair were white like wool, as white as*
snow, and his eyes were like blazing fire.

***15** His feet were like bronze glowing in a furnace, and his voice was like the sound*
*of rushing waters. **16** In his right hand he held seven stars, and out of his mouth*
came a sharp double-edged sword. His face was like the sun shining in all its
brilliance.

***17** When I saw him, I fell at his feet as though dead. Then he placed his right*
*hand on me and said: "Do not be afraid. I am the First and the Last. **18** I am the*
Living One; I was dead, and behold I am alive for ever and ever! And I hold the
*keys of death and Hades. **19** "Write, therefore, what you have seen, what is now*
and what will take place later.

Revelation 1:12-19 (NIV)

It is important to read through each of these passages to fully realise how long Jesus stayed on the earth and how many people saw Him, touched Him and spoke with Him after His resurrection. We are not speaking about a small group of people who fleetingly saw Him. He stayed and taught and explained things to them for 40 days before they began their ministries in Israel and throughout the Roman Empire. Plus, as we have seen, the apostles Paul and John met Him, face to face, even years later.

If the resurrection was a fraud, then how could the early Church have grown in the spectacular way that it did in the city of Jerusalem? That was the very place where the resurrection is said to have happened? If it was a fraud then the people of Jerusalem would be very well placed to disprove it.

If nothing else, they would be able to go to the tomb and bring out the dead body of Jesus. Alternatively, virtually everybody in Jerusalem would have had a neighbour or a relative or a friend who was part of this so called hoax. If it was a fraud it would have leaked out somewhere. We have seen from the many Bible references just how numerous the people were who had seen Jesus physically. It ran into hundreds, probably thousands, of people. These were in Jerusalem and elsewhere.

Yet, there is no evidence that any of these people privately confided in their friends or relatives that it was a hoax. Neither did any of them ever say or that they had been mistaken, or that they had imagined it. On the contrary, thousands more people in Jerusalem turned to Jesus Christ and began to follow Him, precisely because of His resurrection.

They were not in the same position you or I are in. We are living many years later and in different parts of the world. Therefore, we are unable to check out the facts for ourselves in the locality. However, they were locals and were able to check all the facts for themselves. Yet, far from disproving or denying the resurrection, they knew for sure that it had happened. The church in Jerusalem became very large in a short space of time and they all continued to believe in the resurrection, despite the persecution that came to them as a result of believing in it.

Alternative explanation 2 – What if the Jewish and/or Roman authorities stole the body?

Again, this makes no sense at all, as one can demonstrate:

a) Why would they do that? They could only lose by doing so.

The main reason that the Jewish authorities wanted Jesus to be crucified was because they feared and envied His growing fame and popularity. Therefore why would they seek to enhance His reputation even further by helping to falsely convince people that He had risen from the dead?

They knew that Jesus had prophesied that He would rise from the dead. That was one of the reasons why a large guard was posted at His tomb. They knew that He said it would happen. Therefore it makes no sense for them to steal His body or to cooperate with anyone else doing so.

b) If either group had stolen the body, i.e. the Romans or the Jewish authorities, then the other group would have exposed it

It would make no sense for either the Jewish authorities or the Roman authorities to assist in building up the reputation of Jesus and His followers. Thus if either had, for some unknown reason, chosen to take the body, then the other group would have tried to prevent them doing so. They would at least have revealed that the other group had done so. They would not cooperate in the stealing of the body, or in concealing it later.

c) Even if they had stolen the body, they would then have displayed it later

If, for whatever reason, the Jewish or Roman authorities had taken the body then they would have revealed it. When they began to see how many people were following Jesus and believing in His resurrection, they would have gone and got the body and displayed it publicly.

They would have said *"Actually He is not risen at all – here is His body, we had it all along"*. We know that they never did that. But, we can be certain that if they had got the body, they would have displayed it. So, we know they didn't have His body and that they could not find it either.

Alternative explanation 3 – "The Swoon Theory"

A few people have half-heartedly put forward the idea that Jesus did not actually die on the cross at all. They suggest that He simply fainted and appeared to be dead. They argue that perhaps He was then put in to the tomb where He later revived and came out again, causing His disciples to mistakenly imagine that He had risen from the dead. However, this theory is plainly impossible, for many reasons:

a) We know He died - the Romans made sure of that

The Romans knew how to execute people. They did not get it wrong. Roman soldiers were experts in killing and they knew death when they saw it. That is why they did not bother to break Jesus' legs, which is what they did if people were too slow in dying. They could clearly see He was already dead.

Plus, Jesus had many additional wounds over and above those that men normally received when crucified. He had a crown of thorns put on His head. He had also been flogged beforehand with a whip, which would have torn open His back and legs. That in itself would cause great loss of blood. Moreover, a spear had been thrust in to His chest.

All that had happened in addition to a complete crucifixion on the cross, whereby His wrists and feet were nailed on to the wood and He then had to struggle in agony to lift Himself up to gain every breath that He took. That is how men died on the cross. They reached the point where they could no longer lift themselves up to breathe.

This was because their arms were outstretched. That places great pressure on the chest and makes it impossible to breathe unless they lift their chest up. Thus Jesus had to keep putting pressure on his nailed wrists and feet to lift Himself. The pain would have been terrible. Therefore, how could anyone survive all of that?

b) Even if He did somehow survive, how could He recover?

The swoon theory would require Jesus, despite His many horrific injuries, to regain consciousness in the tomb and then unwrap his own body. That would not be easy, because He was wrapped with cloth. Then He would have to single-handedly roll away a heavy stone in order to escape.

After that He would have to overpower a large group of Roman soldiers. All of this would have to be done after great loss of blood, the agony of the crucifixion, a deep stab wound in the chest from a spear, and then three days without food, water, or any medical attention. It is plainly impossible.

c) Even if He did somehow "revive" like this, how could He then be strong and healthy enough to convince hundreds or even thousands of people that He was resurrected and that He was the Son of God?

Even if we can somehow believe all of these extraordinary ideas, if He was able to crawl out of the tomb then he would be a physical wreck at best. Yet we know that He was able to walk briskly for several miles on the road to Emmaus. And, whilst doing so, He was alert enough to give a long lecture on the various prophecies in the Bible that were about Himself. How could He do that on feet that had just had long Roman nails driven through the heel bones, let alone all the other wounds?

d) Also, it would make Jesus a liar

The swoon theory requires Jesus Himself to be a liar and a hoaxer rather than His disciples. In effect, it means Him pretending to have risen from the dead and pretending to be the Son of God. Yet, if you read everything that He said in the gospels and look at everything else that He did, does He sound like a liar? Clearly not. Moreover, if this had somehow happened, Jesus would still have had to die later at some point. If so, He would have had to leave His body behind then. But He never did.

Alternative explanation 4 – That the women ran to the wrong tomb

This explanation is too silly to take seriously, but I will deal with it for completeness. The idea is that Mary Magdalene and the other women who went to the tomb of Jesus early on the morning of the resurrection somehow went to the wrong tomb. Then, when finding it empty, they just assumed that He must have risen from the dead!

If this absurd theory had been true then the mistake would have been quickly corrected. The Jewish and/or Roman authorities, on learning about the rumours of a resurrection, would have gone to the correct tomb. Then they would have displayed the body publicly to disprove all the rumours.

They clearly did not and could not do so, because they did not have His body. Moreover, even if the women had somehow been mistaken on day one, we know that from then on they saw Jesus and spoke to Him on many occasions. Therefore, even if they could somehow have been mistaken at the beginning, they would still need from that point on to have been deliberately lying about the many subsequent appearances and meetings with Jesus. The apostles would all have to be lying too.

Alternative explanation number 5 – That it was all an hallucination

We can imagine one person hallucinating about something, but not hundreds of people all at the same time and in the same way. Moreover, if there is an hallucination it would only happen on one occasion, not on many subsequent occasions involving the same people and/or different people.

Also, even where hallucinations do happen it is generally with emotionally disturbed and unbalanced people. Yet we know that the disciples and followers of Jesus were sane, sober and balanced. If nothing else, we know it from the writings that they later produced. Thus, this theory too must be discarded.

Other evidence about Jesus Christ outside of the Bible

Some people argue that perhaps Jesus never existed at all. They are not prepared to believe the Bible and assume that there is no other evidence that Jesus even existed. They wrongly imagine that the only place where Jesus is referred to is in the Bible. However, the existence of Jesus Christ is an historical fact. There is more evidence for His existence than there is for that of Julius Caesar or any other famous person of that era.

It is not only the Bible that tells us about Jesus Christ. He is referred to by the secular historians of the time, not least Josephus, a Jewish historian who worked for the Romans. Josephus was not a Christian and yet he referred to Jesus, as did others. He also referred to the fact that Jesus' disciples were claiming that He had risen from the dead.

Conclusion

We are therefore faced with an inescapable conclusion - that the bodily resurrection of Jesus really did happen. It takes much more faith to believe the various alternative theories than it does to believe in the resurrection. Yet, why should it be considered hard to believe in the resurrection? What is difficult about it?

If God is God and is capable of creating the world and everything in it, then why could He not raise Jesus from the dead? The main reason why people do not want to believe in the resurrection is simply because they do not want to have to believe in and follow Jesus Christ, or do what He says.

If you are troubled about the resurrection or have difficulty believing it, then read Paul Little's book *"Know Why You Believe"*. Also read Frank Morison's book *"Who Moved the Stone?"* Those two books will help you greatly. For me, coming to be convinced of the truth of the resurrection was a turning point in my life. There was a moment where I came to the stark realisation that the resurrection was undeniably true.

At that point I knew that I should hand my whole life over to Jesus Christ and follow Him with all my heart. Yet, even when I came to that point of realising that the resurrection really was true, I still resisted for several more months, because I did not *want* to hand my life over to Him. Thus, believing in the resurrection is necessary, but it is not enough. We must go on from there to realise who and what Jesus is and to repent and believe in Him.

Jesus had repeatedly prophesied beforehand about His own resurrection

The resurrection of Jesus took the disciples by surprise, but it shouldn't have done, because He had already told them many times that it would happen. He spoke about it publicly, such that even the unbelievers and officials knew He had said it:

20And He said to them, "But who do you say that I am?" And Peter answered
and said, "The Christ of God." 21But He warned them and instructed them not
to tell this to anyone, 22saying, "The Son of Man must suffer many things and

be rejected by the elders and chief priests and scribes, and be killed and be raised
up on the third day."

Luke 9:20-22 (NASB)

31 And he began to teach them that the Son of man must suffer many things, and
be rejected by the elders and the chief priests and the scribes, and be killed, and
after three days rise again.

Mark 8:31 (RSV)

31 because he was teaching his disciples. He said to them, "The Son of Man is
going to be betrayed into the hands of men. They will kill him, and after three
days he will rise." 32 But they did not understand what he meant and were afraid
to ask him about it.

Mark 9:31-32 (NIV)

31 Then He took the twelve aside and said to them, "Behold, we are going up to
Jerusalem, and all things which are written through the prophets about the Son
of Man will be accomplished. 32 "For He will be handed over to the Gentiles,
and will be mocked and mistreated and spit upon, 33 and after they have
scourged Him, they will kill Him; and the third day He will rise again." 34 But
the disciples understood none of these things, and the meaning of this statement
was hidden from them, and they did not comprehend the things that were said.

Luke 18:31-34 (NASB)

9 As they were coming down from the mountain, Jesus commanded them, saying,
"Tell the vision to no one until the Son of Man has risen from the dead."

Matthew 17:9 (NASB)

22 When they came together in Galilee, he said to them, "The Son of Man is
going to be betrayed into the hands of men. 23 They will kill him, and on the third
day he will be raised to life." And the disciples were filled with grief.

Matthew 17:22-23 (NIV)

62 The next day, the one after Preparation Day, the chief priests and the
Pharisees went to Pilate. 63 "Sir," they said, "we remember that while he was
still alive that deceiver said, 'After three days I will rise again.' 64 So give the
order for the tomb to be made secure until the third day. Otherwise, his disciples
may come and steal the body and tell the people that he has been raised from
the dead. This last deception will be worse than the first." 65 "Take a guard,"
Pilate answered. "Go, make the tomb as secure as you know how." 66 So they
went and made the tomb secure by putting a seal on the stone and posting the
guard.

Matthew 27:62-66 (NIV)

The difference between "resurrection" and "resuscitation"

Jesus was physically *'resurrected'*. That is a very important word. Nobody else has ever been resurrected in the way that Jesus was. Yet, one day, all of us will be. Many have been raised from the dead in the sense of being *'resuscitated'*. There was Lazarus, the brother of Mary and Martha. Plus there was the 12 year old daughter of Jairus. Also, a large number of people rose from their graves on the day of the crucifixion:

51At that moment the curtain of the temple was torn in two from top to bottom. The earth shook and the rocks split. 52The tombs broke open and the bodies of many holy people who had died were raised to life. 53They came out of the tombs, and after Jesus' resurrection they went into the holy city and appeared to many people. 54When the centurion and those with him who were guarding Jesus saw the earthquake and all that had happened, they were terrified, and exclaimed, "Surely he was the Son of God!"

Matthew 27:51-54 (NIV)

All of these people were merely resuscitated in their ordinary mortal bodies. That means that they physically came back to life, having been dead, but they would all then age and die again later. That was not so with Jesus. His resurrection body is eternal, as ours will be. Jesus did not die again later. He stayed on the earth for 40 days after His resurrection and met with His disciples and others and taught them. Then, when He had finished teaching them, He rose into Heaven in His resurrection body:

The ascension of Jesus

6So when they met together, they asked him, "Lord, are you at this time going to restore the kingdom to Israel?" 7He said to them: "It is not for you to know the times or dates the Father has set by his own authority. 8But you will receive power when the Holy Spirit comes on you; and you will be my witnesses in Jerusalem, and in all Judea and Samaria, and to the ends of the earth." 9After he said this, he was taken up before their very eyes, and a cloud hid him from their sight. 10They were looking intently up into the sky as he was going, when suddenly two men dressed in white stood beside them. 11"Men of Galilee," they said, "why do you stand here looking into the sky? This same Jesus, who has been taken from you into Heaven, will come back in the same way you have seen him go into Heaven."

Acts 1:6-11 (NIV)

This event is called "*the ascension*" because Jesus ascended, or rose, into Heaven. That is where He has been ever since. He is there now, waiting for the time of His return to the earth. That is when He will "*restore the Kingdom to Israel*", as the disciples asked about above. Israel will then be the leading nation on the Earth and Jesus will be their King.

CHAPTER 12

SALVATION IS NOT EARNED BY OUR OWN EFFORT OR MERIT. IT IS A FREE GIFT BY GOD'S GRACE (UNDESERVED FAVOUR) IN RESPONSE TO OUR FAITH

One of the hardest things for people to understand is that the forgiveness of our sins and the granting of salvation, in terms of being justified, are not things that we can earn or deserve through living a good life or through our own merit. The Bible specifically deals with this in the following passages:

And he said to the woman, "Your faith has saved you; go in peace."
Luke 7:50 (ESV)

[8]For it is by grace you have been saved, through faith—and this is not from yourselves, it is the gift of God— [9] not by works, so that no one can boast.
Ephesians 2: 8-9 (NIV)

For no human being will be justified in his sight by works of the law, since through the law comes knowledge of sin.
Romans 3:20 (RSV)

he saved us, not because of righteous things we had done, but because of his mercy. He saved us through the washing of rebirth and renewal by the Holy Spirit,
Titus 3:5 (NIV)

[1]Therefore, since we are justified by faith, we have peace with God through our Lord Jesus Christ. [2]Through him we have obtained access to this grace in which we stand, and we rejoice in our hope of sharing the glory of God.
Romans 5:1-2 (NIV)

It was Jesus, not us, who did what was needed to pay the penalty for our sins. He alone has made possible our justification. It is all achieved by Jesus and not by us. Thus, there is nothing for us to boast about at any stage.

Salvation is by God's grace, through our faith, not by our own good works or merit

This question of how we gain God's forgiveness is perhaps the most widely misunderstood issue in Christianity. If you asked a cross section of people how a person can achieve salvation, most of them would give you a similar answer. It would be along the lines of *'living a good life'*, *'being kind to others'*, *'going to church',* 'etc. They would use different words, but they would mean that salvation, in terms of going to Heaven, is achieved by you *earning* it or *deserving* it through your own good conduct during your life.

Heaven is assumed to be a place that *"good"* people go to. That makes sense to people. It fits in with how they imagine it must operate. By human reasoning, it seems fair that Heaven is for 'good' people and Hell is for 'bad' people. However, I have noticed that no matter who I speak to, their definition of a "good" person always seems to include themselves. All of us are self-righteous in our own way.

Most of us would not recognise ourselves as being self-righteous, but that's what we are by nature. Having spoken about the Gospel one to one with hundreds of people over the years, I have found this to be a common theme. Few people, other than genuine Christians, consider themselves to be bad, or to have done much wrong. It is the norm to view oneself as good, or at least mainly good.

To understand real Christianity correctly, we need to grasp a very surprising fact which goes against all our instincts. It is that to get to Heaven and to have eternal life is something that we can never earn or deserve through our own efforts or goodness. There is nothing you can ever do to be good enough to earn a place in Heaven. What you would have to do, in theory, would be to live your entire life from birth to death without ever doing anything wrong whatsoever.

Even one sinful thought, action or word at any point would ruin everything. It would be like driving all your life without breaking the speed limit but then for one moment, on one day, you go over the speed limit. You would be guilty and liable to a fine regardless of the fact that this was the only time you had ever done it. In God's eyes anyone who sins at all is a sinner. That makes you unacceptable to Him and unworthy to be in His presence. It is all or nothing.

Usually people argue back that if, on balance, they are *"mostly good*" then surely that will be enough. Their assumption is that God must operate some kind of weighing scale system whereby He weighs up your good deeds alongside your bad deeds. Then if the good deeds outweigh the bad deeds that makes you a good person overall, who therefore deserves to go to Heaven. That is what most people think.

I know because literally hundreds of them have told me something like that when I have been sharing the Gospel. Indeed, I have rarely ever heard anything other than that. Though it sounds reasonable, it is completely wrong. It shows a total lack of understanding of how God actually operates. I often say to people that Heaven is a place reserved exclusively for bad people and that no 'good' people are allowed.

They then look puzzled and I explain that nobody can get into Heaven if they *think* that they are a good person. We need to get this straight right now. You are not a good person. Neither am I. Nobody living on your street is a good person. Nobody living in your town is a good person. There is no such thing as a "good" person. Even the best things we do aren't good enough to be acceptable to God. See how Isaiah puts it:

For all of us have become like one who is unclean,
And all our righteous deeds are like a filthy garment;
And all of us wither like a leaf,
And our iniquities, like the wind, take us away.
Isaiah 64:6 (NASB)

To God, the definition of a good person is someone who is like Him. That means someone who is utterly perfect, righteous, holy and sinless at all times. In other words, nobody is good except God alone. The only goodness that is acceptable to God is total, perfect, continuous, 100% goodness. The problem is that none of us have that. Mere relative goodness, where you can show you are 30% better than me, will not do. Look at how Jesus put it:

18A certain ruler asked him, "Good teacher, what must I do to inherit eternal life?" 19"Why do you call me good?" Jesus answered. "No one is good—except God alone.

Luke 18:18-19 (NIV)

Jesus was being provocative with the ruler. He meant that nobody is truly good except God alone. That is the point I am making above. Jesus also meant that He Himself was God. He was testing the ruler as to where he stood on that point. So, what we could say is that there is no way into Heaven for anybody who seeks to rely on their own goodness or virtue as *the means* of getting in. The only way that you can enter Heaven or receive eternal life is as a free gift.

It has to come by God's *"grace"*, through *"faith"*, not by doing it yourself or earning it. Jesus Christ died for the 'ungodly', for 'sinners' and for His 'enemies'. You will not be able to get anywhere until you realise that you belong in all of those categories and accept that you can't save yourself. You deserve nothing other than God's judgment, and punishment. The same is true of everybody else too:

6You see, at just the right time, when we were still powerless, Christ died for the ungodly. 7Very rarely will anyone die for a righteous person, though for a good person someone might possibly dare to die. 8But God demonstrates his own love for us in this: While we were still sinners, Christ died for us. 9Since we have now been justified by his blood, how much more shall we be saved from God's wrath through him! 10For if, while we were God's enemies, we were reconciled to him

through the death of his Son, how much more, having been reconciled, shall we be saved through his life!

Romans 5:6-10 (NIV)

"Grace" means God's *undeserved favour.* In other words, it means *getting* something that you do *not* deserve. It is similar to the concept of *"mercy"*, which means *not* getting what you *do* deserve. A person who imagines that he might be able to build up enough of his own merit or good deeds to earn a place in Heaven, is completely missing the point. You may as well abandon the idea now, because you will never be able to earn or deserve a place in Heaven. That is not the way that God saves people or allows people into Heaven:

For I tell you that unless your righteousness surpasses that of the Pharisees and the teachers of the law, you will certainly not enter the kingdom of Heaven.

Matthew 5:20 (NIV)

Jesus means that even the extremely legalistic religious observance of the Scribes and Pharisees was of no use. That is because it just wasn't good *enough.* These devout Jewish men devoted their whole lives to trying (unsuccessfully) to obey every tiny detail of the Law of Moses plus thousands of their own man-made laws as well. But it was all no use, because that is not the way to get right with God or to be viewed by Him as righteous. You cannot get to Heaven by good deeds or by trying to obey the Law of Moses or any other set of rules:

nevertheless knowing that a man is not justified by the works of the Law but through faith in Christ Jesus, even we have believed in Christ Jesus, so that we may be justified by faith in Christ and not by the works of the Law; since by the works of the Law no flesh will be justified.

Galatians 2:16 (NASB)

he saved us, not because of deeds done by us in righteousness, but in virtue of his own mercy, by the washing of regeneration and renewal in the Holy Spirit,

Titus 3:5 (RSV)

There are millions of people who may seem to us to be Christian because they are 'religious'. They observe all sorts of religious rules and regulations. They go to church, and perhaps even help to lead at church. But, they may not be saved or forgiven. God can see their heart and He knows whether their worship of Him is real. It may be shallow or insincere or just for show.

Or it may be that they only go to church because they were brought up in church and it's become a habit. Sometimes people just like the tradition or the ritual. Only God knows those who are really His. Look how Isaiah describes it:

The Lord says:
"These people come near to me with their mouth
and honour me with their lips,
but their hearts are far from me.
Their worship of me
is made up only of rules taught by men.
Isaiah 29:13 (NIV)

We must therefore examine ourselves and see whether or not we are real and sincere or just following man-made rules and traditions which cannot save us. How then do we achieve righteousness in God's eyes? Look at what Paul says in his letter to the Galatians:

10All who rely on observing the law are under a curse, for it is written: "Cursed
is everyone who does not continue to do everything written in the Book of the
Law." 11Clearly no one is justified before God by the law, because, "The
righteous will live by faith." 12The law is not based on faith; on the contrary,
"The man who does these things will live by them."13Christ redeemed us from
the curse of the law by becoming a curse for us, for it is written: "Cursed is
everyone who is hung on a tree." 14He redeemed us in order that the blessing
given to Abraham might come to the Gentiles through Christ Jesus, so that by
faith we might receive the promise of the Spirit.

Galatians 3:10-14 (NIV)

Apostle Paul means that if you seek to rely on observance of the Law of Moses (or your own version of that, i.e. your own rules for what makes a good person) then you must *always* obey *all* of it. If not, then the very law that you seek to obey in order to earn righteousness will merely demonstrate your guilt by showing you to be a lawbreaker.

The very law that you are trying to keep to prove your own righteousness just becomes a 'curse' to you. It both proves your guilt and increases your guilt. The only way to be saved is to willingly allow all of your sins to be transferred onto Jesus. When He was on the cross (or "tree") He took that curse of the law on Himself so that it would not be on you. Consider these passages:

38"Therefore, my brothers, I want you to know that through Jesus the
forgiveness of sins is proclaimed to you. 39Through him everyone who believes
is justified from everything you could not be justified from by the law of Moses.

Acts 13:38-39 (NIV)

Him who knew no sin he made to be sin on our behalf; that we might become the righteousness of God in him.

2 Corinthians 5:21 (NASB)

See also what Paul says to the Romans:

Therefore no one will be declared righteous in his sight by observing the law; rather, through the law we become conscious of sin.

Romans 3:20 (NIV)

Since they did not know the righteousness that comes from God and sought to establish their own, they did not submit to God's righteousness.

Romans 10:3 (NIV)

Even if you were to attempt to obey all the Law of Moses, you still could not be saved that way, because you could never manage to obey it *all* or to keep it up *all the time*. Nobody ever has, except Jesus. What then was the main purpose of the Law of Moses? Paul says it is **to enable us to see our sin**. In other words, God did not give the Jewish people the Law of Moses so that they could be saved by keeping it.

Contrary to what many assume, that was never its purpose. It was given so that they could see clearly, from their failure to keep it, that they were sinners. It proved that they needed God's forgiveness. It was like a mirror in which they could see themselves for what they were – sinners, just like you and me. A mirror does not improve your appearance. It merely tells you what you look like.

Salvation is based on our faith, not our works

Apostle Paul emphasises that salvation is not obtained through your own good works or deeds, or by keeping the Law of Moses, but only because of God's grace. That means it is solely based on God's undeserved favour, which He freely gives as a gift to those who have faith. **Salvation must be received as a free gift or it cannot be received at all**.

You cannot earn it, no matter what you do, and no matter who you are. Paul knew that it was no use seeking to gain any righteousness for himself by observing and obeying the Law. He wanted only to have the righteousness that comes from having faith in Christ:

7But whatever things were gain to me, those things I have counted as loss for the sake of Christ. 8More than that, I count all things to be loss in view of the surpassing value of knowing Christ Jesus my Lord, for whom I have suffered the loss of all things, and count them but rubbish so that I may gain Christ, 9and may be found in Him, not having a righteousness of my own derived from the Law, but that which is through faith in Christ, the righteousness which comes from God on the basis of faith,

Philippians 3:7-9 (NASB)

The writer of the letter to the Hebrews also emphasises the vital importance of believing or having faith:

And without faith it is impossible to please Him, for he who comes to God must believe that He is and that He is a rewarder of those who seek Him.

Hebrews 11:6 (NASB)

If you were able to earn salvation by your own good works then you would be able to boast about it. You could strut into Heaven telling others that you were there as of right and that you had deserved it and achieved it by yourself, through your own merit.

Few people would speak about their own self-righteousness and merit as openly as I have just put it above. But in our own way, more subtly perhaps, that is exactly what most of us wrongly imagine about ourselves. If we do we are deluded because we have no basis to boast whatsoever:

27 Where, then, is boasting? It is excluded. On what principle? On that of
observing the law? No, but on that of faith. 28 For we maintain that a man is
justified by faith apart from observing the law.

Romans 3:27-28 (NIV)

1 What then shall we say that Abraham, our forefather according to the flesh,
discovered in this matter? 2 If, in fact, Abraham was justified by works, he had
something to boast about—but not before God. 3 What does Scripture say?
"Abraham believed God, and it was credited to him as righteousness." 4 Now to
the one who works, wages are not credited as a gift but as an obligation.
5 However, to the one who does not work but trusts God who justifies the
ungodly, their faith is credited as righteousness. 6 David says the same thing
when he speaks of the blessedness of the one to whom God credits righteousness
apart from works:

7 Blessed are those
whose transgressions are forgiven,
whose sins are covered.
8 Blessed is the one
whose sin the Lord will never count against them.

Romans 4:1-8 (NIV)

To explain the concept of the free gift another way, imagine that Queen Elizabeth II was having a banquet to celebrate her jubilee and she wanted to invite a wide range of people to come to share it with her. She and her staff would select names and send out invitations. Suppose one of those invitations was received by you.

That is not such a strange idea, since the Queen does often invite ordinary people like you and me. Could you say that you "*deserved*" to be at that banquet or that you have a "*right*" to be at it? You could not. The only appropriate way that you can go is to accept the invitation gratefully.

Imagine instead that you were to write back to the Queen to accept her invitation and saying *"You chose the right person when you invited me. I feel sure I deserve to be here. I'm quite a bit better than my neighbours in the way I live"*. Few people would ever write such a foolish letter, but many would *think* it in their hearts when dealing with God.

Or, what would happen if, instead of simply accepting the invitation graciously with a thank you letter you were to write back to the Queen sending her a cheque for £500? Imagine you told her that instead of receiving the invitation as a free gift, you preferred to *"pay"* for it by giving her that cheque because you didn't want to *"feel beholden"* to her. What would her reaction be? It would be viewed as extreme rudeness and presumption for you to imagine that you could reject the free gift and instead buy or earn your place at the Queen's banquet.

But what if you offered her £1000 or £10,000? Would that make it better? Would there be a figure for which you could buy an invitation? Whatever you offered to pay, the insult to the Queen would be the same. Therefore, all your assets combined together and even multiplied by a million would still not be enough to buy your way in.

The Queen has no need of your money or mine. You can never buy her attention in the way that wealthy people sometimes 'buy' time and attention from politicians. She would be disgusted by your offer of money and would reject it, even if you were a billionaire.

Let's now look at this illustration again, but with God instead of the Queen. Also, instead of offering Him money, think in terms of offering your own righteousness or goodness. Neither you nor I come remotely close to having enough of these qualities to deserve to enter Heaven on our own merit.

Thus, quite apart from being an insult to God, it is simply no use you trying to get into Heaven that way. The problem is that you just have not got any righteousness to offer. Neither have I. Only one person has ever lived a perfect life, such that on the basis of His own life He deserves to go to Heaven. That is Jesus Christ Himself.

Nobody else has ever had any righteousness in themselves, not even the apostles who wrote the New Testament. They wrote about themselves as being sinners and unworthy. The apostle Paul even referred to himself as *"the chief of sinners"*.

He knew that because of his enormous knowledge and the abundance of divine revelation that had been given to him, a lot more was expected of him than of us.

Thus failings on his part would be viewed as major sins even if they would be viewed as minor if we did them. If Paul saw himself as a great sinner, then how can you or I imagine ourselves to be worthy? Would you say that you are better than the apostle Paul, or Peter, or John? We could not even say that we are equal to them?

Yet even if somehow you were equal to apostle Paul, it would still not be good enough, because even he knew that he was a sinful man. If so, then so are you. Salvation, forgiveness and eternal life can only be given to those who are willing to receive it all as a free gift. They must know that they have nothing sufficient to offer in return and no possible basis for deserving or earning any of it.

They realise that if they are to get into Heaven they must do so based solely on the righteousness of Jesus Christ, not their own. There is a kind of pride and arrogance involved if we try to earn our way into Heaven. Therefore salvation has to be based on our faith, not on our obedience to any system of law. The same was true for Abraham. He was saved solely by faith:

13It was not through the law that Abraham and his offspring received the promise that he would be heir of the world, but through the righteousness that comes by faith. 14For if those who depend on the law are heirs, faith means nothing and the promise is worthless, 15because the law brings wrath. And where there is no law there is no transgression. 16Therefore, the promise comes by faith, so that it may be by grace and may be guaranteed to all Abraham's offspring—not only to those who are of the law but also to those who have the faith of Abraham. He is the father of us all.

Romans 4:13-16 (NIV)

20Yet he did not waver through unbelief regarding the promise of God, but was strengthened in his faith and gave glory to God, 21being fully persuaded that God had power to do what he had promised. 22This is why "it was credited to him as righteousness." 23The words "it was credited to him" were written not for him alone,

Romans 4:20 - 23 (NIV)

It takes humility to realise that you just aren't good enough and that you need instead to rely on God's grace and mercy. Too many of us would rather starve than receive "charity". That attitude is foolish. We need God's grace and His mercy. We would be fools to refuse them and to try instead to make our own way to Heaven. Yet, that's exactly what many of us attempt to do. When we are saved, (i.e. justified or made righteous) God views us as having all the righteousness that Jesus Christ has.

It is almost as if you were to borrow Jesus Christ's identity papers or bank card and have access to His entire bank account. It is as if Jesus made you a joint signatory with a duplicate cheque book and authorised you to write cheques on His infinite bank account. You would then effectively have as much money as He has and be able to write cheques for any amount, however large, just as He could.

It is the same with sharing His righteousness. We are treated as if we had as much righteousness as Him. Imagine a man who goes to a cash machine. In his left hand he has his own bank card for his overdrawn bank account. In his right hand he has a valid duplicate copy of Jesus' bank card from His infinite bank account.

What would you say if, instead of inserting Jesus' bank card into the machine and having access to the infinite riches in His bank account, he was to reach instead for his own card and use that, leaving Jesus' card unused?

Would he not be a fool to do that? Yet that is exactly what we do if we try to rely on our own pathetic self-righteousness, rather than relying on what Jesus did for us on the cross when He paid for our sins Himself. To make such a foolish choice would be proud and sinful in itself.

It may be that someone would do that because they say they feel *"unworthy"* to use Jesus' righteousness. But, though that sounds superficially humble, it isn't. It is foolish, proud, ungrateful and rebellious. It means arrogantly insisting on standing on our own two feet when the only wise and humble thing to do is to rely on God's help and *"accept His charity*", i.e. His grace and mercy. It also implies that what Jesus did wasn't good enough.

If God views you as having all the righteousness of Jesus Christ, then He can allow you into Heaven without being inconsistent or breaking His own rules. That is because in God's eyes a legal transaction or exchange has taken place. All of your sin is transferred on to Jesus Christ, and all of His infinite righteousness is transferred to, or shared with, you.

The technical term for this is *"imputed righteousness"*. It means that instead of having righteousness of your own, someone else's righteousness is imputed to you. It is credited or transferred to your account, as if it was your own. When I have said to people that I feel an assurance that I am going to go to Heaven, they have often been surprised. Some have said that I am being presumptuous or boastful. Their mindset is that you can only get to Heaven through being a good person. They therefore assume that I must be saying that I believe I am very good. Yet my assurance of salvation and of going to Heaven is not based on me being a good person.

I am not claiming to be a good person. On the contrary, I am claiming to be a bad person. The basis for my assurance of salvation is simply that I know that I have repented and believed in Jesus Christ. I have put my trust in Him and I am relying solely on Him, and on His righteousness, (or in the terms of our earlier analogy, His 'bank card') as the only basis to permit me to enter Heaven.

It is only because Jesus Christ suffered and died in my place on the cross that I can know for sure that my sins, past, present and future, have been paid for and punished. Jesus took all the punishment in my place.

Therefore I am not boasting or being arrogant at all when I say that I am confident I am going to Heaven. My confidence is not in myself, but in Jesus and His trustworthiness. I know what He has done for me and I know that He can be relied on, whereas I cannot be. I have nothing to offer in myself. Neither have you. Even apostle Paul had no righteousness in himself:

Here is a trustworthy saying that deserves full acceptance: Christ Jesus came into the world to save sinners—of whom I am the worst.

1 Timothy 1:15 (NIV)

If apostle Paul could not describe himself as being any better than that, what does it say for us? That is why I said above that Christianity is exclusively for bad people. It is for those who know that they are bad, and who have absolutely no illusions about being good. Ironically, it is only non-Christians who imagine themselves to be good people.

Genuine Christians, who have truly repented, never think that. They know too well how sinful they are to ever imagine that they are good. Real Christians know that their own 'bank account' is overdrawn and worthless. And they are not too proud to rely on Jesus' righteousness or 'bank card' instead. God has not saved us because we are impressive people or better than others. On the contrary, He tells us the opposite. We have absolutely nothing to boast about in ourselves:

27 but God has chosen the foolish things of the world to shame the wise, and God has chosen the weak things of the world to shame the things which are strong,
28 and the base things of the world and the despised God has chosen, the things that are not, so that He may nullify the things that are, 29 so that no man may boast before God. 30 But by His doing you are in Christ Jesus, who became to us wisdom from God, and righteousness and sanctification, and redemption, 31 so that, just as it is written, "let him who boasts, boast in the Lord."

1 Corinthians 1:27-31 (NASB)

There is something very deep in our hearts which makes us want to cling to relying on our own (imagined) goodness and merit and seeking to earn our own way into Heaven. Though it doesn't look, at first sight, like a presumptuous or proud thing to do, it clearly is.

In fact, if you wanted to insult Jesus and dishonour what He did for us, could there be any more effective way of doing so than simply to refuse to accept His help and to choose instead to try to do it for yourself?

For a clearer understanding of the meaning of the word 'salvation' and the different senses in which the word is used in the Bible, see chapter 22. That will help you to see the differences in meaning between *"justification, "sanctification*" and "*glorification"*. Each of these are part of an ongoing process which the Bible calls salvation.

Understanding the definitions of those three words, and how they refer to different stages in the process of salvation, will prevent a lot of confusion. The word we have been focusing on in this chapter is "*justification*". That is the first part of salvation. It is based solely on what Jesus did, not on what we do. "*Sanctification*", which begins after we have been justified, is different.

We do have a part to play in the process of sanctification, but not in our justification. The final stage of salvation, i.e. "*glorification*", is also dependent solely on God. He alone causes it to happen when we are resurrected in our new and perfect resurrection bodies. So, like justification, that is solely God's work, not ours.

CHAPTER 13

AN OVERVIEW OF HOW TO BE SAVED - THE FOUR STEPS WE NEED TO TAKE

[1]Therefore let us leave the elementary teachings about Christ and go on to maturity, not laying again the foundation of repentance from acts that lead to death, and of faith in God, [2]instruction about baptisms, the laying on of hands, the resurrection of the dead, and eternal judgment.

Hebrews 6:1-2 (NIV)

In the verses above, the writer to the Hebrews (probably apostle Paul in my view), sets out the six basic things we need to know. He refers to them as *"the elementary teachings about Christ"*. He may have viewed them as elementary, i.e. basic, but in most churches today these six things are not widely known or taught. The first four of the elementary or basic teachings have to do with what we need to do to become Christians. The fifth and sixth are about what lies ahead, i.e. resurrection and judgment.

We shall look closely at these fifth and sixth points in later books in this series. For now I propose to focus on the first four points or steps. I intend to set out an overview of these in this chapter and then look at them separately, and in closer detail, in the next four chapters.

The four steps we need to take to become a Christian are:

1) repent

2) believe (or have faith)

3) be baptised in water

4) 'receive' the Holy Spirit, also referred to as being 'baptised in', or 'filled with', the Holy Spirit

We need to emphasise all four steps, not just one in particular

I have set out all four of these steps alongside each other, as a combined "*package*" just as the writer of the letter to the Hebrews does. Indeed, I believe that that is what the whole Bible does. All four steps are needed and they all belong together. If you look at particular verses in the Bible, one or another of these steps will be emphasised, depending on the context and on what the letter or book is focusing upon. However, we must not take any one of these steps in isolation and treat that particular one as if it was the only one, or even the most important one. All four steps are important and they all need to be taken. If not, it's possible that we may not actually become a Christian at all. Or, even if we do, we may be missing something very important, which leaves us deficient or stunted. If so, we may not grow properly as a Christian, and will probably have various problems that we could have avoided if we had taken all four steps properly.

There are groups, though rare nowadays, who focus on repentance more than on the other three steps. Repentance is crucial, but it is still wrong to over-emphasise it and downplay the other steps. Repentance by itself is not enough. Likewise, other groups focus excessively or exclusively on believing and elevate that to the central place.

Some even allow believing (or faith) to take the place of some or all of the other steps. That's wrong too. For example, believing without repenting is not enough. In fact, it's hard to see how you can truly say you do believe if you aren't also repenting. If you really believed, you would repent.

Alternatively, a small minority put an excessive and unbalanced emphasis on being baptised in water, as if that alone could save you. That said, there are far more people who do the opposite. They deny, or object to, the need for baptism in water at all. They say it doesn't matter or isn't essential. Some object to water baptism very strongly.

In particular, many believe that baptism is something that we can and should do to babies. But that is not biblical. The Bible never speaks of infant baptism, not even once. Yet, those who believe in it say that if a person was baptised as a baby then the job has been done and they therefore do not need to be baptised again when they are old enough to believe for themselves. Many get very uptight about this and will get angry if the need for baptism as a believer is even mentioned.

Lastly, there is the step of receiving the Holy Spirit, or being *"filled with"*, or "*baptised* in", the Holy Spirit. This fourth step probably causes even more confusion and controversy than baptism in water. Some people get very tense and defensive about the baptism in the Holy Spirit. They are suspicious of those who believe that this step is needed.

Alternatively, others who do realise the importance of this fourth step, can get a superior and divisive attitude. Such people can tend to look down on those who do not understand what it means to be baptised in the Holy Spirit. They can then despise those who have not experienced that, or who are not sure whether they have.

So, my point is that many people only emphasise one or more of these steps and avoid, ignore or downplay the others. However, the Bible emphasises them all.

It is, therefore, not open to us to pick and choose which of these four steps we wish to emphasise. We need to understand and take *all four* steps and *hold them all together in balance.* We have no valid reason, and no authority, to do otherwise. Now let's look briefly at each of the four basic steps and seek to define them:

1) REPENT

This step means to realise and admit that you are sinful, selfish and wrong, that you have ignored, disobeyed and offended God and that you have rebelled against Him and what He stands for. It then means to turn away from those sins, to stop rebelling, and to go in the opposite direction. So, when we repent, it means that we accept that it is we who are wrong, not God or other people.

We therefore accept that it is we who need to change, turn around, and get right with God. You can never get right with God, or enter into a relationship with Him, unless you realise that you aren't right with Him at the moment. Until you grasp that basic point you can't get anywhere or be in the right place to take any of the other three steps.

So, repentance is a vital first step. It makes you capable of understanding and taking the other steps. A person who hasn't repented just isn't ready or able to go any further. Repentance is the vital platform or foundation upon which all the other steps rest. So, it's crucial and must not be missed out or made too little of. That is why the writer to the Hebrews refers to the "*foundation of repentance*".

It would be fair to say that repentance is primarily directed towards God the Father. It is mainly He whom we have offended and to whom our repentance needs to be made. It is His laws that we have broken and rebelled against, and His fatherhood over us that we have rejected. He is the one before whom we stand condemned, and whose wrath we face, unless we are rescued from it. Please note that repentance is discussed in much greater detail in Chapter 14.

2) BELIEVE (OR HAVE FAITH)

Each of the other steps is, likewise, largely directed towards one in particular of the three members of the Trinity. As we have said, repentance is mainly directed towards God the Father. When we believe, however, it is Jesus Christ, (the Son of God and the Second Person of the Trinity) that we are mainly dealing with. Our belief, or faith, must primarily be in (or on) the Lord Jesus. We are to believe in who and what He is, and in what He did on the cross to pay the penalty for our sins.

This is not something merely mental or passive. It means we are to put our faith into action by trusting in Him and accepting His Lordship over us. That means to accept Him as your Saviour and rely solely on Him, and His death on the cross, to pay the penalty for your sin and to remove your guilt. It also means accepting Him as your Lord and King and recognising your duty to follow and obey Him from now on.

Otherwise, if you do not regard Him as Saviour, Lord and King, then how can you meaningfully say that you believe in Him? The Bible says He is all of those things. Taking the second step, believing, also means realising who Jesus Christ really is. That involves understanding His immense status and the exalted position He occupies. He is the most important person in the whole world.

It also means putting your whole trust in Him to save you, not trusting in yourself or in your own merit. This step, believing or having faith, is discussed in much greater detail in Chapter 15. So, having repented towards God the Father, we must then believe in, have faith in, and put all our trust in, the Lord Jesus Christ. That is the second step and, for many people, that is as far as they ever go. But the Bible shows clearly that there is still more to do:

3) BE BAPTISED IN WATER

This third step is frequently viewed as controversial. People have strong views and get very sensitive about this. They generally do so because their own particular denomination has taken a stance about what water baptism (or "Christian baptism") involves, how it should be done, and when, and whether it is even needed at all.

In taking such stances, which are often held very passionately, people rarely get their views from the Bible itself. They tend to get them from their own traditions, or what their own denomination does and says. I would urge you instead to try hard to make sure that you get your views on baptism directly from the Bible, not from what you have heard from others or have been used to.

This is not easy to do. You will have to make yourself do it. Otherwise, your instincts and habits will cause you to follow whatever group you happen to belong to. Therefore, take a good look at what the Bible actually says about baptism in water. Seek to do what the people in the New Testament did, nothing more, nothing less, and nothing else.

Resolve just to believe and do what you see clearly written in the Bible, not what you have seen demonstrated by those around you. Then most of the confusion and controversy will evaporate away. It will then become much clearer what you need to do and how. Simply ask yourself *"What did they do in the New Testament, and how and when did they do it?"*

What you will find in the Bible is that as soon as a person had repented of their sins and put their trust in the Lord Jesus Christ, they were then *immediately baptised in water.* They did not wait until some later time when they had matured or passed an exam or reached any particular stage or age. They went straight ahead and got baptised in water. They saw it as a priority.

As for *what* they did, it was very simple; they went to a place nearby where there was water and submerged themselves in it fully. They went completely under the water and then rose up again. It was not done by sprinkling water on their heads. More importantly, it was not done to them as babies. They made the decision to do it themselves. And it was by full immersion under the water.

So, baptism in water was only for those who were old enough to know what they were doing. They were not necessarily adults; they could be children, but they were not babies. They had all repented and believed for themselves before being baptised in water. There is no trace of any infant baptism anywhere in the Bible.

In fact, there is no example recorded anywhere in the New Testament of any practice other than that which I have described above, i.e. full immersion under the water, of believers, who are old enough to decide for themselves. (See chapter 16 for a fuller analysis of baptism in water and why it matters.) Therefore, we can say that baptism in water is the third step after we have repented and believed, and that it means being fully submerged under water. Baptism in water has a number of effects and meanings, and they all matter:

a) baptism in water symbolises and tells the world about the fact that we have repented towards God.

b) it also represents our choosing to 'die' to our own selfish aims, ambitions and desires. That means to abandon them or give them up. As we go down into the water it symbolises our death. We die to ourselves and to all that is worldly, carnal and selfish. We also turn away from what we have been doing so far, which is living for ourselves, with ourselves at the centre. We then resolve instead to live for, and follow, the Lord Jesus Christ.

When we are baptised in water we are effectively saying that the person we have been all our lives until this moment, is now dead. He is in the grave under the water. We identify ourselves with Jesus Christ in His death. It is as if the person that we have been until now has therefore died and been *"buried"* under the water and is no more.

We are therefore *"cut off"* from our old self. We are no longer under the power of our selfish nature as we have been. That *"old man"* we once were has died. Therefore he can no longer rule over us unless we choose to let him. However, there is even more to it, and in a more positive sense. We are also cut off from the negative and sinful baggage of our past life.

There is much that we leave behind in the water, or *"grave"*, as we rise up. All of this is symbolic, of course. But, it is much more than just symbolic. Things really happen when we are baptised in water. We really are cut off from, and set free from, many evil and harmful things. These things would otherwise continue to plague us and hinder our growth as disciples if we were not baptised in water.

That is one reason why it is so sad that so many people are taught that they do not need to be baptised in water. Or they are told that it need not be done in the way it was in the first century, as shown in the pages of the New Testament. People who are told that they don't need baptism in water are missing out on something very important that God wants us all to have and to benefit from.

Moreover, being baptised is also an issue of obedience, whatever view we take about the benefits it provides. In other words, *we are commanded to be baptised.* The Bible also clearly tells us *how* to do it. It is not open to us to say that baptism in water isn't necessary. Neither can we substitute another way of doing it instead of the biblical way, which is always, without exception, by full immersion in water.

Christian baptism is primarily directed towards Jesus Christ, the Second Person of the Trinity. We are to be baptised in His name, or *into* his name. That is why Christian baptism in water differs from the water baptism that John the Baptist practised.

John's baptism was purely a baptism of *repentance*. Christian baptism in water means much more. It means we are identifying with Jesus in His death and resurrection and that we have unmistakably linked ourselves to Him publicly. Then everybody can see we are believing in Him and trusting only in Him.

That is why the demons hate and fear Christian baptism in water. They will always seek to discourage or obstruct you from taking this crucial step. The Devil knows how significant baptism is. He is behind a great deal of the confusion, defensiveness and hostility which are so common wherever baptism in water is discussed. Baptism in water is discussed in much greater detail in Chapter 16.

4) "RECEIVE" THE HOLY SPIRIT, (ALSO KNOWN AS BEING "BAPTISED IN" OR "FILLED WITH" THE HOLY SPIRIT)

This is the fourth step. Obviously, this step primarily involves the Holy Spirit, the Third Person of the Trinity. However, it also involves Jesus Christ, because it is He, Jesus Christ, who *"baptises"* us in the Holy Spirit. Jesus Christ is the one who *causes* us to *"receive",* or *"be baptised in"*, or *"filled with"* the Holy Spirit. So, one of Jesus Christ's many roles is to be the one who baptises people in the Holy Spirit. Men do not do it. Jesus does it.

Like baptism in water, the subject of receiving the Holy Spirit or being baptised in the Holy Spirit, is a highly controversial and widely misunderstood area. People take up all sorts of aggressive, emotional and unthought-out positions. They tend to feel sure that their own denomination's view on this subject is obviously the right one. They also assume that their own experience, or lack of experience, represents what is normal, proper and correct.

Few people ever question their own stance or seriously consider any other view. However, whatever our own personal experience may, or may not be, that is not, and never can be, the basis for our theology. Our own experience must not be what we rely upon in arriving at an understanding of what it means to 'receive' the Holy Spirit.

Our beliefs and practices need to come solely from the Bible, not from what others say, or from what our own denomination teaches, or from what our own individual experiences have been. If we rely on any of those things we could arrive at an infinite number of different conclusions, all of which could be wrong.

So, we must look solely at what the Bible says and at what the disciples did in the first century. This is set out in the New Testament, in particular in the book of Acts and some of the letters. Let those be our guide and the only basis for our understanding. This complex subject of receiving the Holy Spirit will be more fully explained in chapter 17.

However, for the moment, the key point to make is that the practice in the New Testament period was that when a person had repented, believed, and been baptised in water, they then took the fourth and final step. That was to receive the Holy Spirit. My suggestion to you is that you and I are no different from the people in the first century. So, it follows that we need to do exactly the same as them.

We therefore need to receive the Holy Spirit, i.e. be baptised in, or filled with, the Holy Spirit. We should not neglect to take this step. This is not some personal idea of my own. Neither do I believe that I am over-emphasising or exaggerating what the Bible says about the importance of receiving the Holy Spirit. The Bible presents this fourth step as being crucially important.

Moreover, it applied to everybody. This was not seen as something solely for the apostles, or only for certain special people. Neither is there anything in the Bible to suggest that the baptism in the Holy Spirit was only for people of that era, i.e those who lived in the first century. There is no reason, why we should suppose that. The Bible does not say it. That idea is a purely man-made one, with no biblical basis.

If receiving the Holy Spirit was only for the people of the first century, or only for people of certain types or roles, such as apostles, then why not likewise limit repentance, or believing, or baptism in water solely to such people? It would be equally logical, or illogical.I will seek in chapter 17 to elaborate upon all of this. I will try to explain more fully what it means to receive the Holy Spirit, why it matters and how it ought to be done.

For now I would aim only to bring this important point to your attention and to emphasise its importance. It is the fourth step that every believer needs to take if he is to get fully in line with the biblical way of becoming a Christian and to receive everything that God intends for us, without missing anything out.

Some general points about being saved

I now want to make a few further points about how a person comes to be "*saved*" or "*born again*" or "*converted*". I will also make some general points about salvation, and especially about the vital need for sincerity, i.e. genuineness. If we try to become a Christian insincerely, without really meaning it, and especially if our repentance isn't real, then nothing will happen.

We will remain unsaved, no matter what words we may have said. It would all be meaningless ritual and would have no effect. Christianity is not about formulas or forms or words with some magical powers in themselves. Far from it. These steps are to be taken only by those who *really mean it* and are *genuine*.

Salvation is available to everybody. Nobody is excluded or disqualified.

Having made that very serious point, I also need to say, on the other hand, that forgiveness and salvation are freely available to everybody. Jesus Christ died on the cross to pay the penalty for our sins, not His own, because He had no sin. Therefore salvation is available to anyone who wants it, if they will meet God's simple conditions. Jesus died once and it was on behalf of us all. No one is excluded from the offer of salvation. Let's look at some passages which emphasise that fact:

3This is good, and pleases God our Saviour, 4who wants all men to be saved and to come to a knowledge of the truth.

1 Timothy 2:3-4 (NIV)

21'And it shall be that everyone who calls on the name of the Lord will be saved.'
Acts 2:21 (NASB)

"For Christ also died for sins once for all, the righteous for the unrighteous, that He might bring us to God, being put to death in the flesh but made alive in the spirit."

1 Peter 3:18 (NIV)

"For God so loved the world that he gave his one and only Son, that whoever believes in him shall not perish but have eternal life.

John 3:16 (NIV)

But not everybody will actually be saved

So, we know that Jesus' death on the cross was capable of paying the price for the sin of every person, even though there are billions of us. There are no limitations on Jesus Christ. He has an infinite capacity to take all our punishment upon Himself. However, some people have taken this to mean that therefore everyone will actually be saved, regardless of what they do or believe.

Sadly, there is no basis for that assumption in the Bible. Although Jesus is capable of bearing the sin of everyone who comes to Him, not everyone will actually *choose* to benefit from what He did on the cross. It is reserved for those who meet His very simple (but not easy) conditions. The first two essential foundations, which many people fail to put in place, are to repent and believe:

9That if you confess with your mouth, "Jesus is Lord," and believe in your heart
that God raised him from the dead, you will be saved. 10For it is with your heart
that you believe and are justified, and it is with your mouth that you confess and
are saved. 11As the Scripture says, "Anyone who trusts in him will never be put
to shame." 12For there is no difference between Jew and Gentile—the same
Lord is Lord of all and richly blesses all who call on him, 13for, "Everyone who
calls on the name of the Lord will be saved."

Romans 10:9-13 (NIV)

We do not need to be clever or impressive to believe in Jesus. The simplest and most lowly person can manage it easily. Yet, the high and the mighty, the rich and the powerful, the proud and the self-sufficient, find it very difficult. It is especially hard for those who consider themselves to be intellectual. They are often put off by the very simplicity of the Gospel.

The idea that by believing in Jesus we can receive forgiveness and salvation seems too easy. Many of us therefore assume there must be more to it and that we have to achieve something or reach some high standard. The answer is no - we don't!

God deliberately chose to make belief or faith the key to salvation, rather than ability or achievement. That way salvation would be possible for, and available to, everybody. The poor and simple, the uneducated and downtrodden, can easily grasp and respond to this.

Those of us whose lives are more privileged therefore need to humble ourselves and get in line with what God requires by putting our trust in Jesus alone to save us. It is a life or death matter. Listen to what Jesus Himself said:

I told you that you would die in your sins; if you do not believe that I am the one I claim to be, you will indeed die in your sins."

John 8:24 (NIV)

The above verse seems a harsh one. Yet, take note that it was said by Jesus personally. If we do not believe in Him and put our trust in Him then we will die in our sins! That means that when we die we will still be carrying the full burden and guilt of our sins. If so, we will need to pay the eternal penalty for them ourselves at the Day of Judgment. Yet, if we do believe in Him, then our sins are forgiven and the burden of guilt is removed from us. If so, then we have so much to look forward to for all eternity:

9However, as it is written: "No eye has seen, no ear has heard, no mind has conceived what God has prepared for those who love him"

1 Corinthians 2:9 (NIV)

So, that is a picture of how much God loves us. However the experience of knowing God's love is available only to those who believe in Jesus Christ. We will not all be saved. We will not all go to Heaven. The majority of people will not be saved God has laid down very clear conditions for us receiving His forgiveness and salvation.

The benefit of what Jesus did on the cross is available to all of us, but only provided we meet His conditions. Thus we can rule out any suggestion of "*universalism*". That is the false idea that everyone will be saved. In fact the Bible tells us that only a minority of people will be saved. And it would seem to be a small minority:

13Enter through the narrow gate. For wide is the gate and broad is the road that leads to destruction, and many enter through it. 14But small is the gate and narrow the road that leads to life, and only a few find it.

Matthew 7:13-14 (NIV)

Many people are going to fail or refuse to become real Christians. Given the terrible consequences that that will produce for them, we now need to look very closely at what God's conditions are and how we can make sure we meet them properly.

God's conditions in more detail - repent, believe, be baptised in water and receive the Holy Spirit

When we take these steps and genuinely mean it, then we are born again and we receive eternal life. The Holy Spirit Himself comes to live within us, such that He can then be our guide, helper and comforter. He will assist us and empower us from then on to live the Christian life as a disciple of the Lord Jesus Christ.

The Holy Spirit comes to live in us because there is no way that we can successfully carry on the Christian life in our own strength or virtue. That is because we do not have enough strength and we do not have any real virtue in ourselves.

But are you genuine and sincere or are you shallow and phoney?

Only we can tell whether we ourselves are genuine and sincere. Nobody else knows the true motives of our hearts. But, if we are sincere, then it is possible for us to have assurance of our own salvation. That means that you can know that Jesus has paid the penalty for your sins, that God has forgiven you, that the Holy Spirit has come to live in you and that you have eternal life. This is clearly expressed in this passage:

11 And this is the testimony: God has given us eternal life, and this life is in his
Son. 12 Whoever has the Son has life; whoever does not have the Son of God
does not have life. 13 I write these things to you who believe in the name of the
Son of God so that you may know that you have eternal life.

1 John 5:11-13 (NIV)

That is a strong statement and there are others like it in the Bible. However, I cannot tell you whether your repentance and belief/faith are genuine. You must decide that. But be careful, because there are many people who complacently assume they have eternal life but have, in fact, only made a false or shallow repentance.

Perhaps there was no real repentance at all. Or they may have just casually announced that they believe in Jesus Christ, but without any clear understanding or heartfelt conviction about it. Many such lukewarm, casual people are in our churches today. They struggle with the Christian life and often fizzle out and fall away, because they have never been born again to begin with.

Often the problem is that Church leaders reassure such people too easily. They hastily tell people that they are saved and can be sure of it when, in fact, they aren't yet saved. That's why I am very wary of ever telling anybody else that they are a genuine believer. I have done that in the past, only to see such people fall away badly later on and give up on their faith completely. There are many people in churches today who are only nominally Christian.

They may be church members or churchgoers but it could just be for social reasons, e.g. to make friends, or because they have an interest in the culture, music, liturgy, or trappings of church life. I have found that such people can be the hardest to talk to about the real Gospel.

They assume that because they go to church they are obviously already Christians and don't need to do or believe anything extra or different. They can be highly offended by the suggestion that what they have may not be enough.

I therefore wish to emphasise as much as possible the need for earnestness and sincerity in taking each of these steps. God knows what the real attitude of your heart is. You can't deceive Him. He knows whether you mean what you are saying. If you merely *say* these things and don't *mean* them, then it will count for nothing. In fact it would only be an insult to God.

If however you sincerely mean what you say and take the steps with a genuine desire to become a real Christian, then you will be saved. You can have complete assurance of that fact, not because I say so, but because the Bible says so. (See chapter 21 for more detail on assurance of salvation.)

Above all, ensure that you are sincere and serious and that you really mean what you say. God is eager to be found by those who are genuinely seeking Him:

13 'You will seek Me and find Me when you search for Me with all your heart.
Jeremiah 29:13 (NASB)

CHAPTER 14

STEP ONE IN DETAIL - REPENT

"...God...commands all people everywhere to repent.
Acts 17:30 (NIV)

20 Then he began to upbraid the cities where most of his mighty works had been
done, because they did not repent. 21 "Woe to you, Chora'zin! woe to you, Beth-
sa'ida! for if the mighty works done in you had been done in Tyre and Sidon,
they would have repented long ago in sackcloth and ashes. 22 But I tell you, it
shall be more tolerable on the day of judgment for Tyre and Sidon than for you.
23 And you, Caper'na-um, will you be exalted to Heaven? You shall be brought
down to Hades. For if the mighty works done in you had been done in Sodom,
it would have remained until this day. 24 But I tell you that it shall be more
tolerable on the day of judgment for the land of Sodom than for you."

Matthew 11:20-24 (RSV)

12 "Even now," declares the LORD,
"return to me with all your heart,
with fasting and weeping and mourning."
13 Rend your heart
and not your garments.
Return to the LORD your God,
for he is gracious and compassionate,
slow to anger and abounding in love,
and he relents from sending calamity.
Joel 2:12-13 (NIV)

There were some present at that very time who told him of the Galileans whose
blood Pilate had mingled with their sacrifices. 2 And he answered them, "Do
you think that these Galileans were worse sinners than all the other Galileans,
because they suffered thus? 3 I tell you, No; but unless you repent you will all
likewise perish. 4 Or those eighteen upon whom the tower in Silo'am fell and
killed them, do you think that they were worse offenders than all the others who
dwelt in Jerusalem? 5 I tell you, No; but unless you repent you will all likewise
perish."

Luke 13:1-5 (RSV)

46He told them, "This is what is written: The Christ will suffer and rise from the
dead on the third day, 47and repentance and forgiveness of sins will be preached
in his name to all nations, beginning at Jerusalem.

Luke 24:46-47 (NIV)

[10]Godly sorrow brings repentance that leads to salvation and leaves no regret, but worldly sorrow brings death.

2 Corinthians 7:10 (NIV)

When a person makes a bad start in the Christian life, or if they fail to become a Christian at all, the most common reason, amongst those I have dealt with, is lack of genuine repentance. Repentance about your sin is the foundation upon which the whole of your Christian life has to be built. It must come first and it must be solid, or else a person may fail to be genuinely born again.

Alternatively, even if they are somehow saved and they do become a Christian, inadequate repentance will mean that they will experience ongoing weakness and problems. They will fail to grow properly as a Christian because their foundation is inadequate. It would be like trying to build a three storey building on top soil without a foundation. Even if it could be built, it would not last.

The word *'repent'* literally means to change your mind. But, it must always involve a change in your actions as well. So, if a car is travelling along the A1 trunk road in a northbound direction then the driver can *"repent of driving north"* by coming off the road, turning round and driving back along the A1 southbound.

You cannot repent simply in your mind. That would be like deciding to go south, but instead carrying on driving north. That would be meaningless. Repentance must involve changed *conduct.* Otherwise whatever you were thinking in your mind can't have been sincere.

You must turn away from any idols that you may have set up, whatever they may be. You must also give up any behaviour which is an abomination to God, or indeed anything which grieves Him or is contrary to His commands:

"Therefore say to the house of Israel, Thus says the Lord God: Repent and turn away from your idols; and turn away your faces from all your abominations.

Ezekiel 14:6 (RSV)

Repentance has a number of ingredients and all need to be present for repentance to be genuine. It must involve recognising that you truly are a sinner, and that you are wrong. You must see yourself as being at fault. For many people, this is a real stumbling block. They simply do not see themselves as blameworthy or sinful. They don't *want* to see it and *won't admit it,* even to themselves.

[12]There is a kind who is pure in his own eyes,
Yet is not washed from his filthiness.

Proverbs 30:12 (NASB)

Some of us even take the view that it is God who is wrong and that our own conduct, views and attitudes are correct. If we think that way we are profoundly mistaken and need to change:

29 "But the house of Israel says, 'The way of the Lord is not right.' Are My ways not right, O house of Israel? Is it not your ways that are not right? 30 "Therefore I will judge you, O house of Israel, each according to his conduct," declares the Lord GOD. "Repent and turn away from all your transgressions, so that iniquity may not become a stumbling block to you.

Ezekiel 18:29-30 (NASB)

Some other people can just about manage to see themselves as sinful, but only to a slight degree. They will make all sorts of excuses to justify themselves and minimise their own guilt. They may even reluctantly acknowledge that they are a sinner. However, in their own private thoughts, they see themselves as not very sinful compared to other people. If so, that person will struggle to become a Christian. It reveals that they have no true understanding of what their own sin is or how appalling it is in God's eyes.

It isn't how we compare to other people that matters, but how we compare to Jesus. If we measure ourselves alongside Him, we will get the point and realise why God says we are sinful. But if we only compare ourselves to other people we can miss the point completely and imagine ourselves to be doing very well.

There are no such things as *"small sins"* or *"unimportant sins"*. All sin is terrible and is seen by God as a deadly poison which He cannot tolerate. For example, look at God's view of sin in the book of Proverbs. Note the strength of God's feelings on the subject:

The LORD detests all the proud of heart.
Be sure of this: They will not go unpunished
Proverbs 16:5(NIV)

We need to face this issue and work out whether we are really sinners or not. If you cannot grasp this you will not be able to get started in the Christian life. Or, if you do start then you will go forward in a crippled condition, unable to develop properly.

You have got to abandon all ideas of self-righteousness. You are not righteous. Neither is anybody else. You, like everybody else, are a deeply sinful person. We all have a heart that is rotten and corrupt. You and I are completely unworthy to be in God's presence. Look how the Bible describes us:

The heart is deceitful above all things
and beyond cure

Who can understand it?
Jeremiah 17:9 (NIV)

[2] ***But your iniquities have separated.***
you from your God;
your sins have hidden his face from you,
so that he will not hear.
Isaiah 59:2 (NIV)

It is therefore futile for you to compare yourself favourably with others and to feel reassured by that. Being better than others is not enough, even if you are ten times better than them. We are all like passengers on the Titanic without a place in the life boats. We are all going down, even if you are better than the rest of us. In that context it is irrelevant for any of us to argue that we are better than other people. Maybe you are better. Who knows? However, the chances are that you are not.

But if we are all on the Titanic as it is sinking, it would not matter anyway. Our situations are all identical. We all face God's judgment and are all unacceptable to Him, whatever levels of merit or virtue we each have in ourselves. Perhaps it would help to convince you if you look at what the prophet Isaiah says about his own righteousness:

All of us have become like one who is unclean,
and all our righteous acts are like filthy rags;
we all shrivel up like a leaf,
and like the wind our sins sweep us away.
Isaiah 64:6 (NIV)

Then remember what apostle Paul says about himself:

Here is a trustworthy saying that deserves full acceptance: Christ Jesus came into the world to save sinners—of whom I am the worst.
1 Timothy 1:15 (NIV)

However, Paul's statement that he was such a bad sinner was not because he never did anything good. It was because he realised that no matter how many good things he did, it could never make him righteous in God's eyes. Look what he said about his own *good* deeds, not his bad deeds:

[4]***though I myself have reasons for such confidence. If anyone else thinks he***
has reasons to put confidence in the flesh, I have more: [5]***circumcised on the***
eighth day, of the people of Israel, of the tribe of Benjamin, a Hebrew of
Hebrews; in regard to the law, a Pharisee; [6]***as for zeal, persecuting the church;***
as for legalistic righteousness, faultless. [7]***But whatever was to my profit I now***
consider loss for the sake of Christ. [8]***What is more, I consider everything a loss***

compared to the surpassing greatness of knowing Christ Jesus my Lord, for whose sake I have lost all things. I consider them rubbish, that I may gain Christ.

Philippians 3:4-8 (NIV)

Apostle Paul is describing what his own righteousness (not his bad behaviour) looks like in God's eyes. Even his best qualities and behaviour are described as being *"loss"*, meaning of no value. In the King James translation Paul's meaning is expressed more clearly. It translates it as Paul saying that his own good works are *'dung'*. In fact, the Greek word he uses is even stronger and actually means *human excrement.*

Paul used very strong language to get the message across. The NIV tones it down, presumably to avoid giving offence. This is apostle Paul talking about our best works, i.e. our best deeds, best behaviour and best thoughts. Even they, let alone our usual or worst standards, are insufficient. They are just excrement in comparison to God's holiness.

That means that even at our best, on one of our best days, when we think we are acting at our best standard, we are still inadequate and unimpressive. In short, we have no righteousness at all in ourselves. Think further about how God considers your sin.

If it was true that God looks upon your sin or mine as being trivial, then why was Jesus Christ prepared to go to the cross and die to be punished for it? Your sin was sufficiently serious in the eyes of God the Father, the Son of God and the Holy Spirit, for them all to consider it necessary for Jesus, to go to the cross and die because of it. Therefore, how can it possibly be insignificant?

Jesus did not only die for people who do extraordinary sins on a large scale, like Adolf Hitler. He also died for the likes of you and me. We may not be famous or spectacular in our sinfulness. But we are equally unacceptable and lost from God's perspective. You, and I and Adolf Hitler are all going down together on the same Titanic, unless and until we repent.

Therefore, we must begin by taking a frank and realistic look at ourselves as we truly are. Decide now to abandon all delusions about yourself being righteous or being better than some other people.

Consider the blunt way that Jesus spoke to people who were self-righteous. He had no time at all for self-righteousness. Note also which group of people is most prone to self-righteousness, i.e. thinking more highly of themselves than they should. It is mainly those who are actively involved in *organised religion.* Thus it was the Scribes, Sadducees, Pharisees and Rabbis that Jesus usually criticised most sharply, not the ordinary people. Consider this story that Jesus told:

9 To some who were confident of their own righteousness and looked down on
everyone else, Jesus told this parable: 10 "Two men went up to the temple to
pray, one a Pharisee and the other a tax collector. 11 The Pharisee stood by
himself and prayed: 'God, I thank you that I am not like other people—robbers,
evildoers, adulterers—or even like this tax collector. 12 I fast twice a week and
give a tenth of all I get.' 13 "But the tax collector stood at a distance. He would
not even look up to Heaven, but beat his breast and said, 'God, have mercy on
me, a sinner.' 14 "I tell you that this man, rather than the other, went home
justified before God. For all those who exalt themselves will be humbled, and
those who humble themselves will be exalted."

Luke 18:9-14 (NIV)

The Pharisees belonged to the more conservative wing of Judaism, which believed most fully in the Old Testament. Their views were the closest to the truth. This man therefore had a good knowledge of the Bible. His beliefs and doctrines were more accurate than most people's. However, he also had an inflated view of his own righteousness. So, when he went into the temple to pray he demonstrated that he had no idea how sinful he was.

He mistakenly imagined himself to be better than the other man, merely because of what he knew and because of the prestige of the group he belonged to. The tax collector's job involved dishonesty, corruption and collaboration with the Roman occupying forces. All of that made him despicable in the eyes of people around him. He therefore had no illusions about himself being good or superior. He clearly saw himself as a sinner. He knew that he had no righteousness to offer and could only rely on God's mercy.

Jesus therefore said of him that he went home "justified" and forgiven, whereas the Pharisee did not. Therefore, take on board the point of the story. Jesus told it so that you and I should copy the tax collector's attitude, not the Pharisee's. We are to regard this tax collector as our model when it comes to repentance. (though not when it comes to his previous life, prior to his repentance).

Even today, it is still true that it is 'religious' people who find it hardest to repent and be saved. I find it hard to talk about sin to people in churches. They tend to resent it and feel that it is not relevant to them because they go to church. But they are very mistaken. There is great sinfulness in all our hearts, even if we have been going to church all our lives, and even if we are church leaders:

"Both prophet and priest are godless;
even in my temple I find their wickedness,"
declares the LORD.

Jeremiah 23:11 (NIV)

The Lord says:
"These people come near to me with their mouth
and honour me with their lips,
but their hearts are far from me.
Their worship of me
is made up only of rules taught by men.
Isaiah 29:13 (NIV)

Respectability is not the same as righteousness

Criminals, prostitutes, drug addicts and people who have obviously failed or fallen in a very noticeable way often find it much easier to repent. They have fewer illusions about themselves. If you are, on the face of it, a more "respectable" person, then beware. You may be in real danger of not being able to see your own sinfulness.

You may mistake your own respectability for righteousness. They are not the same thing. No matter how respectable you seem to be, even if you are a doctor or a vicar or a Prime Minister, there is absolutely no righteousness in you at all. You will never find salvation until you realise that:

8 If we claim to be without sin, we deceive ourselves and the truth is not in us.
9 If we confess our sins, he is faithful and just and will forgive us our sins and
purify us from all unrighteousness. 10 If we claim we have not sinned, we make
him out to be a liar and his word has no place in our lives.
1 John 1:8-10 (NIV)

40 Let us examine our ways and test them,
and let us return to the LORD.
Lamentations 3:40 (NIV)

We have to get the message that we are sinful and that our own sin, not just other people's sin, is serious. Then our repentance must involve a genuine sorrow for that sin and a real apology to God for it. We cannot simply acknowledge it casually as if we had bumped into someone's trolley in a supermarket where we instinctively say a quick and cheerful "*Sorry*".

Our sorrow and repentance towards God needs to be deep, heartfelt and real. It should be like that of a man who, through his own negligence or drunken driving, has killed a couple's only child on the road and the Court tells him to go and apologise personally to the parents of that child. Picture that scene, and imagine how you would feel if it was you making that apology, in the parents' living room, surrounded by framed photographs of their dead child. Think about how you would speak to those parents and how you would phrase your apology.

What would be the tone in which you would ask for their forgiveness? Can you even contemplate doing it glibly or light-heartedly? Imagine saying something like this: "*Yes, it's a shame I killed your son, but these things happen. I do generally tend to drive more safely than other people most of the time.*" It would be totally inappropriate. The apology would need to be deep and genuine or it would be only an insult.

That depth of remorse and grief is what we ought to express towards God for what we have done to Him and to our fellow men, whom He created. Even more relevantly, it is partly your sin and mine which caused God's own Son to have to be crucified. That is an awesome responsibility bearing down on your shoulders.

You, like me, are partly to blame for Jesus needing to die. Therefore the illustration I used above about the parents of the child you had killed is, to some extent, an appropriate analogy for how we need to speak to God the Father about our sin. It brought about the death of His only begotten Son.

So, when you repent towards God the Father for your sins, remember what your sin did to His Son. Try to hold that in your mind, and reflect on it. It will help you to guard against glibness. Look at the tone and depth of King David's repentance which he wrote about in Psalm 51:

1 Have mercy on me, O God,
according to your unfailing love;
according to your great compassion
blot out my transgressions.
2 Wash away all my iniquity
and cleanse me from my sin
3 For I know my transgressions,
and my sin is always before me.
4 Against you, you only, have I sinned
and done what is evil in your sight;
so you are right in your verdict
and justified when you judge.
5 Surely I was sinful at birth,
sinful from the time my mother conceived me.
6 Yet you desired faithfulness even in the womb;
you taught me wisdom in that secret place.
7 Cleanse me with hyssop, and I will be clean;
wash me, and I will be whiter than snow.
8 Let me hear joy and gladness;
let the bones you have crushed rejoice.
9 Hide your face from my sins
and blot out all my iniquity.
10 Create in me a pure heart, O God,

and renew a steadfast spirit within me.
Psalm 51:1-10 (NIV)

Look also at the prophet Isaiah's attitude towards his own sinfulness:

"Woe to me!" I cried. "I am ruined! For I am a man of unclean lips, and I live among a people of unclean lips, and my eyes have seen the King, the LORD Almighty."

Isaiah 6:5 (NIV)

Consider also the attitude of the group to whom apostle Peter preached for the first time in Acts Chapter 2. Peter tells them straight-forwardly who Jesus really is and how wrongly they had acted in crucifying Him. Here are some excerpts from his speech. Note how direct he is and also the effect it has on them in bringing them to a place of godly sorrow and conviction:

22"Men of Israel, listen to this: Jesus of Nazareth was a man accredited by God
to you by miracles, wonders and signs, which God did among you through him,
as you yourselves know. 23This man was handed over to you by God's set purpose
and foreknowledge; and you, with the help of wicked men, put him to death by
nailing him to the cross. 24But God raised him from the dead, freeing him from
the agony of death, because it was impossible for death to keep its hold on him.
Acts 2:22-24 (NIV)

Peter then went on to say:

36"Therefore let all Israel be assured of this: God has made this Jesus, whom
you crucified, both Lord and Christ." 37When the people heard this, they were
cut to the heart and said to Peter and the other apostles, "Brothers, what shall
we do?" 38Peter replied, "Repent and be baptized, every one of you, in the name
of Jesus Christ for the forgiveness of your sins. And you will receive the gift of
the Holy Spirit.

39The promise is for you and your children and for all who are far off—for all
whom the Lord our God will call." 40With many other words he warned them;
and he pleaded with them, "Save yourselves from this corrupt generation."
Acts 2:36-40 (NIV)

Peter's straight talking touched their hearts and convicted them in their consciences so that 3000 people were moved to repent and believe in Jesus on that day. They were cut to the heart by the gravity of their own sin, and by the directness of Peter's preaching. But contrast that attitude with what Jeremiah says is the heart attitude of most human beings, i.e. shameless, brazen, indifference to God, with no repentance for sin:

Are they ashamed of their loathsome conduct?
No, they have no shame at all;
they do not even know how to blush.
So they will fall among the fallen;
they will be brought down when I punish them,"
says the LORD.

Jeremiah 6:15 (NIV)

Repentance involves turning around and changing

However, repentance is even more than just acknowledging our sin, feeling sorry about it and genuinely apologising to God. It also involves a definite decision to *turn away* from our sin. That does not mean that we must never sin again, or that if we do ever sin again then we have not genuinely repented. Nobody can manage not to sin ever again. The fact is that we will carry on sinning until the day we die, even if we do genuinely repent.

What is meant is that at the point of your repentance you must genuinely resolve to yourself that you will reject sin and *aim* to turn away from it and to change your life, with God's help. Salvation is by God's grace, through faith. However, real faith and real repentance always produce a changed life and changed conduct.

Thus, although we are not saved by our good deeds or our changed life, a truly saved person will always go on to change in their attitudes and conduct and to *"bear fruit"*. That is why Jesus said *"you will know them by their fruit"*.

Look at how James explains it. This passage from James is relevant to both repentance and faith. For each of these, God will judge the genuineness of it by what we *do*, not what we *say:*

14What good is it, my brothers, if a man claims to have faith but has no deeds?
Can such faith save him? 15Suppose a brother or sister is without clothes and
daily food. 16If one of you says to him, "Go, I wish you well; keep warm and well
fed," but does nothing about his physical needs, what good is it? 17In the same
way, faith by itself, if it is not accompanied by action, is dead. 18But someone
will say, "You have faith; I have deeds. "Show me your faith without deeds, and
I will show you my faith by what I do. 19You believe that there is one God.
Good! Even the demons believe that—and shudder.

James 2:14-19 (NIV)

See also what the prophet Ezekiel says. In this passage he is speaking directly on God's behalf, i.e. voicing God's words to Israel and to us. Again, it is made clear that the genuineness of our repentance will be shown by what we *do* and by what we *get rid of* in our lives:

[30]"Therefore, O house of Israel, I will judge you, each one according to his ways, declares the Sovereign LORD. Repent! Turn away from all your offenses; then sin will not be your downfall. [31]Rid yourselves of all the offenses you have committed, and get a new heart and a new spirit. Why will you die, O house of Israel? [32] For I take no pleasure in the death of anyone, declares the Sovereign LORD. Repent and live!

Ezekiel 18:30-32 (NIV)

God wants us to actually change, in our actions and in our heart attitudes. The responsibility is on us to *want* that change and to *seek to do what God wants* instead of what we have been doing previously. Repentance needs to be seen much more as something we do, rather than just something we say. Look how John the Baptist expressed this point. He didn't mince his words:

[7]But when he saw many of the Pharisees and Sadducees coming to where he was baptizing, he said to them: "You brood of vipers! Who warned you to flee from the coming wrath? [8]Produce fruit in keeping with repentance. [9]And do not think you can say to yourselves, 'We have Abraham as our father.' I tell you that out of these stones God can raise up children for Abraham. [10]The axe is already at the root of the trees, and every tree that does not produce good fruit will be cut down and thrown into the fire.

Matthew 3:7-10 (NIV)

The key phrase John the Baptist used was that we must *"bear fruit"*. That is that our repentance must be evidenced by a changed life. That means that we stop doing certain things and start doing other things, in such a way and to such an extent, that it is apparent to others. If your repentance does not produce any "fruit" then John the Baptist would not view it as valid or real.

Don't be "stiff necked" or stubborn about repenting

Do not be stiff-necked, as your fathers were; submit to the LORD. Come to the sanctuary, which he has consecrated forever. Serve the LORD your God, so that his fierce anger will turn away from you.

2 Chronicles 30:8 (NIV)

Often, the greatest obstacle to repentance, besides pride, is stubbornness. We can know that we are wrong or sinful but refuse to admit it. Don't be like that. When you know something is true about yourself, just admit it to God and repent of it. If you are willing to humble yourself and repent in that way, then God will hear you and respond to you graciously:

Because your heart was responsive and you humbled yourself before God when you heard what he spoke against this place and its people, and because you

humbled yourself before me and tore your robes and wept in my presence, I have heard you, declares the LORD

2 Chronicles 34:27 (NIV)

Also, we need to remember that God wants us to change not only in our actions, but in our *reactions*. We are answerable for how we react to the things others do and to sins committed against us. Even then, in fact especially then, God expects us to show restraint and self-control, not to lash out in rage and fury.

So, look at that in yourself and ask whether, when under pressure, or facing provocation, you lash out and lose your self-control. Or, do you keep your temper and respond in a reasonable way? It is a good litmus test. Remember that just because someone has wronged you, it doesn't mean you are free to react in any way you wish. You are always responsible, both for your actions and your reactions.

Practical repentance – steps we need to take

In practical terms, you need to take real steps to do things differently and to change your lifestyle and behaviour. If you have any occult or pornographic books or DVDs then burn them. If you are engaged in sexual activity with your boyfriend or girlfriend or with someone else's husband or wife, then stop immediately. If you are living together with someone you are not married to, then move out. Or ask them to do so, if it is your house.

NB. It would not be a good idea to solve such a problem by getting married to a non-Christian person you may be living with. It may mean you would no longer be having sex outside of marriage, but it would also mean that you would be marrying a non-Christian. We must never do that as it is a recipe for disaster:

Do not be yoked together with unbelievers. For what do righteousness and wickedness have in common? Or what fellowship can light have with darkness?

2 Corinthians 6:14 (NIV)

If however you are already married to an unbeliever then apostle Paul says you should stay with them (if they will let you do so) and seek to share the good news of Jesus with them too:

12To the rest I say this (I, not the Lord): If any brother has a wife who is not a believer and she is willing to live with him, he must not divorce her. 13And if a woman has a husband who is not a believer and he is willing to live with her, she must not divorce him. 14For the unbelieving husband has been sanctified through his wife, and the unbelieving wife has been sanctified through her believing husband. Otherwise your children would be unclean, but as it is, they

are holy. [15]But if the unbeliever leaves, let him do so. A believing man or woman is not bound in such circumstances; God has called us to live in peace.

1 Corinthians 7:12-15 (NIV)

If you have been stealing then you need to stop and you need to return the goods that you have stolen, or pay for them. If you have been gossiping then you need to stop and put right the damage that you have caused, by telling the truth where you have falsely slandered people. Your sins might also mean that you need to go and personally apologise to some of the people that you have wronged. This will not always be possible, because you will have wronged so many people in your life that you cannot possibly find them all and speak to each one. It would take years, so don't apologise to everyone.

Plus, don't go and apologise to someone if it will only cause them pain and stir up more trouble or bitterness, for example, if something is firmly in the past. Ask God to help you to know which people need you to go to them and which don't. For a very practical example of what real repentance is like, look at Zaccheus, the corrupt tax collector, whom Jesus met in Jericho. Jesus had dinner at his home and he was so convicted that he made a dramatic and decisive repentance and he showed it by his actions:

[1]He entered Jericho and was passing through. [2]And there was a man called by the name of Zaccheus; he was a chief tax collector and he was rich. [3]Zaccheus was trying to see who Jesus was, and was unable because of the crowd, for he was small in stature. [4]So he ran on ahead and climbed up into a sycamore tree in order to see Him, for He was about to pass through that way. [5]When Jesus came to the place, He looked up and said to him, "Zaccheus, hurry and come down, for today I must stay at your house." [6]And he hurried and came down and received Him gladly. [7]When they saw it, they all began to grumble, saying, "He has gone to be the guest of a man who is a sinner." [8]Zaccheus stopped and said to the Lord, "Behold, Lord, half of my possessions I will give to the poor, and if I have defrauded anyone of anything, I will give back four times as much." [9]And Jesus said to him, "Today salvation has come to this house, because he, too, is a son of Abraham.

Luke 19:1-9 (NASB)

Make sure you really mean it

God knows those people who are genuine and those who don't really mean it. He knows whether you have made a real commitment to turn away from sin and to change your life, or whether you are just play-acting. If you were to tell me that you had repented, I would not know whether you really had or not. I have no way of knowing for certain what is really going on in your heart. However God knows, and what's more, *you* know.

You do not know if anyone else is genuine, but you do know whether you are genuine when you say something. If you are not genuine, then do not pretend to repent. Only repent if you mean it sincerely. Otherwise, you are just mocking God and it will not be effective anyway, because God knows where you really stand:

And you, my son Solomon, acknowledge the God of your father, and serve him with wholehearted devotion and with a willing mind, for the LORD searches every heart and understands every motive behind the thoughts. If you seek him, he will be found by you; but if you forsake him, he will reject you forever.

1 Chronicles 28:9 (NIV)

Repentance does not need to be done in any fancy way or with any particular formula or elaborate form of words. It does however need to be sincere. Only you can know whether you are. If you aren't, then ask God to help you to see the full gravity and dreadfulness of your sin. Remember, God is watching and testing you to see whether you are genuine and whether your repentance is truly heartfelt:

This is the one I esteem: he who is humble and contrite in spirit, and trembles at my word.

Isaiah 66:2(b) (NIV)

Repentance is probably the most neglected aspect of Christianity, at least in the Western world and in modern times. In previous centuries when the Gospel was preached, sin, judgment and repentance were spoken about openly. Now, they are glossed over, if they are even mentioned at all. It is partly because they are so under-emphasised, even ignored, in the modern church that I have tried to emphasise them so strongly within this book. In part I am trying to redress the balance. Moreover, it is clearly right that repentance should be emphasised as being the foundation for salvation. That is precisely what God does in the New Testament.

If you look at Matthew's gospel you will see that before Jesus began His public ministry, John the Baptist was sent on ahead of Him to prepare the way for the coming of the Messiah. John the Baptist was, in effect, the last of the Old Testament prophets. In a sense, he was the greatest of them all. He was sent by God to go ahead of Jesus Christ and to prepare the people for Him. John the Baptist therefore had a ministry that went on for some years.

He spent most of His time out in the open countryside, not in grand buildings. Probably more than a million people went to hear him in the open air and to baptise themselves in rivers like the Jordan to demonstrate their repentance. It is no coincidence that the very first recorded word spoken in public by John the Baptist was "*repent*":

[1]*In those days John the Baptist came, preaching in the Desert of Judea* [2]*and saying, "Repent, for the kingdom of Heaven is near."*

Matthew 3:1-2 (NIV)

The ministry of John the Baptist was focused very strongly upon repentance. He spoke of it with great urgency and emphasis. He did so because God wanted to ensure that genuine repentance was in place as a solid foundation before Jesus Christ began His public teaching ministry and before people were invited to follow and believe in Him.

In other words, Jesus' ministry was built upon the foundation that John the Baptist built, namely repentance. If that does not persuade you to emphasise repentance and to put it first, take a look at the first words that Jesus Himself spoke publicly in His own ministry. He too began it with the word *"repent"*, just like John the Baptist did:

Repent, for the kingdom of Heaven is at hand.

Matthew 4:17 (NIV)

Jesus deliberately chose to ensure that the word 'repent' was also the first word He uttered publicly in His own ministry. As with John the Baptist, it was no accident. It reaffirmed the emphasis that God places on repentance as the foundation for everything else in the Christian life. Three and a half years later it is, again, no coincidence that the apostle Peter used similar words when addressing the crowds at the very beginning of his ministry:

[38]***Peter replied, "Repent and be baptized, every one of you, in the name of Jesus Christ for the forgiveness of your sins. And you will receive the gift of the Holy Spirit.***

Acts 2:38 (NIV)

Repent, then, and turn to God, so that your sins may be wiped out, that times of refreshing may come from the Lord,

Acts 3:19(NIV)

The downplaying of repentance in the modern church

It is equally no coincidence that the Devil has done everything he can to downgrade the importance of repentance. He has managed to persuade multitudes of people that it does not really matter much and that preachers should not speak about it or emphasise it.

He has had great success in the Western church in getting many Christian leaders to leave repentance out of their message altogether, or to just mention it briefly, with awkwardness and apology, rather than boldness and urgency. One of the reasons why Christian ministers and teachers choose not to talk about repentance is that they are too embarrassed and afraid to do so.

There is the fear that it will offend people and be controversial. They also fear that it will make them appear old-fashioned or even judgmental. Yet, our duty is to explain the Gospel in the same way that Jesus explained it. We have no right, or need, to change it or to 'improve' it.

Note what apostle Paul says when he is on trial before King Agrippa. He is explaining what he has been preaching. See how Paul also emphasises repentance right at the outset, as the very first thing he tackles when he preaches the Gospel, just like John the Baptist, Jesus and Peter:

[19]"So then, King Agrippa, I was not disobedient to the vision from Heaven.
[20]First to those in Damascus, then to those in Jerusalem and in all Judea, and to the Gentiles also, I preached that they should repent and turn to God and prove their repentance by their deeds.

Acts 26:19-20 (NIV)

See also how apostle Paul says that we should prove our repentance by our deeds, i.e. by what we do. Mere speech is no proof that a person has really repented. There needs to be some visible and practical change. Something needs to stop, or begin, or change. When God sees that He can be satisfied that our repentance is real. In the past, when seeking to explain the Gospel to somebody I used to mainly look for signs that the person truly believed. Now I focus much more on whether there is any evidence of repentance. That is much easier to assess than the person's beliefs.

Therefore when you repent take real steps to change your lifestyle. Get rid of any known sin that you are involved in. You can only begin with what you know about. From that point on God will bring to your mind, one by one, other sins that you need to repent of and actively put right. But He will not deal with it all in one go. He will take it in stages, provided that you genuinely begin by repenting to the best of your ability at that point.

Repentance is not a negative thing. It is actually very positive and joyful. The experience of Ebenezer Scrooge in *'A Christmas Carol'* is an inspired illustration of what repentance really is and the joy it brings. If you are unsaved, repentance leads to forgiveness and the starting of a relationship with God. If you are already a genuine believer then repentance restores closeness with God, which sin always spoils:

If we confess our sins, he is faithful and just and will forgive us our sins and purify us from all unrighteousness.

1 John 1:9 (NIV)

[12]*As far as the east is from the west,*
So far has He removed our transgressions from us.
Psalm 103:12 (NASB)

Don't be phoney or hypocritical

God sees and knows everything. There is no point even attempting to trick Him or hide things from Him, hoping He won't notice. He can never be deceived and He never misses anything:

Nevertheless, God's solid foundation stands firm, sealed with this inscription: "The Lord knows those who are his," and, "Everyone who confesses the name of the Lord must turn away from wickedness."

2 Timothy 2:19 (NIV)

There are many people in churches who say that they are Christians but are living a double life. They attend church, participate in worship, listen to teaching, and even teach others. Yet, they brazenly lie, cheat, gossip, engage in adultery, or fornication (sex outside of marriage) are lazy, selfish, manipulative, crafty and self-indulgent. This kind of hypocrisy is not something exceptional or rare. It is commonplace.

Insincere, unrepentant Christians make poor employees or work colleagues. They also bring dishonour to the name of Jesus through their attitudes and life style. I am not just speaking about the day to day ways in which we all fail by losing our tempers or being unreasonable, although that is bad enough. I mean blatant and shameless sin, which they have no intention of doing anything about, and for which they feel no sorrow or conviction.

If you challenge their behaviour they will not feel ashamed. On the contrary, they will be defensive and angry and will brazenly deny it, even if they are clearly guilty. They will often even turn on you resentfully and attack you verbally. This happened to me once when I challenged the leader of the church that I was in at that time. I was chairman of the trustees of the church, responsible for paying salaries etc. I went to see the leader privately, one to one, in the biblical way, as out in Matthew 18:15.

I raised with him my growing concerns about his worldly lifestyle and lack of personal honesty. He was developing a reputation in the town as a liar and as a carnal, boastful person. I tried to appeal to him in private, as gently and politely as I could, to look at his life and to repent. But he would not. He was defiant and just attacked me verbally and then tried to undermine me to others.

I then went to speak to the other leaders in the church about this, in the way we are told to do by Jesus in Matthew 18:16. To my surprise, they weren't interested either. They just criticised me for asking questions. Some of them were very hostile, especially one particular man in the leadership team. I couldn't understand it. After some months of this conflict we left that church.

Several months later it all made a lot more sense when it emerged that the leader had left his wife for another woman, and was giving up church ministry. What's more, it emerged that the hostile man in the senior leadership team had also been involved for some time in an adulterous affair. No wonder he had been so touchy about the questions I was putting to the leader. He had been doing even worse things himself, although I did not know it at the time.

Do not be brass faced about your sin

In many churches today, even among some leaders, there is blatant ongoing sin, for which those individuals feel no shame. They are not repenting and don't intend to repent. They are *"brass-faced*". That brazenness comes from repeatedly refusing to repent. It begins in smaller ways, as people sin here and there and "get away with it". At least they imagine they are getting away with it, because other people don't find out and don't stop them. So they carry on and commit bigger sins, and more frequently.

Whilst this is going on, God will speak to the person through their conscience. The still, small voice of the Holy Spirit will speak quietly to the person to urge them to stop, repent, seek forgiveness and start afresh. However, the person ignores God's voice and suppresses it. They do not want to stop. So they repeatedly ignore their conscience and God's voice.

Unbelievers do this too, but my point is that even believers, and those who call themselves believers, do it. It is a very dangerous thing to do, because although God will try, again and again, to speak to you and to urge you to repent, if you persist in ignoring His voice and go on sinning, then there will come a day when you will no longer be able to hear Him. Moreover, God will eventually step back from you and let you pursue the foolish and sinful path that you have chosen for yourself:

12 "So I gave them over to the stubbornness of their heart,
To walk in their own devices.

Psalm 81:12 (NASB)

When that happens, it is as if your conscience is switched off, as you might turn off a radio. The conscience (or radio) is still there, but not functioning. It cannot pick up the 'transmission'. The biblical phrase for this is that the conscience is "*seared*". That means it becomes leathery and hard, like skin that has been branded with a hot iron. Look how Zechariah describes it:

[8] And the word of the LORD came again to Zechariah: [9] "This is what the LORD
Almighty says: 'Administer true justice; show mercy and compassion to one
another. [10] Do not oppress the widow or the fatherless, the alien or the poor. In
your hearts do not think evil of each other.' [11] "But they refused to pay attention;
stubbornly they turned their backs and stopped up their ears. [12] They made their
hearts as hard as flint and would not listen to the law or to the words that the
LORD Almighty had sent by his Spirit through the earlier prophets. So the
LORD Almighty was very angry. [13] " 'When I called, they did not listen; so when
they called, I would not listen,' says the LORD Almighty.

Zechariah 7:8-13 (NIV)

This is a terrible condition to be in. If you are not listening to God, it is as if you are flying with your radio and your instruments switched off. In the end, it will result in disaster. God will eventually bring along someone or something to expose your sin and to bring judgment. Sometimes, when disaster comes and a marriage or a ministry is destroyed, the person finally repents and sees what a fool they have been.

However, usually they do not, even at that stage. Instead, they abandon even the pretence of being a Christian. Such people find it very hard later on to soften their hearts towards God and seek His forgiveness. They could, if they wanted to, but they usually *don't choose to*. The hardness of their hearts, which has built up over years of disobedience, becomes almost incurable.

Do not harden your heart towards God

We all need to beware of hardening our hearts. I have seen it in some surprising people. The best protection against it is to deliberately soften your heart towards God and to want to hear His voice. Make it your aim to listen to and obey your conscience whenever God speaks to you through it. If you do these things His voice will grow clearer and louder, like a radio being tuned in better and turned up in volume. Note what apostle Paul says:

[4] Or do you show contempt for the riches of his kindness, forbearance and
patience, not realizing that God's kindness is intended to lead you to
repentance? [5] But because of your stubbornness and your unrepentant heart,
you are storing up wrath against yourself for the day of God's wrath, when his
righteous judgment will be revealed.

Romans 2:4-5 (NIV)

To illustrate this further, look at the famous "parable of the sower" which Jesus told. That's what people often call it, but it would be more accurate to call it the *parable of the soils*, because that is what it is really about:

[1]That same day Jesus went out of the house and sat by the lake. [2]Such large crowds gathered around him that he got into a boat and sat in it, while all the people stood on the shore. [3]Then he told them many things in parables, saying: "A farmer went out to sow his seed. [4]As he was scattering the seed, some fell along the path, and the birds came and ate it up. [5]Some fell on rocky places, where it did not have much soil. It sprang up quickly, because the soil was shallow. [6]But when the sun came up, the plants were scorched, and they withered because they had no root. [7]Other seed fell among thorns, which grew up and choked the plants. [8]Still other seed fell on good soil, where it produced a crop—a hundred, sixty or thirty times what was sown. [9]He who has ears, let him hear." [10]The disciples came to him and asked, "Why do you speak to the people in parables?"

[11]He replied, "The knowledge of the secrets of the kingdom of Heaven has been given to you, but not to them. [12]Whoever has will be given more, and he will have an abundance. Whoever does not have, even what he has will be taken from him. [13]This is why I speak to them in parables: "Though seeing, they do not see; though hearing, they do not hear or understand. [14]In them is fulfilled the prophecy of Isaiah: " 'You will be ever hearing but never understanding; you will be ever seeing but never perceiving. [15]For this people's heart has become calloused; they hardly hear with their ears, and they have closed their eyes. Otherwise they might see with their eyes, hear with their ears, understand with their hearts and turn, and I would heal them.' [16]But blessed are your eyes because they see, and your ears because they hear. [17]For I tell you the truth, many prophets and righteous men longed to see what you see but did not see it, and to hear what you hear but did not hear it.

[18]"Listen then to what the parable of the sower means: [19]When anyone hears the message about the kingdom and does not understand it, the evil one comes and snatches away what was sown in his heart. This is the seed sown along the path. [20]The one who received the seed that fell on rocky places is the man who hears the word and at once receives it with joy. [21]But since he has no root, he lasts only a short time. When trouble or persecution comes because of the word, he quickly falls away. [22]The one who received the seed that fell among the thorns is the man who hears the word, but the worries of this life and the deceitfulness of wealth choke it, making it unfruitful. [23]But the one who received the seed that fell on good soil is the man who hears the word and understands it. He produces a crop, yielding a hundred, sixty or thirty times what was sown."

Matthew 13:1-23 (NIV)

In the parable that Jesus tells, the seed represents God's Word and the four types of soil represent four types of person, or rather four types of heart attitude:

a) The Path

This is the person whose heart is so hard, unrepentant and indifferent that the 'seed' of God's Word cannot even germinate. The birds just eat it up and it has no effect. It is as if God's Word just bounces off them.

b) Rocky Ground

This person is not quite so hard or indifferent as the person whose heart is like the path. Here, although his heart is stony, there is at least a thin layer of poor quality soil. So the seed of God's Word can germinate, but it cannot grow for long, because it cannot take root.

c) Soil full of weeds

This weed-infested soil represents people who receive God's Word and it begins to germinate and grow but, in the end, it is choked and crowded out by other competing interests or priorities. It could be career, worldly friends, a carnal relationship with an unbeliever, or the pursuit of money. It could be anything that captivates and distracts you.

d) The Good Soil

This is the humble person whose heart is soft, teachable and willing to repent. The seed therefore germinates, and grows to a full sized plant. This person continues as a Christian and bears much fruit in their life over the years.

How this applies to you – make the effort to dig, weed and soften the "*soil*" of your heart

The kind of heart you have developed over your life so far is largely what determines how you respond to God's Word when you hear it. The point of the parable is that it is up to you to work on the 'soil' of your own heart. You must dig it and soften it to enable yourself to hear and act on God's Word. The responsibility for the state of your heart is yours. It is not something beyond your control.

It may be a painful and difficult process to change it, but it is worth the effort. If your heart is hard and stony like the path or the rocky ground, then God's Word, (represented by the seed) will not be able to get through to you in order to germinate. The "birds" will eat it before it has any effect on you.

Or, even if God's Word begins to affect you, like the seed that germinates in the rocky ground, it cannot put down any deep roots in your life, because your heart is too hard. If you are like that, make a decision now to persistently and deliberately do everything you can to soften your heart. You can do that by taking every opportunity to repent, to obey God, to humble yourself, and to read the Bible.

As you do those things diligently it is just like a gardener digging into rocky ground, taking out stones and putting in compost and manure to improve it. As he does that, and keeps on doing it, the soil will steadily improve. Our hearts are just the same. It is our responsibility to soften it and not to let it remain hard or stony.

If the problem is weeds, the gardener tackles it by removing and preventing them so that his soil has fewer of them. You can do the same by removing things from your life which you know are likely to distract you or lead you into temptation or bad company. You might not have realised that God expects you to do anything about those things, but He does. If not, why bother to tell the parable?

There is no point telling us that the condition of the 'soil' of our hearts is what determines whether we succeed in the Christian life unless there is some way of improving that soil. There clearly is. Look at King David's experience of how it felt to openly confess his sins to God and get them dealt with, as compared to how it felt if he kept them hidden:

3When I kept silent about my sin, my body wasted away
Through my groaning all day long.
4For day and night Your hand was heavy upon me;
My vitality was drained away as with the fever heat of summer. Selah.
5Iacknowledged my sin to You,
And my iniquity I did not hide;
I said, "I will confess my transgressions to the LORD";
And You forgave the guilt of my sin. Selah.
6Therefore, let everyone who is godly pray to You in a time when You may be found;
Surely in a flood of great waters they will not reach him.
Psalm 32:3-6 (NASB)

Note though that we need to repent while we have the chance to do so because the time for doing so can be lost. Therefore, the right time to repent is always now. Never postpone it:

6Seek the LORD while He may be found;
Call upon Him while He is near.
7Let the wicked forsake his way

And the unrighteous man his thoughts;
And let him return to the LORD,
And He will have compassion on him,
And to our God,
For He will abundantly pardon.
Isaiah 55:6-7 (NASB)

[20]***"Harvest is past, summer is ended,***
And we are not saved."
Jeremiah 8:20 (NASB)

Therefore focus on softening your heart. Work at learning how to humble yourself and to confess your sins. Keep away from temptations, bad influences or immoral TV programs. Reset your computer to block all pornographic content, as you would set it for a child. That will keep temptation away and prevent any problems developing. Continually repent and confess your sins, instead of hiding or denying them.

Regularly ask God to help you to soften your heart and to make you more conscious of your sin and of His coming judgment. Ask Him to increase your ability to hear Him speaking to you through your conscience. He will quickly respond to prayers like that and your heart will change. As it does, you will succeed more and more in becoming a genuine Christian and a real disciple.

[13] ***He who conceals his sins does not prosper,***
but whoever confesses and renounces them finds mercy.
[14] ***Blessed is the man who always fears the LORD,***
but he who hardens his heart falls into trouble.
Proverbs 28:13-14 (NIV)

Also, learn to ask God to give you a correct and realistic view of yourself, your smallness and how brief your life is. Realising that will help you repent and will also reduce your pride and self-sufficiency. Consider the following passages:

"Show me, LORD, my life's end
and the number of my days;
let me know how fleeting my life is.
[5] ***You have made my days a mere handbreadth;***
the span of my years is as nothing before you.
Everyone is but a breath,
even those who seem secure.
[6] ***"Surely everyone goes around like a mere phantom;***
in vain they rush about, heaping up wealth
without knowing whose it will finally be.
Psalm 39:4-6 (NIV)

***The sacrifice acceptable to God is a broken spirit;
a broken and contrite heart, O God, thou wilt not despise.***
Psalm 51:17 (RSV)

You will seek me and find me when you seek me with all your heart.
Jeremiah 29:13 (NIV)

No temptation has seized you except what is common to man. And God is faithful; he will not let you be tempted beyond what you can bear. But when you are tempted, he will also provide a way out so that you can stand up under it.
1 Corinthians 10:13 (NIV)

The point of this last verse is that it is possible to avoid particular sins *if we want to*. Though we will face temptation, God has promised that He will help us to find a way out, or way of escape, if we *want* Him to. The snag is that often we do not actually want to avoid the sin. The truth is *we like our sins*. Therefore we prefer to yield to the temptation. If we change our attitude and seek God's help, we can really start to win victories over sins and habits. We won't become perfect, but we can make progress.

However, we have to want it, and that is far from automatic. A person can easily "play at" Christianity, attending church and saying all the right sounding phrases, but not genuinely wanting to repent. Many people have a curiosity about the Gospel. God may be drawing them to Himself but, because their hearts are hard and cold, they do not respond to God. A good example of that attitude is the Roman governor, Felix. He liked to talk to apostle Paul, when Paul was in prison:

22Then Felix, who was well acquainted with the Way, adjourned the proceedings. "When Lysias the commander comes," he said, "I will decide your case." 23He ordered the centurion to keep Paul under guard but to give him some freedom and permit his friends to take care of his needs. 24Several days later Felix came with his wife Drusilla, who was a Jewess. He sent for Paul and listened to him as he spoke about faith in Christ Jesus. 25As Paul discoursed on righteousness, self-control and the judgment to come, Felix was afraid and said, "That's enough for now! You may leave. When I find it convenient, I will send for you." 26At the same time he was hoping that Paul would offer him a bribe, so he sent for him frequently and talked with him. 27When two years had passed, Felix was succeeded by Porcius Festus, but because Felix wanted to grant a favour to the Jews, he left Paul in prison.
Acts 24:22-27 (NIV)

Felix had a growing understanding. And he had an outstanding teacher in Paul. He also felt conviction and knew he was hearing the truth. But he still held back. There is no evidence that he ever repented or became a Christian, despite two years contact with the apostle Paul. What a waste of a chance to really learn about

God's Word and to grow as a Christian! Felix apparently threw it all away by choosing not to repent.

The way your awareness of sin will increase in future

It is only after you become a Christian and begin the process of maturing, or sanctification, that you will realise just how sinful you really are. Whatever level of sinfulness you may think you have at the moment, you will have underestimated it. The longer you go on in the Christian life the more acutely aware you become of the true extent of your own sinfulness.

Awareness of sin is a little like consciousness of the bacteria on your hands. The average school boy would probably not give them a thought. He would not even be aware of bacteria at all, or care about them, even if told. However, his mother would be much more aware of bacteria on her hands and would give it some serious thought.

So, her hands would be cleaner than her young son's hands, and have fewer bacteria. Yet she would be more concerned about their cleanliness and would pay more attention when handling things than her son does. If however we were then to look at a professional chef, his hands would be even cleaner than the mother's hands, having fewer bacteria. Yet he would be even more concerned than her about the bacteria that remain, and would consider them an even bigger problem.

However, if we were then to look at a consultant surgeon, perhaps one who operates on tiny babies born prematurely, we may well find that before operating he washes his hands with the utmost carefulness for many minutes and thus has even fewer bacteria than a chef. Yet the few remaining germs on his hands would cause him even greater concern still. He would be acutely conscious of his hands and their cleanliness and the vital need to disinfect them. It would be at the forefront of his mind every day when at work.

That analogy works quite well to show how a Christian, as he matures in the Christian life, actually sins less in absolute terms. He gradually gains mastery over bad habits, thought patterns, and attitudes and begins to slowly weed them out, or reduce them, with God's help. Yet, even though the sin in his life is getting less than it used to be in absolute terms, the fact that he is maturing means his ability to see his own sin increases.

Also his concern about his own sin increases. Therefore it is ironic that even though the level of sin gets less and less *in absolute terms*, a real Christian becomes more and more concerned about it *in relative terms.* So, practically speaking, you have to begin by facing up squarely to the reality of your own sin and your need for repentance.

If you do not get this right, then you will not get anything right. You may fail even to become a Christian. Or, if you do, then only a very weak one. If you can get this right however, and repent properly, then you will make excellent progress in the Christian life. You will rapidly mature in your first one to two years. Repentance is a little bit like the elastic in a catapult.

The more you pull back the elastic, i.e. the stronger the repentance, the farther you will be propelled forward in the early stages of the Christian life. The less however that you pull back the elastic in terms of your repentance, the more likely it is that you will make a feeble start. There will be no propulsion to get you started, or momentum to keep you going.

The vital importance of forgiving other people

We have looked closely at the need for us to repent of our sins, but what about other people's sins towards us? What should we do? What should our attitude and response be? The answer is clear, but it's not easy. We are commanded to forgive others. Then we are to leave it to God to judge and punish them if they do not repent, or to bless and forgive them if they do:

Do not take revenge, my friends, but leave room for God's wrath, for it is written: "It is mine to avenge; I will repay," says the Lord.

Romans 12:19 (NIV)

If we do not forgive others, and instead hold onto the bitterness and resentment and nurse our anger, it grows inside us like a tumour. That cancer of bitterness will not necessarily hurt the other person, but it will certainly damage you. It will affect, and even ruin, your life and will rob you of peace and joy. That is true even if the person who wronged you is wicked and you were an innocent party. The same principle still applies.

Forgiveness therefore means letting it go and handing over to God the responsibility for judging and punishing the wrong done to you. He has promised He will do that. Therefore, if you know He is going to judge it all, then why do you need to usurp the responsibility for doing so? You are the wrong person to judge or punish the wrongdoer. You do not have total wisdom, knowledge and understanding as God does. He knows exactly how to handle it, and He will do so, in His time, not yours.

If you let go of the wrong and hand it all over to God, you will be set free from bitterness. You will feel better and a burden will lift. This is a true of any wrong done to you, whether large or small. So you will benefit if you forgive everyone who has wronged you. If you seek to be the 'judge and executioner' yourself then you are usurping God's role. It's as if you are saying to God *"No, I will be the judge, not you. I will repay them myself"*.

That would be rebellion. Tragically, when we are wronged by others, it can often lead us into sin ourselves as we adopt that attitude of seizing God's role as judge. Even worse it can cause us to sin in other ways too as we seek to get even, which can often mean repaying one wrong with another wrong. Instead, God wants us to do the very opposite and to forgive other people when they do wrong to us:

.....as the Lord has forgiven you so you must forgive each other.
Colossians 3:13 (NIV)

In fact, God insists that we forgive others and He even goes as far as to make it a condition of His forgiving us:

14"For if you forgive others for their transgressions, your Heavenly Father will
also forgive you. 15"But if you do not forgive others, then your Father will not
forgive your transgressions.
Matthew 6:14-15 (NASB)

But how do we forgive people in practical terms? If has to begin with prayer. We need to ask God to give us the grace to be able to forgive. In ourselves we may not be capable of it. But He can give us the ability to do it, if we ask. We also need to realise that forgiveness is a *decision,* not a *feeling*. We do not need to wait until the hurt or anger has gone. We must forgive the person now, even if those angry feelings continue, which they are likely to do.

Forgiveness does not depend on feelings. It is something you do as a decision of your will. Therefore you can do it even if you are unable to stop feeling anger/hurt/bitterness. Simply decide to speak the words of forgiveness, and let the feelings come later.

I should also add that this does not mean that we are never to sue people or go to the police. We can do those things if we are wronged, (and if that is the right thing to do). The point is that you then leave it to a lawyer or to the police to act and even to dwell on it, instead of you doing so. God has put in place civil authorities and police for that very purpose. They are doing His work and are a part of His judgment of wrongdoers.

But even when we do go to the police, we personally are still to forgive and release the offender from our thoughts. Then we can leave it to the police, or others, to deal with it instead of us seeking vengeance ourselves. (See the chapters on forgiveness in Book Two in this series for a lot more detail on how to forgive other people and what it really involves).

CHAPTER 15

STEP TWO IN DETAIL - BELIEVE

And without faith it is impossible to please him, for whoever would draw near to God must believe that he exists and that he rewards those who seek him.

Hebrews 11:6 (ESV)

"........ for you will die in your sins unless you believe that I am he"

John 8:24 (b) (RSV)

But these are written that you may believe that Jesus is the Christ, the Son of God, and that by believing you may have life in his name.

John 20:31 (NIV)

"Truly, truly, I say to you, he who hears My word, and believes Him who sent Me, has eternal life, and does not come into judgment, but has passed out of death into life.

John 5:24 (NASB)

28 Then they said to him, "What must we do, to be doing the works of God?"
29 Jesus answered them, "This is the work of God, that you believe in him whom he has sent."

John 6:28-29 (RSV)

For this is the will of my Father, that everyone who sees the Son and believes in him should have eternal life; and I will raise him up at the last day."

John 6:40 (RSV)

Truly, truly, I say to you, he who believes has eternal life.

John 6:47 (RSV)

9 that if you confess with your mouth Jesus as Lord, and believe in your heart that God raised Him from the dead, you will be saved."

Romans 10:9 (NASB)

These things I have written to you who believe in the name of the Son of God, so that you may know that you have eternal life.

1 John 5:13 (NASB)

"Of Him all the prophets bear witness that through His name everyone who believes in Him receives forgiveness of sins."

Acts 10:43 (NASB)

38"Therefore let it be known to you, brethren, that through Him forgiveness of
sins is proclaimed to you, 39and through Him everyone who believes is freed
from all things, from which you could not be freed through the Law of Moses.

Acts 13:38-39 (NASB)

29And he called for lights and rushed in, and trembling with fear he fell down
before Paul and Silas, 30 and after he brought them out, he said, "Sirs, what
must I do to be saved?" 31 They said, "Believe in the Lord Jesus, and you will be
saved, you and your household."

Acts 16:29-31 (NASB)

25Jesus said to her, "I am the resurrection and the life; he who believes in me,
though he die, yet shall he live, 26 and whoever lives and believes in me shall
never die. Do you believe this?"

John 11:25-26 (RSV)

We have just spent a whole chapter looking at passages in the Bible which emphasise repentance. Now, we shall look at verses which focus on *believing*. These passages assume that you have already repented. In this chapter, we are going to examine what believing in Jesus Christ is all about and exactly what the Bible means when it requires us to "*believe*" in or "*have faith*" in or to "*trust*" in Jesus Christ.

In one sense these are simple, everyday words, but in the Bible they have very specific meanings. Therefore, there is a danger of misunderstanding, or underestimating, what is involved. The Bible tells us that it is only by believing in Jesus Christ that we can ever be forgiven and saved. There is no other way. It is a vital requirement.

Therefore, given that so much depends on us *"believing"* in Jesus Christ, we need to make sure that we clearly understand what believing or faith involves and remove all vagueness. We need a really clear grasp of exactly what we have to know, understand, believe and do before we can truly say we *believe* or *have faith* in the full biblical sense.

So, in this chapter, I will seek to set out and briefly explain all the basic essentials that we need to know, understand and believe. But these things are not just about having intellectual "head knowledge". Real faith will always be accompanied by action as we seek to put what we believe into practice. Real faith is not defined in terms of good works, i.e. "fruit" or "actions". It is about trust, which is an attitude of the heart.

However, real faith always leads on to us producing fruit and taking action. That is why God always looks for fruit (or good works) afterwards as the only way of telling whether our faith was real or not. We have to believe in Jesus in the sense of knowing who and what He is, but also in trusting in Him alone to save us. We also need to "*confess*" that belief, which means to speak it out openly. To confess means to *"say the same as"*. That means you need to say the same about Jesus as God the Father says about Him. In basic terms, that means to admit and declare that He is Lord, Saviour and King and that He died on the cross to pay the penalty for our sins and then rose from the dead.

What does it really mean to believe in Jesus?

If we are to qualify to benefit to from the death of Jesus Christ by being justified and forgiven we have to believe in Him. More accurately, we must believe **on** Him. That does not mean simply to believe that He exists, or even to believe that He is the Son of God, It is not enough in itself, even to believe that He is the Saviour, or that He died on the cross to take the penalty for sin.

All of those things are true and it is right for us to believe them all. However, in a certain sense, even those facts can be just head knowledge. It is perfectly possible for us to believe all those things as mere facts and still not be saved. Indeed, I fear that that is a very common condition and is true of many people.

What is needed is for us to believe **on** Jesus Christ in the sense that a man believes in a rope bridge when he steps on it to begin to walk across a deep ravine. It is one thing to have head knowledge that the rope bridge exists and even what it is made of. It is quite another thing to put your trust in it and step onto it and begin walking.

That is the kind of faith Jesus requires us to have in Him. He wants us to stake everything we have on Him and to rely on nobody else and nothing else except Him. In one sense, therefore, believing, or having faith, means to *trust*. An example of this was Abraham's willingness to leave his home and go to search for the Promised Land, when he did not yet even know where it was.

Even more starkly, there was his willingness to sacrifice his (adult) son Isaac, through whom God had promised to give Abraham a multitude of descendants. That was an extraordinary act of trust. Abraham demonstrated his faith by trusting God to raise Isaac from the dead, which is what Abraham fully expected to happen.

So, when God saw his faith He was satisfied that Abraham (and Isaac) had real faith and God therefore called off the test and did not make Abraham and Isaac go through with it. However, the key point is that Abraham showed his faith by obeying and trusting:

[8]By faith Abraham obeyed when he was called to go out to a place that he was to receive as an inheritance. And he went out, not knowing where he was going. [9]By faith he went to live in the land of promise, as in a foreign land, living in tents with Isaac and Jacob, heirs with him of the same promise.

Hebrews 11:8-9 (ESV)

[17]By faith Abraham, when he was tested, offered up Isaac, and he who had received the promises was in the act of offering up his only son, [18]of whom it was said, "Through Isaac shall your offspring be named." [19]He considered that God was able even to raise him from the dead, from which, figuratively speaking, he did receive him back.

Hebrews 11:17-19 (ESV)

Believing means obeying and trusting - it's not just intellectual

In other words, we are required to believe in Jesus Christ in the sense that we must put our trust in Him and rely upon Him alone to obtain salvation. That means that we recognise that there is only one way that we can go to Heaven and that is through Him. There is only one way that we can be considered righteous in God's eyes. That is for the righteousness of Jesus Christ to be transferred over to us.

We have to accept that there is no other way to be saved except through Him. We must abandon all ideas of earning salvation or deserving it on the basis of our own merit. Instead we must stake everything we have on Jesus Christ and trust in Him alone for our salvation, based on what He did for us on the cross.

When the man in the illustration above walks across a rope bridge high above a ravine, there is nothing else that can hold him up in the air other than that rope bridge. If it breaks then he will fall. Yet he knows that in himself he cannot cross that ravine or hold himself in the air and that the rope bridge is his only way. He may have anxieties about whether it will bear his weight. Those anxieties may be so great that he is not prepared to set foot on it.

Yet, if the question was raised as to whether this man really *"believes"* in the rope bridge, all of us would agree that the answer would be found by looking at whether he steps on to it and walks across. The very fact that he is stepping onto it demonstrates that he really does believe in it sufficiently to risk everything he has on it, even his own life. If he will not step on it, how can he say he truly believes in the rope bridge?

A person can genuinely believe on the Lord Jesus Christ and yet, understandably, still have moments of doubt that trouble them from time to time. That is natural and happens to most people. The key is whether, in spite of all that, you still put your trust in Him and continue to rely solely upon Him for salvation. It is the same for the man on the rope bridge. He may have his moments of anxiety, when he walks across and feels the wind blowing him. But the question is does he continue walking across it or does he turn back? If he carries on walking across then he is showing that he is putting his faith in the bridge, even if his mind is troubled with doubts.

That is the kind of belief or faith that is meant when the Bible speaks of believing in Jesus. It does not mean merely an academic belief or just agreeing with certain doctrines or beliefs. Likewise, merely knowing about the types of rope, wood and metal that the rope bridge is made of is important, but not enough, if you aren't convinced that it will take your weight.

Having a really good knowledge of the Bible and of doctrine is extremely important. Even so, that is not what is meant by believing in, or believing on, Jesus Christ. A man can have wrong or incomplete ideas about certain doctrines but still genuinely believe in and trust in the Lord Jesus Christ in the sense needed for salvation.

For example, good and honest people hold different views as to exactly what will happen before the return of Jesus Christ and exactly what the sequence of events will be. Yet despite holding different viewpoints on these things, such men can all be genuinely saved. That's because they still sincerely believe in, and on, Jesus Christ and trust in Him alone for their salvation.

Equally we might hold different views about the use of spiritual gifts, or how we should conduct church meetings, or how we should dress, or whether to drink alcohol, or other forms of practice and procedure. But those are not paramount. I do not say that they are not important. It is very important that we believe correctly what the Bible teaches and have a good understanding of it.

Yet our salvation, or being born again, is not based upon passing an examination on Scripture knowledge. It does not require us to be highly educated or academic. The smallest child, or an old man lying on his death bed with only minutes to live, can understand all that they need to believe to put their trust in Jesus Christ. Yet the most learned professor can totally miss the point.

Believing is, therefore, not an academic exam and it is not just about head knowledge. Instead, it is primarily about sincerely *putting our trust* in Jesus Christ and resolving to *follow Him* with devotion and loyalty. You could also say that believing in Jesus is about *'calling on Him'* or *'calling out to Him'* in our distress to ask Him to save us:

for "whoever will call on the name of the Lord will be saved."
Romans 10:13 (NASB)

To the church of God which is at Corinth, to those who have been sanctified in Christ Jesus, saints by calling, with all who in every place call on the name of our Lord Jesus Christ, their Lord and ours:

1 Corinthians 1:2 (NASB)

and he said, "I called out of my distress to the LORD, And He answered me I cried for help from the depth of Sheol; You heard my voice.

Jonah 2:2 (NASB)

18The LORD is near to all who call upon Him,
To all who call upon Him in truth.
19He will fulfill the desire of those who fear Him;
He will also hear their cry and will save them.

Psalm 145:18-19 (NASB)

Nevertheless, though I want to emphasise all of that, there are still certain basic essential facts that we do need to understand and believe in order to be able to meaningfully put our trust in him. Otherwise, if you did not know or understand who Jesus is, what He is and what He did, then what basis would you have to put any trust in Him? So, we do need to have at least some basic knowledge of the facts that the Bible teaches.

I will seek to list and explain these essential facts. I will break it all down into a series of basic statements of what we need to know and believe. After each one I will present a series of Bible verses to back it up. Rather than fully explain each of these, I will generally let the Bible speak for itself. If any of them are not clear, please refer back to the relevant chapter in this book where the point was covered in detail.

I am going to try to provide you now with a solid, thorough explanation of what we need to believe. However, I am not saying that you must fully understand or know all of these things in order to be saved. I have seen dying people come to believe in Jesus in the final minutes of their lives and validly put their trust in Him. They did not know or understand all of these points below. But they were still saved.

Even so, I want to be reasonably thorough with you. Hopefully, you are not in the final few minutes of your life. We therefore have the time to get things very clear, so as to avoid errors and wrong thinking later on.

A summary of the basic things we really need to know and believe in order to be saved:

A) THAT GOD EXISTS, THAT HE IS THE ONE TRUE GOD AND THERE IS NO OTHER GOD.

Turn to me and be saved,
all you ends of the earth;
for I am God, and there is no other.
Isaiah 45:22 (NIV)

To you it was shown, that you might know that the LORD is God; there is no other besides him.

Deuteronomy 4:35 (RSV)

[25] ***For great is the LORD and most worthy of praise; he is to be feared above all gods.*** [26] ***For all the gods of the nations are idols, but the LORD made the Heavens.***

1 Chronicles 16:25-26 (NIV)

so that all the peoples of the earth may know that the LORD is God and that there is no other.

1 Kings 8:60 (NIV)

B) THAT GOD EXISTS IN THREE SEPARATE PERSONS: GOD THE FATHER, THE SON OF GOD AND THE HOLY SPIRIT.

NB In the verses that follow two, or even all three, of the Persons of the Trinity are referred to. Clearly therefore, they are each distinct and separate Persons. Yet, each of them clearly had divine status. That is they are each spoken of as being fully God in their own right.

[14]***May the grace of the Lord Jesus Christ, and the love of God, and the fellowship of the Holy Spirit be with you all.***

2 Corinthians 13:14 (NIV)

[16]***After being baptized, Jesus came up immediately from the water; and behold, the Heavens were opened, and he saw the Spirit of God descending as a dove and lighting on Him,*** [17]***and behold, a voice out of the Heavens said, "This is My beloved Son, in whom I am well-pleased."***

Matthew 3:16-17 (NASB)

[18]Then Jesus came to them and said, "All authority in Heaven and on earth has been given to me. [19]Therefore go and make disciples of all nations, baptizing them in the name of the Father and of the Son and of the Holy Spirit,

Matthew 28:18-19 (NIV)

[1]Jesus, full of the Holy Spirit, returned from the Jordan and was led by the Spirit in the desert,

Luke 4:1 (NIV)

[54]Jesus replied, "If I glorify myself, my glory means nothing. My Father, whom you claim as your God, is the one who glorifies me.

John 8:54 (NIV)

[13]And I will do whatever you ask in my name, so that the Son may bring glory to the Father.

John 14:13 (NIV)

[26]But the Counselor, the Holy Spirit, whom the Father will send in my name, will teach you all things and will remind you of everything I have said to you.

John 14:26 (NIV)

[28]I came from the Father and entered the world; now I am leaving the world and going back to the Father."

John 16:28 (NIV)

[24]"Father, I want those you have given me to be with me where I am, and to see my glory, the glory ou have given me because you loved me before the creation of the world.

John 17:24 (NIV)

[2]according to the foreknowledge of God the Father, by the sanctifying work of the Spirit, to obey Jesus Christ and be sprinkled with His blood: May grace and peace be yours in the fullest measure.

1 Peter 1:2 (NASB)

[20]But you, beloved, building yourselves up on your most holy faith, praying in the Holy Spirit, [21]keep yourselves in the love of God, waiting anxiously for the mercy of our Lord Jesus Christ to eternal life.

Jude 1:20-21 (NASB)

[13]Who has directed the Spirit of the LORD,
Or as His counsellor has informed Him?
[14]With whom did He consult and who gave Him understanding?
And who taught Him in the path of justice and taught Him knowledge

And informed Him of the way of understanding?
Isaiah 40:13-14 (NASB)

17 But He answered them, "My Father is working until now, and I Myself am
working." 18 For this reason therefore the Jews were seeking all the more to kill
Him, because He not only was breaking the Sabbath, but also was calling God
His own Father, making Himself equal with God. 19 Therefore Jesus answered
and was saying to them, "Truly, truly, I say to you, the Son can do nothing of
Himself, unless it is something He sees the Father doing; for whatever the
Father does, these things the Son also does in like manner.

20 "For the Father loves the Son, and shows Him all things that He Himself is
doing; and the Father will show Him greater works than these, so that you will
marvel. 21 "For just as the Father raises the dead and gives them life, even so
the Son also gives life to whom He wishes. 22 "For not even the Father judges
anyone, but He has given all judgment to the Son, 23 so that all will honour the
Son even as they honour the Father. He who does not honour the Son does not
honour the Father who sent Him.

John 5:17-23 (NASB)

C) THAT NONETHELESS, THOSE THREE INDIVIDUAL PERSONS TOGETHER FORM ONE GOD. SO, IT IS TRUE TO SAY THAT GOD IS ONE.

In the beginning God created the Heavens and the earth.
Genesis 1:1 (NIV)

(Note in this verse, the very first in the Bible, we are presented with God as a Trinity. The way the word for '*God*' is written in the Hebrew is to use the plural noun "*Elohim.*" That means three (or more) persons. Then it immediately uses the verb "to create". But it is in the singular form, not plural. The putting together of a noun in plural form and a verb in singular form would be a serious grammatical error if it wasn't for the fact that God is a Trinity. Effectively, it says "In the beginning, God (plural noun for <u>three</u> or more persons) He created (verb in singular form, i.e. <u>one</u> person creating). Isn't that an extraordinary way for God to start page 1 of the Bible? God is telling you at the very outset that He is not just one Person but that, even so, He is still one God.

Hear, O Israel: The LORD our God, the LORD is one.
Deuteronomy 6:4 (NIV)

I and the Father are one.
John 10:30 (NIV)

Thus says the LORD, the King of Israel and his Redeemer, the LORD of hosts: "I am the first and I am the last; besides me there is no god.

Isaiah 44:6 (RSV)

I will remain in the world no longer, but they are still in the world, and I am coming to you. Holy Father, protect them by the power of your name—the name you gave me—so that they may be one as we are one.

John 17:11 (NIV)

I have given them the glory that you gave me, that they may be one as we are one:

John 17:22 (NIV)

4There are different kinds of gifts, but the same Spirit. 5There are different kinds of service, but the same Lord. 6There are different kinds of working, but the same God works all of them in all men.

1 Corinthians 12:4-6 (NIV)

4There is one body and one Spirit, just as also you were called in one hope of your calling; 5one Lord, one faith, one baptism, 6one God and Father of all who is over all and through all and in all.

Ephesians 4:4-6 (NASB)

D) THAT GOD CREATED EVERYTHING, INCLUDING US, AND THAT WE BELONG TO HIM.

In the beginning God created the Heavens and the earth.

Genesis 1:1 (NIV)

Hezekiah prayed before the LORD and said, "O LORD, the God of Israel, who are enthroned above the cherubim, You are the God, You alone, of all the kingdoms of the earth. You have made Heaven and earth.

2 Kings 19:15 (NASB)

By faith we understand that the universe was formed at God's command, so that what is seen was not made out of what was visible.

Hebrews 11:3(NIV)

1In the beginning was the Word, and the Word was with God, and the Word was God. 2He was with God in the beginning. 3Through him all things were made; without him nothing was made that has been made.

John 1:1-3 (NIV)

Who has a claim against me that I must pay? Everything under Heaven belongs to me

Job 41:11 (NIV)

For every living soul belongs to me, the father as well as the son—both alike belong to me. The soul who sins is the one who will die.

Ezekiel 18:4 (NIV)

6 "You alone are the LORD
You have made the Heavens,
The Heaven of Heavens with all their host,
The earth and all that is on it,
The seas and all that is in them
You give life to all of them
And the Heavenly host bows down before You.

Nehemiah 9:6 (NASB)

E) THAT WE ARE UNWORTHY AND HAVE SINNED, TRANSGRESSED AND REBELLED AGAINST GOD AND HAVE OFFENDED AND ANGERED HIM.

2 God looks down from Heaven
on the sons of men
to see if there are any who understand,
any who seek God.
3 Everyone has turned away,
they have together become corrupt;
there is no one who does good,
not even one.

Psalm 53:2-3 (NIV)

for all have sinned and fall short of the glory of God,

Romans 3:23(NIV)

If we claim to be without sin, we deceive ourselves and the truth is not in us.

1 John 1:8 (NIV)

F) THAT WE ARE THEREFORE CONDEMNED IN GOD'S EYES AND, UNLESS WE ARE FORGIVEN, WE WILL BE ETERNALLY SEPARATED FROM HIM WHEN WE DIE AND FACE HIS JUDGMENT. WE WILL THEN GO TO ETERNAL PUNISHMENT IN THE LAKE OF FIRE BECAUSE OF OUR SIN.

But your iniquities have separated
you from your God;
your sins have hidden his face from you,
so that he will not hear.
Isaiah 59:2 (NIV)

But because of your stubbornness and your unrepentant heart, you are storing up wrath against yourself for the day of God's wrath, when his righteous judgment will be revealed.

Romans 2:5 (NIV)

For the wages of sin is death, but the gift of God is eternal life in Christ Jesus our Lord.

Romans 6:23 (NIV)

The LORD replied to Moses, "Whoever has sinned against me I will blot out of my book.

Exodus 32:33 (NIV)

I will punish the world for its evil,
the wicked for their sins.
I will put an end to the arrogance of the haughty
and will humble the pride of the ruthless.
Isaiah 13:11(NIV)

Just as man is destined to die once, and after that to face judgment,
Hebrews 9:27 (NIV)

[8]He will punish those who do not know God and do not obey the gospel of our Lord Jesus. [9]They will be punished with everlasting destruction and shut out from the presence of the Lord and from the majesty of his power

2 Thessalonians 1:8-9 (NIV)

But the cowardly, the unbelieving, the vile, the murderers, the sexually immoral, those who practice magic arts, the idolaters and all liars—their place will be in the fiery lake of burning sulphur. This is the second death."

Revelation 21:8 (NIV)

G) THAT NOTHING WE CAN DO ON OUR OWN BEHALF CAN SAVE (JUSTIFY) US BY GIVING US FORGIVENESS OR RIGHTEOUSNESS IN GOD'S EYES. WE ARE NOT GOOD ENOUGH AND NONE OF OUR WORKS OR DEEDS WILL EVER BE GOOD ENOUGH TO SAVE US. IN GOD'S EYES, EVEN OUR BEST DEEDS ARE INADEQUATE.

Therefore no one will be declared righteous in his sight by observing the law; rather, through the law we become conscious of sin.

Romans 3:20 (NIV)

know that a man is not justified by observing the law, but by faith in Jesus Christ. So we, too, have put our faith in Christ Jesus that we may be justified by faith in Christ and not by observing the law, because by observing the law no one will be justified.

Galatians 2:16 (NIV)

11 Clearly no one is justified before God by the law, because, "The righteous will
live by faith." 12 The law is not based on faith; on the contrary, "The man who
does these things will live by them." 13 Christ redeemed us from the curse of the
law by becoming a curse for us, for it is written: "Cursed is everyone who is hung on a tree."

Galatians 3:11-13 (NIV)

For we maintain that a man is justified by faith apart from observing the law.

Romans 3:28 (NIV)

8 For it is by grace you have been saved, through faith—and this not from
yourselves, it is the gift of God— 9 not by works, so that no one can boast.

Ephesians 2:8-9 (NIV)

he saved us, not because of righteous things we had done, but because of his mercy. He saved us through the washing of rebirth and renewal by the Holy Spirit,

Titus 3:5 (NIV)

H) THAT JESUS CHRIST IS NOT ONLY A MAN, BUT IS DIVINE (GOD). HE IS THE SECOND PERSON OF THE TRINITY, THE SON OF GOD. HE THEN BECAME A REAL HUMAN BEING, WHILST AT THE SAME TIME REMAINING THE SON OF GOD.

I intend to include a lot of verses in this section because there are so many people who refuse to accept that Jesus is divine, i.e. that He is God. Therefore, I aim to show that this is very clearly what the Bible teaches.

Thomas said to him, "My Lord and my God!"
John 20:28 (NIV)

In the beginning was the Word, and the Word was with God, and the Word was God.

John 1:1(NIV)

(NB - "The Word" is one of the many titles or names of Jesus Christ)

[9]The true light that gives light to every man was coming into the world. [10]He was
in the world, and though the world was made through him, the world did not
recognize him. [11]He came to that which was his own, but his own did not receive
him. [12]Yet to all who received him, to those who believed in his name, he gave
the right to become children of God—

John 1:9-12 (NIV)

And the Word was made flesh, and dwelt among us, (and we beheld his glory, the glory as of the only begotten of the Father,) full of grace and truth.
John 1:14 (KJV)

"I myself have seen, and have testified that this is the Son of God."
John 1:34 (NASB)

[15]"But what about you?" he asked. "Who do you say I am?" [16]Simon Peter
answered, "You are the Christ, the Son of the living God." [17]Jesus replied,
"Blessed are you, Simon son of Jonah, for this was not revealed to you by man,
but by my Father in Heaven.

Matthew 16:15-17 (NIV)

[15]He is the image of the invisible God, the firstborn over all creation. [16]For by
him all things were created: things in Heaven and on earth, visible and invisible,
whether thrones or powers or rulers or authorities; all things were created by
him and for him. [17]He is before all things, and in him all things hold together.
Colossians 1:15-17 (NIV)

For in Christ all the fullness of the Deity lives in bodily form,
Colossians 2:9 (NIV)

[25]The woman said, "I know that Messiah" (called Christ) "is coming. When he
comes, he will explain everything to us." [26]Then Jesus declared, "I who speak
to you am he."

John 4:25-26 (NIV)

Then those who were in the boat worshiped him, saying, "Truly you are the Son of God."

Matthew 14:33 (NIV)

***31** The Jews took up stones again to stone him. **32** Jesus answered them, "I have
shown you many good works from the Father; for which of these do you stone
me?" **33** The Jews answered him, "It is not for a good work that we stone you
but for blasphemy; because you, being a man, make yourself God."*

John 10:31-33 (RSV)

***36** do you say of him whom the Father consecrated and sent into the world, 'You
are blaspheming,' because I said, 'I am the Son of God'? **37** If I am not doing
the works of my Father, then do not believe me; **38** but if I do them, even though
you do not believe me, believe the works, that you may know and understand
that the Father is in me and I am in the Father." **39** Again they tried to arrest
him, but he escaped from their hands.*

John 10:36-39 (RSV)

***3** So the sisters sent to him, saying, "Lord, he whom you love is ill." **4** But when
Jesus heard it he said, "This illness is not unto death; it is for the glory of God,
so that the Son of God may be glorified by means of it."*

John 11: 3-4 (RSV)

"Yes, Lord," she replied, "I believe that you are the Messiah, the Son of God, who is to come into the world."

John 11:27 (NIV)

***11**And whenever the unclean spirits beheld him, they fell down before him and
cried out, "You are the Son of God." **12**And he strictly ordered them not to make
him known.*

Mark 3:11-12 (RSV)

***66**When it was day, the Council of elders of the people assembled, both chief
priests and scribes, and they led Him away to their council chamber,
saying, **67**"If You are the Christ, tell us." But He said to them, "If I tell you,
you will not believe; **68**and if I ask a question, you will not answer. **69**"But from
now on the Son of man will be seated at the right hand of the power of
God." **70**And they all said, "Are You The Son of God, then?" And He said to
them, "Yes, I am." **71**Then they said, "What further need do we have of
testimony? For we have heard it ourselves from His own mouth."*

Luke 22:66-71 (NASB)

***1**In the past God spoke to our forefathers through the prophets at many times
and in various ways, **2**but in these last days he has spoken to us by his Son, whom
he appointed heir of all things, and through whom he made the universe. **3**The
Son is the radiance of God's glory and the exact representation of his being,
sustaining all things by his powerful word. After he had provided purification
for sins, he sat down at the right hand of the Majesty in Heaven. **4**So he became*

as much superior to the angels as the name he has inherited is superior to theirs.
Hebrews 1:1-4(NIV)

[8] But to the Son He says:
"Your throne, O God, is forever and ever;
A scepter of righteousness is the scepter of Your kingdom.
[9] You have loved righteousness and hated lawlessness;
Therefore God, Your God, has anointed You
With the oil of gladness more than Your companions.
Hebrews 1:8-9 (ESV)

But we see Jesus, who was made a little lower than the angels, for the suffering of death crowned with glory and honor, that He, by the grace of God, might taste death for everyone.
Hebrews 2:9 (ESV)

[14]Inasmuch then as the children have partaken of flesh and blood, He Himself likewise shared in the same, that through death He might destroy him who had the power of death, that is, the devil, [15]and release those who through fear of death were all their lifetime subject to bondage. [16] For indeed He does not give aid to angels, but He does give aid to the seed of Abraham. [17]Therefore, in all things He had to be made like His brethren, that He might be a merciful and faithful High Priest in things pertaining to God, to make propitiation for the sins of the people. [18]For in that He Himself has suffered, being tempted, He is able to aid those who are tempted.
Hebrews 2:14-18 (ESV)

[14] Seeing then that we have a great High Priest who has passed through the Heavens, Jesus the Son of God, let us hold fast our confession. [15] For we do not have a High Priest who cannot sympathize with our weaknesses, but was in all points tempted as we are, yet without sin.
Hebrews 4:14-15(ESV)

You may have heard people saying that Jesus isn't the Son of God. They even suggest that Jesus never claimed to be so, or that His disciples never claimed it on His behalf. As you can see above, He was very clear in saying that He was the Son of God and therefore equal to God. Thus, cults like the Jehovah's Witnesses make a huge error on this point. Likewise, those who say He was God, but that He never really became a man, are also wrong.

I) THAT JESUS CHRIST LIVED A SINLESS LIFE AND THEN DIED AN UNJUST DEATH, WHICH HE DID NOT DESERVE, IN ORDER TO BE PUNISHED IN OUR PLACE AND PAY THE PENALTY FOR OUR SINS. THAT WAS HOW GOD THE FATHER VIEWED JESUS' DEATH. HE WAS PUTTING HIS OWN SON, JESUS, TO DEATH TO BE THE SACRIFICE THAT PAYS FOR OUR SIN.

He committed no sin, and no deceit was found in his mouth.
1 Peter 2:22 (NIV)

Yet it was the LORD's will to crush him and cause him to suffer,
and though the LORD makes his life a guilt offering,
he will see his offspring and prolong his days,
and the will of the LORD will prosper in his hand.
Isaiah 53:10 (NIV)

6Who, being in very nature God,
did not consider equality with God something to be grasped,
7but made himself nothing,
taking the very nature of a servant,
being made in human likeness.
8And being found in appearance as a man,
he humbled himself
and became obedient to death—
even death on a cross!
Philippians 2:6-8 (NIV)

For Christ died for sins once for all, the righteous for the unrighteous, to bring you to God. He was put to death in the body but made alive by the Spirit,
1 Peter 3:18 (NIV)

He is the atoning sacrifice for our sins, and not only for ours but also for the sins of the whole world.
1 John 2:2 (NIV)

18And he is the head of the body, the church; he is the beginning and the
firstborn from among the dead, so that in everything he might have the
supremacy. 19For God was pleased to have all his fullness dwell in him, 20and
through him to reconcile to himself all things, whether things on earth or things
in Heaven, by making peace through his blood, shed on the cross.
Colossians 1:18-20 (NIV)

25He said to them, "How foolish you are, and how slow of heart to believe all
that the prophets have spoken! 26Did not the Christ have to suffer these things

and then enter his glory?" [27]And beginning with Moses and all the Prophets, he explained to them what was said in all the Scriptures concerning himself.

Luke 24:25-27 (NIV)

[23] The former priests were many in number, because they were prevented by death from continuing in office, [24] but he holds his priesthood permanently, because he continues forever. [25] Consequently, he is able to save to the uttermost those who draw near to God through him, since he always lives to make intercession for them. [26] For it was indeed fitting that we should have such a high priest, holy, innocent, unstained, separated from sinners, and exalted above the Heavens. [27] He has no need, like those high priests, to offer sacrifices daily, first for his own sins and then for those of the people, since he did this once for all when he offered up himself.

Hebrews 7:23-27 (ESV)

so Christ was sacrificed once to take away the sins of many people; and he will appear a second time, not to bear sin, but to bring salvation to those who are waiting for him.

Hebrews 9:28 (NIV)

J) THAT WHEN THE LORD JESUS CHRIST WAS ON THE CROSS, THE BURDEN AND THE GUILT OF ALL THE SIN OF THE WORLD WAS PUT UPON HIM AND GOD THE FATHER POURED OUT HIS WRATH, ANGER AND PUNISHMENT UPON HIM, INSTEAD OF ON US.

He himself bore our sins in his body on the tree, so that we might die to sins and live for righteousness; by his wounds you have been healed

1 Peter 2:24 (NIV)

Christ redeemed us from the curse of the law by becoming a curse for us, for it is written: "Cursed is everyone who is hung on a tree."

Galatians 3:13 (NIV)

(NB - This verse above is a hard one to understand. It means that when Jesus was dying on the cross, God's curse, which is what we all deserve and would otherwise receive, was redirected to Him. It was put upon Him so that it need not be put on us).

[21]Once you were alienated from God and were enemies in your minds because of your evil behavior. [22]But now he has reconciled you by Christ's physical body through death to present you holy in his sight, without blemish and free from accusation—

Colossians 1:21-22 (NIV)

Consequently, just as one trespass resulted in condemnation for all people, so also one righteous act resulted in justification and life for all people.

Romans 5:18 (NIV)

[1]Therefore, there is now no condemnation for those who are in Christ Jesus, [2]
because through Christ Jesus the law of the Spirit who gives life has set you free
from the law of sin and death. [3] For what the law was powerless to do because
it was weakened by the flesh, God did by sending his own Son in the likeness of
sinful flesh to be a sin offering. And so he condemned sin in the flesh,

Romans 8:1-3 (NIV)

For he has rescued us from the dominion of darkness and brought us into the kingdom of the Son he loves,

Colossians 1:13 (NIV)

[13] And you, who were dead in trespasses and the uncircumcision of your flesh,
God made alive together with him, having forgiven us all our trespasses,
[14] having cancelled the bond which stood against us with its legal demands; this
he set aside, nailing it to the cross.

Colossians 2:13-14 (RSV)

K) THAT THE LORD JESUS DIED AND THEN ROSE FROM THE DEAD. HE WAS RESURRECTED, PHYSICALLY AND LITERALLY. HE THEN ASCENDED PHYSICALLY INTO HEAVEN 40 DAYS LATER. HE IS NOW ALIVE AND IN HEAVEN, IN HIS RESURRECTION BODY, WAITING TO RETURN TO THE EARTH.

Praise be to the God and Father of our Lord Jesus Christ! In his great mercy he has given us new birth into a living hope through the resurrection of Jesus Christ from the dead,

1 Peter 1:3 (NIV)

[5]The angel said to the women, "Do not be afraid; for I know that you are looking
for Jesus who has been crucified. [6]"He is not here, for He has risen, just as He
said. Come, see the place where He was lying. [7]"Go quickly and tell His
disciples that He has risen from the dead; and behold, He is going ahead of you
into Galilee, there you will see Him; behold, I have told you." [8]And they left the
tomb quickly with fear and great joy and ran to report it to His disciples. [9]And
behold, Jesus met them and greeted them. And they came up and took hold of
His feet and worshiped Him.

Matthew 28:5-9 (NIV)

*[9]And after He had said these things, He was lifted up while they were looking
on, and a cloud received Him out of their sight. [10]And as they were gazing
intently into the sky while He was going, behold, two men in white clothing stood
beside them. [11]They also said, "Men of Galilee, why do you stand looking into
the sky? This Jesus, who has been taken up from you into Heaven, will come in
just the same way as you have watched Him go into Heaven."*

Acts 1:9-11 (NASB)

*[3]For I delivered to you as of first importance what I also received, that Christ
died for our sins according to the Scriptures, [4]and that He was buried, and that
He was raised on the third day according to the Scriptures, [5]and that He
appeared to Cephas, then to the twelve. [6]After that He appeared to more than
five hundred brethren at one time, most of whom remain until now, but some
have fallen asleep; [7]then He appeared to James, then to all the apostles; [8]and
last of all, as to one untimely born, He appeared to me also.*

1 Corinthians 15:3-8 (NIV)

*[3]Or don't you know that all of us who were baptized into Christ Jesus were
baptized into his death? [4]We were therefore buried with him through baptism
into death in order that, just as Christ was raised from the dead through the
glory of the Father, we too may live a new life. [5]If we have been united with him
like this in his death, we will certainly also be united with him in his
resurrection.*

Romans 6:3-5 (NIV)

L) THAT WE MUST REPENT TOWARDS GOD THE FATHER FOR OUR SINS AND SINCERELY TURN AWAY FROM OUR SINS AND GENUINELY CHANGE IN OUR ATTITUDES, BEHAVIOUR AND LIFESTYLE.

*[1]Now in those days John the Baptist came, preaching in the wilderness of Judea,
saying, [2]"Repent, for the kingdom of Heaven is at hand."*

Matthew 3:1-2 (NASB)

From that time Jesus began to preach and say, "Repent, for the kingdom of Heaven is at hand."

Matthew 4:17 (NASB)

" .... God...... commands all people everywhere to repent"

Acts 17:30 (NIV)

*[36]"Therefore let all the house of Israel know for certain that God has made Him
both Lord and Christ--this Jesus whom you crucified." [37]Now when they heard
this, they were pierced to the heart, and said to Peter and the rest of the apostles,*

"Brethren, what shall we do?" [38]*Peter said to them, "Repent, and each of you be baptized in the name of Jesus Christ for the forgiveness of your sins; and you will receive the gift of the Holy Spirit.*

Acts 2:36-38 (NASB)

"Therefore repent and return, so that your sins may be wiped away, in order that times of refreshing may come from the presence of the Lord;

Acts 3:19 (NIV)

[19]*"So then, King Agrippa, I was not disobedient to the vision from Heaven.*
[20]*First to those in Damascus, then to those in Jerusalem and in all Judea, and to the Gentiles also, I preached that they should repent and turn to God and prove their repentance by their deeds.*

Acts 26:19-20 (NIV)

M) THAT WE MUST BE BAPTISED IN WATER, BY FULL IMMERSION, IN THE NAME OF THE FATHER, THE SON AND THE HOLY SPIRIT. THIS MUST BE DONE BY US AS A REPENTANT BELIEVER, NOT DONE TO US AS AN INFANT. ANY PAST BAPTISM AS A BABY DOES NOT COUNT AS REAL BAPTISM.

"Go therefore and make disciples of all the nations, baptizing them in the name of the Father and the Son and the Holy Spirit,

Matthew 28:19 (NASB)

Peter said to them, "Repent, and each of you be baptized in the name of Jesus Christ for the forgiveness of your sins; and you will receive the gift of the Holy Spirit.

Acts 2:38 (NASB)

So then, those who had received his word were baptized; and that day there were added about three thousand souls.

Acts 2:41 (NASB)

[12]*But when they believed Philip preaching the good news about the kingdom of God and the name of Jesus Christ, they were being baptized, men and women*
alike. [13]*Even Simon himself believed; and after being baptized, he continued on with Philip, and as he observed signs and great miracles taking place, he was constantly amazed.*

Acts 8:12-13 (NASB)

[47] *"Can anyone keep these people from being baptized with water? They have*
received the Holy Spirit just as we have." [48] *So he ordered that they be baptized*

in the name of Jesus Christ. Then they asked Peter to stay with them for a few days.

Acts 10:47-48 (NIV)

29 And he called for lights and rushed in, and trembling with fear he fell down before Paul and Silas, 30 and after he brought them out, he said, "Sirs, what must I do to be saved?" 31 They said, "Believe in the Lord Jesus, and you will be saved, you and your household." 32 And they spoke the word of the Lord to him together with all who were in his house. 33 And he took them that very hour of the night and washed their wounds, and immediately he was baptized, he and all his household. 34 And he brought them into his house and set food before them, and rejoiced greatly, having believed in God with his whole household.

Acts 16:29-34 (NASB)

Crispus, the leader of the synagogue, believed in the Lord with all his household, and many of the Corinthians when they heard were believing and being baptized.

Acts 18:8 (NASB)

When they heard this, they were baptized in the name of the Lord Jesus.

Acts 19:5 (NASB)

'Now why do you delay? Get up and be baptized, and wash away your sins, calling on His name.'

Acts 22:16 (NASB)

3 Or do you not know that all of us who have been baptized into Christ Jesus have been baptized into His death? 4 Therefore we have been buried with Him through baptism into death, so that as Christ was raised from the dead through the glory of the Father, so we too might walk in newness of life. 5 For if we have become united with Him in the likeness of His death, certainly we shall also be in the likeness of His resurrection,

Romans 6:3-5 (NASB)

N) THAT WE MUST "RECEIVE" THE HOLY SPIRIT, OTHERWISE REFERRED TO AS BEING "FILLED WITH" OR "BAPTISED IN" THE HOLY SPIRIT.

7 And he was preaching, and saying, "After me One is coming who is mightier than I, and I am not fit to stoop down and untie the thong of His sandals. 8 "I baptized you with water; but He will baptize you with the Holy Spirit."

Mark 1:7-8 (NASB)

[16]"I will ask the Father, and He will give you another Helper, that He may be
with you forever; [17]that is the Spirit of truth, whom the world cannot receive,
because it does not see Him or know Him, but you know Him because He abides
with you and will be in you.

John 14:16-17 (NASB)

"But the Helper, the Holy Spirit, whom the Father will send in My name, He will teach you all things, and bring to your remembrance all that I said to you.

John 14:26 (NASB)

And do not get drunk with wine, for that is dissipation, but be filled with the Spirit,

Ephesians 5:18 (NASB)

[13]"But when He, the Spirit of truth, comes, He will guide you into all the truth;
for He will not speak on His own initiative, but whatever He hears, He will
speak; and He will disclose to you what is to come. [14]"He will glorify Me, for
He will take of Mine and will disclose it to you. [15]"All things that the Father
has are Mine; therefore I said that He takes of Mine and will disclose it to you.

John 16:13-15 (NASB)

[1]It happened that while Apollos was at Corinth, Paul passed through the upper
country and came to Ephesus, and found some disciples. [2]He said to them, "Did
you receive the Holy Spirit when you believed?" And they said to him, "No, we
have not even heard whether there is a Holy Spirit." [3]And he said, "Into what
then were you baptized?" And they said, "Into John's baptism." [4]Paul said,
"John baptized with the baptism of repentance, telling the people to believe in
Him who was coming after him, that is, in Jesus." [5]When they heard this, they
were baptized in the name of the Lord Jesus. [6]And when Paul had laid his hands
upon them, the Holy Spirit came on them, and they began speaking with tongues
and prophesying.

Acts 19:1-6 (NASB)

O) THAT FORGIVENESS AND ETERNAL LIFE WITH GOD ARE AVAILABLE TO ANYONE WHO MEETS GOD'S CONDITIONS. THOSE ARE TO REPENT, BELIEVE, BE BAPTISED IN WATER AND RECEIVE THE HOLY SPIRIT.

[9]If we confess our sins, he is faithful and just and will forgive us our sins and
purify us from all unrighteousness.

1 John 1:9 (NIV)

[15]And He said to them, "Go into all the world and preach the gospel to all
creation. [16]"He who has believed and has been baptized shall be saved; but he
who has disbelieved shall be condemned.

Mark 16:15-16 (NASB)

They said to the woman, "We no longer believe just because of what you said; now we have heard for ourselves, and we know that this man really is the Saviour of the world."

John 4:42 (NIV)

"I tell you the truth, whoever hears my word and believes him who sent me has eternal life and will not be condemned; he has crossed over from death to life.

John 5:24 (NIV)

[7]Therefore Jesus said again, "I tell you the truth, I am the gate for the sheep.
[8]All who ever came before me were thieves and robbers, but the sheep did not
listen to them. [9]I am the gate; whoever enters through me will be saved. He will
come in and go out, and find pasture. [10]The thief comes only to steal and kill
and destroy; I have come that they may have life, and have it to the full.

John 10:7-10 (NIV)

38 Let it be known to you therefore, brethren, that through this man forgiveness
of sins is proclaimed to you, 39 and by him every one that believes is freed from
everything from which you could not be freed by the law of Moses.

Acts 13:38-39 (RSV)

[9]That if you confess with your mouth, "Jesus is Lord," and believe in your heart
that God raised him from the dead, you will be saved. [10]For it is with your heart
that you believe and are justified, and it is with your mouth that you confess and
are saved. [11]As the Scripture says, "Anyone who trusts in him will never be put
to shame." [12]For there is no difference between Jew and Gentile—the same
Lord is Lord of all and richly blesses all who call on him, [13]for, "Everyone who
calls on the name of the Lord will be saved."

Romans 10:9-13 (NIV)

[11]And this is the testimony: God has given us eternal life, and this life is in his
Son. [12]He who has the Son has life; he who does not have the Son of God does
not have life. [13]I write these things to you who believe in the name of the Son
of God so that you may know that you have eternal life.

1 John 5:11-13 (NIV)

[16]"For God so loved the world that he gave his one and only Son, that whoever
believes in him shall not perish but have eternal life. [17]For God did not send his
Son into the world to condemn the world, but to save the world through him.
[18]Whoever believes in him is not condemned, but whoever does not believe

stands condemned already because he has not believed in the name of God's one and only Son.

John 3:16-18 (NIV)

And without faith it is impossible to please Him, for he who comes to God must believe that He is and that He is a rewarder of those who seek Him.

Hebrews 11:6 (NASB)

P) THAT THERE IS NO OTHER WAY TO GOD AND THAT NO MAN, RELIGION, SYSTEM, ACTIVITY OR FORMULA CAN SAVE US. ONLY THE LORD JESUS CHRIST HIMSELF CAN SAVE US BECAUSE OF HIS DEATH ON THE CROSS, WHEN HE TOOK OUR PUNISHMENT IN OUR PLACE.

35The Father loves the Son and has placed everything in his hands. 36Whoever believes in the Son has eternal life, but whoever rejects the Son will not see life, for God's wrath remains on him."

John 3:35-36 (NIV)

23Jesus said to her, "Your brother will rise again." 24Martha answered, "I know he will rise again in the resurrection at the last day." 25Jesus said to her, "I am the resurrection and the life. He who believes in me will live, even though he dies; 26and whoever lives and believes in me will never die. Do you believe this?"
27"Yes, Lord," she told him, "I believe that you are the Christ, the Son of God, who was to come into the world."

John 11:23-27 (NIV)

I told you that you would die in your sins; if you do not believe that I am he, you will indeed die in your sins."

John 8:24 (NIV)

Jesus answered, "I am the way and the truth and the life. No one comes to the Father except through me.

John 14:6 (NIV)

Salvation is found in no one else, for there is no other name under Heaven given to men by which we must be saved."

Acts 4:12 (NIV)

42 And he commanded us to preach to the people, and to testify that he is the one ordained by God to be judge of the living and the dead. 43 To him all the prophets bear witness that everyone who believes in him receives forgiveness of sins through his name."

Acts 10:42-43 (RSV)

Q) THAT IF WE DIE WE WILL EVENTUALLY BE PHYSICALLY RESURRECTED. WE WILL THEN HAVE ETERNAL AND INDESTRUCTIBLE "RESURRECTION BODIES" WHICH WILL NEVER DIE. THIS IS TRUE BOTH FOR BELIEVERS AND UNBELIEVERS. THE RESURRECTION BODY OF AN UNBELIEVER WILL NEVER BE DESTROYED, EVEN IN THE LAKE OF FIRE.

***19**Your dead will live;*
Their corpses will rise
You who lie in the dust, awake and shout for joy,
For your dew is as the dew of the dawn,
And the earth will give birth to the departed spirits.
Isaiah 26:19 (NASB)

Multitudes who sleep in the dust of the earth will awake: some to everlasting life, others to shame and everlasting contempt.

Daniel 12:2 (NIV)

Now God has not only raised the Lord, but will also raise us up through His power.

1 Corinthians 6:14 (NASB)

23 Jesus said to her, "Your brother will rise again." 24 Martha said to Him, "I
know that he will rise again in the resurrection on the last day."

John 11:23-24 (NASB)

having a hope in God, which these men cherish themselves, that there shall certainly be a resurrection of both the righteous and the wicked.

Acts 24:15 (NASB)

12 Now if Christ is preached, that He has been raised from the dead, how do some among you say that there is no resurrection of the dead?
13 But if there is no resurrection of the dead, not even Christ has been raised;
14 and if Christ has not been raised, then our preaching is vain, your faith also is vain.
15 Moreover we are even found to be false witnesses of God, because we testified against God that He raised Christ, whom He did not raise, if in fact the dead are not raised.
16 For if the dead are not raised, not even Christ has been raised;
17 and if Christ has not been raised, your faith is worthless; you are still in your sins.
18 Then those also who have fallen asleep in Christ have perished.
19 If we have hoped in Christ in this life only, we are of all men most to be pitied.
20 But now Christ has been raised from the dead, the first fruits of those who are asleep.

[21]For since by a man came death, by a man also came the resurrection of the dead.

1 Corinthians 15:12-21 (NASB)

[35]But someone will say, "How are the dead raised? And with what kind of body do they come?" [36]You fool! That which you sow does not come to life unless it dies; [37]and that which you sow, you do not sow the body which is to be, but a bare grain, perhaps of wheat or of something else. [38]But God gives it a body just as He wished, and to each of the seeds a body of its own. [39]All flesh is not the same flesh, but there is one flesh of men, and another flesh of beasts, and another flesh of birds, and another of fish. [40]There are also Heavenly bodies and earthly bodies, but the glory of the Heavenly is one, and the glory of the earthly is another. [41]There is one glory of the sun, and another glory of the moon, and another glory of the stars; for star differs from star in glory. [42]So also is the resurrection of the dead It is sown a perishable body, it is raised an imperishable body; [43]it is sown in dishonour, it is raised in glory; it is sown in weakness, it is raised in power; [44]it is sown a natural body, it is raised a spiritual body. If there is a natural body, there is also a spiritual body.

1 Corinthians 15:35-44 (NASB)

[51]Behold, I tell you a mystery; we will not all sleep, but we will all be changed, [52]in a moment, in the twinkling of an eye, at the last trumpet; for the trumpet will sound, and the dead will be raised imperishable, and we will be changed.

1 Corinthians 15:51-52 (NASB)

[10]that I may know Him and the power of His resurrection and the fellowship of His sufferings, being conformed to His death; [11]in order that I may attain to the resurrection from the dead.

Philippians 3:10-11 (NASB)

R) THAT JESUS CHRIST WILL RETURN PHYSICALLY TO THIS EARTH. HE WILL THEN RULE AS KING OF ISRAEL AND KING OF THE WHOLE WORLD. IN OTHER WORDS, HE WILL ESTABLISH THE KINGDOM OF GOD AND BRING IT TO COMPLETION.

Nathanael answered Him, "Rabbi, You are the Son of God; You are the King of Israel."

John 1:49 (NASB)

So Pilate asked Him, saying, "Are You the King of the Jews?" And He answered him and said, "It is as you say."

Luke 23:3 (NASB)

[16]For the Lord Himself will descend from Heaven with a shout, with the voice of the archangel and with the trumpet of God, and the dead in Christ will rise first. [17]Then we who are alive and remain will be caught up together with them in the clouds to meet the Lord in the air, and so we shall always be with the Lord.

1 Thessalonians 4:16-17(NASB)

"Where is He who has been born King of the Jews? For we saw His star in the east and have come to worship Him."

Matthew 2:2 (NASB)

And above His head they put up the charge against Him which read, "THIS IS JESUS THE KING OF THE JEWS."

Matthew 27:37 (NASB)

Now to the King eternal, immortal, invisible, the only God, be honour and glory forever and ever. Amen.

1 Timothy 1:17 (NASB)

[15]which He will bring about at the proper time--He who is the blessed and only Sovereign, the King of kings and Lord of lords,

1 Timothy 6:15 (NASB)

"These will wage war against the Lamb, and the Lamb will overcome them, because He is Lord of lords and King of kings, and those who are with Him are the called and chosen and faithful."

Revelation 17:14 (NASB)

[13]"I kept looking in the night visions, And behold, with the clouds of Heaven One like a (Son of Man was coming, And He came up to the Ancient of Days And was presented before Him. [14]"And to Him was given dominion, Glory and a kingdom, That all the peoples, nations and men of every language Might serve Him His dominion is an everlasting dominion Which will not pass away; And His kingdom is one Which will not be destroyed.

Daniel 7:13-14 (NASB)

[15]From His mouth comes a sharp sword, so that with it He may strike down the nations, and He will rule them with a rod of iron; and He treads the wine press of the fierce wrath of God, the Almighty. 16And on His robe and on His thigh He has a name written, "KING OF KINGS, AND LORD OF LORDS."

Revelation 19:15-16 (NASB)

And he was saying, "Jesus, remember me when You come in Your kingdom!"

Luke 23:42 (NASB)

***6So when they had come together, they were asking Him, saying, "Lord, is it at
this time You are restoring the kingdom to Israel?" 7He said to them, "It is not
for you to know times or epochs which the Father has fixed by His own
authority;***

Acts 1:6-7 (NASB)

***29"Brethren, I may confidently say to you regarding the patriarch David that
he both died and was buried, and his tomb is with us to this day. 30"And so,
because he was a prophet and knew that God had sworn to him with an oath to
seat one of his descendants on his throne, 31he looked ahead and spoke of the
resurrection of the Christ, that He was neither abandoned to hades, nor did His
flesh suffer decay. 32"This Jesus God raised up again, to which we are all
witnesses.***

Acts 2:29-32 (NASB)

***4Then I saw thrones, and they sat on them, and judgment was given to them And
I saw the souls of those who had been beheaded because of their testimony of
Jesus and because of the word of God, and those who had not worshiped the
beast or his image, and had not received the mark on their forehead and on their
hand; and they came to life and reigned with Christ for a thousand years. 5The
rest of the dead did not come to life until the thousand years were completed.
This is the first resurrection. 6Blessed and holy is the one who has a part in the
first resurrection; over these the second death has no power, but they will be
priests of God and of Christ and will reign with Him for a thousand years.***

Revelation 20:4-6 (NASB)

Conclusion

I have set out above a fairly thorough list of the basic truths that we need to believe and understand to be able to meaningfully put our trust in Jesus Christ and rely on Him to be our Saviour. Obviously, each of these things can be studied in much greater detail, as they are deep and complex issues.

Yet, at the same time they are also simple truths which can be accepted by a small child. God will judge you and deal with you according to your level of understanding, ability, age and experience. If you are a small child then less will be expected of you. But if you are an adult then God will expect you to seek to understand these facts properly so that you can fully put your trust in the Lord Jesus Christ.

If some of these basic essentials do not make sense to you, or you have a problem believing some of them, then ask God to open your mind and to give you the understanding, knowledge or faith that you need. Then start reading the Bible every day.

If you do your part, God will help you and give you the understanding that you need. However, do it with humility. Don't have the self-important and patronising attitude that you will *"sit in judgment"* on God's Word, deciding which parts of it you *"agree with"* and which parts you don't.

Instead approach it with respect, aiming to learn from it. If you approach the Bible with a childlike and humble heart, wanting to learn from it, not to criticize it, then the Bible will open up to you in an amazing way. You will find yourself able to understand it and to believe it.

So, if a man does not have faith then he can get it. And, it is his duty to set about getting it. The way that we get that faith is through reading and studying God's written Word, the Bible:

Consequently, faith comes from hearing the message, and the message is heard through the word of Christ.

Romans 10:17 (NIV)

How to get faith if you don't yet have it

The apostle Paul is realistic enough to talk about the problem of how a person can come to believe or have faith if they do not believe already. In short, the answer he gives is that faith comes by hearing. That means by hearing the Word of God read out in public. Obviously, if you can read, faith also comes by reading the Word of God for yourself. Thus, if you have any difficulty in believing the essential ingredients of what needs to be believed, then set about seriously studying God's Word for yourself. Then faith will come to you.

Why not begin by reading the gospel of Mark? It is the shortest and simplest gospel. Then read the gospel of Luke. It is the only gospel which claims to be in chronological order. Then read the book of Acts, which is the continuation of Luke's gospel. It goes on from the crucifixion and resurrection of Jesus through the first thirty or so years of the early church to show how the church developed.

Then go back and read John's gospel and then Matthew's gospel. Each of these have very different styles, and were written for different audiences. Then look at Paul's letter to the Romans, which is very deep and concentrated teaching. Then just carry on right through the New Testament. Then go back to the Old Testament and read Genesis and Exodus so that you can understand better how the world was formed by God as our Creator.

You will see how sin came in to the world when "*the fall*" happened. That brought God's judgment upon us all, because we all share the same fallen nature as Adam and Eve. The remainder of the Old Testament then shows how God slowly set about creating and developing the nation of Israel. He did so in order that His son could come as our Saviour and Lord, through being born as a baby in the land of Israel.

If you do not already have the faith to honestly say that you understand and believe all these things and genuinely trust in the Lord Jesus Christ to save you, then do not pretend to have it. Instead, diligently set about getting that faith by asking God for it persistently. Pray to Him and ask Him sincerely to open your mind so as to be able to understand the Bible. That is a prayer that God will delight to answer.

Then, set about methodically reading the Bible with the right heart attitude and you will find that genuine saving faith will come to you. You will gain understanding, knowledge and faith when you approach God's Word in that sincere and teachable way. However, you won't get it if your heart is proud, casual or indifferent. God is a rewarder of those who *diligently* seek Him, but not of those who are flippant, lazy, brazen, or don't truly want to know.

But without faith it is impossible to please Him, for he who comes to God must believe that He is, and that He is a rewarder of those who diligently seek Him.
Hebrews 11:6 (NKJV)

So, be diligent and persistent. Set out to read and understand the whole Bible and to keep studying until genuine faith comes to you.

CHAPTER 16

STEP THREE IN DETAIL - BE BAPTISED IN WATER

15 ***And He said to them, "Go into all the world and preach the gospel to all creation. 16"He who has believed and has been baptized shall be saved; but he who has disbelieved shall be condemned.***

Mark 16:15-16 (NASB)

18And Jesus came up and spoke to them, saying, "All authority has been given to Me in Heaven and on earth. 19"Go therefore and make disciples of all the nations, baptizing them in the name of the Father and the Son and the Holy Spirit,

Matthew 28:18-19 (NASB)

For all of you who were baptized into Christ have clothed yourselves with Christ.
Galatians 3:27 (NASB)

Baptism, which corresponds to this, now saves you, not as a removal of dirt from the body but as an appeal to God for a clear conscience, through the resurrection of Jesus Christ,

1 Peter 3:21 (RSV)

And now why do you wait? Rise and be baptized, and wash away your sins, calling on his name.'

Acts 22: 16 (RSV)

The Bible clearly commands us not only to repent and believe, but to go further and be baptised in water as well. Even so, there are sincere and genuine people who hold different opinions about baptism in water and exactly how and when it should be done. I would want to try my hardest not to fall out with other people or to lose relationships based on disagreements about baptism. However, the Bible is quite clear about baptism in water, so I have a duty to be clear too.

I would urge you to look at what the Bible has to say about it and then put it into practice, rather than just fit in with what other people say, or what your particular church denomination says. When this book was at draft stage I showed it to many people to get comments and advice. To my surprise, a number of people immediately focused on baptism in water. They urged me not to emphasise it, or even mention it, as it is such a controversial subject.

I was taken aback by the strength of feeling. One said *"Why not just focus on the essentials?"* By that they meant repentance and believing (or faith). They implied that baptism in water is a minor side-issue or non-essential, though they did not go so far as to say that explicitly. They advised me that if I emphasised the need for baptism in water for believers, as opposed to infant baptism, then I would upset people and that they might then reject everything else, including what the Bible says on repentance and believing.

I saw the point they were making. But I could not in good conscience take their advice, even if my approach does mean that I will offend people. If I was to take their approach, where would it end? I might as well feel free to leave out, or tone down, any of the other uncomfortable things that the Bible says, and there is no shortage of those. I have no authority to rewrite or edit the Bible so as to make it less offensive or more marketable. Neither does anybody else.

The reason, therefore, that I have to include, and emphasise, baptism in water in this book is simply that the Bible does so. There is no other reason to do so. No other reason is needed. There is no getting around the fact that the Bible teaches the need for baptism in water for believers. That means those old enough to repent and believe for themselves. It is not for babies.

If the Bible taught infant baptism anywhere, even once, I would include it in this book and teach it myself. But it doesn't and I would challenge anybody to point to even one verse which supports it, even indirectly Likewise, if the Bible ever said *"baptism in water is purely optional"* then I would say that too, but it doesn't. Therefore, baptism for believers has to remain in this book, not because I believe in it, or because it is something I have done myself. It is in this book because it is in the Bible, and for no other reason.

Baptism means full immersion i.e. being submerged under the water

So, let us begin by looking at what baptism in water is. The word '*baptise*' simply means to completely dip something under water, in the same way that you would with a sheep dip. Thus a farmer when dipping his sheep is, in the literal sense of the Greek word, baptizing them. It means to completely submerge them beneath the water.

Strangely, the word baptise is the original Greek word. The reason we use the original Greek word rather than our own English words *submerge* or *immerse* is because at the time that the King James Bible was being translated, shortly before 1611, a fierce debate was raging about how baptism should be done.

Some felt that it should be by sprinkling with water on the head and that it should be done to babies. Others argued that it should be done only with those who are old enough to believe and decide to be baptised for themselves, and that it should be done by full immersion in water. Rather than offend either group the translators of the King James Bible chose simply to use the original Greek word '*baptizein*' as a transliteration. They just Anglicised the very Greek word itself, to create the word '*baptise*', without translating it at all. Then it was up to every man to give it whatever meaning that he believed it had. That was how the King James translators chose to get themselves out of a very tight corner.

There ought not to be any controversy over what the Greek word 'baptizein' means. Its meaning is totally clear and beyond any doubt. In fact, in 1860 a leading scholar, and Bible translator, Thomas J. Conant (1802 - 1891) was working on the translation of the American Standard Version (and the Revised Standard Version). He argued that we should stop using the words '*baptism*' and '*baptise*' altogether.

Instead he said that we should translate the original Greek words into English (i.e. '*submerge*' or '*immerse*') just as we do with all the rest of the words in the Bible. Thus, he wanted to simply translate it as '*submerge*' or '*immerse*' every time the Greek word '*baptizein*' was in the text. That was clearly the right approach but he could not get the committees to accept what he said. It was too controversial for them.

Their reasons for not taking this obviously correct step were presumably the same as with the translators of the King James Bible in 1611. They feared a backlash of criticism from all those people whose denominational tradition was to practise baptism by sprinkling with water. The reason that is done is simply because the person being 'baptised' is only a baby and would not react well to being dipped under the water.

So, the error of baptising babies led on, for practical reasons, to the error of sprinkling rather than submerging. It was not done because the Bible says so, because it doesn't. So, Thomas Conant left the translation committee and wrote a book *called 'The meaning and use of baptizein'*. In that book he gives 236 examples of the use of the Greek word '*baptizein*' in both the New Testament and secular Greek literature. In fact he chose every instance where the word was ever used in the whole New Testament and in all surviving secular Greek literature.

He found, without any exceptions whatsoever, that it always meant 'submerge or immerse'. That is to plunge someone or something entirely under the water. For example it was used to refer to a ship sinking in the sea and so forth. In the whole of Greek literature of any kind there is no other use ever made of that word. Doesn't that settle it? If so, what are we doing sprinkling people's foreheads with water? It is entirely unbiblical.

So, for example, the way that we ought to have translated Mark 16:16 would be:"He who has believed and has been *submerged in water* shall be saved...." If we translated 'baptizein' like that, as we ought to, there being no valid reason not to, then it would make the meaning unmistakable. Instead of this it is being obscured.

Baptism is for believers, not for babies

Moreover, if we look at what actually happened in the first century, from the early years of the Church, through to the end of the book of Acts, we can see that baptism was solely for believers who could decide for themselves. It was not for babies. Likewise earlier, the baptism that John the Baptist gave was usually in a river. People would go into the river Jordan and they would bend down into the water by themselves and become completely submerged. John the Baptist did not do it for them. They baptised themselves, though John was present, as were the crowds as well. It was not done to infants.

Also, within Judaism, long before John the Baptist, great importance was placed on ritual washing. That involved going into a large bath called a *'mikhvah'* in which you submerged yourself to indicate your repentance and to symbolize your cleansing from sin. Likewise, this ritual washing was not done to babies, but only by those old enough to decide for themselves. That is the background concerning Jewish ritual baptism and the baptism of John.

We should keep that background in mind when considering how Christian baptism in water was later practised during the period of the book of Acts. These earlier Jewish forms of baptism and the baptism of John the Baptist *were never done to babies*. It was always by full immersion under the water and only for believers. Therefore that was the model for Christian baptism in water.

I must emphasise however, that when the New Testament speaks about baptism in water it is speaking about being baptised in, or into, the name of the Father, the Son and the Holy Spirit. It is *not* the same as the earlier baptism of John the Baptist, which was purely a baptism of repentance from sin. John's baptism was given as a preparation for the arrival of the Messiah, Jesus Christ, whose ministry was shortly due to begin. Neither is John's baptism the same thing as the long established practice of baptism in a mikhvah bath that was widely practiced within Judaism for ritual cleansing purposes.

To be baptised in the name of the Father, Son and Holy Spirit means to be openly identified with the Lord Jesus, as His disciple. That, of course, involves repenting towards God the Father and believing in the Lord Jesus too. It is also about openly and publicly declaring that you are now His follower, as a prelude to receiving the Holy Spirit. That usually occurred immediately after baptism in water. Christian baptism in water is also a symbolic act. It means that we identify with Jesus' death as we go down into the water:

[3]Or don't you know that all of us who were baptized into Christ Jesus were baptized into his death? [4]We were therefore buried with him through baptism into death in order that, just as Christ was raised from the dead through the glory of the Father, we too may live a new life.

Romans 6:3-4 (NIV)

Baptism in water also visually demonstrates our repentance and signifies the washing away of our sins through publicly putting our trust Jesus Christ and identifying ourselves with His sacrificial death on our behalf:

having been buried with Him in baptism, in which you were also raised up with Him through faith in the working of God, who raised Him from the dead.

Colossians 2:12 (NASB)

[1]Therefore if you have been raised up with Christ, keep seeking the things above, where Christ is, seated at the right hand of God. [2]Set your mind on the things above, not on the things that are on earth. [3]For you have died and your life is hidden with Christ in God.

Colossians 3:1-3 (NASB)

Baptism therefore symbolizes a number of things, all of which are important. One of its most important meanings is that the *"old self"* or the carnal, fleshly, sinful, self-centred person you have always been up to this point, is symbolically put to death and *"buried":*

[12]having been buried with him in baptism and raised with him through your faith in the power of God, who raised him from the dead. [13]When you were dead in your sins and in the uncircumcision of your sinful nature, God made you alive with Christ. He forgave us all our sins, [14]having cancelled the written code, with its regulations, that was against us and that stood opposed to us; he took it away, nailing it to the cross.

Colossians 2:12-14 (NIV)

Apostle Paul goes further in his letter to the Romans and refers to this concept of the old self or the old man being "crucified" with Christ:

[6]knowing this, that our old self was crucified with Him, in order that our body of sin might be done away with, so that we would no longer be slaves to sin;

Romans 6:6 (NASB)

Therefore, when we are baptised in water we are symbolically identifying ourselves with Jesus in His death. It is as if our old self, the sinful person we have been, is put on a cross alongside Jesus to be identified with Him, even in His crucifixion. The symbolism involved in the act of being baptised in water is very important. Our baptism is meant to be a crucial turning point in our lives. It produces big changes and cuts us off from our rebellious, sinful, unbelieving, non-Christian past.

Paul is speaking of this in Colossians 2 and Romans 6 above. So, as we go down under the water in Christian baptism, we are to ask God to cut us off from the "*old man*" or *"old self"*, i.e. our sinful, carnal nature which has been used to keep us in bondage to sin for so many years. We are also to ask God to give us a fresh start as a new person or a *"new creation"* in Christ:

[17]Therefore, if anyone is in Christ, he is a new creation; the old has gone, the new has come!

2 Corinthians 5:17 (NIV)

We are also described by Paul in Galatians 3 as having *"put on Christ"*. It is as if He was a garment that we could wear:

[26]For you are all sons of God through faith in Christ Jesus. [27]For all of you who were baptized into Christ have clothed yourselves with Christ.

Galatians 3:26-27 (NASB)

Though the symbolism in baptism is important, it is far more than just symbolic. God will truly cut you off from, and set you free from, a lot of bad things from your past as your old self symbolically *"dies"* in the water of baptism. Many of the problems, sins, addictions and hang-ups that Christians are plagued by could be avoided, or reduced, if they were properly baptised. Look how strongly apostle Peter puts it when he refers to baptism in this next passage. He says ".... *baptism now saves you....* "

[20]who once were disobedient, when the patience of God kept waiting in the days of Noah, during the construction of the ark, in which a few, that is, eight persons, were brought safely through the water. [21]Corresponding to that, baptism now saves you--not the removal of dirt from the flesh, but an appeal to God for a good conscience--through the resurrection of Jesus Christ,

1 Peter 3:20-21 (NASB)

Peter is using the word *'baptism'* as a collective word to embody and represent all the steps that are needed in order to be saved. It must be so, because he would otherwise be saying that baptism alone is what saves us and that is clearly not true. The same happens elsewhere in the Bible where the single word *'repent'* or *'believe'* is, likewise, used as a form of shorthand to stand for all the steps combined.

However, even though Peter is obviously using the word 'baptism' to stand for and to include within it all the other steps, i.e. repentance and faith, that come before baptism, it still has to be faced that he is including baptism within the whole process of being saved. We certainly can't say that Peter is minimising the significance or importance of baptism.

Neither can these verses be safely ignored by those who want to argue that baptism is a non-essential detail that comes after we are saved. We need to raise the status of baptism and see it as a key part of the whole process of being saved. Baptism in water is in the Bible, and it is emphasised, for a reason. It is meant to benefit us and to have a real and lasting impact. We cannot safely leave it out of Christianity or change it to become, instead, something which we do to babies.

We must never forget that Jesus commanded us to be baptised. It is not optional.

Apart from anything else, it is a matter of obedience to what the Bible says. Jesus *commanded* us to be baptised in water. That instruction was repeated within the New Testament many times. There can be no doubt that we are commanded to be baptised in water. Therefore Christian water baptism ought really to be treated as a part of repenting, believing in the Lord Jesus Christ, and putting our trust in Him.

It is the way that we openly declare and demonstrate that we have done so. We are saying publicly that we have cut ourselves off from our old life of sin and rebellion and begun a new life. However, baptism is much more than just a symbol. It is really important, and perhaps even essential, for our salvation. At any rate, I have no authority to say that it is *not* essential. Neither does anybody else. I personally would not want to ignore the command that Jesus has given for us to get baptised in water.

As for the question of *when* to get baptised in water, there are different viewpoints on this. Many churches today have baptism classes. People are taken through a series of lessons on what the Gospel is and what they need to believe and why. At the end of that course they are then all baptised. I do not necessarily criticize that. If that is done sincerely, then I am sure that God will bless it and use it. However, that is not the way that baptism was practiced in the early church.

In the Bible, as soon as a person made the decision to repent, believe in Jesus and follow Him, they got baptised *there and then*, without waiting. The person would simply look for a river, a lake, a mikhvah bath or the sea and go immediately to fully immerse himself in water. This was to demonstrate in public the fact of his conversion and the start of his new life trusting in Jesus Christ. More importantly, it was to obey what Jesus commanded. Today many of us tend to be very casual about all this, whereas they took their conversion, and its public proclamation, very seriously in the first century. They regarded it as a major life-changing event, which needed to be visibly and publicly proclaimed:

[34]The eunuch answered Philip and said, "Please tell me, of whom does the prophet say this? Of himself or of someone else?" [35]Then Philip opened his mouth, and beginning from this Scripture he preached Jesus to him. [36]As they went along the road they came to some water; and the eunuch said, "Look! Water! What prevents me from being baptized?" [37]And Philip said, "If you believe with all your heart, you may." And he answered and said, "I believe that Jesus Christ is the Son of God."[38]And he ordered the chariot to stop; and they both went down into the water, Philip as well as the eunuch, and he baptized him.

Acts 8:34-38 (NASB)

In this passage Philip explains the Gospel to this man from Ethiopia, and he accepts it and believes in Jesus Christ. He then sees some water and asks to be baptised immediately. Evidently, Philip approved of that. That was the normal way to do it. We would do well to adopt this. Apostle Paul himself was baptised very quickly after he became a believer:

[17]So Ananias departed and entered the house, and after laying his hands on him said, "Brother Saul, the Lord Jesus, who appeared to you on the road by which you were coming, has sent me so that you may regain your sight and be filled with the Holy Spirit." [18]And immediately there fell from his eyes something like scales, and he regained his sight, and he got up and was baptized;

Acts 9:17-18 (NASB)

Indeed Ananias, who took care of Paul when he was first converted, told Paul that there was no need to wait to get baptised:

[12]"A certain Ananias, a man who was devout by the standard of the Law, and well spoken of by all the Jews who lived there, [13]came to me, and standing near said to me, 'Brother Saul, receive your sight!' And at that very time I looked up at him. [14]"And he said, 'The God of our fathers has appointed you to know His will and to see the Righteous One and to hear an utterance from His mouth. [15]'For you will be a witness for Him to all men of what you have seen and heard. [16]'Now why do you delay? Get up and be baptized, and wash away your sins, calling on His name.'

Acts 22:12-16 (NASB)

Likewise, we see from Acts chapter 18 that the people in Corinth believed and were baptised. The clear implication is that they got baptised straight away, as soon as they came to repent and believe:

[8]Crispus, the leader of the synagogue, believed in the Lord with all his household, and many of the Corinthians when they heard were believing and being baptized.

Acts 18:8 (NASB)

Apostle Paul operated in the same way when he baptised the Philippian jailer immediately after the man was converted:

[31]They said, "Believe in the Lord Jesus, and you will be saved, you and your household." [32]And they spoke the word of the Lord to him together with all who were in his house. [33]And he took them that very hour of the night and washed their wounds, and immediately he was baptized, he and all his household.

Acts 16:31-33 (NASB)

The practice of baptizing babies is entirely man made and unbiblical

I should mention here that some people have actually used the passage above about the Philippian jailor as a basis for supporting the practice of infant baptism. They do so by arguing that if this man and *"all his household"* were baptised, then that, presumably, may have included children and even babies. Therefore they argue that we should baptise babies. However, that is based on extraordinarily weak logic. It is pure supposition and is no proper basis for creating the practice of baptising babies, which is not found anywhere in the Bible.

More importantly, we can actually prove, categorically, that the Philippian jailor's family did *not* include any babies. I say that because we are told in the very next verse that his whole household were not only baptized, but also *believed*, which babies cannot do:

[34] And he brought them into his house and set food before them, and rejoiced greatly, having believed in God with his whole household.

Acts 16:34 (NASB)

So, whatever ages his family members were, the one thing we know for sure is that they were all old enough to believe for themselves. Otherwise, the Bible would not say that they did so. God thinks of everything and I believe He deliberately included verse 34 in the chapter to demolish the false arguments which He knew people would later make in support of infant baptism, based on the earlier parts of chapter 16. It also illustrates how vital it is to read every verse in its full and proper context, so as not to misunderstand it.

In any event, the word translated *'household'* in the passage about the Philippian jailor would also include the employees or slaves that worked in his house. That was common practise in those days, especially for a man senior enough to be in charge of a jail. So, applying the same flawed logic used by those who support infant baptism, we could equally seek to use that passage to argue today for the compulsory baptism of our staff or employees!

A far better way to understand the reference to his household is simply to conclude that, following his own conversion, he went and told the Gospel message to all his family and even his slaves and employees. Then they quickly believed and repented and were eager to be baptised in water, of their own free will, just as he had been.

Remember, those relatives and/or slaves/staff had also got apostle Paul with them. They may well have already heard Paul explain the Gospel earlier as well, while in the prison. So, the key point is that we have to assume that each member of that household made a decision of their own to get baptised in water. There is nothing in that passage, or in any other passage in the Bible, to support the idea of anybody baptising a baby. Every baptism in the Bible involves a person old enough to decide for themselves.

While we are on this theme of infant baptism, it may also assist to look at another passage which is sometimes used, or rather misused, to give the false impression that the Bible supports the baptizing of babies. I refer to the passage about Cornelius the Gentile in Acts chapter 10. He was converted, in a very unusual manner, or sequence, because he was baptized in the Holy Spirit before being baptized in water. However, the operative point, for our purposes in this chapter, is that he was baptized in water, and so were all those who were with him, after listening to apostle Peter's preaching:

43 Of Him all the prophets bear witness that through His name everyone who believes in Him receives forgiveness of sins." 44 While Peter was still speaking these words, the Holy Spirit fell upon all those who were listening to the message. 45 All the circumcised believers who came with Peter were amazed, because the gift of the Holy Spirit had been poured out on the Gentiles also. 46 For they were hearing them speaking with tongues and exalting God. Then Peter answered, 47 "Surely no one can refuse the water for these to be baptized who have received the Holy Spirit just as we did, can he?" 48 And he ordered them to be baptized in the name of Jesus Christ. Then they asked him to stay on for a few days.

Acts 10:43-48 (NASB)

Strangely, although this passage makes no mention whatsoever of infants, it has been squeezed very hard by some people to make it fit that purpose and to help justify infant baptism. However, just by looking back earlier in the same chapter, one can again demonstrate that that interpretation is impossible.

If we look at verse two (see below) we see that not only Cornelius, but also his household, *"feared God"*. Clearly, if they were old enough to be able to do that, then they were not babies, or even young children. So, the argument, which was already feeble to begin with, evaporates completely:

Now there was a man at Caesarea named Cornelius, a centurion of what was called the Italian cohort, ² a devout man and one who feared God with all his household, and gave many alms to the Jewish people and prayed to God continually.

Acts 10:1-2 (NASB)

The main origin of infant baptism is that it comes from a misunderstanding of circumcision. Jewish baby boys were circumcised on the eighth day in order that they could be physically marked as members of the Jewish race. It also meant that they could become partakers in the promise made to the physical descendants of Abraham, Isaac and Jacob.

However, those particular aspects of the promises made to Abraham, Isaac and Jacob were only available, both then and now, to *Jewish* people, not to Gentiles. Baptism is not the same as circumcision and it is a major mistake to confuse the two things. Circumcision is not a basis for infant baptism. Neither is it a precedent for how, or when, baptism should be done.

By getting baptised in the biblical way a person starts the Christian life well. There is a definite cutting off from the old life and an obvious start of a new life. That helps people to avoid problems of half-heartedness, confusion and compromise, where a person does not want to be known openly as a Christian. Baptism in water is an unmistakable event. It means that you are publicly and decisively revealed to be a Christian. There is no hiding it. That is a good thing and helps you to make a strong and clean start in your new Christian life.

Look at the Bible for yourself and try to forget, for a moment, everything that people have ever told you about baptism. Then form your own conclusions about baptism in water solely from what is written there. As I engage in that exercise, I can see no other way of doing baptism in water than the way that it was practiced in the first century, namely full immersion in water. And it should be immediately after a person repents, not months or years later.

A summary of where many churches have gone wrong on the subject of baptism in water

In the majority of churches baptism in water is handled in the opposite way from what God intended. Let us examine the various ingredients in turn and compare what the Bible says with what we generally see happening:

Biblical baptism:	**How most churches actually do baptism**:
1) full immersion under the water	1) sprinkling with water
2) done *by* people old enough to believe and repent for themselves	2) done *to* babies too young to understand anything
3) done as part of the process of becoming a Christian	3) done to make a baby into a Christian. That is baptism *by itself* is seen as giving salvation to the baby, which is not true. Thus multitudes of nominal Christians assume that they are Christians and are saved, just because their parents had them baptised. I was speaking to a girl some time ago called Alexia who told me she was a Christian. I asked her when she had become a Christian and she replied, perfectly seriously, *"When I was baptised as a baby"*. She really thought that event had saved her.
4) done by a person immediately after they have repented and believed	4) done either: *to* a person as a baby, many years before they repent/believe OR done *by* a person long after they have repented and believed. It is seen as non-urgent - just whenever you get round to it.
5) always done by every new believer and considered to be obviously essential	5) not always done at all - very much an optional extra for those who want it.

I feel I ought to add another point to address a practice which has become increasingly popular, but which is problematic. That is the idea that before getting baptised a person is expected, or even required, to stand with a microphone and '*give their testimony*' to all those present. In larger churches, that could mean addressing hundreds of people.

It is not that there is anything wrong with doing this in itself. On the contrary, giving one's testimony is a good thing. It enables the Gospel to be proclaimed to any unbelievers in the audience. It also helps those present to gauge whether the person getting baptised really believes and repents.

However, there is a problem, and even a danger, with this approach. Firstly, this practice is not biblical. That is, there is no indication in the book of Acts, or in any of the letters, that any new convert was ever required to give his testimony or demonstrate his bona fides in any other way before being baptised. Doing so might bring some advantages. But the point is *it isn't what the apostles did.* Moreover, I believe there were good reasons why they didn't do this and those reasons still apply today.

One problem that can arise where a succession of people come to the lectern, one after the other, to give their testimony, is that it feeds pride. It is evident that for some of them it can turn into a competitive performance in which they are anxious not be outdone by the others. Therefore, instead of them making simple, sincere statements, one sometimes hears detailed accounts which draw too much attention to the one giving the testimony rather than to God or the Gospel.

So, for those who are already prone to pride and exhibitionism, this practice of requiring them to give their testimony publicly, especially to a large audience, can become a temptation which may cause them to stumble. Conversely, for those who are shy by nature, or who are less educated or less articulate, the prospect of being baptised in front of a large audience can come to be seen as an ordeal. It can make them wary or even afraid of being baptized at all.

There are people who have refrained from being baptized, or have put it off until later, because they dread the prospect of having to speak in public, and especially to have to speak about themselves. I know this because they have told me. This second problem is actually my main concern.

Of course, if Jesus or the apostles had commanded us to give our testimony in public before being baptised, then there could be no argument on the point. We would all need to do it, whatever we might feel about it. But they neither commanded it nor practiced it themselves. It is a wholly man-made practice, as indeed is so much else of what has come to be seen as normal church practice.

We have no right to impose our own ideas, traditions and preferences on other people and, least of all, to make such things appear to be an essential part of the process of becoming a Christian. It is one thing to *allow* people to give their testimony if they *wish* to do so. But it is quite another thing to *require* it of them.

Indeed, I believe that it is not wise even to allow the practice to become the norm. If we do that, there is effectively no alternative but for new believers to go along with it, even if it is not formally insisted upon by a church. Traditions and familiar practices can easily become so rigid that they might as well be made into rules, because the reality is that they are seen as such.

That said, some churches are actually going so far as to make it part of their written constitution or rules that every person being baptised *must* give their testimony. I came across this recently in the case of a particular evangelical church. My own conviction is that man-made rules such as that, which do not come from the Bible, should not be imposed on people, notwithstanding any advantages they might be felt to offer.

We should not require, or even ask, people to do anything more than the Bible requires, especially in relation to such a crucially important issue as baptism. The apostles kept it very simple and so should we. For even one person to avoid getting baptized due to shyness or a sense of social or academic inferiority is a tragedy. Yet I fear that there are many for whom that is the case.

So, if that applies to you and you are choosing to avoid or delay water baptism because you don't want to give your testimony to a large audience, then be reassured. You do not *need* to do that if you prefer not to. You can just be baptised at home in the bath, or at a swimming pool, and with only a handful of people present, if that is what you feel is right for you.

The importance of baptism in water from the Devil's perspective

It is odd that so much of the Church has got baptism so very wrong. If there were to be errors you would ordinarily expect them to be randomly spread out, so that in some ways we might operate biblically and in other ways not.

However, the reality is that with baptism most churches tend to get just about everything completely wrong. In fact most churches do the exact opposite of what God says on almost every aspect of baptism.

That cannot be a mere coincidence. It has clearly been orchestrated and arranged on purpose. It shows all the signs of being a satanically coordinated plot or scheme. It looks very much like the Devil has gone out of his way to try to make sure that baptism is messed about with. The Devil wants it to be either done wrongly, or not done at all.

That emphasis on undermining baptism suggests that the Devil considers baptism in water to be very important. Why would he go to so much trouble to deceive us and to confuse our thinking and our practice on the whole subject of baptism if it wasn't vitally important?

Indirectly we can take encouragement from the fact that this is an area where there is so much false teaching and error. It can help to convince us that baptism really matters to God and is extremely useful and necessary for us.

CHAPTER 17

STEP FOUR IN DETAIL - 'RECEIVE' OR BE 'BAPTISED IN' THE HOLY SPIRIT

21 So Jesus said to them again, "Peace be with you; as the Father has sent Me,
I also send you." 22 And when He had said this, He breathed on them and said
to them, "Receive the Holy Spirit.

John 20:21-22 (NASB)

5 for John baptized with water, but you will be baptized with the Holy Spirit not many days from now."

Acts 1:5 (NASB)

8 but you will receive power when the Holy Spirit has come upon you; and you shall be My witnesses both in Jerusalem, and in all Judea and Samaria, and even to the remotest part of the earth."

Acts 1:8 (NASB)

16 But this is what was uttered through the prophet Joel:
17 "'And in the last days it shall be, God declares,
that I will pour out my Spirit on all flesh,
and your sons and your daughters shall prophesy,
and your young men shall see visions,
and your old men shall dream dreams;
18 even on my male servants and female servants
in those days I will pour out my Spirit, and they shall prophesy.

Acts 2:16-18 (ESV)

38 Peter said to them, "Repent, and each of you be baptized in the name of Jesus
Christ for the forgiveness of your sins; and you will receive the gift of the Holy
Spirit. 39 For the promise is for you and your children and for all who are far
off, as many as the Lord our God will call to Himself."

Acts 2:38-39 (NASB)

31 And when they had prayed, the place where they had gathered together was shaken, and they were all filled with the Holy Spirit and began to speak the word of God with boldness.

Acts 4:31 (NASB)

14 Now when the apostles in Jerusalem heard that Samaria had received the word
of God, they sent them Peter and John, 15 who came down and prayed for them
that they might receive the Holy Spirit. 16 For He had not yet fallen upon any of

them; they had simply been baptized in the name of the Lord Jesus. [17]Then they began laying their hands on them, and they were receiving the Holy Spirit.

Acts 8:14-17 (NASB)

[17] So Ananias departed and entered the house, and after laying his hands on him said, "Brother Saul, the Lord Jesus, who appeared to you on the road by which you were coming, has sent me so that you may regain your sight and be filled with the Holy Spirit."

Acts 9:17 (NASB)

[15] And as I began to speak, the Holy Spirit fell upon them just as He did upon us at the beginning. [16] And I remembered the word of the Lord, how He used to say, 'John baptized with water, but you will be baptized with the Holy Spirit.'[17] Therefore if God gave to them the same gift as He gave to us also after believing in the Lord Jesus Christ, who was I that I could stand in God's way?"

Acts 11:15-17 (NASB)

[5] and hope does not disappoint, because the love of God has been poured out within our hearts through the Holy Spirit who was given to us.

Romans 5:5 (NASB)

[21]Now He who establishes us with you in Christ and anointed us is God, [22]who also sealed us and gave us the Spirit in our hearts as a pledge.

2 Corinthians 1:21-22 (NASB)

Pursue love, yet desire earnestly spiritual gifts, but especially that you may prophesy.

1 Corinthians 14:1 (NASB)

[14] Guard, through the Holy Spirit who dwells in us, the treasure which has been entrusted to you.

2 Timothy 1:14 (NASB)

This chapter is longer and more complicated than I would have wished, due to the many unbiblical traditions that need to be tackled in addition to looking at what the Bible says.

In the other chapters in this book I have got straight down to business and have simply set out what the Bible says. That is the basis on which we have looked at issues like our sin, God's holiness, His impending judgment, Hell, the Lake of Fire, our urgent need to repent and what it means to believe. In each of these things I have looked at what the Bible says and have not spent much time looking at the unbiblical traditions of the various churches, or at what men say.

However, when it comes to the issue of 'receiving', being 'baptised in', or 'filled with', the Holy Spirit, it is going to take longer. That is because, as well as looking at what the Bible says, we are also going to have to examine a number of different things that churches have taught which differ from what the Bible says. These manmade ideas and practices cause widespread confusion and make it much harder for this subject even to be discussed at all, let alone understood accurately.

The time spent examining and disproving each of these unbiblical ideas and practices will perhaps be tiresome to those who are new to Christianity and who have no church background. However, those who have spent some time in churches will have come across one of more of these errors and been confused or misled by them. Therefore they will benefit from looking at them.

What makes things even harder is that the whole subject of the baptism in the Holy Spirit, and in particular the use of spiritual gifts, tends to arouse intense feelings. Therefore few people seem to be able to talk calmly about these issues. The norm is to become angry and closed-minded and to condemn anybody who does not agree with the stance taken by one's own denomination.

So, in this chapter I will need to spend a disproportionate amount of time looking at what other people think, or allege, as well as looking at what the Bible says. We shall also have to look at alternative views on the meaning of words, and also as to what happened, or didn't happen, in the churches that are written about in in the Book of Acts.

We shall even have to consider whether the gifts of the Holy Spirit have entirely ceased, at some point between the first and fifth centuries, such that they are not meant for us at all. That is absolutely not my view, but I shall still need to address it, because it is so widely held and has done so much to undermine the Church and to stifle the work of the Holy Spirit.

An explanation as to why, in this chapter, I use the long and cumbersome phrase "*receive or be baptised in*" the Holy Spirit.

You might be wondering why I have used, and continue to use, such a long, cumbersome phrase as "*receive, or be baptised in, the Holy Spirit.*" I shall explain it more fully below but, for now, let me say that it is because I want to avoid giving the impression that 'receiving' the Holy Spirit is different from being 'baptised in' or even 'filled with' the Holy Spirit. My own belief is that each of these phrases, and a number of others too, are used in the Bible to describe the very same event or experience.

Thus, if I was to choose only one phrase and use that, by itself, to the exclusion of the others, it may give the impression to some readers that I am seeking to draw a distinction between them. It is actually likely to do so, because that is exactly what many people do.

However, as I shall explain later, I take the view that the expressions 'receiving the' Holy Spirit, being 'baptised in' the Holy Spirit, being 'filled with the' Holy Spirit, and others too, are alternative phrases used in the Bible for the same experience. That is one of the things that I will seek to prove below.

The first, and biggest, problem is that so many people get their beliefs about the baptism in the Holy Spirit from men's ideas and denominational tradition rather than from the Bible.

The confusion, misinformation and controversy that arises so frequently in this area occurs because most people get their beliefs about the Holy Spirit from their own *experiences,* or from what they have been *told* or have *seen others doing,* rather than *from the Bible.* The effect of all that is that there is probably more error, conflict and confusion generated on this topic than on any other.

It is ironic that the Third Person of the Trinity, the Holy Spirit, should be the object of such contention and intolerance, given the gentleness which is the hallmark of His character. So, this is a controversial topic, and many leaders therefore completely avoid teaching about the Holy Spirit, for that very reason.

However, we cannot do that, because the Bible repeatedly speaks about the importance of receiving or being filled with or being baptised in the Holy Spirit. This event or experience is presented as a crucial part of the process of becoming a Christian. Therefore it is not something which we can ignore, or even downplay.

Accordingly, how can anyone leave this subject of the baptism in the Holy Spirit out of their preaching of the Gospel, even if the topic is controversial? We have no alternative but to present all of what the Bible says, as honestly and clearly as possible, even at the risk of offending people.

Furthermore, in writing about receiving the Holy Spirit, whilst I will sometimes refer to my own personal experiences, I will not rely on those experiences to define or prove anything. I will try to base everything I say solely on what the Bible says. My own experiences are no authority for anything. Neither is anybody else's experience, nor the traditional teaching of anybody's denomination. The Bible must be our only authority for any conclusions we arrive at with any doctrine or practice. That is just as true when we are discussing the baptism in the Holy Spirit as with any other issue or doctrine.

If we make the mistake of relying on our own or other people's experience, or on our traditions or denominational background, we will end up reading the Bible through a lens or filter, just as we might attach to a camera. That filter will distort our understanding and we will then *read into* the Bible whatever we already think, or have been told, even when it's *not* there on the page.

We will also edit out and ignore anything which contradicts our existing views, even when it clearly *is* on the page. We usually don't even realise we are doing any of that unconscious editing.

That is how powerful pre-existing ideas can be. They are so blinding they can cause us to miss a barn door from ten yards away, even when it is clearly there on the page. Without ever saying so out loud, we will tend to assume that our own existing ideas, traditions and practices must obviously be right.

Therefore, it will be assumed that anything which challenges our pre-conceived ideas must obviously be wrong and it is then automatically screened out, before it even registers. Let that not be true of you. Take a different approach, which very few people take.

Try asking yourself: *"Where am I getting my ideas from? Are they from the Bible or from somewhere else?"* Having asked yourself that, why not examine again, completely afresh, the question of receiving, or being baptised in, the Holy Spirit?

Look very closely at what the Bible actually says, and at what the first century disciples did, rather than at your own tradition. Then ask yourself "*Is what I do and think in line with Scripture, or am I just copying what I've seen other people doing and assuming it must be right?"* Above all, make sure you carefully check my views, your own views, and every other person's views, against what the Bible says.

As you do so, pray for God to protect you from any errors or manmade ideas and to show you what the Bible really means in this area. Then seek to form your own view, with God's help, of what the Bible actually teaches. Start from a blank sheet of paper and make an effort to put to one side every tradition and every belief or custom that you have ever been taught or have grown used to. That is very difficult and won't happen unless you are consciously seeking to do it.

Also, let us all try to approach this important subject of the Holy Spirit with gentleness and humility. Let's not attack each other if we disagree. You may find you disagree with me. That is alright, so long as your own belief has come from a thorough study of the Bible, rather than being a mere knee-jerk reaction to the fact that you are hearing something you're not used to, or which is not what your denomination does.

The exercise of spiritual gifts, and even the very discussion of the baptism in the Holy Spirit, are so controversial that they have been effectively banned by most churches.

Probably the main reason why there is so little understanding of the baptism in the Holy Spirit is that there is little or no teaching about this issue in most churches. Even discussion of it is rare, because it is seen as an acutely sensitive topic, about which people get extremely uptight, defensive and suspicious. There are a number of reasons for that.

It's partly due to bad teaching, which has caused many to accept, without question, that the gifts of the Holy Spirit ceased in the first century, or at some point afterwards, and are not meant for us today. It is also partly due to people's liking for manmade tradition, which causes most Christians to prefer to persist with whatever practices, or non-practices, they grew up with and are used to.

However, perhaps the strongest reason for the widespread rejection of the use of spiritual gifts, the baptism in the Holy Spirit, or even the supernatural as a whole, is that so many people have been appalled by demonic counterfeits. They have seen a lot of misguided, unbiblical and even crazy things being done by others.

Then, as a knee-jerk reaction to those counterfeits, they have rejected everything that is in any way supernatural, regardless of whether it is true or false. One can understand why people make that error, but the fact still remains that it is a terrible mistake.

Instead, the proper response to seeing false, unbiblical, demonic counterfeits of spiritual gifts is to ask oneself "*What is the authentic, biblical, God-given gift that is being counterfeited here*?" The point is that no currency forger produces fake £9 or $9 notes. They do not invent things for which there is no genuine article. Therefore they only ever produce forgeries of real notes.

Thus, the very fact that a forgery or counterfeit exists actually tells us that, somewhere else, there is something genuine which is being imitated. So, far from rejecting everything out of hand and throwing out the baby with the bath water, we should resolve even more firmly to seek diligently for the genuine. I would urge you to be wise enough to do that and also to be patient enough to persist until you find it, no matter how many false things you may have witnessed to date.

Why do we need to receive, or be baptised in, or filled with, the Holy Spirit?

Before we look at defining the baptism in the Holy Spirit, or at identifying exactly when it occurs, let's look briefly at *why* it occurs and what this event or experience is meant to produce or achieve. Receiving, or being baptised in, the Holy Spirit has a number of purposes, all of which are important:

a) It completes the process of becoming a Christian, which is consistently presented, in the Bible, as consisting of repenting, believing, being baptised in water and then receiving the Holy Spirit.

b) It is a seal and serves as an indication that God now recognises you as a genuine believer.

c) From that point on, the Holy Spirit makes available to you the many gifts of the Holy Spirit, sometimes called "*spiritual gifts*".

d) The Holy Spirit also helps us, over a long period of time, to grow into fruitful disciples of Jesus Christ through being *"sanctified"* or made holy. That involves growing within our characters the *"fruit of the Spirit"* i.e. the qualities of love, joy, peace, patience, kindness, goodness, faithfulness, gentleness and self-control. (See chapter 22 for more details on sanctification).

e) The Holy Spirit also guides you into the truth, which Jesus spoke of in John 16:13

f) The baptism in the Holy Spirit is also the means by which we receive the *power* to do the things that we are called to do.

Why are so many alternative phrases used in the Bible to refer to 'receiving', being 'filled with' or 'baptised in' the Holy Spirit? Do they all refer to exactly the same event, or are there any differences in meaning?

Have you ever made a list of all the different words and phrases used in the book of Acts and the New Testament letters to refer to the event, or experience, of receiving the Holy Spirit? There are actually several different phrases, including the following:

a) To 'receive' the Holy Spirit

b) To be 'baptised in' the Holy Spirit

c) To be 'filled with' the Holy Spirit

d) To have the Holy Spirit 'fall upon' you

e) To have the Holy Spirit 'come upon' you

f) To have the Holy Spirit 'given to us'

g) To “receive the gift of the Holy Spirit”

h) For the Holy Spirit to be ‘poured out’

Opinions differ widely as to whether these phrases are all synonyms and refer to exactly the same event or experience, or whether they have different meanings. It is beyond the scope of this short chapter to examine that complex question in any depth. Therefore, let me save time by moving directly to the conclusion that I have reached.

That is that these various phrases are used so inter-changeably in the Bible that it is impossible to build any convincing case for saying that they each have separate meanings. In short, I believe they all refer to the very same event or experience, which is meant to occur at conversion or at some point very shortly afterwards, usually on the same day.

As we have seen, the biblical model for becoming a Christian is that the four basic steps of repenting, believing, being baptised in water and then receiving (or being baptised in or filled with) the Holy Spirit all occurred in quick succession. Very often they all occurred on the same day. If they did not, it was seen as a departure from the norm and as being less than ideal. Yet, there are many people who hold strong views to the contrary.

Some believe that receiving the Holy Spirit is the inevitable and automatic result of repenting and believing and, therefore, that it occurs, quietly and imperceptibly, at the very moment of conversion. Others insist that being baptised in the Holy Spirit is a distinctly separate event from ‘receiving’ the Holy Spirit, and that it occurs later. They therefore refer to it as a ‘second blessing’.

However, my own conclusion is, firstly, that it is more biblical, and also more helpful, to see the receiving of the Holy Spirit and the baptism in the Holy Spirit as being one and the same. Secondly, it is always portrayed in the Book of Acts as a distinctly identifiable event, which is clearly noticeable to you yourself and to others. Thirdly, I believe that it needs to be seen as being part of the overall process of becoming a Christian, not as a separate and subsequent event, which we should expect to happen later.

Accordingly, it is right to expect that it will be a noticeable, or even an unmistakable, event and wrong to think of it as occurring automatically, invisibly, inaudibly and imperceptibly at the moment of conversion. That said, I believe that it is also wrong to assume that one must wait for this event, or prepare for it, on the basis that there must be a period of delay, while one ‘tarries’, as the Pentecostal phrase goes.

Some of the main schools of thought as to what it means to receive the Holy Spirit and as to whether that is, or isn't, the same as being baptised in the Holy Spirit.

I can only deal with these various beliefs very briefly because there are a number of them and to deal with them fully would take far too long and is outside the scope of this book. However, I can, at least introduce you to the basic ideas, so that you are aware of them and will not be surprised or puzzled if you come across them elsewhere. Then, once we have looked briefly at these different opinions and practices I will focus thereafter on what I believe the Bible actually says.

In particular, I will seek to focus on what the early Church did, in the Book of Acts and the letters. I say that because my strong conviction is that we are meant to do exactly what they did then, not to follow the traditions, customs and practices of whatever denomination we may be part of. Let me firstly set out, the main schools of thought, or approaches to the baptism in the Holy Spirit, that exist today, before going on to look at what, in my view, the Bible says:

a) 'Cessationism' – the belief that the baptism in the Holy Spirit, and the gifts of the Holy Spirit were only for the first century or, as others would say, for the first few centuries. Those who hold this view would include most of those who come from a Reformed tradition. They believe that, in every case, the Holy Spirit is 'received' automatically at conversion and that there are no separate or subsequent events, experiences or gifts. Thus they do not accept that any valid gifts of the Holy Spirit are in operation today. Many would therefore go so far as to say that anybody purporting to operate in any of the spiritual gifts is, by definition, either false or deluded or is operating with demonic assistance.

b) The belief that although everyone receives the Holy Spirit at conversion, automatically and imperceptibly, one is later 'baptised in' or 'filled with' the Holy Spirit as a distinctly identifiable, but entirely separate and subsequent, event or experience. It is at this later point that they believe the gifts of the Holy Spirit can then begin to operate. This is referred to as a "second blessing" and is the view taken by those who come from a Pentecostal or Charismatic background, all of whom believe that the gifts are for today.

c) Some groups who are within the broadly Pentecostal and Charismatic wings of the Church, do believe in the baptism in the Holy Spirit, and do seek to operate in spiritual gifts, but, regrettably, they do so in unbiblical ways. For example, they fail to follow the instructions and guidelines laid down in the New Testament, in particular those given by Paul in 1 Corinthians chapter 14 (See below). Whilst they may be operating in genuine spiritual gifts, such people act with immaturity and even carnality. Therefore, they may well be speaking or acting, some of the time, through their own selves, or in their own 'flesh', rather than under the anointing of the Holy Spirit. This may be because they are careless and/or disobedient. Alternatively, it may be that they are simply unaware of what the Bible says, due to lack of sound teaching, or even lack of any teaching at all.

d) Others are even more misguided and go even further in the wrong direction. Therefore, while purporting to believe in, and operate in, the gifts of the Holy Spirit, they may actually be operating under the power and influence of a demon. This is what I referred to earlier as a 'counterfeit' of the spiritual gifts. It is this group which has done most damage to the Church as a whole by discrediting the whole subject of the baptism in the Holy Spirit. Many then look upon the crazy and unbiblical behaviour or such people, and the false prophecies they make, and are put off the whole thing. Thus they reject the genuine because they have seen the false. Many a person has also been driven into the camp of the cessationists precisely because of the dreadful counterfeits which they have witnessed or heard about.

My own conclusions as to what it means to receive or be filled with or baptised in the Holy Spirit?

In this chapter I am going to seek to base everything I say on what the Bible says, not on my experiences or anybody's traditions or customs. Therefore, let's begin at the beginning and look at what Jesus said would happen to the disciples:

"But the Helper, the Holy Spirit, whom the Father will send in My name, He will teach you all things, and bring to your remembrance all that I said to you.
John 14:26 (NASB)

"When the Helper comes, whom I will send to you from the Father, that is the Spirit of truth who proceeds from the Father, He will testify about Me,
John 15:26 (NASB)

"But when He, the Spirit of truth, comes, He will guide you into all the truth; for He will not speak on His own initiative, but whatever He hears, He will speak; and He will disclose to you what is to come.
John 16:13 (NASB)

4 Gathering them together, He commanded them not to leave Jerusalem, but to wait for what the Father had promised, "Which," He said, "you heard of from Me; 5 for John baptized with water, but you will be baptized with the Holy Spirit not many days from now." 6 So when they had come together, they were asking Him, saying, "Lord, is it at this time You are restoring the kingdom to Israel?" 7 He said to them, "It is not for you to know times or epochs which the Father has fixed by His own authority; 8 but you will receive power when the

Holy Spirit has come upon you; and you shall be My witnesses both in Jerusalem, and in all Judea and Samaria, and even to the remotest part of the earth."

Acts1:4-8 (NASB)

Jesus made this last statement during the 40 days He spent with His disciples, after His resurrection, but before His ascension into Heaven. While Jesus was physically present on the Earth, His followers could receive Him into their homes. Jesus could literally be invited to dinner and He was, many times. However, since His ascension into Heaven, Jesus has not been physically present with us.

Therefore, from then on, the task of working in the life of each believer, to develop them into a mature disciple of Jesus Christ, has been transferred over to the Holy Spirit. He is now the main member of the Trinity who is empowering us and helping us to grow, become sanctified and be guided into the truth.

The Day of Pentecost - when the disciples were baptised in the Holy Spirit

When Jesus was present on the Earth in His physical body He did all of those things for His disciples Himself. So, during His earthly ministry, He did not ask the Holy Spirit to perform those roles. The new arrangement did not begin until some days after Jesus' ascension when, on the Day of Pentecost, (a Jewish feast) the Holy Spirit came upon the disciples in a dramatic way. This was the first time it happened, but it has been happening to Christians ever since, right up to today. Let's now look at how it began:

1 When the day of Pentecost had come, they were all together in one place. 2 And
suddenly there came from Heaven a noise like a violent rushing wind, and it
filled the whole house where they were sitting. 3 And there appeared to them
tongues as of fire distributing themselves, and they rested on each one of
them. 4 And they were all filled with the Holy Spirit and began to speak with
other tongues, as the Spirit was giving them utterance. 5 Now there were Jews
living in Jerusalem, devout men from every nation under Heaven. 6 And when
this sound occurred, the crowd came together, and were bewildered because
each one of them was hearing them speak in his own language.

7 They were amazed and astonished, saying, "Why, are not all these who are
speaking Galileans? 8 "And how is it that we each hear them in our own
language to which we were born? 9 "Parthians and Medes and Elamites, and
residents of Mesopotamia, Judea and Cappadocia, Pontus and Asia, 10 Phrygia
and Pamphylia, Egypt and the districts of Libya around Cyrene, and visitors
from Rome, both Jews and proselytes, 11 Cretans and Arabs--we hear them in
our own tongues speaking of the mighty deeds of God." 12 And they all continued

in amazement and great perplexity, saying to one another, "What does this mean?" [13]***But others were mocking and saying, "They are full of sweet wine."***
Acts 2:1-13 (NASB)

After this had occurred, apostle Peter stood up and explained to the onlookers what had just happened. He told them that it was actually from God and was a fulfilment of a prophecy made by the prophet Joel:

[14] ***But Peter, taking his stand with the eleven, raised his voice and declared to them: "Men of Judea and all you who live in Jerusalem, let this be known to you and give heed to my words.*** [15] ***For these men are not drunk, as you suppose, for it is only the third hour of the day;*** [16] ***but this is what was spoken of through the prophet Joel:***

[17] ***'AND IT SHALL BE IN THE LAST DAYS,' God says,***
'THAT I WILL POUR FORTH OF MY SPIRIT ON ALL MANKIND;
AND YOUR SONS AND YOUR DAUGHTERS SHALL PROPHESY,
AND YOUR YOUNG MEN SHALL SEE VISIONS,
AND YOUR OLD MEN SHALL DREAM DREAMS;
[18] ***EVEN ON MY BONDSLAVES, BOTH MEN AND WOMEN,***
I WILL IN THOSE DAYS POUR FORTH OF MY SPIRIT
And they shall prophesy.
[19] ***'AND I WILL GRANT WONDERS IN THE SKY ABOVE***
AND SIGNS ON THE EARTH BELOW,
BLOOD, AND FIRE, AND VAPOR OF SMOKE.
[20] ***'THE SUN WILL BE TURNED INTO DARKNESS***
AND THE MOON INTO BLOOD,
BEFORE THE GREAT AND GLORIOUS DAY OF THE LORD SHALL COME.
Acts 2:14-20 (NASB)

A closer look at the prophet Joel's original prophecy and what it implies about the extent, and duration, of the 'pouring out' of the Holy Spirit

As we saw, there is a widespread belief that the pouring out of the Holy Spirit, which apostle Peter tells us began on the Day of Pentecost, was only for the days of the apostles, in the Book of Acts. It is therefore assumed that it has all ceased long ago. This approach is known as 'cessationism'.

However, I believe there is no basis for that belief and that it is a wholly man made idea, which the Bible does not support in any way. I will address that controversy further below, but there is a point which is worth making here which arises out of Joel's original prophecy.

The points to note are, firstly, that Joel says that God's Spirit will be poured out on "*all mankind*". That plainly doesn't mean all people, because most people do not repent or believe, or become Christians at all. However, it does strongly imply that the pouring out of God's Spirit will occur all over the world, amongst all nations and races.

If the cessationist viewpoint was correct, that would not be the case, because within the 30 year period of the book of Acts, or even in the first few centuries AD, the Gospel did not spread very far outside of Europe and Asia Minor. That limited coverage can hardly be described as "*all mankind*" and thus would not fulfil Joel's prophecy.

Secondly, the prophecy set out above, and also the subsequent verses at the end of chapter two and throughout chapter three of Joel, are evidently referring to the "*Day of the LORD*". However, that will not even begin until after the Church age has ended.

The Day of the LORD refers to the period of judgment and of the setting up of God's Kingdom on Earth which will only occur when Jesus returns. Accordingly, my point is that the pouring out of God's Spirit, to which Joel refers, would appear to be something which begins prior to, and then continues until, the Day of the LORD, an event which is still future.

Accordingly, the view which I have set out above of the meaning of Joel's prophecy is only an inference, not a direct statement, by any means. Yet, for what it is worth, the impression given, especially alongside the earlier point about 'all mankind', is that the pouring out of the Holy Spirit will be extensive, both geographically and in terms of its duration. In both senses, that does not support the idea that the gifts of the Holy Spirit have ceased, either in the first century, or at any point since then.

The role the Holy Spirit plays in the process of sanctification and of becoming a disciple

To receive the Holy Spirit means that He comes to live within you. Then He is not merely *alongside* you, but *inside you*, comforting, helping, empowering and guiding you. His help is needed to enable you to live the Christian life because it is so difficult. However, the Holy Spirit's help is also needed in our "*sanctification*", which means being made holy.

Sanctification is the second stage of the overall process that we call "*salvation*" or being *"saved"*. The Bible reveals that we are "*deemed righteous*" or "*justified*" in legal terms, at the moment when our sins are forgiven due to what Jesus did for us on the cross.

However, from then on, we also need to keep growing in maturity, such that we actually become holy in our own thoughts, speech and actions. This life-long process of sanctification, or growing in holiness, is not what makes us justified or forgiven. Only Jesus' death on the cross in our place can achieve that.

What sanctification does do is to change us from the inside out, so that we gradually (and it is gradually) become more and more like Jesus Christ in the way we live. You could say that the words *"saved"* or *"salvation"* have three tenses in the Bible:

a) *"Justification"* - This is salvation in the past tense. Once it has happened it is complete and final. It cannot be increased or improved upon. It is something that Jesus has achieved for us and has given to us. We have been forgiven, justified, and made righteous. So, when speaking of justification, we can accurately say we *"have been saved",* i.e. in the past tense.

b) *"Sanctification"* is the ongoing process of salvation which is now taking place in the present tense. We are meant to be continually being sanctified, from the moment we are justified, until the moment we die. This life-long task of sanctification is what the Holy Spirit helps you with, so that you can actually change, become holy and grow in the fruit of the Spirit. So, sanctification is the present tense of salvation, such that we can say we *"are being saved".*

c) *"Glorification"* - this is the final stage of the process of salvation and it only occurs when we die. At that point our very sin nature itself will be taken away from us. Then we will be fully saved. We will be set free from the very presence of sin within us. So, at our conversion we were set free from the penalty of sin (by justification). Later we are gradually set free from the power of sin, (by sanctification). It is when we refer to our future glorification that we can use the future tense and say that we *"will be saved."*

It is only at this final stage, i.e. when we die and are glorified and our sin nature is removed, that we can say we have been completely saved in every sense, and every tense, of that word. We are then set free even from the presence of sin. It will be gone forever and sin will never again trouble us. So, we can say that glorification reflects the future tense of the process of salvation, i.e. we *will be* glorified. So, in summary, we might say:

a) we *have been* saved (justified - i.e. instantly deemed righteous in legal terms)

b) we *are being* saved (sanctified - i.e. gradually being made holy in our day to day lives)

c) we *will be* saved (glorified - i.e. instantly losing our sin nature after we die)

So, when we read in the Bible of "*salvation*", or being "*saved*" we always need to be clear as to which of these three meanings, or tenses, is being referred to. In this chapter on the Holy Spirit, we are mainly looking at the second meaning, or present tense of salvation, i.e. sanctification. Indeed, one of the main reasons why we all need the baptism in the Holy Spirit is so that He can help us to become sanctified or holy.

For a fuller explanation of these three stages of salvation, please refer to chapter 22. However, there is another major reason why we need the Holy Spirit. That is so that He can provide us with the *"gifts of the Holy Spirit"*. There is a wide range of supernatural gifts which enable us to serve the Lord Jesus Christ more effectively. Using the various gifts of the Holy Spirit helps us to do things which we could never do in or by ourselves, through our own natural ability.

The gifts of the Holy Spirit or 'spiritual gifts'

Let's look briefly at this point at what apostle Paul has to say about the gifts of the Holy Spirit. For now, we shall just seek to familiarise ourselves with the concept and we will then look at this more closely later in the chapter:

4Now there are varieties of gifts, but the same Spirit. 5And there are varieties of ministries, and the same Lord. 6There are varieties of effects, but the same God who works all things in all persons. 7But to each one is given the manifestation of the Spirit for the common good. 8For to one is given the word of wisdom through the Spirit, and to another the word of knowledge according to the same Spirit; 9 to another faith by the same Spirit, and to another gifts of healing by the one Spirit, 10 and to another the effecting of miracles, and to another prophecy, and to another the distinguishing of spirits, to another various kinds of tongues, and to another the interpretation of tongues. 11But one and the same Spirit works all these things, distributing to each one individually just as He wills.

1 Corinthians 12:4-11 (NASB)

Each of the gifts are meant to be used by the people to whom they are given. They are intended to be for the benefit of the individual to whom they are given and also the whole Church. They are not natural talents like musicality or being good at maths. They are supernatural gifts, which the Holy Spirit provides.

We shall look in closer detail below at the gifts of the Holy Spirit, but before we do so, let us examine another controversial question. That is whether we are *all* meant to receive, or be baptised in, the Holy Spirit, or just *some* of us. Also, are we all supposed to operate in spiritual gifts or just some of us?

Are we all supposed to receive, or be baptised in, the Holy Spirit and should we all operate in spiritual gifts?

We have seen earlier what happened to the apostles on the day of Pentecost when they first spoke in tongues. They were the very first people to receive the Holy Spirit in the way the New Testament speaks of this. Let's now look, in the passage below and in the passages set out in the following sections, at some other examples of how other people subsequently received the Holy Spirit and His gifts in the first 30 years of the Church.

This was seen then as an entirely normal, and even essential part of becoming a new Christian. Consider firstly how apostle Peter dealt with a very large crowd of about 3000 people who were all converted on the same day. Note the emphasis that Peter gives to them being about to receive the Holy Spirit:

37 Now when they heard this, they were pierced to the heart, and said to Peter
and the rest of the apostles, "Brethren, what shall we do?" 38 Peter said to them,
"Repent, and each of you be baptized in the name of Jesus Christ for the
forgiveness of your sins; and you will receive the gift of the Holy Spirit. 39 For
the promise is for you and your children and for all who are far off, as many as
the Lord our God will call to Himself." 40 And with many other words he
solemnly testified and kept on exhorting them, saying, "Be saved from this
perverse generation!" 41 So then, those who had received his word were
baptized; and that day there were added about three thousand souls. 42 They were
continually devoting themselves to the apostles' teaching and to fellowship, to
the breaking of bread and to prayer.

Acts 2: 37-42 (NASB)

Why does Peter say that 'the promise', which includes the Holy Spirit, is for *"all who are far off, as many as the Lord our God will call to Himself"*?

Did you notice the words that Peter spoke in verse 39 above? Let's break his statement down into two basic parts. He says that 'the promise' of receiving the gift of the Holy Spirit, is for:

a) "all who are far off"

b) "as many as the Lord our God will call to Himself".

If Peter thought that the baptism in the Holy Spirit and/or the gifts or the Holy Spirit were only for a particular group of people, limited by race, time, geography or any other factor, he surely could not have made either of those statements. Firstly, how could the promise be to those who are 'far off' if it can only happen to the people of Peter's own day and/or to those who lived in or close to Jerusalem, or even to those who lived within The Roman Empire?

Secondly, we saw that the promise of receiving the gift of the Holy Spirit is for "*as many as the Lord our God will call to Himself.*" That being so, how can it be argued that there are any people whom God would later call to Himself, throughout the last 20 centuries, who would *not* be eligible to receive the gift of the Holy Spirit?

Surely, God is making that promise to *all* of those people who were going to be saved in the 20 or more centuries after Peter spoke those words. At any rate, anyone who thinks otherwise would need to explain how it could be that God intended to limit the receiving of the Holy Spirit, or His gifts, to a select few.

It surely makes no sense to limit any part of the promise to any particular group, race, geographical area or time in history. To put it another way, anybody who says that the promise of receiving the gift of the Holy Spirit is limited in any of these ways, needs to explain why "the forgiveness of sins" is still available to us now, in the 21st century but the baptism in the Holy Spirit is not.

They would also need to spell out what they base that belief upon. I say that because it would seem to contradict the plain words of the promise made in that passage. Furthermore, I cannot think of any other passage of Scripture which even indirectly implies, however remotely, that the receiving of the Holy Spirit, or the receipt of His gifts, was going to be limited to any group, area or period of time.

Let's look at more New Testament passages where we see *everybody* present receiving the Holy Spirit and also showing *clear evidence* of having done so, such that it would appear to be the norm.

See how the need to receive the Holy Spirit is again emphasized in this next passage from Acts chapter 8. Note also how it seems plain that *all* of the people present received the Holy Spirit, and in such a way that that fact was *apparent* to everybody else. It also gives no indication that it was limited only to some of them:

14 Now when the apostles in Jerusalem heard that Samaria had received the word of God, they sent them Peter and John, 15 who came down and prayed for them that they might receive the Holy Spirit. 16 For He had not yet fallen upon any of them; they had simply been baptized in the name of the Lord Jesus.
17 Then they began laying their hands on them, and they were receiving the Holy Spirit.

[18] Now when Simon saw that the Spirit was bestowed through the laying on of the apostles' hands, he offered them money, [19] saying, "Give this authority to me as well, so that everyone on whom I lay my hands may receive the Holy Spirit." [20] But Peter said to him, "May your silver perish with you, because you thought you could obtain the gift of God with money! [21] You have no part or portion in this matter, for your heart is not right before God.

Acts 8: 14-21 (NASB)

Consider also the following passages where we see that the Holy Spirit 'fell upon' *all* those present, not just a few exceptional individuals:

[44] While Peter was still speaking these words, the Holy Spirit fell upon all those who were listening to the message. [45] All the circumcised believers who came with Peter were amazed, because the gift of the Holy Spirit had been poured out on the Gentiles also. [46] For they were hearing them speaking with tongues and exalting God. Then Peter answered, [47] "Surely no one can refuse the water for these to be baptized who have received the Holy Spirit just as we did, can he?"

Acts 10:44-47 (NASB)

[15] And as I began to speak, the Holy Spirit fell upon them just as He did upon us at the beginning. [16] And I remembered the word of the Lord, how He used to say, 'John baptized with water, but you will be baptized with the Holy Spirit.'[17] Therefore if God gave to them the same gift as He gave to us also after believing in the Lord Jesus Christ, who was I that I could stand in God's way?"

Acts 11:15-17 (NASB)

Let's now look more closely at Acts 8:14-17 and consider why the words 'receive' and 'fallen upon' are used interchangeably, and also why the latter was seen as being evidence of the former

We have already seen this passage from Acts 8, but I would like to zoom in and examine it more closely because it reveals some very interesting insights as to exactly what is meant by 'receiving' the Holy Spirit. In addition it tells us a lot about *when* it occurs, and also what the *evidence* is that it has occurred. I say that because, as we saw, one school of thought, which is widespread today, is that the Holy Spirit is always, and automatically, received at the moment when a person first repents and believes. We might call that the moment of 'conversion'.

However, Acts 8:14-17 presents a major difficulty for those who hold that view, or rather those who make that assumption, because the Bible never expressly says that that is the case. On the contrary, it strongly suggests that that is not so, as I hope to demonstrate from these verses. Let's now look at them again:

[14] Now when the apostles in Jerusalem heard that Samaria had received the word of God, they sent them Peter and John, [15] who came down and prayed for them that they might receive the Holy Spirit. [16] For He had not yet fallen upon any of them; they had simply been baptized in the name of the Lord Jesus. [17] Then they began laying their hands on them, and they were receiving the Holy Spirit.

Acts 8:14-17 (NASB)

Look carefully at each phrase in the passage. We see at first that the people of Samaria have received the Word of God. That is they have heard the Gospel preached following the death and resurrection of Jesus. The reason why that is considered newsworthy is that the Samaritans were not fully Jewish, being of mixed race. Therefore they were not a group that the apostles would have expected to go to, as they were not part of Israel and were viewed as Gentiles.

At any rate, Peter and John went to investigate. When they got there, and had assessed the situation, we see that, although the Samaritans had repented and believed the Gospel, Peter and John evidently did not think that the new Samaritan believers had received the Holy Spirit. We know that, because Peter and John then prayed for them to receive the Holy Spirit, in verse 15.

However, what is especially important is *why* Peter and John concluded that these new believers had not received the Holy Spirit, even though we are expressly told that they had already been baptised in water. Moreover, we are told that that baptism in water had been done in the name of Jesus. It was not merely John's baptism of repentance, as was the case in Acts 19, when apostle Paul asked a group of people in Ephesus if they had received the Holy Spirit. The crucial point is that Peter and John reached the conclusion that the Holy Spirit "*had not yet fallen upon*" the Samaritans.

Do you see the significance of that? Peter and John plainly did not think that '*receiving*' the Holy Spirit was something that occurred automatically, or inevitably, at the moment when a person first believed. Neither did they think that the Holy Spirit "*falling upon*" a person only occurred in certain cases, or that this event was in any way different from, or subsequent to, '*receiving*' the Holy Spirit.

Indeed, far from seeing the receiving of the Holy Spirit as being something different from, or prior to, the Holy Spirit 'falling upon' a person, Peter and John thought that this very noticeable event was what constituted 'receiving' the Holy Spirit.

At the very least, we have to infer from Peter and John's words that this experience of the baptism in the Holy Spirit, whereby the Holy Spirit 'falls upon' a person, is the *evidence* of their having received the Holy Spirit, even if it is not the moment at which that receiving actually takes place.

What else can we conclude, given that it is so clear that Peter and John were not satisfied by the fact that those new believers in Samaria had "*simply been baptized in the name of the Lord Jesus*".

How many of us today would use the word *'simply'* to describe the steps taken by a person who had repented, believed and been baptised in water? Most of us would agree that that series of steps is actually far more than many people in our churches have ever done.

Therefore, few people today would point to such a person and conclude that they lacked anything, least of all tell them that they have not yet received the Holy Spirit. Yet we have to face the fact that that is exactly what Peter and John did.

One suspects that they would not be invited back to speak again in most of our churches today. Their blunt words, and their direct approach, would be seen as controversial and 'divisive'. On the same theme, let us look next at how apostle Paul dealt with another group of brand new converts in Ephesus, many years after the Day of Pentecost.

Paul realised very quickly that they had not received the Holy Spirit. Moreover he too then said so, directly and assertively, just as Peter and John had done years before with the new believers in Samaria:

1 It happened that while Apollos was at Corinth, Paul passed through the upper
country and came to Ephesus, and found some disciples. 2 He said to them, "Did
you receive the Holy Spirit when you believed?" And they said to him, "No, we
have not even heard whether there is a Holy Spirit." 3 And he said, "Into what
then were you baptized?" And they said, " Into John's baptism." 4 Paul said,
"John baptized with the baptism of repentance, telling the people to believe in
Him who was coming after him, that is, in Jesus." 5 When they heard this, they
were baptized in the name of the Lord Jesus. 6 And when Paul had laid his hands
upon them, the Holy Spirit came on them, and they began speaking with tongues
and prophesying. 7 There were in all about twelve men.

Acts 19:1-7 (NASB)

We see in the passage above that Paul met a group of people in Ephesus who had believed in Jesus Christ and had repented. So, neither repentance nor faith were missing. However, Paul could sense that they had not yet received the Holy Spirit. They had not yet been baptised in water either.

Instead of probing into such matters, most church leaders today would have accepted these men just as they were. They would not have intervened or advised them to do anything further. However, that was not Paul's approach. He was concerned and was not satisfied with their situation.

He therefore had them baptised in water straight away and then he laid his hands on them to pray for them to receive the Holy Spirit. As Paul did this, the Holy Spirit 'came on' them and they spoke in tongues, just as had happened to the apostles in Acts chapter two, many years earlier.

The point is that that means that these people in Ephesus, who had repented and believed and who would be fully accepted as Christians in most churches today, had not yet 'received' the Holy Spirit at the point when Paul arrived. It follows, therefore, that there must be many people in our churches today who, likewise, have repented and believed but have not yet received the Holy Spirit.

That may be a controversial statement, but what else can we possibly conclude? It would appear to be self-evident. Another point which emerges clearly from this episode, and indeed all of the other passages we have seen, is that this experience of receiving the Holy Spirit, and of immediately speaking in tongues and prophesying, was not restricted just to the 12 apostles, or even to the 120 disciples on the day of Pentecost.

I would suggest to you that it happened consistently to most people, though admittedly not to absolutely everybody, for the first 30 years of the church, which the book of Acts covers. If so, that means it would have happened to hundreds of thousands of believers, given how fast the church grew, and it carried on long after that as well.

It was a normal part of the process of becoming a Christian, until the fourth century, when the churches were taken over and contaminated by the Emperor Constantine. From that point onwards they began to degenerate into what we now know as the Roman Catholic church. However, outside of the Roman Catholic church, the experience of being baptised in the Holy Spirit continued, just as in the book of Acts, and has done so to this day.

The unusual sequencing of events that we see in the experience of Cornelius the Gentile

We have seen that, ordinarily, in most of the passages in the Book of Acts, people received the Holy Spirit after they had been baptised in water. However, that was not always the case. Let's look now at a more unusual situation where apostle Peter dealt with Cornelius, a Gentile (non-Jewish) believer. He believed in God and had repented, even though he was not a Jew.

Peter then explains the Gospel to Cornelius and all the others who are with him. Peter tells them who Jesus is and what He did. As he spoke, the men repented and believed his message. Then the Holy Spirit 'fell upon' them and they spoke in tongues, even without Peter asking for any of that, or laying hands on them.

Moreover, note also that, despite Luke having just referred to this same event as the Holy Spirit 'falling upon' them, Peter then immediately refers to it as them having 'received' the Holy Spirit. Luke, who wrote the Book of Acts, is evidently happy for both words to be used to describe the very same event. More to the point, so is the Holy Spirit, who inspired him to write it.

***44**While Peter was still speaking these words, the Holy Spirit fell upon all those who were listening to the message. **45** All the circumcised believers who came with Peter were amazed, because the gift of the Holy Spirit had been poured out on the Gentiles also. **46**For they were hearing them speaking with tongues and exalting God. Then Peter answered, **47**"Surely no one can refuse the water for these to be baptized who have received the Holy Spirit just as we did, can he?" **48**And he ordered them to be baptized in the name of Jesus Christ. Then they asked him to stay on for a few days.*

Acts 10:44-48(NASB)

This episode in Acts chapter 10 is an unusual situation because Cornelius, and those with him, received the Holy Spirit *before being baptised in water*. That is not the usual biblical order. Baptism in water almost always came before receiving the Holy Spirit, but it was different on this occasion.

Peter had only just realised that the Gospel was supposed to be preached to Gentiles as well as to Jews and that they no longer needed to become Jews, as they always had to up to that time.

If Peter and the others had realised all of that previously they would have had Cornelius baptised in water already. However, it had never occurred to Peter to baptise these Gentile believers because, up to this point, he didn't even consider Gentiles to be eligible to become Christians at all.

That is an example of how a fixed mindset can even cause a man to miss what God is expressly saying. Remember that Peter had got this blind spot despite the fact that he had heard Jesus say, prior to His ascension, that He wanted the apostles to go and make disciples *of all nations*, not just among the Jews:

***19**"Go therefore and make disciples of all the nations, baptizing them in the name of the Father and the Son and the Holy Spirit, **20**teaching them to observe all that I commanded you; and lo, I am with you always, even to the end of the age."*

Matthew 28:19-20 (NASB)

Peter had still not realised that Jesus really meant what He had said and that the Gospel was also to be preached to the Gentiles. That shows how we can so easily miss things if we get our ideas from traditions, or from what we are used to, rather than from what the Bible actually says. At any rate, the point is that each of these men with Cornelius in Acts 10 received the Holy Spirit.

They then began to speak in tongues, just as the apostles had done, and just as Paul's converts did later. I would suggest that this step of receiving the Holy Spirit, and then immediately operating in the gifts of the Holy Spirit, was the norm and was intended for almost everybody.

In the passages we have looked at above, the people concerned all received the Holy Spirit and it would appear that they all spoke in tongues and/or prophesied as a result. That is the clear impression and nothing is stated to the contrary. Receiving, or being baptised in, the Holy Spirit was not just for the apostles. Nor was it restricted to any other particular group or class of people or for any limited period of time.

Therefore I suggest that we are all meant to be baptised in the Holy Spirit and that we are all meant to receive the gifts of the Holy Spirit. However, I would freely concede that we are not all going to receive the *same* gifts. We will inevitably differ in what specific gifts we are given, just as we all differ in our natural gifts and talents.

The Day of Pentecost was only about seven weeks after the resurrection, whereas the incidents with Peter and Cornelius and then with Paul at Ephesus, were much later, many years after the resurrection. Yet it is plain that they all still received the Holy Spirit in the same way and that most of them spoke in tongues and/or prophesied.

Nothing had changed and nothing had been abandoned during these years, so why should we imagine that anything should change at any time after this? That said, the Bible does not say that we must all operate in any particular gift of the Holy Spirit. For example, we cannot say that we must *all* speak in tongues, because apostle Paul specifically says that we do not all do so:

27Now you are Christ's body, and individually members of it. 28And God has appointed in the church, first apostles, second prophets, third teachers, then miracles, then gifts of healings, helps, administrations, various kinds of tongues. 29All are not apostles, are they? All are not prophets, are they? All are not teachers, are they? All are not workers of miracles, are they? 30All do not have gifts of healings, do they? All do not speak with tongues, do they? All do not interpret, do they? 31But earnestly desire the greater gifts. And I show you a still more excellent way.

1 Corinthians 12:27-31 (NASB)

Nevertheless, it seems clear that Paul does still expect that we will all operate in *some* gift of the Holy Spirit, even if not tongues or any other particular gift.

Therefore the passage from 1 Corinthians 12 can't be used as a basis for arguing that we don't need to, or aren't meant to, operate in *any* of the spiritual gifts.

That does not follow at all. Neither can what Paul says be taken to mean that we do not need to receive the Holy Spirit, or that receiving the Holy Spirit is automatic or inevitable, or that it happens without us being aware of it.

Note also this next passage from Acts chapter 15 concerning the Council meeting which took place in Jerusalem, several years after the resurrection. At this meeting the status of Gentile believers was discussed, including the question of whether they can become Christians without first becoming Jewish as an intermediate step.

In that meeting the question of receiving the Holy Spirit was also addressed:

6The apostles and the elders came together to look into this matter. 7After there had been much debate, Peter stood up and said to them, "Brethren, you know that in the early days God made a choice among you, that by my mouth the Gentiles would hear the word of the gospel and believe. 8"And God, who knows the heart, testified to them giving them the Holy Spirit, just as He also did to us; 9and He made no distinction between us and them, cleansing their hearts by faith.

Acts 15:6-9 (NASB)

The key point from the above passage, for our purposes in this chapter, is that apostle Peter is telling the Council that not just the apostles, and not just the Jews, but also the Gentiles, were to receive the Holy Spirit. Moreover, they were to do so *in the same way* as the apostles and all other Jewish believers had done.

I suggest to you therefore that receiving the Holy Spirit or "the baptism in the Holy Spirit" is intended to be *for every believer, not just a select few*. It also seems clear that it is meant for us today, not just for people in the past. At any rate, there is no biblical reason to think otherwise. Whilst we have seen above that not everybody spoke in tongues, the strong implication is that most, or at least many, of them did.

If not, it surely would not have been emphasised as it was. At the very least, the clear impression given is that speaking in tongues, and the other gifts too, were a completely normal part of church life. They were by no means limited to a minority of people, or just in exceptional cases.

In any case, the real burden of proof must be on those who assume that the gifts as a whole do *not* apply any longer to prove their case and also to show what authority or evidence they base it on. In doing so they would need to explain why *any* of the people in these passages spoke in tongues or prophesied, because we can see that many of them clearly did. The real question therefore is, did *any* of them do so.

Instead of asking that, too many of us are focusing on whether or not *all* of them did so. Then people are saying *"If they didn't all operate in spiritual gifts, then that justifies me in not doing so"*.

However, why would we want to look for reasons or excuses *not* to operate in the gifts of the Holy Spirit? We should surely just be seeking to do exactly what they did in the Book of Acts, not trying to justify doing otherwise.

How do we reconcile what Jesus said in John 20:22 with what He also said later in Acts 1:4-5 and Acts 1:8?

One of the main verses used by those who argue that there is a difference between 'receiving' and being 'baptised in' the Holy Spirit is John 20:22. Therefore let's take a look at it and then compare it with Acts 1:4-5 and Acts 1:8.

21 So Jesus said to them again, "Peace be with you; as the Father has sent Me, I also send you." 22 And when He had said this, He breathed on them and said to them, "Receive the Holy Spirit.

John 20:21-22 (NASB)

This was said by Jesus after His resurrection but before His ascension. More to the point, it was said before the events of the Day of Pentecost when the apostles first spoke in tongues. Yet, we are told that Jesus breathed on them saying "*Receive the Holy Spirit*", and the clear implication is that they did so, there and then. If so, why was there no visible or audible evidence that they had received the Holy Spirit?

Secondly, why is this the only instance in the whole New Testament where this unusual, two stage approach appears to be taken? In every other case the phrases 'receive', 'baptised in' or 'filled with' are quite clearly used interchangeably to refer to the same event. Indeed, sometimes two phrases are used in the same passage to describe the very same incident, as we saw above in Acts 10.

I have to admit that I can't provide a fully satisfactory explanation of exactly what Jesus meant by the word 'receive' in John 20:22. Neither can I explain satisfactorily why He did not follow the same pattern or model that we see consistently in the Book of Acts concerning other individuals or groups who are baptised in the Holy Spirit.

In other words, I can't fully explain why Jesus, having already breathed on the apostles for them to 'receive' the Holy Spirit, should then speak to them a short time later to tell them that they were subsequently going to be 'baptised in' the

Holy Spirit and why He spoke of that as a future event. I shall set out the relevant passages below:

Gathering them together, He commanded them not to leave Jerusalem, but to wait for what the Father had promised, "Which," He said, "you heard of from Me; [5] for John baptized with water, but you will be baptized with the Holy Spirit not many days from now."

Acts 1:4-5 (NASB)

but you will receive power when the Holy Spirit has come upon you; and you shall be My witnesses both in Jerusalem, and in all Judea and Samaria, and even to the remotest part of the earth."

Acts 1:8 (NASB)

As stated, many have relied on John 20:22, in conjunction with Acts 1:4-5 and Acts 1:8 to argue that these two events or concepts or 'receiving' and being 'baptised in' the Holy Spirit are separate and distinct. The problem is that the rest of the book of Acts does not support that point of view. It may possibly be that Jesus chose to adopt an unusual, or even a unique, approach in the case of the apostles. One cannot be sure.

Accordingly, it seems safest, in my view, to be guided by the combined evidence of all the New Testament passages as to what is meant by 'receiving', being 'baptised in' and being 'filled with' the Holy Spirit. When one does that, one is obliged to conclude that they all seem to be portrayed as alternative phrases for the very same event or experience.

One of the key purposes of the baptism in the Holy Spirit is that we are then meant to be guided towards the truth by the Holy Spirit.

Have you ever noticed that one of the key roles of the Holy Spirit and, also, by clear implication, of the baptism in the Holy Spirit, is that we are meant, from then on, to be guided into the truth? Consider what Jesus said on this point:

[13] But when He, the Spirit of truth, comes, He will guide you into all the truth; for He will not speak on His own initiative, but whatever He hears, He will speak; and He will disclose to you what is to come.

John 16:13 (NASB)

This process of being guided into the truth is what is meant to happen as a result of the influence of the Holy Spirit. However, if that is so, why is it that, so frequently, we see the exact opposite actually happening? Instead of growing in knowledge of the Bible, gaining accurate doctrine, and growing in understanding, discernment, insight and all round wisdom, vast numbers of Christians, or rather 'churchgoers' seem to be going further into error and deception.

One sees very little evidence of people being guided into truth, which would tend to suggest that few people today are genuinely receiving the Holy Spirit. Or, even if they are, they are perhaps refusing to allow the Holy Spirit to operate, either in giving His gifts, or in guiding them into truth.

At any rate, the current levels of biblical illiteracy, openness to deception and compromise with the world are not much of an advert for today's Church. We are plainly in desperate need of the help of the Holy Spirit in guiding us into the truth and, in particular, towards a proper love for the Bible, which is being so grievously neglected by so many.

Have you ever asked yourself whether you personally are consistently being led away from error and towards the truth? In my own case, I feel very sure that I am being. There is not a month or even a week, that goes by in which I do not learn something new from the Bible. I keep on and on discovering new facts, gaining insights, seeing the connections between one passage of Scripture and another, and growing in all round understanding, especially of how God's Word is meant to be applied.

In particular, I keep on finding errors in my own previous thinking or assumptions. Then, one by one, I replace those mistaken beliefs with the truth. The best way that I can explain it is to say that God keeps on and on opening my eyes, and my mind, to see things that I had not previously noticed or understood in His Word. I describe these discoveries, or revelations, as insights, which God is increasingly giving to me.

In part, I believe that that ongoing process of discovery and the sharpening of my understanding is because I consistently put in the time and the effort to study His Word. I do so because I sincerely want to know the truth, and also to know where I have, until now, been mistaken, ignorant or deceived. It is a fact that God tells the man who cares, and who really wants the truth for its own sake.

However, I believe that my on-going process of discovery is also partly because the Holy Spirit is doing for me exactly what Jesus spoke of in John 16:13 and is guiding me into the truth. I believe that that, in turn, is because of the baptism in the Holy Spirit. Ask yourself therefore whether you are also moving steadily away from errors and deceptions and towards the truth and a growing knowledge of God's Word.

If you are not, then it would be wise to ask why not and to address your mind to God's Word and the extent to which you are studying it. However, it would also be right to ask yourself whether you have actually been baptised in the Holy Spirit.

Why did the early Church, in the Book of Acts, lay hands on people to receive the Holy Spirit?

In most (but not all) cases in the New Testament, once a new believer had been baptised in water, someone would lay their hands on them immediately and pray for them to receive the Holy Spirit. The person praying and laying their hands upon a new believer is not the one who causes them to receive the Holy Spirit. The only one who does that is Jesus Himself. Jesus is the one who baptises us in the Holy Spirit. We learn this from John the Baptist:

6John was clothed with camel's hair and wore a leather belt around his waist, and his diet was locusts and wild honey. 7And he was preaching, and saying, "After me One is coming who is mightier than I, and I am not fit to stoop down and untie the thong of His sandals. 8"I baptized you with water; but He will baptize you with the Holy Spirit."

Mark 1:6-8 (NASB)

29The next day he saw Jesus coming to him and said, "Behold, the Lamb of God who takes away the sin of the world! 30"This is He on behalf of whom I said, 'After me comes a Man who has a higher rank than I, for He existed before me.' 31"I did not recognize Him, but so that He might be manifested to Israel, I came baptizing in water." 32John testified saying, "I have seen the Spirit descending as a dove out of Heaven, and He remained upon Him. 33"I did not recognize Him, but He who sent me to baptize in water said to me, 'He upon whom you see the Spirit descending and remaining upon Him, this is the One who baptizes in the Holy Spirit.' 34"I myself have seen, and have testified that this is the Son of God."

John 1:29-34 (NASB)

So then, if Jesus Christ Himself is the One who gives the Holy Spirit to us, or baptises us in the Holy Spirit, what is the role of the person who prays for us and lays hands upon us? The answer is that they are, at most, a helper, who can guide and advise us. They are not the source, or the giver, of the baptism in the Holy Spirit. That is Jesus alone. The person who prays for us, and lays hands upon us, merely helps us to receive the Holy Spirit.

They show us what to do and what to ask for and they help us to ask. We are not dependent upon that person. We can receive the Holy Spirit without such a person's help. Remember Cornelius in Acts chapter 10. He, and those around him, received the Holy Spirit while they were just listening to apostle Peter preaching. Nobody had laid hands on any of them, or even prayed for them.

Accordingly, you do not necessarily have to have the help of any person to receive the Holy Spirit. You can be alone if necessary.

The points made above should encourage you to be confident that you will receive the Holy Spirit if you ask, even if you have no fellow believer who is able and willing to pray for you and lay their hands on you. Human help and support is useful, but not essential. You can receive the Holy Spirit even when you are on your own, just as I did (see below).

We benefit from a fellow believer praying with us and laying hands upon us to ask Jesus to baptise us in the Holy Spirit. That is the normal, biblical model which we should, ideally, follow. However, it does not *have* to be done that way.

Jesus can baptise you in the Holy Spirit even if you are alone, with nobody to pray for you or lay hands on you. It can happen even if nobody in your church understands any of this, and even if they all actively oppose it. No man can deny you the freedom to receive the Holy Spirit from Jesus. It may be that there is nobody willing or able to help you, or that nobody in your church believes in this.

However, if they say it is not for today, you can simply ask God the Father and the Lord Jesus yourself, directly. Jesus will be glad to do this for you. It is His wish, and the Father's wish, that every one of His disciples should receive the Holy Spirit. Therefore, He will not deny you when you ask:

11 "Now suppose one of you fathers is asked by his son for a fish; he will not give him a snake instead of a fish, will he? 12 "Or if he is asked for an egg, he will not give him a scorpion, will he? 13 " If you then, being evil, know how to give good gifts to your children, how much more will your Heavenly Father give the Holy Spirit to those who ask Him?"

Luke 11:11-13 (NASB)

It is interesting that in this verse we are told by Jesus to ask God the Father to give us the Holy Spirit. So, although Jesus is the one who actually baptises us in the Holy Spirit, we can, and should, ask the Father. He will then answer that prayer through His Son, Jesus Christ. This is an illustration of how the Father, Son and Holy Spirit work together in perfect cooperation.

So, to reiterate, if you are alone, with nobody suitable or willing to help you, or pray with you, do not feel thwarted or discouraged. Just ask God the Father and the Lord Jesus Christ directly, for yourself. Then believe that your own prayer will be answered.

Note also from the above passage from Luke 11 that we can be confident that if we *sincerely* ask God to give us the Holy Spirit then He is the One whom we will receive, not a demonic counterfeit. If we pray sincerely, then God will never give us something bad. Neither will He allow the Devil to give us something false instead of the Holy Spirit.

In other words, if we genuinely ask God for the Holy Spirit, then He will not allow any demon to give us something false instead. If a human father can be trusted not to give his child a scorpion when he asks for an egg, then how much more can God be trusted? Therefore if you are a genuine believer, and are sincerely seeking to receive the Holy Spirit, do not fear that you will receive anything false. Go ahead and ask to receive the Holy Spirit with confidence.

However, I would stress again the need for you to be *genuine and sincere,* because it has to be said that there is a danger here. If we allow another person to lay hands on us, we could receive a demonic spirit if that is what *they* have. In other words, if they themselves are not genuine and are operating in an unbiblical way, with false teaching, a carnal lifestyle and false spiritual manifestations, then they could pass on to you what they have.

Therefore it is essential that you examine the 'fruit' that comes from their lives. Also test the accuracy of their doctrine closely before you allow anybody to lay hands on you to receive the Holy Spirit. If there is any doubt about that person, you should not let them lay hands on you and you can simply pray by, and for, yourself.

What are tongues? Why does God give such a strange gift?

When people received the Holy Spirit in the New Testament it would appear that the fact that it had happened was obvious to everyone else. That is because they began to speak in tongues or they prophesied or operated in some other gift. I personally feel that they all operated in some gift, but if you disagree then we can surely say that most or, at the very least, many of them did.

In other words, it was by no means limited or restricted. That was true then, and I suggest that it is still true today. Let's now look specifically at what tongues are and why that particular gift was given and, in my view, still is given. We will then go on to look at the other spiritual gifts too:

Apostle Paul's explanation of how spiritual gifts operate

Let us look at 1 Corinthians chapter 14:

1Pursue love, yet desire earnestly spiritual gifts, but especially that you may
prophesy. 2For one who speaks in a tongue does not speak to men but to God;
for no one understands, but in his spirit he speaks mysteries. 3But one who
prophesies speaks to men for edification and exhortation and consolation. 4One

who speaks in a tongue edifies himself; but one who prophesies edifies the church. [5]Now I wish that you all spoke in tongues, but even more that you would prophesy; and greater is one who prophesies than one who speaks in tongues, unless he interprets, so that the church may receive edifying.

[6]But now, brethren, if I come to you speaking in tongues, what will I profit you unless I speak to you either by way of revelation or of knowledge or of prophecy or of teaching? [7]Yet even lifeless things, either flute or harp, in producing a sound, if they do not produce a distinction in the tones, how will it be known what is played on the flute or on the harp? [8]For if the bugle produces an indistinct sound, who will prepare himself for battle?

[9]So also you, unless you utter by the tongue speech that is clear, how will it be known what is spoken? For you will be speaking into the air. [10]There are, perhaps, a great many kinds of languages in the world, and no kind is without meaning. [11]If then I do not know the meaning of the language, I will be to the one who speaks a barbarian, and the one who speaks will be a barbarian to me. [12]So also you, since you are zealous of spiritual gifts, seek to abound for the edification of the church.

[13]Therefore let one who speaks in a tongue pray that he may interpret. [14]For if I pray in a tongue, my spirit prays, but my mind is unfruitful. [15]What is the outcome then? I will pray with the spirit and I will pray with the mind also; I will sing with the spirit and I will sing with the mind also. [16]Otherwise if you bless in the spirit only, how will the one who fills the place of the ungifted say the "Amen" at your giving of thanks, since he does not know what you are saying? [17]For you are giving thanks well enough, but the other person is not edified.

[18]I thank God, I speak in tongues more than you all; [19]however, in the church I desire to speak five words with my mind so that I may instruct others also, rather than ten thousand words in a tongue. [20]Brethren, do not be children in your thinking; yet in evil be infants, but in your thinking be mature. [21]In the Law it is written, "by men of strange tongues and by the lips of strangers I will speak to this people, and even so they will not listen to me," says the Lord.

[22]So then tongues are for a sign, not to those who believe but to unbelievers; but prophecy is for a sign, not to unbelievers but to those who believe. [23]Therefore if the whole church assembles together and all speak in tongues, and ungifted men or unbelievers enter, will they not say that you are mad? [24]But if all prophesy, and an unbeliever or an ungifted man enters, he is convicted by all, he is called to account by all; [25]the secrets of his heart are disclosed; and so he will fall on his face and worship God, declaring that God is certainly among you.

26 What is the outcome then, brethren? When you assemble, each one has a
psalm, has a teaching, has a revelation, has a tongue, has an interpretation Let
all things be done for edification. 27 If anyone speaks in a tongue, it should be
by two or at the most three, and each in turn, and one must interpret; 28 but if
there is no interpreter, he must keep silent in the church; and let him speak to
himself and to God. 29 Let two or three prophets speak, and let the others pass
judgment. 30 But if a revelation is made to another who is seated, the first one
must keep silent. 31 For you can all prophesy one by one, so that all may learn
and all may be exhorted; 32 and the spirits of prophets are subject to
prophets; 33 for God is not a God of confusion but of peace, as in all the churches
of the saints.

1 Corinthians 14:1-33 (NASB)

Take a close look at the passage above. Ideally read it and re-read it two or three times. Wouldn't you agree that what Paul is speaking about, and what he views as normal, is very different from what most of our churches are like today? Paul clearly saw the widespread and active use of spiritual gifts as being entirely right and proper.

Yet, in most Western churches today, what Paul says in 1 Corinthians chapter 14 is almost entirely ignored. At any rate, it certainly isn't practiced. It is glossed over and not even thought about, let alone preached on. If it was it would raise too many uncomfortable questions, such as *"Why doesn't our church do these things?*

However, anybody who teaches that the gifts of the Holy Spirit are *not* meant to be used by us today will have great difficulties in explaining away what Paul says. Therefore, those people who hold that view generally ignore 1 Corinthians 14 entirely, which is why it is very rarely preached on.

Speaking in tongues, both in the New Testament, and today, is not mere babbling or making gibberish sounds. The gift of tongues, when given by the Holy Spirit, should involve a real language, whether human or angelic. It will have complex and detailed structure, grammar and syntax, just like any other language.

That is how the various foreigners present on the day of Pentecost all heard their own language being spoken. The only foreign language I can speak, up to a point, is French, because I once worked in France. However, if I hear a language like Russian or Chinese or German, even though I can't understand it, I can tell very clearly that the person is speaking in a proper language with clear rules and vocabulary. I know it isn't gibberish and that the speaker isn't just making up sounds by themselves.

It is the same with the gift of tongues. It sounds like a real language. That's because it *is* a real language, whether human or angelic. It is just one that you don't know. The point is that God knows it and He understands it. However, I should add that that is not necessarily the experience of every person. I know people myself for whom tongues is very limited. That fact can make a person feel inferior or threatened, because what they have does not sound very fluent or extensive.

I have no wish to suggest that anybody is inferior. That is the last thing I would wish to do. Yet, if what you have got so far is limited just to a few words or phrases, then please do not be content to stay at that level. Ask God to give you more, so that you can begin to speak in tongues with the full fluency and range that is available to others.

So, whilst I fully accept that nobody is inferior or second rate, that is still no reason for anybody to stay where they are. Instead, press on and seek for all that God has to offer. When we speak in tongues, we are saying words which the Holy Spirit Himself puts into our mouths.

We may be praying prayers that He wants us to pray, even though we do not know what we are praying about. We may also be praising God and worshiping Him in our spirit with a greater fluency and depth than we would be capable of in our own language, using only our minds, if we were not aided by the Holy Spirit.

The purposes and benefits of the gift of tongues in particular

The gift of tongues has a number of purposes and benefits. Let us examine these:

a) Speaking in tongues enables us to praise and worship God with a depth and content that we could not achieve by ourselves.

b) The gift of tongues enables God to put into our mouths specific prayers and requests which we would never think of, or even know about, for ourselves. There could be a person for whom nobody is praying, or perhaps an urgent situation which needs prayer, but nobody is aware of it. Through praying in tongues God can then put prayers into the mouths of His people which would not otherwise be prayed. I believe many situations and people have been prayed about in that way and that God has then answered those prayers.

> ***26In the same way the Spirit also helps our weakness; for we do not know how to pray as we should, but the Spirit Himself intercedes for us with groanings too deep for words;***
>
> ***Romans 8:26 (NASB)***

c) The gift of tongues, when used in private as part of our own devotional time, has the effect of strengthening us personally in our 'inner man' or spirit. We each have a spirit and the gift of tongues enables our own spirit to speak to God with a freedom we would not otherwise have, if we were confined solely to what our minds can think of. When praying in tongues we are praying "*in the Holy Spirit*" rather than just praying in and through our own minds:

> [20] ***But you, beloved, building yourselves up in your most holy faith and praying in the Holy Spirit,***
>
> ***Jude 20 (ESV)***

Remember, our spirit is not the same thing as our mind. When we pray with our minds, in our own native language, it is not the same as when we allow the Holy Spirit to enable our own spirit to pray. Praying in tongues bypasses our mind. This strengthens and benefits us, as well as helping those other people or situations that we may, unknowingly, be praying for.

d) Tongues when spoken out loud at a meeting, are a supernatural sign. It can benefit another person if he hears someone speaking in tongues and recognises his own language being spoken. The same is true if the tongue is interpreted through the gift of interpretation. That is another of the gifts of the Holy Spirit. Either way, the other person, who may even be an unbeliever, can then understand what has been said. That may get through to him and bring him to repentance, and to faith, in ways that ordinary speech may not achieve. The late Derek Prince, a well-known Bible teacher, told many stories of how non-Christians have visited a church and been amazed to hear people praying out loud in the visitor's native language, even though the person speaking does not know that language. The person is actually speaking in tongues, but the visitor understands it.

   On one occasion a Welshman, who was not a Christian, was travelling abroad, in South America I believe, and went to a South American church together with some English speaking friends. A local man then began to pray out loud in tongues publicly. He didn't know it, but he was speaking perfect Welsh. The Welsh speaking visitor was amazed and said to the English speaking person who had brought him that the man had been speaking in detail, in Welsh, about some sins which he (the Welsh visitor) had committed. He was the only person in the room who knew what was being said, because he was the only Welsh speaker. It convicted him very deeply and he repented and believed. There are many other instances where things like that have occurred. It would occur even more often if more people believed that the gifts of the Holy Spirit are for today and allowed them to be used in churches.

e) Perhaps most important of all, tongues are also a supernatural sign or seal of approval. It is meant to demonstrate to you, and to others, that your conversion is real and has been accepted by God, that you really are a Christian and, therefore, have received the Holy Spirit. In the book of Acts and in the letters of the New Testament it seems that they assumed that new believers would either speak in tongues or prophesy immediately when they received the Holy Spirit. Therefore tongues was the main evidence they looked for, at least in the immediate sense. Later on they would be looking for fruit to emerge in that person's life. Conversely, the absence of tongues or prophecy or any other gift at the outset, was generally seen as an indication that the person had not yet completed the process of becoming a Christian. Can you imagine how much offence would be taken if apostle Paul visited many of our churches today and began to challenge people as he did in Acts chapter 19? Paul would be thrown out of most churches today.

My own experience of the baptism in the Holy Spirit

I repented and believed at 2:30pm on 8 June 1981. That is the point at which I began the biblical process of becoming a Christian. At that moment, though I had not yet been baptised in water, I believe I was justified (made righteous in God's sight) and my sins were forgiven. Thankfully, I had heard about the Gospel from people who believed that the need to receive the Holy Spirit, and to operate in the gifts of the Holy Spirit, still applied. So, I was prayed for.

They laid their hands on me in the biblical manner, asking God to baptise me in the Holy Spirit. I wanted that to happen and I was praying for it myself. However, so far as I could tell at the time, nothing supernatural appeared to happen to me. Indeed, nothing seemed to happen at all. I did not speak in tongues, or feel anything strange in any way. I felt disappointed, and confused.

Therefore I just continued to pray to receive the Holy Spirit and to receive spiritual gifts, in particular the gift of tongues. Weeks and months passed and I persisted in praying and asking others to pray for me too. Still nothing happened, so far as I could tell.

What I did do, however, was to eagerly read the Bible, study it, memorize it and tell others about the Gospel. God used me in some surprising ways and I was effective in evangelism, telling many people about Jesus and seeing some come to faith as a result.

All this occurred without me ever having spoken in tongues. Yet, rather strangely, one of the new converts whom I had led to faith was baptised in the Holy Spirit at the very outset. He had a very powerful and life changing experience and began to speak in tongues long before I did.

I believe that throughout this time of waiting, which lasted nearly two years, I was already a real Christian. I believe I had started out on "*the Way*". (See chapter 21) I had been forgiven and justified in God's sight because of my repentance and my faith in Jesus Christ. However, I had not yet been baptised in water and, in my view, I had not yet been baptised in the Holy Spirit.

Then, quite out of the blue, there came a day of dramatic breakthrough. It was early on the morning of my 21st birthday in 1983, nearly two years after I had first repented and believed. I was sitting on my bed in my student room and I suddenly felt a release whereby I felt free to speak in tongues. It was not forced upon me. Yet, somehow, I felt able to do it and I began to speak. However, I had perfect liberty to stop if I had wanted to.

The point was that I suddenly felt prompted to begin to speak out loud, but not in English. As I opened my mouth, and began to speak, words flowed easily and quickly. Moreover, I felt a powerful *emotional release* too. I had felt so buttoned up and reserved beforehand. I had felt shy of showing any emotion. In particular, I had been very sensitive about anybody hearing me attempt to speak in tongues.

That had been a real stumbling block for me and was probably the main thing that kept me bound up during those two years. However, I didn't realise that then. At any rate, I found myself suddenly able (but not compelled) to speak in tongues. It came out in a torrent and I didn't want it to stop. I just kept on and on for about 2 hours!

What made it stranger, and more memorable, was that it was accompanied by weeping. As soon as I began to speak in tongues I also began to cry, which was something I had never done before then. I had always been, and still am, particularly reserved, even for a person from England, which is a country that specialises in being reserved.

I wasn't sad. It was a joyful experience and was a release of a lot of pent up emotion. I think God was also doing some deep work inside me, putting some things right that needed to be dealt with. So two breakthroughs were made simultaneously. God enabled me to speak in tongues, and He also enabled me to cry. That too was an ability, or a freedom, that I needed but had lacked.

I believe that God touched me powerfully in my spirit that day. Some things were also being dealt with at an emotional level. When the Holy Spirit comes into a person's life it seems to me that He begins to change us from the inside. I remember that as this weeping and praying in tongues continued, I did not want it to stop. I was concerned that if I stopped I might not be able to start again. I had spent two years feeling paralysed in this area of speaking in tongues and didn't want to risk going back to that.

However, eventually, I stopped. Then, after a moment, in which I felt unsure as to whether it would be possible to start again, I resumed. Happily, there was no difficulty at all in starting again. From that day onwards, I have been able to speak in tongues whenever I choose to. The gift is entirely in my hands. It has been left to me to decide whether and when to use it.

Why did it take me two years to be baptised in the Holy Spirit?

So, why did it take me two years to be baptised in the Holy Spirit and speak in tongues while others experienced it immediately? What held me back? I have reflected on this and I believe the following factors all combined to prevent me from receiving the baptism in the Holy Spirit, or at least from operating in the spiritual gifts:

a) I was tense and keyed up. I felt shy and awkward about speaking in tongues out loud in front of others, or even by myself. I was afraid that I would begin to attempt it, but fail, and be embarrassed.

b) I had wrongly thought that it would be something God would *do to me*, or impose on me. I assumed it would come down on me from above without me needing to be active or do anything. So, I kept waiting for God to do something, but I think He was waiting for me to just speak and get started.

c) I had never been baptised in water. Oddly, for a group of believers whose Bible knowledge was otherwise so good, the people who had led me to faith never told me that I needed to be baptised in water. Perhaps they felt shy about saying it, given that so many people take offence at being told that. I don't know. They either never told me, or I never heard them. At any rate, I didn't get baptised in water. I assumed that the baptism in water I had had as a baby, in the Catholic church, was sufficient. I did not know then that it wasn't and that I was being disobedient to what the Bible clearly teaches about baptism in water.

I feel that these three factors, combined together, held me back. In the end God, in His mercy, intervened and rescued me. If not, I could have gone on like that for decades, as many people do. So, God made an exception with me, as He did with Cornelius, in Acts chapter 10. He allowed me to receive the Holy Spirit before I was baptised in water, whereas the New Testament clearly shows that baptism in water should happen first.

I don't recommend what I did. I should have got baptised in water straight away when I first repented and believed. Had I done so, I feel that being baptised in water would probably have produced the breakthrough I needed.

I would then have received the baptism in the Holy Spirit either immediately or very soon after being baptised in water. Still, despite all my errors, ignorance and hang-ups, God intervened and helped me to break through. God also helped me to overcome the silly, but to me very real, barrier of my own shyness and self-consciousness.

God is a very kind and tender parent. He knows each of His children individually and is aware of all their different ways and hang-ups. Therefore, He wisely and sensitively dealt with my specific problems so that I could be free to break through.

The gifts of the Holy Spirit in more detail

We have already seen the gifts of the Holy Spirit discussed by Paul in the earlier passage, 1 Corinthians 14:1-33. There is not space to examine all of these gifts fully in this book, but I will, at least, list them and briefly explain them. These are gifts which are *still available to us today* and we should ask God for them. He wants us to have them.

Don't be shy about it, as I was. Don't hold back. Ask God for these gifts with eagerness, so that you can be more useful to God in the work He is calling you to. Let's look again at the full list of spiritual gifts which apostle Paul sets out for us:

> ***7But to each one is given the manifestation of the Spirit for the common good. 8For to one is given the word of wisdom through the Spirit, and to another the word of knowledge according to the same Spirit; 9to another faith by the same Spirit, and to another gifts of healing by the one Spirit, 10and to another the effecting of miracles, and to another prophecy, and to another the distinguishing of spirits, to another various kinds of tongues, and to another the interpretation of tongues. 11But one and the same Spirit works all these things, distributing to each one individually just as He wills.***
>
> ***1 Corinthians 12:7-11 (NASB)***

Now let's list the nine gifts in turn, in the same order that Paul uses and then define what they are and give some examples of them in operation:

1) The word of wisdom

This means that the Holy Spirit provides you with a specific piece of wisdom, directly from Him, which is needed for the particular situation you are facing. Or, it could be to benefit someone else's situation. A solution or an insight or understanding comes to you from God which meets the need of the moment. It is not from your own mind. It is planted into your mind.

With a word of wisdom, we can help others in ways that we could never do if we just used our own personal wisdom. This is a gift we all need to seek for. Ask God to give you His wisdom in whatever situation you face, so that you can take the right path, or solve a vexed problem. That gift is available to us when we have received the Holy Spirit.

A personal example of an occasion when I have received a word of wisdom is when my son badly injured his finger when he was 13. He got his finger tip caught in a door hinge at school and cut off the end of his finger. He was taken to A&E and then was seen by an orthopaedic surgeon. The finger end was badly damaged and the whole nail was pulled off, plus the fingertip was gone.

I was devastated because my son was a gifted cello player and had won a scholarship to a private school to play the cello. The finger he'd injured was on his left hand and was needed for pressing hard on strings, not just for bowing. Therefore, he needed a full finger with a tip and nail. I spoke to the orthopaedic surgeon, but he said that it was going to be necessary to amputate more of the finger, i.e. right back to the knuckle!

I asked him if he was sure about this and pointed out to him that my son needed the whole finger for cello (and piano). The surgeon was adamant and said that amputation was *"the only way"*. He then called over another orthopaedic surgeon who agreed with what he said. However, I believe that at that moment the Holy Spirit gave me a word of wisdom.

I just knew in my spirit that what I was being told by these two surgeons was wrong. I knew that the finger should not be amputated and that I was being given bad advice. I had no way of knowing that in myself. It was a word of wisdom (and probably also a word of knowledge) from the Holy Spirit. It was not from within myself, or from my own knowledge, because I did not have any knowledge.

So I refused to allow the amputation to go ahead, even though the operation was all lined up and ready to happen within the next hour. I insisted, instead, on being transferred to another surgeon for an official second opinion. That didn't go down well. I then prayed, and rang others to get them to pray, for the next surgeon to give correct advice and to find a way to save and restore the finger.

The next morning, to my great relief, we were put under the care of one of the top hand specialists in the area. Plus, it turned out that he had a daughter who played the cello, so he understood the instrument fully. He knew what was needed and why it mattered so much.

He looked at my son's finger. Unlike the first surgeon, who had said amputation was "the only way", the first words he said were: *"Well, there are at least six different ways of doing this"*. He then described each way, and none of them involved amputation. His view was totally different from that of the first two surgeons! He said he would operate and seek to restore the finger, not to amputate it.

He then operated and took pieces of skin from elsewhere and put them on the badly injured fingertip, which was down to bare bone. Amazingly, over the next year the finger got progressively better. In the end the extent of the healing was astonishing. The nail grew back and so did the flesh at the side and the tip of the finger. Moreover, it was deep enough to enable him to press on the strings of a guitar or cello.

We had been warned that there could be nerve damage and that pressing could be very painful, but it wasn't. The operation was a total success. God also caused the finger to regenerate itself to such an extent that it now looks hardly any different to the other fingers. Now, the point is that I was in a crisis. I was being given wrong medical advice which I was not qualified to disagree with.

Yet, I knew in my spirit that it was wrong. The Holy Spirit had revealed that to me. If I had listened to the first surgeon (and his colleague) instead of to the Holy Spirit, my son would now have a missing finger end. Instead, his finger is virtually perfect and he has no loss of function and no pain either.

Another example of a word of wisdom involved a young man I know. He was a sixth former (aged 17) who was at school, studying for A levels. He had not been wise in his lower sixth form year and had done badly in his chemistry exams. Therefore the teacher told him very firmly that he could not continue to do chemistry in the upper sixth form. He said he would have to give it up and only do physics and biology.

I was being told about this by the young man. He was resigned to this and saw no way round the problem. He had been thrown out of chemistry and that was all there was to it. However, I felt a deep concern rising up inside me. God then gave me a word of wisdom and revealed to me how *He* saw that young man's situation and what should now be done about it.

It was that, although he had been thrown out of chemistry A level, he should nevertheless, turn up for the first lesson of the new school year and just sit down in the class. I said he should tell the teacher that he did not want to stop doing chemistry and then promise to change his ways. He took my advice and turned up, sat down, and spoke to the teacher.

It didn't go down well initially, but he persisted. In the end he was allowed back into the class. He went on to do well in chemistry in the upper sixth form. Ironically, he then took chemistry for his degree, narrowly missing out on first class honours. He then went on to do a Masters degree in chemistry.

Doing that Masters degree then won him a fully paid position to do a PhD in chemistry, which he has recently completed! All of that happened to a lad who had been thrown out of his A level class half way through. The point is that God knew that that young man's future was to be wrapped up in chemistry and that he must not give it up, despite the mess he was in, and despite what his school was telling him.

So, God shared His thoughts with me. He revealed His sense of concern and urgency and gave me a word of wisdom which met the need of the moment. Therefore, what I told that young man wasn't just a good idea, it was a *"God-idea"*.

If I had simply thought up that plan for myself it wouldn't have worked. Also, who would ever have imagined that chemistry was going to be such a vital part of the future of a young man who had just been kicked out of A level? At a human level it made no sense, but it was God's wisdom in operation and reflected God's deeper understanding of the situation and of the future.

That is the difference that a word of wisdom can make. They ought to be much more common, and they would be, if more people were willing to believe that the gifts of the Holy Spirit are for us to use today. By the way, I should add that in my son's case, I think the gift of faith was also involved. (see below).

2) The word of knowledge

This is similar to the word of wisdom, except that it involves being given a specific *fact* or *piece of knowledge* rather than wisdom or understanding. The Holy Spirit reveals a fact to us to help us, or which we can say to another person, which unlocks the situation. It can provide a breakthrough. For example it could be that there is an illness or disease that needs healing.

Or it could be about some problem or danger, of which they would, otherwise, be unaware. For example, I can remember on one occasion being exasperated by some ongoing problems in my business. I was asking God to tell me what on Earth was causing the problems, because I was baffled.

To my great surprise I then heard, in my head, an almost audible voice saying a person's name. I was amazed because it was the last person I would ever have expected. I had no idea that they were causing harm. I believe that God revealed that person's name to me. However, I did not just rely on that, because I knew that I could have been mistaken and so I was not willing to act based solely on that.

Therefore I did not take any action at that point, but I did begin to make a lengthy series of enquiries to check behind the scenes and to find out as much as I could. I wanted to know what this person had been doing and whether or not they were being faithful to me and to the business, which I had always assumed they were.

When I had finished investigated it (very thoroughly and carefully), I found it to be entirely true. They had been causing great harm in the firm and had been deceiving me for a long time. That was a total revelation to me. I could not have figured it out for myself. Or, if I ever had, it would have taken much longer.

So, the purpose of that word of knowledge was not that I should act on it by getting rid of that person, there and then. It was intended to alert me to the real source of the problem, so that I could look into it thoroughly and then take whatever steps were necessary and fair. God is very practical and He still wanted me to go through all the proper steps of an investigatory procedure, even after being alerted by His warning.

God also regularly gave me words of knowledge (and words of wisdom) in my job as a lawyer and a manager. I found myself repeatedly in situations, when handling a client's case, where I just instantly put my finger on some point of detail, or some issue. It then turned out to be the key fact in a case, on which it all turned. Or, God would alert me to a hazard or problem, which I could not have realised for myself.

However, this did not only occur when dealing with staff in my law firm, or when handling client's cases. It also happened within my family, in my capacity as a husband and father. God would give me words of knowledge to alert me to some hazard or danger, or to the real nature of some problem. Sometimes that would be because He wanted me to do something practical about it, but at other times it would be done simply to alert me, so that I could pray about it.

For example I vividly recall an occasion when I was getting ready to leave the house one morning to go to work. It was the day before my daughter's fourth birthday. As I was in the hallway, about to leave, I saw her walking by and I then heard an almost audible voice, in my head, saying: "*Will she make it to her fourth birthday?*"

I was deeply startled by that, in itself. However, I also felt a sudden and strong feeling of alarm and that she was in some kind of danger. Therefore I prayed for her, very earnestly, and asked for God's protection and help. Then I set off for work and the kids were taken to school by my wife.

I was telephoned later, by my wife, and told that when they had arrived at the school, about 15 minutes later, my wife was attending to something with her car and my daughter ran across the car park and then stood behind some other parked car. At that moment, the parked car, which had already got a driver in it, began to reverse out of the parking place.

My daughter was not visible to the driver, as she was too small to be seen through the rear window. She was in the driver's blind spot. My daughter did not realise what was happening and my wife had her back to it and did not see the situation until it was too late.

However, at that very moment, another parent was passing by. She ran over and urgently snatched my daughter up, out of the way of the reversing car, at the very last second and thus saved her life. She was therefore completely uninjured. I fully believe that that incident was a demonically inspired attempt on my daughter's life.

However, it was one which God had warned me about beforehand, by that word of knowledge, such that I was able to pray for her. Therefore the demonic plot was foiled. That is how I see it. However, even if you don't believe that demons play any active part in our lives, the fact is that it was an imminent danger, to which God alerted me, so that I could pray about it and prevent it.

Let me give another example, which is along similar lines, but involved my son, when he was about eight years old. I drove out of our drive way one morning, to go to work, and was approaching the corner of the street on which we lived. At that point, I then suddenly felt a strong sense of danger and alarm, concerning my family. It was very powerful. Moreover, it intensified sharply as I approached the corner itself. So I instantly began to pray for protection for my family.

I also remember very distinctly, as I went around the corner, looking down at the kerbstones at the corner of the junction. I felt my eyes were drawn to look at them and I focused on the kerb. Though I had no idea why at the time, that image of the kerb distinctly registered with me.

Then I continued to drive and, as I went past that corner, the acute feeling of alarm lifted off me and the sense of danger went away. The whole episode can only have taken 10 seconds, but it was as if it was all played out in slow motion.

When I got home that evening I was told that my son had just had an accident when out riding his bike on the street after school. He had fallen off it and he went out with me and showed me where he had hit his head on the kerbstone at the corner of the street. It was at the very spot to which my eye had been drawn that morning, and at which I had felt the most acute level of alarm!

I believe that God had warned me of the danger which was coming up that day and had therefore enabled me to pray about it. Therefore I believe the outcome was totally different. The bang to my son's head hurt him, but caused no injury, whereas my firm belief is that he would, otherwise, have been seriously injured, or even killed.

Each of those incidents concerning my kids were, I believe, examples of the gift of the word of knowledge in operation. Sometimes it involves literal words, as in the first example I gave with the colleague's name being uttered, and in the second, where I heard a voice speaking about my daughter. However, at other times it need not necessarily involve any words. It can simply be knowledge or information which is given by some other means.

I don't recall any words at all in the third example, concerning my son. I didn't even know that it involved him. I just knew, somehow, that there was a danger and that it concerned my family. You could say that I sensed it, but I believe that the Holy Spirit communicated it to me, at the level of my spirit, rather than my mind. He is very varied in how He chooses to go about doing things and so it can happen in all sorts of ways.

I have deliberately chosen to give examples of the word of knowledge, and also the word of wisdom, which show their relevance to everyday life, at work or school or in our personal life, not just at church meetings. They can certainly also be given in a church meeting, but *not only* in that context.

That is worth emphasising, because few people seem to realise that God wants spiritual gifts to be used *in every part of our life, not just in the setting of a church meeting.* Perhaps the most common context where I find God gives me words of knowledge or words of wisdom is where I am sharing the Gospel one to one with a person.

God will often give me a point to make, or an analogy, or illustration, or a question to ask, which is extremely relevant or timely in the life of that person. It just comes out of me, without me even needing to think. I just open my mouth and begin to speak and then realise that I am saying something very relevant and specific, which I didn't know that I was going to say, or wasn't even aware that I knew at all.

That has occurred more times than I could ever remember. So these examples illustrate the point that spiritual gifts are meant to be used regularly and freely, in everyday life, not rarely, or as a last resort, and certainly not only in church buildings.

3) The gift of faith

This is when God gives you the specific faith to believe Him for something, so that you can then pray with greatly enhanced confidence that the prayer will be answered. You might face a difficult situation and you don't have enough faith to ask for help and to believe that that prayer will be answered.

The gift of faith can suddenly lift up the level of your faith so that you can then ask with full confidence, expecting your prayer to be answered. Or, where you face a problem or there is danger, you can step out in faith, believing God will provide for you. With this gift you will attempt things, or ask for things, where you would not otherwise do so.

It transforms your prayers and your actions from mere presumption into stepping out in faith. That's because the gift of faith has been imparted to you from outside of yourself. It is not merely worked up by yourself, in your own strength, or by your own effort. In 1999 I believe God gave me the gift of faith to enable me to set up a new business when all the facts and circumstances seemed to suggest that it would inevitably fail and that there was no point even trying.

However, because I had the gift of faith, I pressed on and refused ever to give up, even though there were a vast number of difficulties to overcome. I couldn't have done it without the gift of faith and probably wouldn't even have been willing to attempt it.

Let me give an example of the operation of the gift of faith in the context of a crisis we faced when a close relative was dangerously ill and it was feared that he may not survive the night. It happened some years ago. He had had an abdominal operation which had gone badly wrong and he then needed a second operation, which was far more invasive, to deal with the severe damage caused by the first one going wrong.

He then had to go into intensive care, where he was unconscious and on a life support machine. We had been praying for him throughout all of this. Then one night, about two weeks after the first operation, and six days after the second operation, there was a decline in his condition and he had to go to the operating theatre again for yet further complications.

However, he was, by now, in a seriously weakened condition overall. Therefore the doctors were speaking in very grave terms. I spoke to his wife in the waiting room at the hospital and I perceived that she did not expect him to survive this third operation and that she believed that death was imminent. We all sat around in the waiting room, in the early hours of the morning, at a weekend, when this third emergency surgery was about to be done.

There were long faces all round and an overwhelming mood of helplessness and despondency. The family in question were not Christians and had no faith and no basis for hope. Then, to add to the gloom, a doctor came in and told us all that if they were to find any more leaks from the intestines then his chances of survival were small, even if they were able to repair such a leak, as they had done in the second operation.

As the doctor said that it was like another hammer blow and the morale of the family sank even lower. It was plain that they had little or no hope and were resigning themselves to face the worst. It was at that moment, when everything looked and sounded so utterly bleak, that I believe God gave me the gift of faith. That then enabled me to handle that challenge and to make a difference. What I then did was also an example of the 'proclamation' of Scripture, which I explain in my Book Six.

However, what I will focus on here is the gift of faith. I felt a welling up inside me of defiance and of a determination not to accept the bad news that we were getting, which had got worse and worse as it went along. Instead I knew in my spirit that I must 'maintain a positive confession' and that I had to begin to speak words of faith, hope and confidence in God's ability and willingness to intervene.

I knew that I also needed to take a stand and to defy the demons' plans, which were to take his life that night, and that I needed to begin to proclaim God's Word into the situation. Therefore, even though I was in a waiting room, surrounded by a large group of relatives who were not Christians, and who did not have any faith, or know the Bible, I knew I needed to speak and pray out loud and with boldness and defiance.

Before doing so, I asked his wife if it was alright with her for me to pray out loud and to read from the Bible and she agreed immediately. Indeed, she was eager. I then began to read out loud from Psalm 103:1-5, Psalm 121 and then Psalm 123:1-3(a). I did so with a warlike attitude of confidence, and even aggression, being determined to reject what Satan wanted for that man and putting all my trust in God to intervene and to bring him through this crisis.

From that point on, something broke in the spiritual 'climate' and the news from then on got better, He survived the night, and, after some weeks, came out of intensive care, firstly onto high dependency, then onto a ward and then, eventually, he went home. By the time he died, which was over two years later, he had become a Christian.

Moreover, his wife was also saved later on. However, on that terrible night of his third operation, when we were anticipating his imminent death, he was an unsaved man, facing a lost eternity. The gift of faith which God gave to me on that occasion, and to me alone, was able to turn the situation around. That is why it is such a vital gift. It turns a plaintive prayer of supplication into a bold, assertive, confident prayer of faith, which is the kind of prayer that God has promised to answer.

I will give another example of the gift of faith, this time in totally different circumstances. It was in the very early days of my brand new law firm, which I had set up as an act of faith, against incredible odds, as I mentioned earlier. There came a day when I was in an acute financial crisis as the cash flow was very severe, due to being a new start business with little or nothing in the pipeline from past work done.

So I rang the Inland Revenue and spoke to someone at the local tax office. They owed me a large amount of money as a tax rebate which was due to me by virtue of me having left my previous business and started all over again. I desperately needed that tax refund to help me with the cash flow crisis I faced in the new firm.

When I spoke to the tax official he was blunt and unhelpful and told me that my file was not even due to be looked at for several more weeks. Even then, he said it would take a number of further weeks for it to be reassessed and for any refund to be paid to me. I pressed him and stressed the urgency, but he was adamant that nothing could be done to speed up the procedure.

Therefore the facts and circumstances were grim and there seemed no hope of any breakthrough. If I had continued just to look at the facts and circumstances, then the position would have remained the same. However, God then gave me the gift of faith and I began to pray about the situation with hugely increased boldness and with a confident expectation of God's intervention on my behalf.

Moreover, later that evening I felt a prompting to go to the very offices of the Inland Revenue, when they were closed, and to pray outside their front door. So that is exactly what I did. I went there, and stood outside, and began to pray with boldness for God to step in and to cut through the maze of red tape and release my money to me very quickly. I also read out passages from God's Word and 'proclaimed' His promises of provision out loud, claiming them, relying upon them, and trusting God to meet my needs and answer my prayers.

About 36 hours later, I got a call from the tax office, without me having contacted them further at all. They said that my full tax refund had just been processed and was now on its way to me! They gave no explanation as to how, or why, this had happened, or how I had jumped the queue. I didn't ask either. I already knew exactly what had happened and who had done it.

It goes to show, yet again, just how much can be accomplished when a Christian prays with real, God-given faith. That is the kind of faith which moves mountains and we all need to ask God to give us far more of it.

By the way, I should add that what I did in praying outside the tax office was nothing at all to do with the so called 'Word of Faith' movement, or the 'prosperity gospel', which you might have heard of. Those things are unbiblical, are not of God and are not what I am speaking of here or advocating.

The gift of faith is given to us achieve God's purposes, not to make us rich or to give us what we want. I hope I have emphasised that strongly enough, but I say more about the errors of the 'Word of Faith' movement in my Book Six.

4) The gift of healing

This gift means that a person is given the faith needed to pray for healing for themselves or another person. They are then supernaturally healed by God's power. This gift is rarely seen in Western churches because our minds are so utterly saturated with unbelief and scepticism.

However, the gift of healing is much more common in the Developing World. In such places, where medical help isn't very available, the people seek much more earnestly for this gift. More people are therefore physically healed by God's miraculous intervention than in the West.

That ought not to be the case, but it is, due to our unbelief, hardness of heart and dullness of mind. This problem of unbelief is not unique to the West, or to the modern day. It has always existed. Indeed, it even had an effect on Jesus Himself and meant that He could not do as many miracles in Nazareth as he could do elsewhere.

That was because the people of His home town knew Him and His family and His humble background as a carpenter/builder. That caused them to despise Him and to think less of Him. In particular, it meant that the locals in Nazareth did not believe that He could even be a prophet from God, let alone the Messiah. Therefore, not only were they full of unbelief, but they actually "took offense" at Him and at His claims about Himself, and gave Him no honour.

However, the operative point, for our purposes here, is that they did not believe that He could heal people. Therefore, because of their unbelief, not His own, He didn't heal many when He was in their presence. In other words, their lack of faith, had a huge bearing on what Jesus was willing, and even able, to do:

55 Is not this the carpenter's son? Is not His mother called Mary, and His brothers, James and Joseph and Simon and Judas? 56 And His sisters, are they not all with us? Where then did this man get all these things?" 57 And they took offense at Him. But Jesus said to them, "A prophet is not without honor except in his hometown and in his own household." 58 And He did not do many miracles there because of their unbelief.

Matthew 13:55-58 (NASB)

By contrast, where people do have faith, and are not crippled by unbelief, we really can see miracles of healing taking place, even in the West. I can recall a situation in a very good church which we were part of in the early 1990s. A particular family had a baby boy who had just been diagnosed as having cerebral palsy.

The doctors spoke gloomily of how he would be unable to walk and that the family would have to alter their home, or move house, so that their son would be able to have a downstairs bedroom in future. However, there was a rising of faith within the church and we all began to pray for him to be healed.

It actually began when the baby's father spoke in church of the news they had been given by the doctors. He said, with resolve and defiance in his voice, that he was not accepting it and that he refused to believe that that was to be his son's future. As he spoke in that confident way, faith spread to the rest of us. I believe it was the gift of faith, which he had received first, but which God then gave to the rest of us as well.

There was also something different about this case, which enabled us to pray with a sense of expectancy that we did not exhibit on other occasions where we had prayed for the sick to be healed. What I mean is that it was not only that God gave us the gift of faith, as discussed above. It was also the fact that the baby was so young which made us feel more able to believe that God could heal him, because it could be done slowly.

That may be irrational, because God is just as capable of doing 'big' or 'quick' miracles as He is of doing 'small' ones, or 'slow' ones. However, for many of us, the reality is that if you face a situation where someone is an adult, with terminal cancer, your faith may just drain away and you are overwhelmed with unbelief.

Yet, if the person you are praying for is a child, such that God has got years in which to heal him, you somehow feel more able to have faith that it can be done, even though it still requires a miracle. Anyway, the point is that we all prayed boldly and expectantly for that boy and God really did move miraculously to heal him. As he grew up, over the space of a few years, his condition improved remarkably and did not take the grim course which the doctors had said it would. Far from being unable to walk, as they had said, the boy got stronger and stronger. He is now completely well and can not only walk, but run, and engage in sports as well as anybody else.

So, his case is an example of what God can, and does, do when people pray for healing with faith, rather than unbelief. Someone might object at this point that perhaps it was a wrong diagnosis and the child never had cerebral palsy to begin with. I don't accept that. I believe the diagnosis was correct.

However, even if that was not the case, the operative point is that that child had something gravely wrong with him, as we could all see for ourselves and, whatever it was, it gradually went away and was healed over a period of time. So, whatever it was that he was healed of, the point is that he was healed, and that it was God who did it.

5) The gift of effecting of miracles (or working of miracles)

This is similar to the gift of healing but more general. Thus it would relate to any supernatural, miraculous intervention. Again it is rare in the West, but it shouldn't be, and wouldn't be, if we were not so saturated in unbelief.

6) The gift of prophecy

Prophecy is *not* divination or fortune telling. That is evil and is of the occult. The gift of prophecy means the ability, by the power of the Holy Spirit, to speak God's truth into a situation. We deliver a message which God wishes to give, but *He does it through us*, in our own native language. It often relates to the future and reveals something which is going to happen. If so, it needs to turn out to be entirely accurate or it should be rejected as false.

Prophecy is always a message *from God to the people.* That is the direction of travel. Thus it differs from the interpretation of tongues (see below) which involves us saying something *to or about God,* such as praise, worship, prayer etc. The main purpose of the gift of prophecy is to edify, exhort and console other people:

1Pursue love, yet desire earnestly spiritual gifts, but especially that you may
prophesy. 2For one who speaks in a tongue does not speak to men but to God;
for no one understands, but in his spirit he speaks mysteries. 3But one who
prophesies speaks to men for edification and exhortation and consolation. 4One
who speaks in a tongue edifies himself; but one who prophesies edifies the
church. 5Now I wish that you all spoke in tongues, but even more that you
would prophesy; and greater is one who prophesies than one who speaks in tongues, unless he interprets, so that the church may receive edifying.

1 Corinthians 14:1-5 (NASB)

Whenever a prophecy or *"prophetic word"* is given it should always be weighed and tested very carefully by those hearing it. It should only be accepted if it is genuinely from the Holy Spirit. That therefore requires people with discernment to be able to know what it is and the courage to say whether it is valid. (see below)

An example from the Bible of a person giving a personal word of prophecy to another person is the account in Acts chapter 21 of Agabus. He told Paul what trouble awaited him if he was to go to Jerusalem, which Paul was determined to do:

[10]As we were staying there for some days, a prophet named Agabus came down
from Judea. [11]And coming to us, he took Paul's belt and bound his own feet
and hands, and said, "This is what the Holy Spirit says: 'In this way the Jews
at Jerusalem will bind the man who owns this belt and deliver him into the
hands of the Gentiles.'" [12]When we had heard this, we as well as the local
residents began begging him not to go up to Jerusalem. [13]Then Paul answered,
"What are you doing, weeping and breaking my heart? For I am ready not only
to be bound, but even to die at Jerusalem for the name of the Lord Jesus." [14]And
since he would not be persuaded, we fell silent, remarking, "The will of the Lord
be done!" [15]After these days we got ready and started on our way up to
Jerusalem.

Acts 21:10-15 (NASB)

So, Agabus was able to tell Paul what lay ahead. Paul was arrested in Jerusalem and imprisoned and ended up being sent to Rome to be tried. Agabus' prophecy allowed Paul and those around him *to be prepared* for what lay ahead and to be able to pray for Paul. Thus, neither Paul nor his friends were caught out or surprised when he was later taken into protective custody in Jerusalem, due to so many people seeking to kill him:

[10]And as a great dissension was developing, the commander was afraid Paul
would be torn to pieces by them and ordered the troops to go down and take him
away from them by force, and bring him into the barracks. [11]But on the night
immediately following, the Lord stood at his side and said, "Take courage; for
as you have solemnly witnessed to My cause at Jerusalem, so you must witness
at Rome also."

Acts 23:10-11 (NASB)

From my own experience, another example of a prophecy relating to the future was one which was given to me in 2004. It came very indirectly from a friend of a friend of a friend of mine. A man called Chris had heard of me from a friend of his called John, who was a friend of my friend, Bob. They all lived over 100 miles from me and I didn't know Chris or John at all. Neither did my friend Bob know Chris, so it was all very much at arm's length.

Yet God gave Chris a very clear, very helpful, word of prophecy concerning my business and it was passed on to me. It was detailed, but it basically related to the fact that I was going to go through a period during which a series of people were going to plunder my business and steal from me. However, he said that I should not be alarmed when it occurred.

He said that God had it all under control and would not allow them to go beyond a certain point and would ensure that the business remained fruitful. He also said that God would repay me seven times over for everything that was stolen from me.

That prophecy came out of the blue, from someone I had never met, but it all proved to be entirely accurate. I therefore knew about this period of difficulty in advance, and was encouraged to keep going and not to be alarmed by it. That really helped me to keep it all in perspective.

It also alerted me to pray about it and to be prepared for it all, which reduced the scale of the losses. So, that prophecy greatly encouraged me. It built up my faith, endurance and hope at a difficult time. That shows how valuable prophecy can be, when it is valid and is genuinely from the Holy Spirit. It is like a word in season which has a huge impact for good. I have always been grateful for that particular word of prophecy and for Chris, the man who gave it, whom I've still never met.

However, the gift of prophecy does not always relate to the future. It is often used to reveal what God feels and wishes us to know about what *has been happening*, or what *is happening now,* or to tell us something about us or about the state of the church. It could be a word of encouragement, correction, guidance or even rebuke. Whatever it is, it should always be carefully weighed and tested by those who hear it.

Nothing should ever be accepted uncritically or passively. In particular, whatever is said must never contradict the Bible. If it does, it is not a genuine prophecy. This gives us yet another reason to study and be familiar with the *whole Bible,* so that our discernment is more thoroughly informed.

7) The gift of distinguishing of spirits

This means the supernatural ability to tell whether something said or done is coming from God, or from a demon, or merely from a person themselves. So, if someone gives a prophecy you might be unsure whether it is a real prophecy from God, or a false demonic counterfeit, or of purely human origin from the person themselves. If so, this gift is of great value.

God reveals to us the *origin or source* of what was said or done by that other person. We really need to seek for this gift today. It is not highly regarded or sought after, but it ought to be as it is desperately needed, given the extent of the deception and apostasy within so many churches. It is a great help to the church when a large number of members have this gift. Let me give an example of one of the times when I have operated in this gift myself:

Many years ago I was Chairman of the Trustees in quite a large charismatic church. The church contained a mixture of some good and bad things. I was struggling to know what to think about some of the carnal, worldly behaviour and false spiritual manifestations that were coming in to the church. It was a highly confusing situation. I knew some things were wrong, but I couldn't quite put my finger on exactly what was going on.

I was even more confused because in some ways the leader of the church was, himself, a major concern to me. I was troubled by his actions and by the way he spoke. Sometimes he seemed to be genuine, but at other times he would surprise me by acting in carnal, manipulative, dishonest and controlling ways. He didn't add up and it was very confusing to me.

However, he was the leader of the church and I naively assumed that he must, therefore, be genuine. Plus I'd seen him do many good things, especially in past years. Yet, now, he was different and something was wrong, even sinister. If it happened today I would weigh him up far quicker, but, in those days I knew so much less. I needed God to step in and give me understanding of what was really going on.

Then one Sunday morning, God gave me a revelation of what the problem really was. I suddenly became able to see what was happening and what lay behind all the confusion. I was sitting listening to the leader speaking at the front of the church when I saw something very strange in his eyes that I had never seen in anybody before.

His eyes and his whole face suddenly changed. His eyes lit up and became someone else's eyes. They were very different and did not even look human. They glowed and looked entirely evil. I was, in fact, looking into the eyes of the demon which was within, or operating through, the leader. I also saw the demon's face in his face, which became contorted. His facial appearance altered dramatically. It was horrible.

It went on for about 10 or 15 seconds and then it stopped. I would, perhaps, have assumed that I must have imagined it. However, there are at least two reasons why I feel sure it was genuine and that God really had revealed to me that a demon was operating in and through the leader of the church, which I would never have guessed or figured out for myself.

The first is that immediately after the service another man, who was older than me, and who was a fellow trustee in the church, came over to me. We looked at each other and I could see he was very concerned. I said *"Did you see what I just saw?"* He looked grimly at me and said *"I did"*.

We then discussed it. Both of us had seen the same things. I don't know if anybody else did. I expect not. I expect they saw nothing at all. The congregation certainly gave no impression of having seen anything.

It was something which probably only the two of us had seen, because only we had operated at that moment in the gift of distinguishing of spirits. I think that because the situation was so serious, and involved the very leader of the church himself, God revealed it to two of us simultaneously, so that each of us could be sure that we were not mistaken.

Secondly, subsequent events seemed to prove the truth of what I had seen. Things went from bad to worse. More and more lies were told. More carnal and manipulative things were done. Eventually, that leader gave up his ministry completely and left his wife for another woman.

I tried to reach out to him, to help him and get him to repent. So did the other man who had seen the demon in his eyes. Yet, in one sense, we both failed. The leader was not willing to listen or to repent. He just hardened his heart.

I couldn't do anything to stop the collapse of the church that followed, but at least God had warned me and enabled me to try to help the leader and others. By the way, I didn't tell others what I'd seen that morning, not even the leader. Its purpose was to help me and the other trustee to understand what was going on, so that we could help the leader and the church. It wasn't meant to be broadcast, at least not on that occasion.

Let me give you another example of an occasion when God enabled me to operate in the gift of distinguishing of spirits. It happened years later and concerned a church member called 'Sandra', about whom I provide a lot more detail in Book 6. I was concerned about her devious, manipulative behaviour, and had grave doubts about her overall spiritual condition.

So, I already knew there were serious problems, but I wasn't sure exactly how serious those problems were, or what was causing them. Therefore, one day, as we were preparing to go to a house group meeting, at which Sandra would be present, I prayed for God's guidance. I asked Him to show me what Sandra was really like and how seriously I ought to take things.

Later that very evening, at the start of the house group meeting, God gave me a vision which vividly revealed Sandra's spiritual condition. I looked over at her and was amazed by what I saw. Her whole face suddenly mutated, while I was watching her, and became like the face of a carved gargoyle statue on a medieval church building. Her face became grey and her skin looked like stone. It was also contorted and looked horribly evil and was covered in pock marks.

Then, after about 10 seconds, during which I had been staring at her face, it suddenly transformed back to what it normally looked like. I knew immediately that God had answered my prayer. He had allowed me to see Sandra's real nature and the gravity of her spiritual condition. That was that there was a demon inside her.

She had, many years earlier, before becoming a Christian, been actively involved in spiritualism. However, so far as I was aware, she had never been delivered of any demons, either at the time of her alleged conversion, or since. I concluded that God was showing me that a demon had entered her back then and that that demon was still there and was having a major effect on her character and behaviour.

I ought to explain, by way of background information, that if anybody gets involved in the occult, such as spiritualism, tarot cards, fortune telling, séances, ouija boards etc, they are likely to have a demon enter into them. That demon will then stay permanently, until and unless it is expelled.

I did not immediately act on what I had seen, or say anything about it. However, I did take it as my cue to investigate the situation much more thoroughly. So, I started to find out what other information I could gather. In particular, I called a meeting with two other highly trusted couples at which I shared with them what I had seen.

We then openly discussed the subject of Sandra, and also her husband, Philip, for the first time. That was because, until then, each of us had been totally confidential about our own individual concerns. When we shared the fragments of information that we each knew, a host of additional events, issues, problems and concerns came to light. It was as if we had each previously had a few pieces of a jigsaw puzzle. However, none of us had had all the pieces until then.

Therefore none of us had been able to see the full picture, or to realise how severe the problem was. So, the effect of the revelation which God gave me was that it galvanised me into calling that meeting, which led, in turn, to the six of us drawing up a detailed catalogue of incidents.

When we then looked together at that long list, the extent and gravity of the situation became obvious to us all. However, we probably wouldn't have reached that stage until much later, if at all, if I hadn't received that guidance.

8) The gift of tongues (private and public)

We need to distinguish between two different ways in which the gift of tongues operates. There are *private* tongues which are purely for your own personal use when you are alone. With that gift you can pray on your own in tongues, i.e. to pray *"in the Spirit"*. That will strengthen and edify you. It is also a means by which God can put prayers into our mouths which He wants us to pray.

Or He can put praise and worship into our mouths even though we can't understand it. I use tongues very regularly in private and I always feel better for it. That is to be expected. Indeed, apostle Paul said he spoke in tongues more than all (any) of the people in Corinth:

I thank God, I speak in tongues more than you all;
1 Corinthians 14:18 (NASB)

What Paul meant by that was that he spoke in (private) tongues more than any other person at Corinth, not more than all of them put together. I clarify that because I've heard people say that he meant that he spoke in tongues more than all of them combined. They then suggest that it meant that the people at Corinth *didn't* generally speak in tongues.

They then put that forward as a justification for them *not* speaking in tongues, i.e. that the people in Corinth didn't speak in tongues very much. It doesn't mean that at all. On the contrary, it just means that Paul used the gift of tongues a lot, to edify himself and to build himself up.

The clear implication is that we should follow Paul's example and use the gift of tongues regularly, not that we should avoid it or ban it. Indeed, Paul tells the Corinthians directly that he wishes they would all speak in tongues and that they would all prophesy.

Clearly that has to mean that *they did not all do so*, or he wouldn't have said it. However that fact cannot be used as an argument *against* speaking in tongues and/or prophesying, because Paul clearly says he wishes they *would* all do so:

Now I wish that you all spoke in tongues, but even more that you would prophesy; and greater is one who prophesies than one who speaks in tongues, unless he interprets, so that the church may receive edifying.
1 Corinthians 14:5 (NASB)

Another form of the gift of tongues is when the gift is for *public* use. It is good in a church meeting, or just when a group of believers are gathered together, for up to two or three people (one at a time) to speak out loud in tongues. They should each then pause and allow what has been said to be interpreted by someone else in the meeting who has the gift of interpretation of tongues. Or it can be interpreted by the person themselves, i.e. the one who gave the original message in tongues.

What is said in tongues will always be directed *from the person towards God.* Tongues enables us to address God more fluently. It will not be a message from God to us, though other things could be referred to within it, as happened in the instance that Derek Prince spoke of, where a Welshman's sins were described within the message in tongues (given by a non-Welsh speaker). That is, the person speaking in tongues was praying to God (in Welsh) *for* the Welshman, not saying something on God's behalf *to* the Welshman.

9) The gift of interpretation of tongues

This is a gift that enables a person to understand what has been said by themselves, or by someone else, speaking publicly in tongues. God gives understanding and then the person interprets it in ordinary speech, in their own language, so that all can understand it. This gift should always be used whenever tongues are spoken publicly.

Tongues are basically directed from the people towards God. Therefore, when the interpretation is given it will, if it is valid, always be in that direction. It will be saying something that is addressed *to God*, not to the people.

So it differs from prophecy, which is about God speaking to the people. A message in that direction would be given directly as a prophecy, not by way of tongues with interpretation. Therefore, it is vitally important that when that interpretation is given, there must be mature people listening to it who are willing to speak up and challenge it if it is not correct.

That is needed to prevent false interpretations being given. Someone else in the meeting also needs to be operating in the gifts of interpretation and/or distinguishing of spirits. That will enable what is being said to be tested and verified.

What should be the manner in which we receive the Holy Spirit? Should it be a distinct and noticeable experience or is it valid for it to be imperceptible?

When we receive the Holy Spirit it is meant to be an event which you can't miss. It is supposed to be very noticeable. Indeed, one of the very purposes of being filled with, or baptised in, the Holy Spirit is to confirm conclusively to ourselves, and to others, that we really have become a Christian. That is one reason why apostle Paul was so easily able to see, and hear, whether a person had, or had not, received the Holy Spirit. In the Bible this event of the baptism in the Holy Spirit is not presented as something quiet, such that you can't tell whether it has happened. You can tell. God doesn't want you to be left in any doubt about it.

So, if we have received the Holy Spirit there should, normally, be a clear sign. Usually it is that we will be able immediately to begin to speak in tongues, and/or to operate in one or more of the other gifts, though probably not all of them. These other gifts will not necessarily come immediately. Some of them could come immediately, for example prophecy or interpretation of tongues. Others may come later, as and when we need them.

I have never heard of anybody having all of the gifts, except for apostle Paul. The sign that most of us should expect to see straight away, is the ability to speak in tongues. It is not just making babbling sounds. It is clear, structured, complex language. It usually flows in full sentences without any effort. and without needing to think or construct it at all.

It has been suggested to me that I am being too dogmatic in suggesting that *most* people can and should speak in tongues. The argument is put to me that there are some people who cannot and do not speak in tongues but, nevertheless, that they are genuine Christians and have received the Holy Spirit.

I wouldn't argue against that. Indeed I know many people who are excellent Christians and mature disciples who have never operated in any spiritual gifts so far as they know. Many of these people that I know, and who are my friends, do not even believe in the gifts being for today.

One question is are such people real Christians? I'm entirely willing to accept that they are. Have they 'received' the Holy Spirit, despite not having, or not using, the gifts? It may well be so. I don't know. It could be that, without realising it, they have been baptised in the Holy Spirit and could operate in spiritual gifts if they chose to do so. I don't know.

What is clear is that they never choose to. That is probably because of their theology, which rules it out. They don't believe that they are *supposed* to operate in spiritual gifts and they don't see *others* doing so. Therefore, they don't do it either.

The real question is not whether such people are Christians, or whether they are saved. I see no basis at all to deny that they are justified and forgiven. The issue is whether they have completed the biblical process of becoming a Christian and whether they have done so in the right manner. In other words, have they been competently or incompetently 'delivered' by the 'midwife' who assisted them at their spiritual birth?

By way of an analogy, if a natural birth in a hospital is handled well, and the child is not damaged or deprived of oxygen, then it will grow and thrive from that point on and develop in the right way. However, if things were not handled correctly in the hospital, due to the incompetence of the midwife, that child could be seriously, and even permanently, damaged and rendered incapable of growing or developing as it should.

Thus, six months later, the baby may still be seven pounds in weight and its arms and legs may not be functioning as they should. Likewise, what if, even after the birth, the baby does not receive colostrum, from the mother? What if the adviser or midwife believes that breast milk is not needed and that bottled milk will suffice?

In such a case, the baby will not be given the boost to its immunity that it would have received if it did receive colostrum from the mother. That is a special substance in the mother's milk which God has created and which He wants every baby to receive in its first feeds, just after it is born. So, in my analogy, the colostrum, which is so helpful to the natural baby, is a little like the baptism in the Holy Spirit for a brand new convert, or spiritual baby.

Nevertheless, we would not say that the baby in the hospital which was starved of oxygen, or which did not receive colostrum, is not a real baby. Neither would we say that it was never born, or that it isn't a human being. There would be no reason to say any of those things. However, what we would say is that the negligence, or wrong advice, of the hospital at the birth stage has damaged that baby.

At the very least, it has deprived it of the crucially important boost to its immune system, which it was meant to receive, and which would have greatly assisted it from then on. Such a baby might then get an infection to which it would not have succumbed if it had received the colostrum, as God intended.

I hope that analogy clarifies the position and helps people to see that I am not attacking those who have not been baptised in the Holy Spirit. Neither am I accusing them of not being real Christians, or of being unsaved or unforgiven. My only aim is to describe and explain the process of becoming a Christian as accurately and biblically as I can and not to leave anything out.

If we do things exactly as they did in the Book of Acts, we maximize the chances of a new believer going on to become a strong disciple. However, if we leave things out, for whatever reason, we do them no favours and give them a poor and inadequate start in their Christian life, the end result of which may be very unfortunate

The Holy Spirit never forces you to receive, or operate in, any of His gifts

Let's address a common area of confusion, which I got wrong myself as a young Christian. You mustn't imagine that the gift of tongues will be *forced upon you*, such that you don't have to do anything at all, or even to speak out. Though the gift of tongues is supernatural, it still operates through your physical tongue. Your tongue is, and always will be, entirely under *your* control.

So, for the gift to begin to operate you do have to *choose to speak.* You have to launch forth and say something. You can't just sit there saying nothing at all and expect the Holy Spirit to take over or do it all for you. He won't. The same applies to prophecy, interpretation, and so on. You have to choose to speak.

The Holy Spirit is the most perfectly well-mannered, gentle, sensitive person you could ever imagine. He does not take over or dominate you or use you like a puppet. He gives gifts, but He gives them to you for you to use, or not to use, *as you freely choose.* The Holy Spirit always respects your free will. He never forces you to do anything.

Many people make the serious mistake (as I did) of never starting to speak in tongues because they wrongly imagine that if it is the real thing it will happen *to* them, automatically and involuntarily, without them needing to do anything or speak at all. They expect to be *"taken over"* like a ventriloquist's dummy or to go into some kind of trance where they speak without any involvement of their own free will. That is all totally mistaken. That is the Devil's way, not the Holy Spirit's.

Indeed, if it happens like that, you can be sure that it is *not* the Holy Spirit who is involved. That is not His way, or His style. By contrast, the hallmark of the Devil and of all his demons is that they always seek to dominate, control and manipulate us. The Holy Spirit never does. So, a medium or spiritualist, when they speak, is under the power and influence of a demon.

That demon will, to some degree, take over and speak through the medium, even overriding their free will. In some cases such mediums may be pure fraudsters, faking it and making it all up for themselves. However, in many other cases, they really are under the dominating power and influence of a demon.

What if nothing happens when we pray to receive the Holy Spirit?

A common explanation, if nothing happens when we pray to receive the Holy Spirit, is simply that the person has been too afraid to speak out loud or too shy to do so in front of others. I was like that myself. It can be that you, yourself, are the blockage. Perhaps the Holy Spirit is just waiting patiently for you to be willing to step out in faith and begin to speak.

So, if you have prayed to receive the Holy Spirit and nothing happens, i.e. there are no tongues, then consider what I have said above. Ask yourself whether you have actually tried to speak. You may not have. The answer could be as simple as that.

You may have just sat there silently and passively, waiting for something to happen. It won't. The Holy Spirit won't ever force you to speak. He will only *enable you to do so.* He always respects your free will (unlike how demons operate) Therefore, go ahead and start to speak. Don't speak English. Just make a sound and continue.

If you have received the gift of tongues, it will flow and you will be able to do it without effort or thinking of what to say. It is best if you do this together with another person who believes that the gifts of the Holy Spirit are for today and who has already received the Holy Spirit themselves and operates in the gifts. They can then encourage and assist you.

However, if there is no such person to help you, then you can still go ahead on your own. Also do not make the mistake of thinking that there must be strong feelings of emotional intensity. That does often happen when a person first speaks in tongues, *but by no means always.*

So do not be put off or discouraged if you feel no different emotionally. That is quite normal. However, if you have prayed to receive the Holy Spirit and have attempted to speak in tongues, but still nothing at all has happened, then there may be one or more other problems. Let's examine what those might be:

Other reasons why sometimes nothing may happen when we pray to receive the Holy Spirit

You need to remember that receiving the Holy Spirit is generally meant to be the fourth and final step in becoming a Christian. There have been some notable exceptions, such as Cornelius the Gentile. He received the Holy Spirit before he was baptised in water. However, I would argue that when that occurred in the New Testament, it was always for some exceptional reason. It's not meant to happen that way normally.

Therefore, if you have prayed to receive the Holy Spirit but nothing has happened, then it may be that God is trying to tell you that something is missing, or that something has been done wrongly or inadequately, in the process of becoming a Christian.

The most likely explanation could be that you may not have taken one or more of the three previous steps which are meant to happen first, before we receive the Holy Spirit. It would be wise, therefore, if you find yourself in this position, to examine yourself and ask yourself whether you have genuinely and properly:

a) **repented** of your sins and turned away from them

b) **believed** in Jesus Christ and put your whole faith and trust in Him, and in Him alone, to save you from your sins

c) **been baptised in water**, as the Bible clearly commands us to do. Remember that this is meant to be done when you are old enough to have repented and believed for yourself. Do not make the mistake which many make, and which I made myself, of assuming that if you have been baptised as a baby that will count. I don't believe it will. (See chapter 16) If that offends you, I can only apologise, but I can't say anything different, because the Bible is so clear on this. So, if that is your position, then don't delay. Go now and be properly baptised in water. Take that third step and obey Jesus' command. Don't neglect or overlook it any further.

Likewise if, on reflection, you think that you have perhaps *not genuinely repented*, or are continuing in some known sin which you know is wrong, then repent properly now. Turn away from any sin or sinful situation which you are aware of.

If you are unclear or confused, just ask God to reveal to you anything you need to repent of which may be a blockage. He will gladly answer that prayer. Also, reread chapter 14 on repentance.

Ask God to make clear to you whether there is something specific in your behaviour or lifestyle that concerns Him. Alternatively, it could be that you have not properly or genuinely believed in, or put your faith and trust in, the Lord Jesus. That's possible. It could be that you have some issues which you are confused or mistaken about.

For example it could be to do with who and what Jesus Christ is. Or it could be about what His death on the cross was all about or why it was needed. Or it could be about whether He rose from the dead. Confusion, error and false teaching are extremely widespread, so this could easily be the problem. Pray and ask God to reveal to you any specific error, deception or significant *doctrinal mistake* you may be affected by. Look also at chapter 15 on believing.

Carefully go through the various points I have set out, which are the basic things a person needs to know, understand and believe. If any of these don't make sense to you, or you don't believe them, or you have been taught something different in the past which you still believe, then ask God to expose any error or deception which may be holding you back. Do this sincerely, with a genuine willingness to be corrected.

One common problem is with people who come out of cults such as the Jehovah's Witnesses. They teach that Jesus Christ is not God, but just a man. Sometimes that error is so deeply ingrained that a person still holds onto it, even after leaving the cult. Or, even if you weren't in a cult, you may just have heard something like that, or been taught it, and it may have taken deep root in your mind. If so, it needs to be corrected.

You can't meaningfully believe in Jesus Christ, if you don't believe that He is the Son of God. If the 'Jesus' that you believe in is just a man, not the God of the Bible, then you would be believing in a false god, instead of the real Jesus. He has to be seen as divine or you are not truly believing in Him in the way the Bible requires you to. You would only be believing in a false god, who is wrongly going by the name Jesus.

For example, I am reminded of a story Derek Prince told about a man with whom he shared the Gospel in Sudan. This man was a Muslim. He wanted to become a Christian and Derek Prince led him in a prayer, but nothing happened. Later it occurred to Derek Prince to question the man closely as to exactly *who* it was that he was praying *to*. It emerged that the man was still praying to Allah, as was his lifelong habit.

That was the problem, because the truth is that 'Allah' is not just an alternative name for the real God of the Bible. That is what many people assume, even in churches. However Allah is actually just the Arabic moon god, whom Mohammed had worshipped when he was a pagan. He simply brought that false god with him into his new religion of Islam and then falsely claimed that it was the God of the Bible. In fact Allah was, still is, and always will be, a demon, just as every other idol or false god is.

Moreover, in addition to having a totally false god, Islam also has a false Jesus, who is not the real Jesus of the Bible. The 'Jesus' of Islam is just an ordinary mortal man, who was not the Son of God, never died on the cross, and never rose from the dead. The counterfeit 'Jesus' of Islam is said to be just a prophet, and, moreover, one who is inferior to Mohammed.

Thus, if a Muslim has this false, manmade substitute for Jesus in mind when they attempt to become a Christian, they will be terribly confused, at best, and will probably not be saved at all. Therefore, they need to be told who, and what, the real Jesus is and also what He did.

Once these errors were cleared up by Derek Prince, and the Muslim man spoke to the real God of the Bible, and prayed in the name of the real Jesus, then he was heard by God and was unmistakably saved.

This same problem also arises with people who have come out of a New Age background. The New Age movement presents many false and distorted versions of Jesus. So it's very possible you could be deceived or misinformed. If so, the Jesus you are following would be a false, distorted, unbiblical, counterfeit, rather than the real Lord Jesus Christ. However, if it is all you have ever been taught, it may seem true to you even though it isn't.

That type of error would cause a total blockage. How can the *real* Jesus answer your prayer and baptise you in the Holy Spirit if you are, in fact, believing in, and praying to, some other false, inaccurate, counterfeit Jesus? Therefore carefully read and reread chapter 15 on believing. Pray about it and ask God to expose any error in your thinking or your knowledge, however small, which might be creating a blockage.

Once you have corrected any errors and taken or retaken any step that was missing or inadequate, then you may now be ready to pray again to receive the Holy Spirit. Hopefully the error or problem will have been removed and you can now receive the Holy Spirit.

If not, and still nothing happens, then just continue to pray earnestly and sincerely. Ask God to reveal the problem, or blockage, or whatever is missing. Keep asking and He will do so. God wants you to receive the Holy Spirit. He is on your side.

Persist therefore until you have found out what the blockage is. Keep on and on asking to receive the Holy Spirit. Do not give up. God is a rewarder of those who diligently seek Him. Therefore be diligent and carry on for as long as it takes. Many people give up even at the first or second obstacle and do not press on. That would be a tragic mistake. Never stop seeking and asking. Keep on and on, for as long as it takes, until your prayer is answered:

7"Ask, and it will be given to you; seek, and you will find; knock, and it will be opened to you. 8"For everyone who asks receives, and he who seeks finds, and to him who knocks it will be opened.

Matthew 7:7-8 (NASB)

In these verses, Jesus Himself is speaking. He tells us to ask, to seek and to knock. However, the clear implication of His words is that we are to *persist* in doing so. He doesn't mean that we should knock once or twice. He means keep on knocking, persistently, until the door is opened.

Why don't we see more of the gifts of the Holy Spirit being used, if they are really from God?

We have to remember that God will not impose Himself or His gifts on us. Therefore, if we reject the gifts, or if we are wary and suspicious of them, we will not be able to operate in them. So, much depends on what the leaders of a particular church say. If they teach that the gifts of the Holy Spirit have ceased, or are not from God at all, then there will be no gifts. You then end up with yet another church where the shutters have been firmly slammed down, keeping out anything of the Holy Spirit. This is very widespread.

At any rate, in Great Britain, we now have a situation where the gifts of the Holy Spirit can be freely used in a small minority of churches, but in most other churches nearby there are no gifts, due to confusion and wrong teaching, Sadly, in those churches, where the gifts of the Holy Spirit are effectively "banned", (though they would never put it that way), even believers who have received the Holy Spirit, and the gifts, will be silenced.

The reality is that in such a church, even those individuals who have been baptised in the Holy Spirit will be pressured, or even intimidated, into not operating in the gifts. Thus, there will be no tongues, interpretation, prophecy, words of wisdom or words of knowledge within the church meetings, even if such things are occurring at an individual level outside of meetings.

This indicates the profound importance of the responsibility that church leaders have to interpret the Bible correctly. They must not reject or forbid genuine gifts which the Holy Spirit wants us to use. We must all be so careful, not only in what we *accept and allow*, but also in what we *reject or forbid*:

39Therefore, my brethren, desire earnestly to prophesy, and do not forbid to speak in tongues. 40But all things must be done properly and in an orderly manner.

1 Corinthians 14:39-40 (NASB)

Even people who have been genuinely baptised in the Holy Spirit are often unable, or unwilling, to operate in spiritual gifts, due to being stifled by fellow church members or leaders.

Even people who have undoubtedly been baptised in the Holy Spirit, and who believe the gifts are for today and have even operated in them elsewhere, can be stifled into silence and inactivity by the people around them. So, if they are in a church which rejects the gifts of the Holy Spirit, forbids tongues or prophecy or prayer for healing and which rejects the supernatural, they will be rendered effectively paralysed. They will be unable to act or speak in any of the Spiritual gifts, even if they could operate elsewhere and have already done so in the past.

As we saw earlier with Jesus' unbelieving, sceptical relatives and neighbours in Nazareth, their negativity, unbelief, and even hostility, can be crippling. However, it is even more basic than that. Quite apart from their unbelief, you can be stifled simply by their disapproval and non-acceptance of the supernatural. That can be the case even if it is never stated expressly, but is only implied or perceived indirectly.

Therefore, for example, one would never be willing to stand up in an English pub and sing 'Danny Boy' or 'The Fields of Athenry' or, indeed, any other song. It would be considered inappropriate and even bizarre behaviour. However, if one was in an Irish pub, especially if it is in a rural area, one would very readily get up and sing, and so would several others. It would be considered perfectly normal and acceptable.

There does not even need to be a sign up in the English pub saying 'No singing allowed here'. You would already know that it is unthinkable. Even if nobody said a word, you would work it out for yourself from the fact that nobody else ever stands up by the bar and sings a song.

That alone would make it clear that you are not welcome to sing there. So, the mere fact that you are *capable* of singing is irrelevant. You still would not do so, because you know perfectly well that others would disapprove, even if only silently, with raised eyebrows and quiet mutterings between themselves.

Accordingly, if you want to operate in the gifts of the Holy Spirit, one of the things you may need to do is to move to a church which permits that and where there are others who also do so and who want you to do so.

Realistically, that is likely to involve you moving to, or even setting up, a small house church, because most traditional, hierarchical, denominational 'clergy led' churches, at least in the UK, have no belief in, or acceptance of, the gifts of the Holy Spirit. Please see my Book Eight for more detail on what is meant by a 'house church' and why they are what we need to be in.

CHAPTER 18

JESUS IS THE ONLY WAY TO SALVATION

Jesus said to him, "I am the way, and the truth, and the life; no one comes to the Father but through Me.

John 14:6 (NASB)

11 I, even I, am the LORD,
and apart from me there is no saviour.
12 I have revealed and saved and proclaimed—
I, and not some foreign god among you.
You are my witnesses," declares the LORD, "that I am God.
Isaiah 43:11-12 (NIV)

"I am the door; if any one enters by me, he will be saved…."
John 10:9(a) (RSV)

so that all the peoples of the earth may know that the LORD is God and that there is no other.

1 Kings 8:60 (NIV)

To you it was shown, that you might know that the LORD is God; there is no other besides him.

Deuteronomy 4:35 (RSV)

24 So the Jews gathered around him and said to him, "How long will you keep
us in suspense? If you are the Christ, tell us plainly." 25 Jesus answered them,
"I told you, and you do not believe. The works that I do in my Father's name
bear witness about me, 26 but you do not believe because you are not among my
sheep. 27 My sheep hear my voice, and I know them, and they follow me.
John 10:24-27 (ESV)

22 He went on his way through towns and villages, teaching, and journeying
toward Jerusalem. 23 And someone said to him, "Lord, will those who are saved
be few?" And he said to them, 24 "Strive to enter by the narrow door; for many,
I tell you, will seek to enter and will not be able.
Luke 13:22-24 (RSV)

13 "Enter through the narrow gate; for the gate is wide and the way is broad that
leads to destruction, and there are many who enter through it. 14 "For the gate
is small and the way is narrow that leads to life, and there are few who find
it. 15 "Beware of the false prophets, who come to you in sheep's clothing, but

inwardly are ravenous wolves.

Matthew 7:13-15 (NASB)

We live in an unusual age in history. The Western church is probably weaker and more lukewarm than it has ever been. And it is more of a mixture of wrong beliefs and false religions than ever before. We see today a strange approach to the idea of '*tolerance*'. All manner of wrong ideas or false religious beliefs will be tolerated freely, but not genuine, biblical Christianity.

A man can believe in Islam, Hinduism, Sikhism, Buddhism, the New Age, yoga, spiritualism, paganism, Roman Catholicism, liberal wishy-washy Christianity, or a mixture of any or all of the above, and nobody will complain. However, if someone believes in genuine, biblical Christianity and says so openly, then people will aggressively object, and seek to silence him. However, there is no getting away from the fact that God says there is no God besides Him:

5"I am the LORD, and there is no other;
Besides Me there is no God
I will gird you, though you have not known Me;
6That men may know from the rising to the setting of the sun
That there is no one besides Me.
I am the LORD, and there is no other,
7The One forming light and creating darkness,
Causing well-being and creating calamity;
I am the LORD who does all these.

Isaiah 45:5-7 (NASB)

The main thing the world objects to is Jesus' claim to be the *only* way to salvation. We could make Jesus far more popular if we were to present Him as *one of* the ways to salvation, or *a* way to reach God, or *a* Prophet or *an example* of how to live. If we were to present Him as just another option then few people would object to Him, or to us. But look how the apostle Peter presents Jesus:

Salvation is found in no one else, for there is no other name under Heaven given to men by which we must be saved."

Acts 4:12 (NIV)

Peter does not pull his punches. He tells it like it is, no matter how much controversy is caused. Look also at what apostle Paul says:

For no one can lay any foundation other than the one already laid, which is Jesus Christ.

1 Corinthians 3:11 (NIV)

Note also how apostle Peter refers to Jesus as being **the** Prophet, namely the very special prophet that Moses had said God would send. This is first referred to in Deuteronomy:

***15 "The Lord your God will raise up for you a prophet like me from among you,
from your brethren—him you shall heed— 16 just as you desired of the Lord
your God at Horeb on the day of the assembly, when you said, 'Let me not hear
again the voice of the Lord my God, or see this great fire any more, lest I die.'
17 And the Lord said to me, 'They have rightly said all that they have spoken. 18 I
will raise up for them a prophet like you from among their brethren; and I will
put my words in his mouth, and he shall speak to them all that I command him.
19 And whoever will not give heed to my words which he shall speak in my name,
I myself will require it of him.***

Deuteronomy 18:15-19 (RSV)

Peter tells us that Jesus is this unique Prophet, whose coming was foretold by Moses:

***19 Repent therefore, and turn again, that your sins may be blotted out, that times
of refreshing may come from the presence of the Lord, 20 and that he may send
the Christ appointed for you, Jesus, 21 whom Heaven must receive until the time
for establishing all that God spoke by the mouth of his holy prophets from of
old. 22 Moses said, 'The Lord God will raise up for you a prophet from your
brethren as he raised me up. You shall listen to him in whatever he tells you.
23 And it shall be that every soul that does not listen to that prophet shall be
destroyed from the people.' 24 And all the prophets who have spoken, from
Samuel and those who came afterwards, also proclaimed these days. 25 You are
the sons of the prophets and of the covenant which God gave to your fathers,
saying to Abraham, 'And in your posterity shall all the families of the earth be
blessed.' 26 God, having raised up his servant, sent him to you first, to bless you
in turning every one of you from your wickedness."***

Acts 3:19-26 (RSV)

So, we know that Jesus is *the* Prophet that Moses said would come, whose words we must listen to or else we would be destroyed. Interestingly, Islam claims that Mohammed is actually this Prophet. But he is not. It is Jesus and only Jesus. At any rate, that is the choice you have to make, as it cannot be both. Either Jesus or Mohammed must be a false prophet, otherwise words have no meaning.

Then look at what apostle John says:

Jesus said to him, "I am the way, and the truth, and the life; no one comes to the Father, but by me.

John 14:6 (RSV)

[11]And this is the testimony: God has given us eternal life, and this life is in his Son. [12]He who has the Son has life; he who does not have the Son of God does not have life.

1 John 5:11-12(NIV)

We know also that the Son of God has come and has given us understanding, so that we may know him who is true. And we are in him who is true—even in his Son Jesus Christ. He is the true God and eternal life.

1 John 5:20 (NIV)

Whether we like it or not, and whether it makes us popular or not, Jesus also makes some startlingly absolute and exclusive statements about Himself. He does so in a stark and uncompromising way which, by today's standards, would be viewed as deeply *"intolerant"*. It entirely contradicts the whole secular/liberal agenda of *"diversity"*. Therefore, if you say that Jesus claims to be the only way to salvation, many people will take offence.

Strangely, the strongest objections are from liberal nominal churchgoers, rather than outright unbelievers. They have fallen for the diversity agenda and say that a Jesus who claims to be the only way to God is not the kind of Jesus that they would want to believe in. Many will accept Jesus as a *teacher* but not as *"Lord"* because, if He is Lord, then that means He is way above every other person or religion. They don't like that. But look at what Jesus Himself says:

[25]Jesus said to her, "I am the resurrection and the life; he who believes in Me will live even if he dies, [26]and everyone who lives and believes in Me will never die. Do you believe this?" [27]She said to Him, "Yes, Lord; I have believed that You are the Christ, the Son of God, even He who comes into the world."

John 11:25-27 (NASB)

"You call me 'Teacher' and 'Lord,' and rightly so, for that is what I am.

John 13:13 (NIV)

Likewise many will accept Him as a *prophet,* but not as *the Son of God.* However, look at what Jesus Himself says just before He is about to raise Lazarus from the dead in John Chapter 11. He calls Himself *"God's Son"*:

[1]Now a man named Lazarus was sick. He was from Bethany, the village of Mary and her sister Martha. [2]This Mary, whose brother Lazarus now lay sick, was the same one who poured perfume on the Lord and wiped his feet with her hair. [3]So the sisters sent word to Jesus, "Lord, the one you love is sick." [4]When he heard this, Jesus said, "This sickness will not end in death. No, it is for God's glory so that God's Son may be glorified through it."

John 11:1-4(NIV)

Note also below how Jesus accepts as true and accurate this amazing comment from Nathanael. He does not contradict him or deny being the Son of God:

49Then Nathanael declared, "Rabbi, you are the Son of God; you are the King of Israel." 50Jesus said, "You believe because I told you I saw you under the fig tree. You shall see greater things than that." 51He then added, "I tell you the truth, you shall see Heaven open, and the angels of God ascending and descending on the Son of Man."

John 1:49-51 (NIV)

Now look at how Jesus speaks to the Samaritan woman at the well and how he openly declares Himself to be the Messiah:

22You Samaritans worship what you do not know; we worship what we do know, for salvation is from the Jews. 23Yet a time is coming and has now come when the true worshipers will worship the Father in spirit and truth, for they are the kind of worshipers the Father seeks. 24God is spirit, and his worshipers must worship in spirit and in truth." 25The woman said, "I know that Messiah" (called Christ) "is coming. When he comes, he will explain everything to us." 26Then Jesus declared, "I who speak to you am he."

John 4:22-26 (NIV)

Then see the response of the Samaritan people in that village and how they clearly knew Him to be the Messiah and the Saviour of the world:

39Many of the Samaritans from that town believed in him because of the woman's testimony, "He told me everything I ever did." 40So when the Samaritans came to him, they urged him to stay with them, and he stayed two days. 41And because of his words many more became believers. 42They said to the woman, "We no longer believe just because of what you said; now we have heard for ourselves, and we know that this man really is the Saviour of the world."

John 4:39-42 (NIV)

There is a widespread school of thought that wants to view Jesus as just a *"good teacher"*. If we choose to see Him that way then He can be fitted in *alongside* other belief systems or religions. Many people think Jesus would not object to such mixtures. They see Him as a liberal with an *"inclusive approach"* who would want to *"promote diversity"* But, it's not true. That is a false view of Jesus. There are a number of reasons for that false view of Him being so widespread:

Reasons why people present a false picture of Jesus as being just one of many alternative ways to God:

a) **That is how many people think and there is a tendency to assume Jesus is like oneself.**

We tend to read into the Bible an assumption that Jesus is rather like us. We can easily reinterpret Him as holding opinions very much like ours. We have to guard against that. All we can validly do is to read the Bible and interpret plainly what Jesus *actually said.* We cannot weave into it any of our own opinions or prejudices. Yet, unless we consciously stop ourselves, we will do that, without even noticing we are doing it.

b) **Because an '*inclusive*' '*liberal,*' '*tolerant*' Jesus who accepts all people, no matter what they believe, seems more attractive to worldly people.**

He is much less threatening and offensive to some of us if viewed in that way. It appeals to our worldly nature and it avoids causing arguments or upsetting people. From a selfish point of view, there would perhaps be certain advantages if Jesus was like that. Yet, the Bible tells us plainly that He is not. Therefore we either have to believe what the Bible says or ignore the Bible and view Him any way we wish. You have to choose. But when you do, you must also take the consequences of your decision.

c) **Because a Jesus who fits in with our preferences and opinions is more convenient.**

Jesus would then be the sort of person that you can keep as a mascot. Following Him would be like joining a fan club. You could add Him into your existing lifestyle without Him challenging you or trying to interfere with your life. That is attractive to many people. Being a "fan" of Jesus, rather than His disciple, offers the appearance of being a Christian, plus an enhanced lifestyle or culture, but without the cost or inconvenience of obeying Him.

The main thing that people do not want Jesus to be is Lord. We instinctively recognise that if we accepted Him as Lord, then He would want to act like a Lord. He would want to rule and reign in our lives like a king. But, that would mean we would not be in charge of our own life anymore. Thus many people reinvent Jesus as someone who fits in with them, rather than accept Him as someone with whom they must fit in.

The real Jesus – the only way to salvation

Let's look at some more of the startling things that Jesus actually says about Himself being the one and only King and Lord. I also want to dwell on the theme of Jesus being the *only* way to be saved, no matter how unpopular that is with those who are politically correct. It is simply a truth, which we must either accept or reject. Consider these passages:

Jesus answered, "I am the way and the truth and the life. No one comes to the Father except through me.

John 14:6 (NIV)

but these have been written so that you may believe that Jesus is the Christ, the Son of God; and that believing you may have life in His name.

John 20:31 (NASB)

And having been made perfect, He became to all those who obey Him the source of eternal salvation,

Hebrews 5:9 (NASB)

Salvation is found in no one else, for there is no other name under Heaven given to men by which we must be saved."

Acts 4:12 (NIV)

When Jesus spoke again to the people, he said, "I am the light of the world. Whoever follows me will never walk in darkness, but will have the light of life."

John 8:12 (NIV)

"Therefore I said to you that you will die in your sins; for unless you believe that I am He, you will die in your sins."

John 8:24 (NASB)

Note how angrily the Jewish authorities reacted when Jesus said the words "*I AM*". It is very significant, because "*I AM*", or "*Yahweh*" in Hebrew, is God's personal name. Thus, Jesus was taking God's personal name and applying it to Himself, making Himself equal to God. That is why they reacted so angrily. They could all see what He was doing. In fact, Jesus emphasises God's personal name, "*I AM*", and applies it to Himself seven times in John's gospel, making what are known as His "*I AM*" statements". That is their main significance, i.e. His claim that He is God and equal to God. That makes Him totally unique in all of world history:

While I am in the world, I am the light of the world.

John 9:5 (NIV)

7 Therefore Jesus said again, "I tell you the truth, I am the gate for the sheep.
8 All who ever came before me were thieves and robbers, but the sheep did not
listen to them. 9 I am the gate; whoever enters through me will be saved. He will
come in and go out, and find pasture.

John10:7-9(NIV)

*[24]The Jews gathered around him, saying, "How long will you keep us in
suspense? If you are the Christ, tell us plainly." [25]Jesus answered, "I did tell
you, but you do not believe. The miracles I do in my Father's name speak for
me, [26]but you do not believe because you are not my sheep. [27]My sheep listen to
my voice; I know them, and they follow me. [28]I give them eternal life, and they
shall never perish; no one can snatch them out of my hand. [29]My Father, who
has given them to me, is greater than all; no one can snatch them out of my
Father's hand. [30]I and the Father are one." [31]Again the Jews picked up stones
to stone him, [32]but Jesus said to them, "I have shown you many great miracles
from the Father. For which of these do you stone me?" [33]"We are not stoning
you for any of these," replied the Jews, "but for blasphemy, because you, a mere
man, claim to be God*

John 10: 24-33 (NIV)

Look also at how Jesus describes Himself in the book of Revelation:

*[12]"Behold, I am coming soon! My reward is with me, and I will give to everyone
according to what he has done. [13]I am the Alpha and the Omega, the First and
the Last, the Beginning and the End. [14]"Blessed are those who wash their robes,
that they may have the right to the tree of life and may go through the gates into
the city.*

Revelation 22:12-14 (NIV)

"I, Jesus, have sent my angel to give you this testimony for the churches. I am the Root and the Offspring of David, and the bright Morning Star."

Revelation 22:16 (NIV)

Take a careful look at all of those remarkable verses above. Does Jesus seem to you from those passages to be someone who is willing to embrace all beliefs and religions and fit in with whatever you choose to believe, without objecting? On the contrary, Jesus sounds from these verses likes someone who thinks that He is God. There is a simple reason for that: He is God.

The Lord Jesus Christ is certainly a man, but at the same time He is also the Second Person of the Trinity. He is God the Son, and is equal to God the Father and God the Holy Spirit. When Jesus speaks, it is God speaking. He is totally unique. Nobody else can match Him. He is God in human form. That is not true of any other religious figure.

Therefore, He is not simply giving opinions or suggestions. He is telling us the truth as a matter of absolute fact. Whatever Jesus says is utterly true. He is not just another voice that we can listen to alongside many others. He is the King of kings and Lord of lords. We are to worship, honour and obey Him in all things. He not only expects that, He commands it and He has every right to do so. He is unique. He is sovereign. He rules as an absolute monarch and He gives commands, without any apology.

The word *"command"* is offensive to modern ears. It is socially unfashionable in the current climate, and it offends our pride. It sounds as if He thinks He is better than us or as if He considers us to be His servants. Our fleshly nature does not like that and recoils against it. Yet, He is better than us. In fact He is more than just "better"; He is perfect, whereas you and I are corrupt, selfish and sinful.

Jesus Christ has to be either a liar, a lunatic or the LORD

Christianity is absolutely unique in comparison to all the other belief systems and religions on the face of the earth. It makes claims about itself which nobody else makes. Just look at the way that Jesus speaks with such absolute authority. There is no way that an ordinary human being could ever speak like He does without being a liar or a lunatic. Yet He is neither of those things, because He is precisely what He says He is.

Therefore He is entitled to speak as He does. Throughout His life no one could ever find Him guilty of any crime or sin of any kind. Even when he was falsely put on trial before the Jewish Sanhedrin, then before King Herod and then Pontius Pilate, no charge against Him could stick. Nobody could find any evidence that stood up. Would that be true of you?

How long would it take for people to dig around in your life or mine and find evidence of hypocrisy, pride, dishonesty, selfishness, greed, impatience, rudeness, unfaithfulness, inconsistency, or a host of other sins or crimes? It would not take long in my life. Yet nobody could do it in Jesus' life. If that is so, then how can He possibly be a lunatic or a liar? It simply does not add up, and our own instinct confirms that. We know it simply by reading the words that He spoke. **The problem is that that leaves us with only one option, which is that He is exactly what He said He is, i.e. the LORD.**

You can try as hard as you like, but there are no other options. He is either a liar or a lunatic or He is the LORD. He cannot be a *mixture* of these three things, i.e. part liar, part lunatic and part telling the truth. Yet He also cannot be *anything else* outside of these three things. You therefore have to pick one of them. In my experience, people agree that He is not insane or a liar, but they shrink back from conceding that He is exactly what He said He is. The main reason they hold back is they don't *want* to accept the implications of that. If Jesus is the LORD, as He says He is, then all the other things He says must also be true.

That has massive implications for our lives. It means that we need to change radically. *But, we don't want to.* Thus, many people reserve judgment on what

Jesus really is and decide not to come to any decision. They leave it hanging in the air. Then they don't have to reach a place which requires them to change or take action. That self-delusion makes them feel better, but it is foolish.

Moving back to our original question, which is whether Jesus is the only way to salvation, we need to look at Him and His claims against the back drop that we have just painted. Look at the things He says about Himself. If you or I said any of those things, then people would laugh at us or even put us into a mental institution, yet not Him.

Even His enemies could not deny that He was doing vast numbers of astonishing miracles in front of large crowds. He did so whilst representatives of the High Priest were standing at close quarters watching His every move and listening to every word. They witnessed almost everything He did, and they could never fault Him or find any way to expose Him or trip Him up. They saw that everything He did was genuine.

Have you ever noticed in the Bible how many times the Sadducees, Pharisees, Scribes, and even members of the Sanhedrin, were present when Jesus was teaching, and that they questioned Him about the things He said? Why were they even there? It was because they were constantly following Him around. The reason they were doing so is that He had performed certain miracles which were viewed as *"Messianic miracles"*.

These were specific miracles that Jewish tradition said could only be done by the Messiah Himself. For example, the healing of a Jewish leper inside the Land of Israel or healing a person born blind, were said to be things that only the Messiah would do. Therefore they were following Him to verify these miracles and to find out whether He really was the Messiah they were all waiting for.

Therefore, when Jesus performed miracles it was necessary for the representatives of the High Priest to follow Him and investigate it all to certify whether they were genuine miracles. If they could have somehow exposed Him as a fraudster or His miracles as fake, then they would have done so. Yet they never did, because they couldn't. On the contrary, they openly acknowledged that He was performing these Messianic miracles.

They could not deny it. They had seen Him do them on many occasions in front of large crowds. Yet they still stubbornly refused to become His disciples. In fact they hated Him all the more, because they felt envious and because He condemned many of their traditions and practices as being false and unbiblical. So, if anybody could have caught Him out or exposed Him as false, they would have done so eagerly.

It simply does not make any sense to believe in Jesus and to try to accept any other religious system or practice at the same time. For example, if Jesus is who He says He is, and if what He says is true, then Hinduism must be false. Equally, Islam, Sikhism and Buddhism must be false. So must Confucianism, Spiritualism, Mormonism, the beliefs of the Jehovah's Witnesses and any other religion or cult.

I have no desire at all to offend anyone, yet, if you examine this, you will have to concede that what Jesus said and what the founders and followers of all cults and religions say are mutually exclusive. **They cannot both be true. It is either Christianity or some other belief, but it cannot be both.** For example, Jesus teaches that He is the Son of God, i.e. the Second Person of the Trinity. Yet, Islam teaches that God has no Son. That is what Mohammed said. Those two statements cannot both be true. One of them must be wrong.

No matter how polite or diplomatic you might wish to be, you will not be capable of explaining how the claims of Jesus about Himself and the teaching of Islam about Jesus can both be true. They simply cannot be. At least one of them is false. Likewise, as we saw earlier, they cannot both be the special Prophet that Moses said would come. If Jesus is that Prophet, which He is, then Mohammed is not. Moreover, the Lord Jesus and Mohammed cannot both be the mediator between God and men. Only one person has that place, and it is Jesus:

5For there is one God and one mediator between God and men, the man Christ Jesus, 6who gave himself as a ransom for all men—the testimony given in its proper time.

1 Timothy 2:5-6 (NIV)

Apostle Peter confirms this further in Acts:

42 And he commanded us to preach to the people, and to testify that he is the one ordained by God to be judge of the living and the dead. 43 To him all the prophets bear witness that every one who believes in him receives forgiveness of sins through his name."

Acts 10:42-43 (RSV)

Now consider Hinduism. This is a polytheistic religion. That means that they have many different gods, in fact millions of gods Yet, Jesus tells us that there is only one God, namely the God of Israel, i.e. the God of Abraham, Isaac and Jacob. He alone is God and there is no other. The Bible clearly teaches that any other 'gods' that people worship are simply demons pretending to be gods. We might feel that it would be convenient and diplomatic if we could simply fit Christianity and Hinduism together. Then we could accept that Hinduism has many gods and that Jesus is just another of them who fits in alongside all the others. But we cannot do so.

If we are honest we will have to concede that we cannot hold these two beliefs at the same time. It would be illogical and absurd. Either there is one God and all other gods are demons masquerading as gods or the Bible is not true. If so, Hinduism could be true, but not if the Bible is true. We can accept one or the other, but we cannot logically accept both. You have to choose. God urges you to choose Him:

"Turn to Me and be saved, all the ends of the earth;
For I am God, and there is no other.
Isaiah 45:22 (NASB)

Look what the Bible says about other gods. These gods referred to below and declared to be false and empty include Hinduism, Buddhism, Islam, Sikhism and so on. They are all false and man-made religions. They do not lead to salvation but to Hell and then the Lake of Fire :

9 All who make idols are nothing,
and the things they treasure are worthless.
Those who would speak up for them are blind;
they are ignorant, to their own shame.
10 Who shapes a god and casts an idol,
which can profit him nothing?
Isaiah 44:9-10 (NIV)

16 Half of the wood he burns in the fire;
over it he prepares his meal,
he roasts his meat and eats his fill.
He also warms himself and says,
"Ah! I am warm; I see the fire."
17 From the rest he makes a god, his idol;
he bows down to it and worships.
He prays to it and says,
"Save me; you are my god."
18 They know nothing, they understand nothing;
their eyes are plastered over so they cannot see,
and their minds closed so they cannot understand.
Isaiah 44:16-18 (NIV)

"Gather yourselves and come;
Draw near together, you fugitives of the nations;
They have no knowledge,
Who carry about their wooden idol
And pray to a god who cannot save.
Isaiah 45:20 (NASB)

16 All the makers of idols will be put to shame and disgraced;
they will go off into disgrace together
17 But Israel will be saved by the LORD
with an everlasting salvation;
you will never be put to shame or disgraced,
to ages everlasting.
18 For this is what the LORD says –
he who created the Heavens,
he is God;
he who fashioned and made the earth,
he founded it;
he did not create it to be empty
but formed it to be inhabited –
he says:
"I am the LORD,
and there is no other.

Isaiah 45:16-18 (NIV)

25 For great is the LORD and most worthy of praise;
he is to be feared above all gods.
26 For all the gods of the nations are idols,
but the LORD made the Heavens.

1 Chronicles 16:25-26 (NIV)

We could go on and on looking at the distinctions between genuine, biblical Christianity and any religion or cult that you could ever think of. At some point, in some way, every religion or cult denies an essential truth about biblical Christianity. Usually they deny the vital truths about *who* Jesus Christ is.

For example, a Jehovah's Witness will not accept that Jesus Christ is *God*, i.e. that He is the Second Person of the Trinity. They say that He is only a man. They are either right or wrong. If they are right, then biblical Christianity would be false. If however we do not want to say that, then we must say that the beliefs of the Jehovah's Witnesses are false. We can't say that *neither* is false.

All of this goes entirely against the grain of modern secular thinking and political correctness. In the modern Western world people do not like to arrive at clear conclusions or call anything *'false'*. Western thinking is now *'relativist'*. Our society believes that there are no absolutes and that all things are relative. Thus a bundle of contradictory things can all be true at the same time and many people are comfortable with that. Relativism enables us not to have to make any clear choices. We can then assume that there is 'merit' in a host of different and conflicting viewpoints and that there is *"truth in all of them somewhere."*

Relativism is relaxed about leaving it at that, without digging any deeper or trying to reach clear conclusions or labelling anything as true or false. That is the way that much of the Western world now thinks. It is so widespread that it is not even considered illogical anymore.

In the past a man who believed two contradictory things at the same time would have been considered to be a fool, but not now. However, if the Bible is true, we have to make a clear decision about the Lord Jesus Christ. He will not allow anything less than our total acceptance of what He teaches. He also insists that we follow Him unreservedly, with all our heart and with absolute loyalty.

To do that we must forsake all other gods and all other competing claims on our lives. And there must be no fudge or compromise. We cannot try to have it both ways by recognising and worshipping other gods and also worshipping the true God at the same time. There is a strong temptation in our day to mix Christianity with other religions so as to fit in better with other people and avoid pressure.

This kind of mixture is called "*syncretism*" and it is very widespread in the Western churches today. There are many joint services where people of different faiths "*come together*" and "*worship together*". This has been participated in by Pope John Paul II and also by Pope Benedict XVI. Very many Anglican, Methodist and other leaders have done the same. However, it is not acceptable to God.

Compare that confused and compromised approach with the firm, clear stance taken by the three friends of the prophet Daniel. They were faced with a crisis when King Nebuchadnezzar of Babylon tried to force them to worship his false gods or else be put to death. Most people went along with it and cooperated in order to avoid being executed. But Daniel's friends did not:

14Nebuchadnezzar responded and said to them, "Is it true, Shadrach, Meshach and Abed-nego, that you do not serve my gods or worship the golden image that I have set up? 15"Now if you are ready, at the moment you hear the sound of the horn, flute, lyre, trigon, psaltery and bagpipe and all kinds of music, to fall down and worship the image that I have made, very well But if you do not worship, you will immediately be cast into the midst of a furnace of blazing fire; and what god is there who can deliver you out of my hands?" 16Shadrach, Meshach and Abed-nego replied to the king, "O Nebuchadnezzar, we do not need to give you an answer concerning this matter. 17"If it be so, our God whom we serve is able to deliver us from the furnace of blazing fire; and He will deliver us out of your hand, O king. 18"But even if He does not, let it be known to you, O king, that we are not going to serve your gods or worship the golden image that you have set up."

Daniel 3:14-18 (NASB)

As it happened, on that occasion, God rescued the three men from the fiery furnace. However, that is the exception. Normally we are not rescued and we have to face the consequences of remaining faithful to the one true God. It shows, however, how seriously God takes the need for us to hold firm to the truth. We must not be joined to any false religion or participate in the worship of any false god. Jesus' claim to be the only way to salvation must either be true or false.

If it is false then He is either lying or mistaken about this. If so, then that claim falls down, and so does everything else about Him. In other words, if He is wrong about that, then He is not worthy of being worshiped, or followed at all. Yet, if He is the only way to salvation, then we have a colossal problem on our hands. I say that because the vast majority of our world doesn't believe in Jesus Christ or follow Him.

If that is so, then it means that most people are not saved, which means that they do not have eternal life. Thus when they die they will stand condemned before God at the Great White Throne judgment. But those people who face that judgment are all around me. They are my friends, family, neighbours and work colleagues. Does that mean they are going to go to Hell and the Lake of Fire unless they repent?

The Bible says they are, which is a terrible thought. I wish that I did not have to believe that last point, and that there was some way round it. I wish that it could somehow be true to say that all men will be saved and that nobody will go to Hell or the Lake of Fire or stand condemned before God. Yet, there is no biblical basis for believing that.

If we believe what Jesus said, and take Him at His word, then there is no other position that we can take. It means that He is the only way to God. That means that salvation cannot be found through anyone else, or in any other belief, system or practice. Saying that is going to make us unpopular. Yet, it is the truth. These are horrifying thoughts. Even to imagine the people we know going to a lost eternity in the Lake of Fire is awful.

Many people deal with that by just ignoring it or blocking it out of their minds. I can't do that. What good would it do to pretend that something isn't true when we know it is? If what Jesus says is true then we urgently need to take action. We must repent and turn to Him. We must also tell others. To simply bury our heads in the sand and not worry about it, which is what most of us do, is surely the worst possible response.

I would urge you to go against the instinct to bury your head, or any other ways of avoiding painful realities. Instead face up to the dilemma head on. Jesus is the only way to salvation. There is no other way to be saved, no matter how unfashionable or controversial it may be to say that. Therefore let's respond to

Him while there is still time. And let us forsake any other gods or philosophies which we may have put in His place.

Look at what Joshua said to the Jewish people after they had escaped from Egypt and just as they were entering the 'Promised Land' of Israel. God spoke through Joshua to warn the people to get rid of any other gods and, instead, to worship God alone.

14"Now fear the LORD and serve him with all faithfulness. Throw away the gods your forefathers worshiped beyond the River and in Egypt, and serve the LORD. 15 But if serving the LORD seems undesirable to you, then choose for yourselves this day whom you will serve, whether the gods your forefathers served beyond the River, or the gods of the Amorites, in whose land you are living. But as for me and my household, we will serve the LORD."

Joshua 24:14-15 (NIV)

Remember also the first commandment which God gave to Moses:

1And God spoke all these words: 2 "I am the LORD your God, who brought you out of Egypt, out of the land of slavery. 3 "You shall have no other gods before me"

Exodus 20:1-3 (NIV)

And we are told again in 2 Kings not to worship any other gods:

37You must always be careful to keep the decrees and ordinances, the laws and commands he wrote for you. Do not worship other gods. 38 Do not forget the covenant I have made with you, and do not worship other gods.

2 Kings 17:37-38 (NIV)

You now have to decide whether to take these commands seriously, or to disobey, dodge or deny them. You must also decide whether Jesus is just one of many equally acceptable ways to get to God, or the one and only way. Be careful how you make that choice because, according to the Bible, your whole eternal future depends on it.

36"He who believes in the Son has eternal life; but he who does not obey the Son will not see life, but the wrath of God abides on him."

John 3:36 (NASB)

CHAPTER 19

HOW TO KNOW WHETHER YOU ARE A REAL CHRISTIAN OR NOT

[5]Examine yourselves to see whether you are in the faith; test yourselves. Do you not realize that Christ Jesus is in you—unless, of course, you fail the test?
2 Corinthians 13:5 (NIV)

Paul tells us that we need to *examine ourselves* to see whether we really are Christians or not. Note that he said that in a letter written to the church in Corinth. It wasn't written to unbelievers. So, Paul did not assume that people in churches must automatically be Christians. We cannot make that assumption either, whether in relation to others or ourselves. We need to pause therefore and look at how to find out whether you are already a real Christian.

This book may come into the hands of all sorts of people, of different levels of knowledge and understanding and from many different backgrounds. You may not necessarily know what you are and whether you have started out on "*the Way*" and become a Christian, or still need to do so. In other words, you may be confused about exactly where you stand.

Some people are obviously not Christians. They may be atheists or followers of some other religion. If that's you, you will know quite clearly that you have never genuinely repented or believed in Jesus Christ and that you are not "on the way". Other people may be quite certain that they are a Christian and with good reason. They know very clearly where they stand, what they believe, and that they have truly repented.

There is probably a much larger group in the middle who are unsure what they are. Perhaps that's you? You may have been brought up in church, or made a decision to follow Jesus Christ years ago, but perhaps you have not kept it up. Perhaps you never quite realised what you were doing when you made that decision?

Or you may be nominally Christian by background, or family connection, but are living in a lukewarm, compromised way. Or perhaps there is active ongoing sin in your life which you know is wrong, but you have never tackled it. You may have been to church all your life, but you don't feel any certainty as to what you are. Maybe your church is wishy-washy, with no clear teaching or preaching about the real Gospel?

Possibly you are unsure whether you have ever really repented, or whether you have genuinely believed in Jesus Christ or given your life to him. If any of these things apply to you, it may be that you don't know whether you are saved already, or still need to be saved.

People can find it very difficult to pin some of these things down and they can be very vague. However, before you can take the step of becoming a Christian, you need to be able to know for sure where you stand now, and exactly what you are at the moment. If you are not yet a genuine Christian, and your sins have not yet been forgiven, then you do not have eternal life, no matter how many times you have been to church. Thus, you would need to make a clear and definite step now to become a Christian and to start out on the way.

There is no single test that will, by itself, show whether you are already a real Christian. However, I will now list many different questions or tests that you can apply to yourself. Go through them all, one, by one and carefully answer them as honestly as you can. Each question, on its own, will not be conclusive proof in either direction. But, taken together, if you weigh up the overall pattern that emerges, you will probably find that most of your responses are pointing in the same direction. If so, then that is probably your answer.

However, if the answers are a confusing mixture, then the safest thing to do is to assume that you are not yet a real Christian. If so, then take the necessary steps to make your position completely certain. This is much too important to leave to chance or to let it remain vague and uncertain.

If you are a person who goes to church or was brought up in church I would urge you not to be complacent just because of that. It may be that what you experienced of church was far removed from real, biblical Christianity. Millions of people all over the world are in churches, even genuine churches, but they are not necessarily real Christians themselves.

Therefore please consider all of the following questions honestly and carefully. Don't be too quick to answer. Ask God to open your eyes and to help you to be brutally frank with yourself. There is no point pretending. You would only be fooling yourself.

A series of questions to help you to diagnose whether or not you are a real Christian at present:

<u>Question 1</u>

Does the question of whether you are already a real Christian bother you? Or, are you unconcerned and complacent about it?

☐ A = You are unconcerned or relaxed about it.

☐ B = It's important to you and you want to be sure

Question 2

Can you point to a specific day or a moment of decision or commitment when you first became a Christian? Or, is it vague? It may be that it is unclear because you have been brought up in a Christian home and you became a Christian so young that you simply cannot remember the day when you first made the decision to follow Jesus Christ. However, even if that is so, was there ever a day later in life, as you grew up, where you made a conscious recommitment, or confirmed that decision?

☐ A = You can't think of any specific day when you ever made a clear decision to become a Christian or to recommit yourself

☐ B = You can think of the day, time and place very clearly

Question 3

Is there an emphasis on repentance in your thinking and prayers? Is your own sin, as opposed to other people's sin, significant to you? Does it concern you? Do you spend much time thinking about your own sins, selfishness and pride? Do you ever feel convicted in your conscience about those sins?

☐ A = In your life there is little or no emphasis on, or thinking about, your own sin or repentance

☐ B = There is substantial and regular emphasis on your own sin and your own need for repentance

Question 4

Can you point to a day or a time when you first knowingly and consciously repented of your own sins?

☐ A = There is no specific day when you can remember repenting

☐ B = You can remember a specific day when you first repented

Question 5

If so, did you deal with specific sins that were real, or was it just vague and non-specific? Did you get down to brass tacks and repent of actual sins?

☐ A = It wasn't specific and you didn't get down to brass tacks about your own particular sins

☐ B = It was specific and you did deal with real sins, not just vague generalities

Question 6

When you read or hear verses from the Bible which describe sin, do you assume it is talking about other people or about you? Do you tend immediately to think of other people who commit those sins, or do you usually recognise that those sins are in you and that you need to change?

☐ A = When you read or hear of sins you tend to assume the Bible is referring to other people. You think of instances where other people commit those sons, rather than yourself.

☐ B = You tend to assume the Bible is speaking about your sins and you easily recognise those sins or faults in yourself.

Question 7

Can you point to any significant/meaningful ways in which, since you decided to repent, you have turned from your sins and genuinely changed your lifestyle and behaviour? For example have you ever stopped doing something like lying, stealing, looking at pornography etc? Is there something specific that has ever changed or stopped?

☐ A = There has not been any significant change of lifestyle or behaviour

☐ B = Your behavior and lifestyle have changed noticeably and you can think of specific sins you have stopped or reduced

Question 8

Have you ever, even for a moment, felt grieved over your own sinfulness? Have you ever felt remorse and conviction about it? Or, even as you read these words now, does that sound alien to you? Do you even understand, from personal experience, what is meant by such words as '*remorse*' and '*conviction*'?

If you have never felt remorse or conviction, then, it is very unlikely that you have ever truly repented. And, if you cannot ever remember feeling those things, then you probably never have felt them. It is not something that you could easily forget.

After you become a Christian the continued cravings that you still feel to engage in sin are a cause of turmoil. It disturbs and unsettles you. The famous seventeenth century puritan writer, John Owen, said *"Sin in the believer is a burden which afflicts him, rather than a pleasure which delights him"*.

☐ A = No you have never felt grief or anguish, remorse or conviction about your sin. Or, you have felt such things only very rarely/slightly.

☐ B = Yes you have felt those things significantly and were deeply troubled by them.

Question 9

Do you find that you have a desire to read the Bible? Is it alive and interesting to you? Do you find it precious and valuable? Alternatively, is it dry and boring to you? Do you rarely look at it, or even avoid it? If you are a real Christian then one of the signs is that the Bible ought to be fresh, living and active to you. God will speak to you through it and continually reveal new things to you. If you are not yet a real Christian, then the Bible is likely to be burdensome to read and irksome to you. It will feel like a dull duty, not a pleasure.

☐ A = The Bible is dry, dull and boring and is an effort to read and you find it hard to understand. You tend to avoid reading it or you read it rarely.

☐ B = The Bible is alive, fresh and interesting, and you want to read it every day and keep finding new things in it. You read it regularly.

Question 10

Do you clearly understand and accept the point that I have been emphasising in this book so far, i.e. that you have got no merit, righteousness or virtue in yourself and that you can never earn your way into Heaven? Or, do those words seem odd to you? Do they jar against your assumptions about yourself, because you basically feel that you are a good person?

☐ A = You feel you do have quite a lot of merit and goodness and that you do expect to get into Heaven because you're better than many other people.

☐ B = You genuinely grasp the fact that you have no righteousness at all in yourself and that your own good deeds can never get you into Heaven.

Question 11

Have you ever asked God for His mercy? Has it ever even occurred to you that you need His mercy?

☐ A = You have never asked for mercy and/or have never felt you needed it.

☐ B = You have asked for God's mercy and you know you need it

Question 12

Do you understand the concept of Jesus dying in your place to take the penalty for your sin and of His righteousness being transferred to you and your sin being transferred to Him? Or, is that a new and strange idea to you as you read it now?

☐ A = The idea seems strange and you don't really get it or see why Jesus died on the cross or what it has to do with you and your sins.

☐ B = It makes sense to you why Jesus died and you can see how His being sacrificed works and why there is no other way to deal with your sin

Question 13

Do you still think in terms of getting into Heaven based on being a good person, or, at least, on being a person who is more good than bad? Do you think, in broad terms, of balancing your good deeds against your bad deeds and hoping that you have been a good enough person?

☐ A = You do think in terms of trying to be a good enough person to get into Heaven. You do see it in terms of weighing scales, and you hope your good deeds will outweigh your bad ones.

☐ B = You realise that it is futile even to think in those terms. You are therefore relying solely on Jesus' death in your place as the payment for your sins, not on trying to be a good person.

Question 14

Have you ever felt the *"fear of the Lord"*? If God's judgment is mentioned, do you ever tremble, and feel apprehensive? Or, are you quite carefree and relaxed about that? Are you able to shrug casually at the idea of God's judgment as if it did not affect you?

☐ A = You don't feel much, if any, fear of God. It doesn't make much sense to you and isn't a factor in your life. Judgment by God doesn't worry you and you don't really think about it

☐ B = Yes, you understand and you do fear God and His judgment. You have known what it is to tremble at the prospect of His judgment

Question 15

Are you, at the moment, involved in any known and obvious sin which you have chosen to continue in? I am not referring simply to the ordinary day to day ways in which we all fail by losing our temper or being impatient or selfish towards other people in minor ways. Those things are bad, and I am not excusing them, but such things will happen even in the lives of genuine believers. I am referring to more sinister actions and thoughts, such as lying, stealing, manipulation, deviousness and also sexual sin, such as adultery or sex outside of marriage.

If you are involved in such things then it is more difficult to see how you can ever have truly repented and become a Christian. Repentance is the first and most crucial ingredient of becoming a Christian. Therefore, you would already have recognised and begun to deal with such sins if you had ever truly repented. Certainly, you would not be able to justify to yourself continuing in such sins if you were a true believer. At the very least you would feel wretched about it, due to the strong sense of conviction at your own wrongdoing.

Yet, it would be perfectly possible to commit such sins quite happily if you are a shallow, superficial or nominal believer. I have come across countless people in churches whose lives involve blatant ongoing sins of that type. I should emphasise that I am not saying that a real Christian can never commit such a sin. They can. It is simply that if they do, they will be wracked with conviction and are likely to repent of it afterwards. If you commit such sins and do not feel convicted to repent and stop, then that is a strong sign that you are not a real Christian.

☐ A = You are involved in specific sins and they don't trouble you. You don't worry about them and you're not seeking to stop. You're content as you are.

☐ B = There have been specific sins but you have stopped them. Or, where such sins continue, you feel convicted of the need to stop and you are seeking to stop.

Question 16

Are you pretentious? Do you wear a "mask" or put on an act when you are with others? Are you two-faced? Are the private things that you say and do different from the public way in which you try to portray yourself? In other words, are you false/phoney/playacting in the way you live? Many people in churches are kidding themselves and others about what they really are.

If you are a real Christian and have truly repented, then God will work in your heart to take away from you any desire to be false or pretentious. At any rate, if you were doing such things, then you would be convicted and would feel a desire to stop it. If however you feel comfortable about being false/phoney, and justify yourself for being those things, then that is a very bad sign.

☐ A = Yes, you are two-faced and phoney. You pretend to be things that you aren't and to have attitudes that you don't really have. You wear a mask to impress people and to hide what you really are.

☐ B = You are not two-faced, or you have stopped being so. You now seek to be sincere, honest and real and are making progress.

Question 17

Do you ever feel a longing for holiness i.e. to be clean and pure and to more closely resemble Jesus Christ's character? Do you ever ask God to change you and to reduce your sin and increase your godliness and holiness?

☐ A = No, you don't feel any such longing. You don't really understand what it means to long to be holy as God is holy. You're content as you are.

☐ B = Yes, you do long for holiness and for God to help you to change. You can identify with what is being referred to here.

Question 18

Do you feel a hatred for sin and long for it to be removed from, or reduced in, your life and character?

☐ A = No, you don't feel any hatred for your sin, or very little. At least you do not hate the sin in yourself, only the sin in other people.

☐ B = Yes, you do increasingly hate your own sin and long to remove it from your own life.

Question 19

Do you long for Jesus Christ to return to the earth? Do you hope and pray for the day when He returns and brings this present age to an end and takes His place as King?

☐ A = No, you don't really ever think about His return, or at least you don't hope and pray for it

☐ B = Yes, you do hope for His return to the earth and long for Him to take up His place as King.

Question 20

Do you reject this world's system and its godless ways? Do the proud, vain, selfish, manipulative, grasping values and standards of this world seem very wrong to you? Do you want to keep out of some of the things that go on at work or in society?

☐ A = No, you feel pretty comfortable with the values and lifestyles of our society and it doesn't bother you. You don't reject or renounce its values. You feel you fit in well with this world.

☐ B = Yes, you feel uncomfortable with much of what goes on and often feel uneasy about things that people do or say as you work or live alongside them. You do reject this world's system and its values.

Question 21

Do you ever worry about or pray for the salvation of other people. Do you ever feel the reality of their "lostness" and their desperate need to know Jesus Christ? Does it concern you that otherwise they will go to Hell and then the Lake of Fire after they die?

☐ A = No, you don't feel any anxiety about those things or identify with any of that. Those things don't seem real to you.

☐ B = Yes, you do sometimes feel those anxieties and feel burdened to pray for family and friends to come to know Jesus.

Question 22

Have you ever told anybody that you are a Christian? Have you ever told anybody what the Gospel is, or at least wanted to do so, but felt too afraid? Or, are you unconcerned about your duty to tell other people about Jesus and/or ashamed of being identified with Jesus Christ?

☐ A = No, you haven't told anybody that you are a Christian or what the Gospel is. You also feel ashamed at being identified with Jesus Christ

☐ B = Yes, you have told people you are a Christian and have told them the Gospel too. You don't feel ashamed of Jesus Christ. Or, even if you do, you force yourself to speak about Him anyway.

Question 23

Have you ever experienced any persecution, ridicule, hostility or opposition from any non-Christians or nominal Christians, due to them objecting to your Christian views, values, or behaviour?

☐ A = No, nobody objects to any of your beliefs, values or behaviour on the basis of you being too Christian.

☐ B = Yes, you have experienced such anti-Christian opposition or hostility on one or more occasions

Question 24

Have you ever been baptised in water, not just as a baby, but at an age when you were old enough to know what you were doing and why? In other words, have you ever been properly baptised as a believer?

☐ A = No, you have never been properly baptised in water. If you have been baptised, it was only as a baby. Or, you did get baptised when you were older, but you didn't really mean it or understand it properly.

☐ B = Yes, you have been properly baptised in water. You were aware of what you were doing and you really meant it.

Question 25

Have you ever received (or been filled with, or baptised in) the Holy Spirit in such a way that you were aware of it? Was it an unmistakable event because you spoke in tongues or began to operate in any of the other gifts of the Holy Spirit?

☐ A = No, you have never knowingly received (or been filled with/baptised in) the Holy Spirit. You are not able to point to any occasion when anything of that nature has ever occurred. Or, you have always been told that you automatically received the Holy Spirit at your confirmation or when you first believed and repented. Or you've never given this question any thought at all and have no idea whether you have ever received the Holy Spirit

☐ B = Yes, you have received the Holy Spirit and you can point to the occasion when it happened. You know that things changed and you spoke in tongues or prophesied or you have operated in some other gifts of the Holy Spirit since then.

Question 26

If you believe you are a Christian, can you look closely at your own life and point to any "fruit" that it has produced? Remember, we saw earlier that fruit is what God looks for to see whether we are real. Can you see a pattern of your life increasingly making a positive difference in the lives of others? Are you a blessing to the poor, the homeless, the lost, the old, the helpless, the sick, the hungry etc etc? Has your life made any difference to the lives of such people? Is the world now a better place for you being in it? Are you salt and light in some way to the people you know?

☐ A = No, you don't really do anything for any such people. Or, if you do, it's at a small level and has not been increasing. It is similar to what any typical unbeliever might do or give. Your life hasn't made any part of the world a better place and your life hasn't touched or affected the lives of any other people around you. In short, you cannot really see any fruit from your life.

☐ B = Yes, you have been increasingly effective and active in doing, giving, helping, caring and volunteering, and also in influencing others. You have increasingly met the physical, financial and spiritual needs of other people and you find you want to do so more and more. In short, you can see fruit growing in your life.

<u>Question 27</u>

What is the position with your money and your financial giving? Do you give your money away on an increasingly large scale? Do you get a real pleasure from giving to the poor or supporting the preaching of the Gospel? Or, do you resent, avoid and resist giving your money away? When you give money away, is it done with coins or is it with notes and cheques? (assuming you are wealthy enough to have notes and cheques, which many people are not). In short, are you generous?

In my experience, though I can never be sure what is in another person's heart, or what their real motives are, I have noticed that financial generosity is one of the clearest tests of what a person really is. Financial giving is one of the main 'fruits' God is looking for from your life. That is one reason why Jesus had so much to say about money and about not being in love with it.

The way you are with your money is a very clear test of whether you are a real Christian or not. Real Christians will, almost always, find their hearts getting more and more tender about the needs of the poor and about the importance of supporting God's work in churches, charities and so on. If you enjoy giving and look forward to it, that's a good sign.

If you don't and, instead, you avoid giving and minimise it, or even resent it, then I would question whether you are a real Christian. That is especially true if you are not just a brand new convert but have been a believer for years.

In my experience, stinginess, i.e. being mean with money, is one of the surest signs that a person has no real relationship with God and that they do not have the Holy Spirit at work in their lives. Moreover, I have observed that financially stingy people almost always have a range of other deep problems. In particular, they tend to have hard and callous hearts. That is not consistent with being a real Christian.

☐ A = No, you don't really give much money away. You don't enjoy giving money away either and you try to avoid it or minimise it. You feel your money is your own and that you need it all and deserve to keep it.

☐ B = Yes, you enjoy giving money away and you have been giving away more and more. Your heart is getting more and more tender about the needs of the poor, the sick, the elderly and the lost etc. You see your money as God's money rather than as your own.

Conclusion

I have been through many different factors in the numbered paragraphs above. The list is not exhaustive. There are many other things that you could ask yourself. It may be that God will bring such questions to mind now, especially if you ask Him to. The key is to go through the above list one by one and to be really frank and truthful with yourself about where you stand. Which direction are your answers mainly pointing in?

Do all or most of them point in the direction of you never having truly repented and handed over your life to Jesus Christ? Do they mostly show that there has been no real change of heart and of behaviour and priorities in your life? Is there little or no sign of fruit growing from your life? If so, then you are probably not really a Christian at all, no matter how many times you have been to church.

If most or all of your answers are option A than that strongly suggests that you are *not* a real Christian. If you have only or mainly ticked B then that would suggest to me that you are a real Christian, provided you weren't just fooling yourself, which a lot of people do. Were you just ticking box B automatically, simply because you "wanted to get the answer right", even where it was not a true reflection of your life? If so, then do the test again more carefully and thoughtfully.

However, this test is only a guide. You need to pray and ask for God's guidance and, ideally, speak to a genuine and mature Christian to seek further advice. There is another type of person who tends to tick box A too readily. They are overly harsh with themselves, seeing no growth or progress even when it is really there.

This is a small minority, especially in the Western churches in this apostate age. However such people do exist and so I mention this in case you are one. People in this sub-category suffer from having excessive scruples. They are so honest that they are too quick to believe that any passage in the Bible which condemns sin or wrong attitudes is relevant to them and aimed at them. They see themselves as one of the least fruitful, least committed, least godly people in the church. In fact, they are usually the opposite.

Such a person is very prone to hear the accusing whispers of a demon. Therefore they are easily robbed of their assurance of salvation. They will therefore tick box A wrongly, when they ought to tick box B. It is the exact opposite of the self-satisfied, complacent person who casually ticks box B every time, when he has no valid basis for doing so.

So, if you feel you may belong to this sub-group and you have ticked box A many times, even though you have a sincere desire to be a disciple of Jesus and to follow Him, then go and take advice from a mature fellow believer or leader. Consider whether your answers involve too many 'false negatives' That said, such people are rare nowadays. Perhaps your answers were a mixture? It may be, therefore, that the genuineness of your conversion is in doubt.

If that is so, then take the opportunity now to make things certain by truly and deeply repenting and getting right with God. Do that even if you have been going to church for years. Remember, it is not going to church that will save you, but rather a genuine repentance and a sincere belief in Jesus Christ and your whole hearted acceptance of Him as your own Lord and Saviour. Nothing else can save you. There is no other way to become a Christian.

I am reminded of a work colleague of mine in the past that I had been speaking to about the Gospel. I believed that he was not yet a Christian because it seemed to me that he had no real repentance. Plus he had so many doubts about the Gospel and the Bible that I felt he didn't really have saving faith either. Nonetheless, he was told by some other Christians in a church he had started attending that he definitely was a Christian already. They were kindly people, but misguided.

They saw him fretting and agonizing about his doubts and about whether he really believed and was really saved. They just wanted to "help" him by enabling him to stop worrying. So they assured him he was already a Christian and that he should be confident of that and stop doubting it. So he took no further steps to become a Christian. He relied on what they told him and assumed that he was already a Christian.

From that point on he continued to go to church. But he was still troubled by the same confusion and unbelief and I felt that there was still no genuine repentance. I could see all that, but he couldn't, because someone had told him that he was a Christian and that there was no question about that. In fact, he was full of doubts and problems. He hadn't genuinely repented, believed, been baptised in water or received the Holy Spirit. Therefore, his problems just continued and increased.

It all ended in disaster. He knew in himself, and eventually said openly, that being a Christian *"wasn't working"*. He had been assured by experienced people that he was a real Christian. He assumed that they must surely know what they were talking about. Oddly, even at the end, he never came to doubt *whether he really was a Christian*. He concluded instead that he *was* one, but that *"Christianity just doesn't work"*. He reached that conclusion because he was in just as much of a mess as ever. In fact his problems were worse.

In the end, everything fell apart completely and he decided that he no longer even believed that there was a God! It was a tragedy brought about by bad advice given to him by well-meaning but very misguided people. These days I never tell anybody that they are a real Christian. All I do now is point them to what the Bible says a person needs to do. Then I urge them to take all four steps, (repeatedly if necessary), until they are given genuine assurance of their own salvation by the Holy Spirit.

Giving that assurance to people is the task of the Holy Spirit. It's not my place to do it, because I would probably get it wrong. So, if you already know in your heart that you are a genuine Christian and the Holy Spirit has given you that assurance, then that is wonderful. But, if you are in any doubt at all, then you need to get right with God now. Don't put it off till later or leave it to chance. Be real with Him. Ask Him to help you now to genuinely repent and to truly become a Christian, with no doubt about it.

Also go ahead and get baptised in water. Then pray to receive the Holy Spirit and to speak in tongues and to prophesy and to receive the other gifts of the Holy Spirit. Why take any chances? Why leave anything in doubt? Why leave anything out? You need to know that you really are a Christian and to put it beyond all doubt.

I recently came across this poem in a book by Chuck Missler (See the section entitled 'Approved Ministries' on the Real Christianity website for details of his ministry). The poem is carved around the door frame of an old church in Germany. It was written in the sixteenth century, probably during the Reformation. The poem takes the form of a series of (imaginary) statements by Jesus Christ about the inconsistencies in our lives between what we claim to *believe,* and what we actually *do*:

Sixteenth century German poem

You call me eternal, then do not seek me.
You call me fair, then do not love me.
You call me gracious, then do not trust me.
You call me just, then do not fear me.
You call me life, then do not choose me.
You call me light, then do not see me.
You call me Lord, then do not respect me.
You call me Master, then do not obey me.
You call me merciful, then do not thank me.
You call me mighty, then do not honour me.
You call me noble, then do not serve me.
You call me rich, then do not ask me.
You call me Saviour, then do not praise me.
You call me shepherd, then do not follow me.
You call me Way, then do not walk with me.
You call me wise, then do not heed me.
You call me Son of God, then do not worship me.
When I sentence you, then do not blame me.

If those words don't convict you and cause you to question yourself and seek to become more committed to Jesus then something is wrong. They are sobering words and they accurately reflect the inconsistencies, hypocrisy and shallowness that I have often seen in myself and still see, all too often.

CHAPTER 20

SUMMARY - HOW DO WE ACTUALLY BECOME A CHRISTIAN? WHAT DO WE NEED TO DO IN PRACTICAL TERMS?

Preparatory steps to help you get ready to become a Christian:

Before we look at exactly how to take the step of becoming a Christian, let's consider what to do if you don't quite feel ready yet. Perhaps you still feel there is some blockage or obstacle which prevents you making a decisive step to put your trust in Jesus. If so, don't rush it. It is extremely important to start your Christian life with a clear and definite decision of your will.

Your will is the part of you that God is most interested in. He wants you to hand it over to Him. To be able to make such a clear decision to become Jesus' disciple you need to be fully convinced that the Gospel is true. If you don't yet feel completely ready to make such a definite decision, you can at least take these sensible preparatory steps. These will help you to get to the stage where you are ready:

a) Prayer

Begin by sincerely asking God for help. Even though you may not yet be a Christian, it is perfectly alright for you to pray to God and ask Him for His help. Ask for this in two specific ways:

i. Ask Him to show you the real extent and seriousness of your own sin and to enable you to see your sin the way that He sees it and to feel what He feels about it.

ii. Ask Him to help you to read the Bible and to understand it and for your eyes and your mind to be opened so that you can believe it. Nobody can understand the Bible just through their own intellect. It requires the help of the Holy Spirit or you will make no sense of it. However, when God opens your eyes, it will make sense.

b) Begin to read the Bible every day

Preferably read the Bible morning and evening, but at least once per day. If you are a non-Christian and are new to the Bible then begin in the New Testament with the gospels. Then follow on with Acts and then on through all the letters of the New Testament until you reach the book of Revelation at the end. If you lack faith, or real repentance, or if you just lack understanding, then reading your Bible on a daily basis like this will provide you with what you need. After you have finished the New Testament then go back and read the whole of the Old Testament. Then start on the whole New Testament

The Bible says faith comes by hearing (or reading). Therefore, if you have not yet got faith then reading the Bible is how you get it. Also, God will provide understanding to you if you really seek for Him diligently and seriously with your whole heart:

You will seek me and find me when you seek me with all your heart.
Jeremiah 29:13 (NIV)

When you read the Bible it is also 'reading you'. It speaks to your heart, and convicts and changes you. You need to be realistic though about how long it will take for you to gain a good overall understanding of the whole Bible. It won't happen overnight. So don't expect that, or you'll get discouraged and give up. Keep pressing on and read as much as you can and take note of all that you do understand. Those things that you don't yet grasp can be looked at again later.

c) Honestly assess where you currently stand
Maybe you already know that you are a sinner and sincerely want to repent. It may be that you already believe all those basic essentials that I have listed earlier in chapter 15. If so, then there is nothing to stop you from becoming a Christian right now.

If you still feel in doubt as to whether you are a sinner, or as to whether you genuinely believe in Jesus, then wait. Keep reading your Bible daily. Keep praying to God to help you to wholeheartedly repent and believe. Also ask him to help you to get past any obstacles or blockages which might be hindering you from becoming a Christian.

If you feel you are ready to make a definite decision of your will to become a Christian, here are some practical steps to take:

If you feel you are ready now to truly repent and believe in Jesus, and you are genuinely serious about it, then go ahead and become a Christian now. There is no set formula for how you go about this, but, from experience, it may be helpful to do it broadly along the following lines:

Step one in becoming a Christian – repent towards God the Father

How to repent – what to do in practical terms:

Get a pad of paper. Put the date at the top and write on it any specific sins, or transgressions or attitudes of rebellion, that you feel aware of in your life. Write down anything that you are doing now or in the past that you can remember. Make the list as long as it needs to be. Ask God to help you remember the things He is most concerned about. He will bring to mind specific sins or transgressions, past or present, that He particularly wants you to repent of. They will be sins that are especially significant in your own life.

God will not bring everything to mind, because it would need a computer to deal with all your sins. What He will do is bring the most important or most relevant ones to mind. To start with it may only be a few. The exact number of sins you write down does not matter so much. What matters is that you seriously repent of them and really mean it.

You do not have to write things down if you prefer not to. You could just speak them out. But, writing does help to make it more real. Plus it is easier, later on, to look at it and feel sure that you really did this and that you meant it. I would advise it. For each of the sins write down the name of the person who may have been affected by it. It could be your wife, children, employer, work colleague, friend or relative etc. Then alongside that name write down what you might be able to do to put it right. Sometimes it will not be possible to put it right. Sometimes it will. It may be that the most you can do is give an apology.

Other times you may be able to repay and put right the damage that you have caused in some practical way. For example, if you have been stealing from your employer or fiddling expenses, then you need to deal with that. It could be very hazardous to go to your employer and openly confess. That could result in dismissal or even prosecution. It is not always necessary to go that far. You need to be guided by your own conscience on that.

There is a need to be practical and wise at the same time as being sincere. If you have been stealing from your employer, then here is a good way to repay, without having to risk getting into serious trouble. You could set about working unpaid overtime for a sufficient period of time to more than pay back what you owe. Calculate on paper and work out how much extra time you need to work secretly without claiming any pay for it.

Then quietly set about doing that extra work without telling anybody. In calculating it, err on the generous side. Make sure you fully repay or even over pay. This is practical repentance. It demonstrates to God that you mean what you say and you are not just being casual or shallow. There may be other ways that you can do it.

Apologies will be needed for many people, especially those closest to you such as your wife, children, parents or close friends. Where it is appropriate, go and see each person and apologise specifically for things that are suitable to raise. Do it unreservedly. Do not qualify your apology or seek to explain or justify your actions. Just straightforwardly apologise. Ideally, tell the person that you have become a Christian and feel you need to repent of what you did or said which has wronged them.

Be careful with this, however. Do not bring up painful things that are in the past and which would only cause even more pain and harm to others if they were to be openly raised again now.

Some things need to be repented of privately, just between you and God. You need to ask for the wisdom to know the difference. If however an apology will help and will not cause harm to that person or to anybody else, then go and directly apologise face to face with the person. They may receive it well, or they may not. But whatever their reaction is, your going to them will please God, and it will help you to properly repent.

However, do not go to people to tell them things you have said or thought about them which they are not aware of. That would only cause pain and upset them for no beneficial purpose. Once you have written out your list of sins and are resolved to deal with them, don't wait until you have spoken to the people on the list. You need to speak out your repentance towards God first. It's important that you tell God out loud that you repent.

Again, there is no formula for this, but it is a good idea to kneel down. You can do it on your own, or even better with a mature Christian to help you, and to be a witness to it. If you are doing this with a genuine and mature believer alongside you, don't be ashamed to speak out loud and don't imagine that they will disapprove of you. They won't. They will just want to help you to get it all out and dealt with. They will have had similar sins in their own past.

Speak your repentance out loud to God the Father directly. Kneeling helps because it puts your body into a humble position. There is a direct relationship between the position of your body and the attitude of your mind. Altering your posture can really help to alter your attitude of mind. You do not have to use eloquent words or indeed any particular form of words. Just speak in your own way with your own vocabulary.

Tell God that you are sorry for the things that you have done and that you recognise that you have sinned against Him and others. Then apologise to Him directly. But only say it if you mean it. If you don't yet mean it then persist with the preparatory steps I set out earlier, i.e. prayer and Bible reading, until you do really mean it. Then ask God the Father for His forgiveness.

Tell Him that you want to turn away from all your sins and that you want to renounce them and stop committing them. At the same time ask Him for His help in turning away from them, because on your own you cannot change or achieve anything. Both you and God will know whether you are sincere in the prayer that you make. Therefore do not be phoney or try to kid God or yourself. Just be straight and come clean with God, without any pretentiousness.

Step two in becoming a Christian - believe in (or on) the Lord Jesus Christ

9 That if you confess with your mouth, "Jesus is Lord," and believe in your heart that God raised him from the dead, you will be saved. 10 For it is with your heart that you believe and are justified, and it is with your mouth that you confess and are saved. 11 As the Scripture says, "Anyone who trusts in him will never be put to shame." 12 For there is no difference between Jew and Gentile—the same Lord is Lord of all and richly blesses all who call on him, 13 for, "Everyone who calls on the name of the Lord will be saved."

Romans 10:9-13 (NIV)

You need to be clear in your own mind that you believe the Bible and that you know and understand the main points that we need to believe in order to be a Christian. Please refer to the list of foundational things that you need to believe that was set out earlier in Chapter 15. I will reproduce the list here in short form, i.e. without the Bible verses in support. Do remember, however, that believing in Jesus is not just a mental attitude that happens only in our minds. If it is real then it will show itself in what we do, i.e. in our actions and words. It will bring about a changed lifestyle. Please now consider this abbreviated list. Do you understand and believe all of these basic things?

THE BASIC ESSENTIALS THAT WE NEED TO BELIEVE:

a) That God exists, that He is the one true God and that there is no other God.

b) That God exists in three separate Persons: God the Father, the Son of God and the Holy Spirit.

c) That nonetheless, those three individual Persons together form One God. So, it is true to say that God is One.

d) That God created everything, including us, and that we belong to Him.

e) That we are unworthy and have sinned, transgressed and rebelled against God and offended and angered Him.

f) That we are therefore condemned in God's eyes. And, unless we are forgiven, we will be eternally separated from Him when we die and face His judgment. We will then go to eternal punishment in the Lake of Fire because of our sin.

g) That nothing we can do on our own behalf can save (justify) us by giving us forgiveness or righteousness in God's eyes. We are not good enough and none of our works or deeds will ever be good enough to save us, because in God's eyes even our best deeds are inadequate.

h) That Jesus Christ is not only a man, but is also divine, (i.e. that He is God). He is the Second Person of the Trinity, the Son of God. He became a real human being, whilst at the same time remaining the Son of God.

i) That Jesus Christ lived a sinless life and then died an unjust death, which He did not deserve, in order to be punished in our place and pay the penalty for our sins. That was how God the Father viewed Jesus' death. He was putting His own Son, Jesus, to death to be the sacrifice that pays for our sin.

j) That when the Lord Jesus Christ was on the cross, the burden and the guilt of all the sin of the world was put upon Him. God the Father poured out His wrath, anger and punishment upon Him, instead of on us.

k) That the Lord Jesus Christ died and then rose from the dead. He was resurrected physically and He ascended physically into Heaven 40 days later. He is now alive and in Heaven, in His resurrection body, waiting to return to the earth.

l) That we must repent towards God the Father for our sins and sincerely turn away from our sins and genuinely change in our attitudes, behaviour and lifestyle.

m) That we must be baptised in water, by full immersion, in the name of the Father, the Son and the Holy Spirit. And this must be done *by* us as a repentant believer, not done *to* us as an infant. Any past baptism as a baby does not count as real baptism.

n) That we must receive the Holy Spirit, otherwise referred to as being "filled with" or "baptised in" the Holy Spirit.

o) That forgiveness and eternal life with God are available to anyone who meets God's conditions. Those are to repent, believe, be baptised in water and receive the Holy Spirit.

p) That there is no other way for any person to get to God. No man, religion, system, activity or formula can save us. Only the Lord Jesus Christ can do it because of His death on the cross, when he took our punishment in our place.

q) That if we die we will eventually be physically resurrected. We will then have eternal and indestructible "resurrection bodies" which will never die. This is true both for believers and unbelievers. The resurrection body of an unbeliever will never be destroyed, even in the Lake of Fire

r) That Jesus Christ will, one day, return physically and literally to this earth. He will then rule as King of Israel and King of the whole world. In other words, He will set up the Kingdom of God and bring it to completion.

Go through the above list and check carefully whether you truly understand and believe each point. If so, speak out loud to God to say to Him that you do believe each of those things. Tell Him that you do put your faith and trust solely and totally in the Lord Jesus Christ for salvation, not in yourself or in your own goodness.

Ask God to give you the forgiveness that is available due to Jesus' death on the cross, so that you can be saved and given eternal life. Ask for the guilt of your sins to be placed on Jesus Christ and for His righteousness to be transferred, or credited, to you. Just ask God in your own simple words and style, using your own vocabulary.

Speak to God the Father and tell Him that you want to follow His Son, the Lord Jesus Christ, as His disciple, (follower) from this moment on and for the rest of your life. Promise God, if you really mean it, that you will give yourself and everything you have to Jesus. Hand over your whole life, and all your ambitions, and plans, so that Jesus Christ will, from now on, be your Lord and the one who decides your priorities. That includes where you go, what you do, and how you live.

Speak out loud and tell God the Father and Jesus that you believe that Jesus Christ is the King of kings and Lord of lords and that you acknowledge Him to be so. Say that you also personally recognise and accept Him as King and Lord in your own life. Then ask God to give you the grace and the help to be Jesus' disciple and to remain faithful to Him.

Remember that being a disciple, and continuing faithfully on "the Way", is not what justifies you or gives you forgiveness. However, it is what is needed to bring you to Christian maturity. More importantly, it is what Jesus commands us to do. The idea of handing over the whole of yourself and your future to Jesus can be scary. You might fear that He cannot be trusted with your future and to make decisions about what you should be and do.

It's natural to be apprehensive about that, but you really don't need to be. He is totally trustworthy and can be relied on to form a plan for your life which is far better than anything you could plan for yourself. God is good and kind and full of mercy. All His plans for your life will be for your good:

For I know the plans I have for you," declares the LORD, "plans to prosper you and not to harm you, plans to give you hope and a future.

Jeremiah 29:11 (NIV)

Having taken each of these steps, then thank God for forgiveness and salvation and for the gift of eternal life. However, do not rely on your feelings. It may be that your emotions will surface at this point. You may be tearful or emotionally moved in some way. Or, more likely, it may be that you are not. Becoming a Christian is primarily a decision of the *will*, not of the *emotions*. God is much more interested in what you *decide* than in what you *feel*.

Therefore do not judge the validity of what you are doing on the basis of whether there is an outward emotional reaction. The emotions are a side-issue here. They may or may not materialise. Instead, simply take God at His word. Claim the forgiveness that you have asked for and believe that you have received it. God is faithful. He can be trusted and relied upon to honour every promise that He makes. Therefore believe Him to do so. On that basis, then give thanks to Him for forgiveness, justification and eternal life.

Step three in becoming a Christian: be baptised in water, preferably in public

If necessary please refer again to Chapter 16 on baptism in water. This is a badly neglected topic. Many people have come to regard it as something peripheral and non-essential, as if it was an "optional add on". Others take the view that they were baptised as a baby and therefore it has already been done. As explained in Chapter 16, that is not a biblical view. Baptism needs to be done when you have genuinely made a conscious decision to repent and believe in Jesus Christ. If all you have had is baptism as a baby then you need to do it again. Whatever was done to you as a baby is not valid baptism in water. At any rate, nobody was ever baptised that way in the Bible.

Therefore, once you have taken these steps, go as soon as you can and get baptised in water. Speak to someone at church, and get baptised in a river, or lake, or in the sea or a swimming pool. Anything will do. However, if for health reasons you cannot do that, then be baptised in a warm bath at home.

If you really can't do even that, I feel sure that God will accept you being baptised in some lesser way, e.g. by sprinkling some water on your head, provided that is all you can manage. God is very reasonable and gracious, but you would need to have a genuine reason to depart from the normal biblical method.

Ideally, do it publicly so that others can witness it. That will help you to get over any problem you may have of being ashamed of being identified with Jesus Christ. The act of baptism in water will help to remove that. It will also let the world, and the Devil, know where you now stand. It will also help to cut you off from your past life as an unbeliever.

That will help you to become free from many things such as habitual sins, addictions or demonic influences in your life. Quite apart from any benefits it brings, we have been commanded to be baptised to demonstrate our repentance and our belief in Jesus. Therefore don't leave it out or neglect it. Don't even delay it. Baptism is very important.

Step four in becoming a Christian: 'receive' or be 'baptised in' the Holy Spirit

Look again at Chapter 17 if you still feel any confusion or uncertainty about this. However, if you feel you do grasp what this means and you want to go ahead and receive the Holy Spirit, then, first of all, make sure you have taken the first three steps properly. Make sure you have genuinely repented, that you really do believe, and that you have been properly baptised in water. If you haven't taken all of these steps properly, then put that right. Take them now.

If you have properly dealt with all three of these steps and you want to receive the Holy Spirit, then the ideal is to get the help of someone else who believes that the baptism in the Holy Spirit is for today, not just for the first century. Find someone who has, him or herself, received the Holy Spirit and spoken in tongues or operated in one or more of the other gifts of the Holy Spirit. Ask them to pray for you and lay their hands on you.

It needs to be a genuine Christian who has a proper, biblical understanding of the need to be baptised in the Holy Spirit. Sadly, most people in British churches, including leaders, do not have that level of knowledge or understanding. Therefore there is a problem. If you were to just ask the first person you see, they may tell you that you don't need to receive the Holy Spirit. Or they may say that you have already received the Holy Spirit automatically.

They may even tell you that the gifts of the Holy Spirit have ceased and are not for today. They may be sincere, but they would be wrong and they would confuse you. God is unlikely to use such a person to help you to receive the Holy Spirit. They will only hold you back and discourage you.

So, try to find a person who does understand and believe the Bible on this subject. They can help you. They can then simply lay their hands on you, i.e. on your head or back, and pray for you to receive the Holy Spirit. As they pray for you pray also for yourself, in your own language, for Jesus Christ to baptise you in the Holy Spirit.

Remember that Jesus Christ *wants* to do that. He's not against the idea. He is in favour of it. He is the very Person who baptises us in the Holy Spirit. You don't need to persuade Him. The main thing is for you to believe that Jesus does want you to receive the Holy Spirit and to expect Him to answer your prayers in this regard.

Try to relax and avoid being stressed or afraid or tensed up if you can. Then be willing to step out and open your mouth to speak. Don't speak in English. Just begin to make sounds and see what comes. Step out boldly and with faith. Go ahead and don't hold back or be shy. Don't be afraid of sounding foolish. My fear of that held me back needlessly for two years.

Don't make my mistake. You may find that you suddenly take off and are away, speaking in a new unknown language immediately. Or, you may not. There could be a delay or blockage which holds you back. If so it could be for a number of reasons. Here are some of the main ones:

a) You may be too tense/uptight/afraid. The Holy Spirit will not force Himself on you. He will wait for you to be ready and relaxed. He wants *you* to be in control of when to speak, not Him.

b) You may not have genuinely or properly repented, believed or been baptised in water. If so, see chapters 10-17 again.

c) The person helping you may not understand or believe any of this. Or he may never have received the baptism in the Holy Spirit himself. If so, try asking someone else (if possible). Or, just go ahead by yourself. You are much better off being alone than being prayed with by someone who doesn't agree with, or believe in, what you are seeking for. They would be tensed up themselves, or even opposing you.

d) There could be some particularly significant sin in your life which God wants you to deal with first. I don't mean that you must deal with or cease all sin. That's not possible this side of death. However, there can sometimes be major sins which God is particularly concerned about. For example you could be involved in some sexual affair or stealing money or living in some immoral way. God may want you to stop that particular sin first before He will recognise you as having genuinely repented. Therefore consider this and ask God to reveal to you any specific sin that He is particularly concerned about, which may be a blockage to you receiving the Holy Spirit.

e) There could be some occult involvement in your past, (or even now), which has still not been dealt with or repented of fully. If so, repent now, fully and unreservedly. If you still possess any occult books or charms or jewellery etc, burn all it now. Ask God to set you free from its hold over you. If you are unsure, ask God to highlight anything relevant.

If you have nobody at all who is suitable and willing to pray with you, do not be discouraged. Go ahead by yourself. Just take all the same steps but pray by yourself. Remember, it is Jesus Christ Himself who baptises us in the Holy Spirit, not the person who prays with us or lays their hands on us. Such a person, if there even is one, is just there to help us and to explain things. They are not essential.

Also, be aware that some people just seem to take longer than others to break through. That ought not to be the case, but it often is. If so, and there is delay, keep on asking and don't give up. Also keep on attempting to speak. Don't just leave it to God alone. Play your part by stepping out in faith and beginning to speak. Let your mouth make sounds and see if God then releases you fully to speak in tongues. If you persist, then He will do so at some point, even if not immediately.

After you have become a Christian – what next?

Tell others

If you have not had a person to be with you and help while you take these steps, and to be a witness, then, instead, go out now and tell others what you have done. It is important that you start as early as possible to let other people know that you have become a believer and have begun your journey along "the Way". This will “help the concrete to set” and become permanent.

The more publicly and openly you acknowledge the Lord Jesus Christ, the quicker you will lose any fear or embarrassment at being associated with Him. Also the bolder you will become in being able to tell other people about Him.

If you keep quiet about your conversion at the start you will find that that silence will turn into a habit and become a major handicap later on. It will hinder your growth and development. Therefore quickly tell at least one person, preferably a mature Christian, what you have done.

Then tell others too, even those close to you, (unless it would put you in physical danger). Don't be worried about not knowing how to explain yourself or how to answer their questions. The object is not to impress people, but to please God. He will be very proud that you are openly associating yourself with Him and learning not to be ashamed of Him. He will also reward you for it.

I am not saying you have to tell everybody. Sometimes it could be unwise to tell certain people. But do at least make sure you tell some people, unless you are in a country where that would be dangerous due to persecution.

Join a biblical church

Then seek to join a good and biblical church. Sadly, today in the Western world, this is not simple. Genuine churches are very hard to find, whereas there are far too many that are liberal, shallow, insincere, compromised and worldly. I give more advice in my Book 8, "*Biblical and unbiblical churches*", about how to find a sincere and genuine biblical church.

Once you have found one, then join it. You may need to drive quite a few miles. Become active in it and seek to learn as much as you can and to gain as much fellowship (i.e. making relationships) as you can with other more mature believers. You need their help, advice and friendship.

However, even after you have joined a genuine church you must continue to be vigilant. You are under a duty to be discerning and careful to make sure that what you are being taught is biblical and accurate. That always remains *your own personal responsibility*. You can't delegate it to anybody, not even to church leaders.

You must always be like the Bereans in Acts 17:11. Search the Scriptures daily to test whatever is being taught and to see whether it is true. Much of what is taught in British and American churches today is not true. The same applies to most of the Western world.

Set about seeking to become an effective disciple

See chapter 23 in this book and also subsequent books in this series, for more detail on this. The key point in becoming an effective disciple is to *want* to be one. You could never become a pianist or a sculptor or dentist without first wanting to be one. Otherwise you would never pay the price or make the effort or do the necessary things to change from what you are now into whatever it is you want to be.

It is just the same with becoming a real disciple. It won't happen automatically. You will become a disciple to the precise extent that you want to. Therefore choose to be a 100% committed disciple. Then actively set out to obey all that God commands us to do in order to become one.

CHAPTER 21

ASSURANCE OF SALVATION, PROVIDED WE PERSEVERE AND CONTINUE ON "THE WAY"

[13]These things I have written to you who believe in the name of the Son of God, so that you may know that you have eternal life.

1 John 5:13 (NASB)

[27] My sheep hear My voice, and I know them, and they follow Me; [28] and I give eternal life to them, and they will never perish; and no one will snatch them out of My hand. [29] My Father, who has given them to Me, is greater than all; and no one is able to snatch them out of the Father's hand.

John 10:27-29 (NASB)

The Spirit of God came upon Azari'ah the son of Oded, [2] and he went out to meet Asa, and said to him, "Hear me, Asa, and all Judah and Benjamin: The Lord is with you, while you are with him. If you seek him, he will be found by you, but if you forsake him, he will forsake you.

2 Chronicles 15:1-2 (RSV)

[12]Take care, brethren, that there not be in any one of you an evil, unbelieving heart that falls away from the living God.

Hebrews 3:12 (NASB)

"These things I have spoken to you so that you may be kept from stumbling.

John 16:1 (NASB)

[15]for some have already turned aside to follow Satan.

1 Timothy 5:15 (NASB)

In this chapter we shall examine a complex and controversial question. That is whether a real Christian can lose his salvation after he has been *genuinely* justified and forgiven. It is a question which is not capable of a short answer. We are not discussing a *false* Christian who has never really repented or believed at all. Such a person has never been saved in the first place. So, he cannot 'lose' his salvation because he had no salvation to begin with.

We are discussing the position of a real Christian who has repented, believed, been baptised in water and even received the Holy Spirit. Can such a person "*fall away*" such that they cease to be a Christian? Is it possible for them to lose their forgiveness and justification and go to Hell and then the Lake of Fire when they die? That is the question and it is not an easy one to answer. There are two main schools of thought about this and we will examine both:

A) People who emphasise assurance of salvation

This group tends to believe in the idea of *"Once saved, always saved"*. By that they mean that a person who has been genuinely saved *cannot* lose his forgiveness and justification, even if he later turns away from the faith, or acts in a way which is very wrong or sinful. There are many Bible passages which indicate that a person can have assurance of salvation and can be confident that they have eternal life. For example, consider the following series of verses:

The LORD redeems the soul of His servants,
And none of those who take refuge in Him will be condemned.

Psalm 34:22 (NASB)

"Truly, truly, I say to you, he who hears My word, and believes Him who sent Me, has eternal life, and does not come into judgment, but has passed out of death into life.

John 5:24 (NASB)

39 "This is the will of Him who sent Me, that of all that He has given Me I lose
nothing, but raise it up on the last day. 40 "For this is the will of My Father, that
everyone who beholds the Son and believes in Him will have eternal life, and I
Myself will raise him up on the last day."

John 6:39-40 (NASB)

33 Who will bring any charge against those whom God has chosen? It is God
who justifies. 34 Who then is the one who condemns? No one. Christ Jesus who
died—more than that, who was raised to life—is at the right hand of God and
is also interceding for us. 35 Who shall separate us from the love of Christ? Shall
trouble or hardship or persecution or famine or nakedness or danger or sword?
36 As it is written: "For your sake we face death all day long; we are considered
as sheep to be slaughtered." 37 No, in all these things we are more than
conquerors through him who loved us. 38 For I am convinced that neither death
nor life, neither angels nor demons, neither the present nor the future, nor any
powers, 39 neither height nor depth, nor anything else in all creation, will be
able to separate us from the love of God that is in Christ Jesus our Lord.

Romans 8:33-39 (NIV)

As the Scripture says, "Anyone who trusts in him will never be put to shame."

Romans 10:11 (NIV)

19 Therefore, brethren, since we have confidence to enter the holy place by the
blood of Jesus, 20 by a new and living way which He inaugurated for us through
the veil, that is, His flesh, 21 and since we have a great priest over the house of
God, 22 let us draw near with a sincere heart in full assurance of faith, having
our hearts sprinkled clean from an evil conscience and our bodies washed with

pure water. [23]Let us hold fast the confession of our hope without wavering, for He who promised is faithful;

Hebrews 10:19-23 (NASB)

[8]who will also confirm you to the end, blameless in the day of our Lord Jesus Christ.

1 Corinthians 1:8 (NASB)

[18]The LORD is near to all who call upon Him,
To all who call upon Him in truth.
[19]He will fulfil the desire of those who fear Him;
He will also hear their cry and will save them.

Psalm 145:18-19 (NASB)

[13]These things I have written to you who believe in the name of the Son of God, so that you may know that you have eternal life.

1 John 5:13 (NASB)

[9]But, beloved, we are convinced of better things concerning you, and things that accompany salvation, though we are speaking in this way. [10]For God is not unjust so as to forget your work and the love which you have shown toward His name, in having ministered and in still ministering to the saints.

Hebrews 6:9-10 (NASB)

[24]Now to Him who is able to keep you from stumbling, and to make you stand in the presence of His glory blameless with great joy,

Jude 24 (NASB)

[22]so much the more also Jesus has become the guarantee of a better covenant. [23]The former priests, on the one hand, existed in greater numbers because they were prevented by death from continuing, [24]but Jesus, on the other hand, because He continues forever, holds His priesthood permanently. [25]Therefore He is able also to save forever those who draw near to God through Him, since He always lives to make intercession for them. [26]For it was fitting for us to have such a high priest, holy, innocent, undefiled, separated from sinners and exalted above the Heavens; [27]who does not need daily, like those high priests, to offer up sacrifices, first for His own sins and then for the sins of the people, because this He did once for all when He offered up Himself. [28]For the Law appoints men as high priests who are weak, but the word of the oath, which came after the Law, appoints a Son, made perfect forever.

Hebrews 7:22-28 (NASB)

These '*assurance passages*' seem to be very clear and firm. Their meaning appears to be that if we are a genuine believer we are assured of going to Heaven when we die and of having eternal life. The question, therefore, is whether it is possible for such a genuine believer to *stop* being a believer. Before we seek to reach any conclusion about that, let us look at the other main school of thought:

B) People who emphasise the warnings in the Bible of the need to persevere to the end

This group tends to highlight those passages in the Bible which contain warnings about the need to persevere to the end. Those *'warning passages'* do appear to say that our salvation could be lost if we deny Jesus Christ, or turn away from Him, or commit serious sins. Consider the following passages very carefully Note that in the first passage, Jesus Himself is speaking:

31So Jesus was saying to those Jews who had believed Him, "If you continue in My word, then you are truly disciples of Mine;

John 8:31 (NASB)

Then the writer of the letter to the Hebrews also tells us that we need to "*hold fast".... "until the end".*

1Therefore, holy brethren, partakers of a heavenly calling, consider Jesus, the Apostle and High Priest of our confession; 2He was faithful to Him who appointed Him, as Moses also was in all His house. 3For He has been counted worthy of more glory than Moses, by just so much as the builder of the house has more honour than the house. 4For every house is built by someone, but the builder of all things is God.

5Now Moses was faithful in all His house as a servant, for a testimony of those things which were to be spoken later; 6but Christ was faithful as a Son over His house--whose house we are, if we hold fast our confidence and the boast of our hope firm until the end. 7Therefore, just as the Holy Spirit says, "today if you hear His voice, 8do not harden your hearts as when they provoked Me, as in the day of trial in the wilderness, 9where your fathers tried Me by testing Me, and saw my works for forty years. 10"Therefore I was angry with this generation, and said, 'they always go astray in their heart, and they did not know My ways'; 11as I swore in my wrath, 'they shall not enter My rest.'"

Hebrews 3:1-11 (NASB)

Then, having made the above points, the writer of the letter to the Hebrews tells us in the next verse to *"take care"* not to have the kind of heart that *"falls away"* from God. His warning would surely be meaningless and absurd if it was not possible to fall away.

Take care, brethren, that there not be in any one of you an evil, unbelieving heart that falls away from the living God

Hebrews 3:12 (NASB)

Note that in verse 12 above, the writer of the letter to the Hebrews is not speaking to unbelievers. He refers to his audience as "*brethren*". That only makes sense if he already considers them to be genuine believers, at least at the moment. Yet, he still warns them of the danger of falling away. It cannot be that he is warning them of something that is purely hypothetical, and which could never happen to them. He warns them soberly against falling away because he views that as a real possibility, even for them.

Now look at how the writer to the Hebrews continues with his warning. He refers to the generation of Israelites who were rescued from Egypt but who went on to become ungrateful and unbelieving, despite all the miracles they had seen. Their attitude angered God, such that He did not let them enter the Promised Land:

13 But encourage one another day after day, as long as it is still called "Today,"
so that none of you will be hardened by the deceitfulness of sin. 14 For we have
become partakers of Christ, if we hold fast the beginning of our assurance firm
until the end, 15 while it is said, "today if you hear His voice, do not harden your
hearts, as when they provoked me." 16 For who provoked Him when they had
heard? Indeed, did not all those who came out of Egypt led by Moses? 17 And
with whom was He angry for forty years? Was it not with those who sinned,
whose bodies fell in the wilderness? 18 And to whom did He swear that they
would not enter His rest, but to those who were disobedient? 19 So we see that
they were not able to enter because of unbelief.

Hebrews 3:13-19 (NASB)

So, the writer, to the Hebrews urges us to learn from their experience and not to behave as that generation did, with ingratitude and unbelief. Instead, we are urged to fear God and to *avoid hardening our hearts*:

1 Therefore, let us fear if, while a promise remains of entering His rest, any one
of you may seem to have come short of it. 2 For indeed we have had good news
preached to us, just as they also; but the word they heard did not profit them,
because it was not united by faith in those who heard. 3 For we who have
believed enter that rest, just as He has said, "as I swore in My wrath, they shall
not enter My rest," although His works were finished from the foundation of
the world. 4 For He has said somewhere concerning the seventh day: "and God
rested on the seventh day from all His works"; 5 and again in this passage,
"They shall not enter My rest."

6 Therefore, since it remains for some to enter it, and those who formerly had
good news preached to them failed to enter because of disobedience, 7 He again

fixes a certain day, "Today," saying through David after so long a time just as
has been said before, "today if you hear His voice, do not harden your
hearts." 8For if Joshua had given them rest, He would not have spoken of
another day after that. 9So there remains a Sabbath rest for the people of
God. 10For the one who has entered His rest has himself also rested from his
works, as God did from His. 11Therefore let us be diligent to enter that rest, so
that no one will fall, through following the same example of disobedience.

12For the word of God is living and active and sharper than any two-edged
sword, and piercing as far as the division of soul and spirit, of both joints and
marrow, and able to judge the thoughts and intentions of the heart. 13And there
is no creature hidden from His sight, but all things are open and laid bare to the
eyes of Him with whom we have to do.

Hebrews 4:1-13 (NASB)

Those are very worrying verses, and should not be brushed aside or ignored. However, we do still need to hold them in balance with the more reassuring words which the writer to the Hebrews goes on to say next. He draws our attention to the fact that although we have to remain faithful to Jesus, He is ready and willing to help us to do so. He fully sympathises with us in our struggles and is able to give us His grace and mercy:

14Therefore, since we have a great high priest who has passed through the
Heavens, Jesus the Son of God, let us hold fast our confession. 15For we do not
have a high priest who cannot sympathize with our weaknesses, but One who
has been tempted in all things as we are, yet without sin. 16Therefore let us draw
near with confidence to the throne of grace, so that we may receive mercy and
find grace to help in time of need.

Hebrews 4:14-16 (NASB)

Now let's look at what apostle Paul has to say on this theme of the need to continue in the faith. It too is sobering:

22yet He has now reconciled you in His fleshly body through death, in order to
present you before Him holy and blameless and beyond reproach-- 23if indeed
you continue in the faith firmly established and steadfast, and not moved away
from the hope of the gospel that you have heard, which was proclaimed in all
creation under Heaven, and of which I, Paul, was made a minister.

Colossians 1:22-23 (NASB)

Note how Paul emphasises above the need for us to *"continue in the faith'."* And he says "*if*". He does not assume that this is automatic or that we will inevitably do so. When writing to Timothy Paul is even more explicit:

[1]But the Spirit explicitly says that in later times some will fall away from the faith, paying attention to deceitful spirits and doctrines of demons, [2]by means of the hypocrisy of liars seared in their own conscience as with a branding iron,

1 Timothy 4:1-2 (NASB)

Paul therefore advises Timothy to guard what he has:

[20]O Timothy, guard what has been entrusted to you, avoiding worldly and empty chatter and the opposing arguments of what is falsely called "knowledge"-- [21]which some have professed and thus gone astray from the faith. Grace be with you.

1 Timothy 6:20-21 (NASB)

Now see how Paul refers, in his letter to the Romans, to the nation of Israel. He describes them as an olive tree on which branches are grafted in, or broken off, depending on their own individual faithfulness:

[17]But if some of the branches were broken off, and you, being a wild olive, were grafted in among them and became partaker with them of the rich root of the olive tree, [18]do not be arrogant toward the branches; but if you are arrogant, remember that it is not you who supports the root, but the root supports you. [19]You will say then, "Branches were broken off so that I might be grafted in." [20]Quite right, they were broken off for their unbelief, but you stand by your faith Do not be conceited, but fear; [21]for if God did not spare the natural branches, He will not spare you, either. [22]Behold then the kindness and severity of God; to those who fell, severity, but to you, God's kindness, if you continue in His kindness; otherwise you also will be cut off.

Romans11:17-22 (NASB)

In this passage, apostle Paul is writing to the largely Gentile church in Rome. He says that that some of the Jewish people have been *"broken off"* for their unbelief, i.e. for not accepting their Messiah. Christians can, likewise, be cut off if they do not continue as they should. Paul's point is that the Jewish people are like a natural olive tree into which we Gentiles have been grafted. So, if even the natural olive branches, the Jews, can be broken off, then so can we be cut off. That is a clear and very disturbing warning to us. Now consider what Peter says:

[20] If they have escaped the corruption of the world by knowing our Lord and Saviour Jesus Christ and are again entangled in it and are overcome, they are worse off at the end than they were at the beginning. [21] It would have been better for them not to have known the way of righteousness, than to have known it and then to turn their backs on the sacred command that was passed on to them.

2 Peter 2:20-21 (NIV)

In this passage Peter goes further. He says that we are actually worse off if we believe and then fall away then if we had never believed. But, when we were unbelievers we were on our way to the Lake of Fire. That must mean, therefore, that a believer who falls away is, likewise, heading for the Lake of Fire. What else can it mean? If it means anything less than that, then Peter's warning would be an inaccurate exaggeration. But we know that that cannot be the case. Therefore the possibility of our *'turning our backs'* on God has to be taken seriously. Now let's consider some longer passages which give further warnings:

[12]"And you, son of man, say to your fellow citizens, 'The righteousness of a righteous man will not deliver him in the day of his transgression, and as for the wickedness of the wicked, he will not stumble because of it in the day when he turns from his wickedness; whereas a righteous man will not be able to live by his righteousness on the day when he commits sin.' [13]"When I say to the righteous he will surely live, and he so trusts in his righteousness that he commits iniquity, none of his righteous deeds will be remembered; but in that same iniquity of his which he has committed he will die.

[14]"But when I say to the wicked, 'You will surely die,' and he turns from his sin and practices justice and righteousness, [15]if a wicked man restores a pledge, pays back what he has taken by robbery, walks by the statutes which ensure life without committing iniquity, he shall surely live; he shall not die. [16]"None of his sins that he has committed will be remembered against him. He has practiced justice and righteousness; he shall surely live. [17]"Yet your fellow citizens say, 'The way of the Lord is not right,' when it is their own way that is not right. [18]"When the righteous turns from his righteousness and commits iniquity, then he shall die in it. [19]"But when the wicked turns from his wickedness and practices justice and righteousness, he will live by them. [20]"Yet you say, 'The way of the Lord is not right.' O house of Israel, I will judge each of you according to his ways."

Ezekiel 33:12-20 (NASB)

In the passage above the prophet Ezekiel is saying that it is possible for a righteous man to change his path and become wicked. If he does then his previous righteous life will not be remembered. In other words, he will be condemned, despite having been righteous up to that point. There would be no point in Ezekiel giving such a warning if it could not occur. Ezekiel also says that if a wicked man turns from his sin then, likewise, his past sinfulness will not be remembered against him either. It works both ways. But the operative point, for our purposes, is that it is possible for a righteous man to fall away. Now let's hear what Jesus says:

[21]"Not everyone who says to Me, 'Lord, Lord,' will enter the kingdom of Heaven, but he who does the will of My Father who is in Heaven will enter. [22]"Many will say to Me on that day, 'Lord, Lord, did we not prophesy in Your name, and in Your name cast out demons, and in Your name perform many

miracles?' [23]"And then I will declare to them, 'I never knew you; depart from me, you who practice lawlessness.'

Matthew 7:21-23 (NASB)

In this grim passage Jesus Himself is directly warning us that on the Day of Judgment, many people will be told by Him that He never knew them. This verse would appear to refer to people who *never were genuine Christians in the first place*, because it says *"I never knew you..."*.

We can deduce from this therefore that, at the very least, there must be many people who assume that they are real Christians, but in fact they are not, and never were. That must be so, because Jesus says He never knew them. That is a very worrying thought in itself, in addition to the quite separate danger of a *real* Christian falling away *after He has known them.*

It means that many of us will, one day, be told that we never were real Christians in the first place. That is very disturbing, especially as it comes from Jesus' own mouth. He is the One who will be judging us. But, what about people who *have* been real Christians, at least for a time? Can such people fall away? If so, how does it occur? Let's look again at one of the most well-known parables Jesus told. We have discussed it earlier in chapter 14 concerning repentance.

The Parable of the soils - i.e. types of heart attitude

[11]"Now the parable is this: the seed is the word of God. [12]"Those beside the road are those who have heard; then the devil comes and takes away the word from their heart, so that they will not believe and be saved. [13]"Those on the rocky soil are those who, when they hear, receive the word with joy; and these have no firm root; they believe for a while, and in time of temptation fall away.

[14]"The seed which fell among the thorns, these are the ones who have heard, and as they go on their way they are choked with worries and riches and pleasures of this life, and bring no fruit to maturity. [15]"But the seed in the good soil, these are the ones who have heard the word in an honest and good heart, and hold it fast, and bear fruit with perseverance.

Luke 8:11-15 (NASB)

This is the famous parable of the sower. However, it ought to be called the parable of the *soils*, because that is what it really speaks about. The soils represent different types of heart attitude. The heart attitude we have, i.e. the quality of our 'soil', determines whether we properly respond to the Gospel in the first place. It also determines whether we persevere and continue as Christians from conversion onwards. It is this post-conversion aspect of the parable that is most alarming. In the parable there are four categories of person, or four types of heart attitude:

1) hard hearted people

The hard ground beside the road, i.e. the path, represents the people whose hearts are so hard to begin with that they never respond at all when they hear the Gospel. When the 'seed' of the Gospel lands on these people it never even germinates. It just bounces off them. These people, therefore, ever were Christians at any time, not even at the start.

2) shallow people

The rocky soil (i.e. thin soil) represents shallow people. They believe for a short time, but the seed of the Gospel takes no firm root. Therefore they germinate, but they quickly fall away. This group may, perhaps, have been real Christians very briefly. It's impossible for us to be sure. Only God knows. However, my impression is that they were real for a while. What we can say is that they do not persist. The seed of the Gospel never puts down takes any deep roots in them. Therefore they quickly fall away, near to the start of the Christian life, assuming they ever got started at all.

3) people who get distracted

The soil that is infested with thorns and weeds represents those people who allow their faith to be choked by various other pressures and distractions in the world. This third group is similar in many ways to the second group, where the seed fell on thin, rocky soil. This third group, whose hearts are like soil that is full of thorns and weeds, may or may not have been real Christians to begin with. Again, only God knows. But the implication is that they were real for a time. At any rate, whatever they were to begin with, they clearly do not continue as Christians. As with the second group, this third group are clearly not saved in the end.

4) sincere and serious people

These people's hearts are portrayed as good deep soil. Their hearts are genuine and honest. This is the only group where the person continues as a Christian to the end and becomes fruitful. This is the only group which is saved in the end. The three other groups are not. The first group never were saved to begin with. The second and third groups probably were genuine for a while, but fell away. The two distinguishing features of this fourth group are:

a) they persevere and they *continue* as Christians to the end, i.e. till death and

b) they *bear fruit,* i.e. their lives are productive and effective in God's service.

So, the point of the parable is that real Christians, can only be identified by those two features i.e.

a) they continue as disciples until death and

b) they bear fruit.

That means their lives change and they produce the fruit of the Spirit (love, joy, peace etc). They are also effective, obedient and productive for Jesus. That is why Jesus warned His disciples that they could only ever know whether a person is a real or false Christian by looking at their fruit, as opposed to their words.

The vital importance of fruit from a person's life as an indicator of what that person really is

Let's now consider a series of verses, all of which focus on the question of fruit. These verses all address the crucial importance of what a person really is and what fruit their lives produce, if any. I have included a long series of passages because I want to demonstrate that the concept of fruit coming from a person's life is a major theme throughout the Bible. I could have chosen very many more.

A person is justified only as a result of their repentance and faith in Jesus. However, the test from that point onwards to determine whether their conversion was real, and/or whether they are still genuine believers, is the quality and quantity of fruit that their lives produce. Please read the following verses carefully. Note the emphasis that is repeatedly given to the subject of fruit:

15"Beware of the false prophets, who come to you in sheep's clothing, but
inwardly are ravenous wolves. 16"You will know them by their fruits. Grapes
are not gathered from thorn bushes nor figs from thistles, are they? 17"So every
good tree bears good fruit, but the bad tree bears bad fruit. 18"A good tree cannot
produce bad fruit, nor can a bad tree produce good fruit. 19"Every tree that does
not bear good fruit is cut down and thrown into the fire. 20"So then, you will
know them by their fruits.

Matthew 7:15-20 (NASB)

33"Either make the tree good and its fruit good, or make the tree bad and its fruit bad; for the tree is known by its fruit.

Matthew 12:33 (NASB)

7So he began saying to the crowds who were going out to be baptized by him,
"You brood of vipers, who warned you to flee from the wrath to
come? 8"Therefore bear fruits in keeping with repentance, and do not begin to
say to yourselves, 'We have Abraham for our father,' for I say to you that from
these stones God is able to raise up children to Abraham. 9"Indeed the axe is
already laid at the root of the trees; so every tree that does not bear good fruit is

cut down and thrown into the fire."

Luke 3:7-9 (NASB)

*43"For there is no good tree which produces bad fruit, nor, on the other hand,
a bad tree which produces good fruit. 44"For each tree is known by its own fruit.
For men do not gather figs from thorns, nor do they pick grapes from a briar
bush. 45"The good man out of the good treasure of his heart brings forth what
is good; and the evil man out of the evil treasure brings forth what is evil; for
his mouth speaks from that which fills his heart.*

Luke 6:43-45 (NASB)

*4"Abide in Me, and I in you. As the branch cannot bear fruit of itself unless it
abides in the vine, so neither can you unless you abide in Me. 5"I am the vine,
you are the branches; he who abides in Me and I in him, he bears much fruit,
for apart from Me you can do nothing. 6"If anyone does not abide in Me, he is
thrown away as a branch and dries up; and they gather them, and cast them
into the fire and they are burned. 7"If you abide in Me, and My words abide in
you, ask whatever you wish, and it will be done for you. 8"My Father is glorified
by this, that you bear much fruit, and so prove to be My disciples.*

John 15:4-8 (NASB)

*16"You did not choose Me but I chose you, and appointed you that you would
go and bear fruit, and that your fruit would remain, so that whatever you ask of
the Father in My name He may give to you.*

John 15:16 (NASB)

*22But the fruit of the Spirit is love, joy, peace, patience, kindness, goodness,
faithfulness, 23gentleness, self-control; against such things there is no law.*

Galatians 5:22-23 (NASB)

*3But immorality or any impurity or greed must not even be named among you,
as is proper among saints; 4and there must be no filthiness and silly talk, or
coarse jesting, which are not fitting, but rather giving of thanks. 5For this you
know with certainty, that no immoral or impure person or covetous man, who
is an idolater, has an inheritance in the kingdom of Christ and God. 6Let no
one deceive you with empty words, for because of these things the wrath of God
comes upon the sons of disobedience. 7Therefore do not be partakers with
them; 8for you were formerly darkness, but now you are Light in the Lord; walk
as children of Light 9for the fruit of the Light consists in all goodness and
righteousness and truth), 10trying to learn what is pleasing to the Lord. 11Do not
participate in the unfruitful deeds of darkness, but instead even expose them;*

Ephesians 5:3-11 (NASB)

All discipline for the moment seems not to be joyful, but sorrowful; yet to those who have been trained by it, afterwards it yields the peaceful fruit of righteousness.

Hebrews 12:11 (NASB)

So we can conclude from these passages that:

a) the purpose and aim of our lives as Christians is that we should bear fruit

b) real Christians do bear fruit

c) false Christians don't bear fruit

d) people who bear fruit will be rewarded and praised

e) people who bear no fruit will be cut off, just as a farmer will eventually chop down a tree if it produces nothing of value

The warning to those who continue to sin wilfully, even after they know the truth of the Gospel

Now let's examine a very grim passage. It clearly seems to be speaking about those who have been real believers but have ended up turning away from their faith. The Bible uses very stark language. It says they have *"trampled under foot the Son of God"*.

26 For if we go on sinning willfully after receiving the knowledge of the truth,
there no longer remains a sacrifice for sins, 27 but a terrifying expectation of
judgment and the fury of a fire which will consume the adversaries. 28 Anyone
who has set aside the Law of Moses dies without mercy on the testimony of two
or three witnesses. 29 How much severer punishment do you think he will
deserve who has trampled under foot the Son of God, and has regarded as
unclean the blood of the covenant by which he was sanctified, and has insulted
the Spirit of grace? 30 For we know Him who said, "vengeance is mine, I will
repay " And again, "the Lord will judge his people." 31 It is a terrifying thing to
fall into the hands of the living God.

Hebrews 10:26-31 (NASB)

The passage above can presumably only be referring to Christians who have been real, at least for a time. It refers to them "*receiving the knowledge of the truth*" and, even more importantly, to them having been "*sanctified*". Sanctification can only occur in the life of a real Christian, not an unbeliever.

Yet, the direct warning is given, even to such people, that they must not go on sinning willfully after receiving the knowledge of the truth (i.e. after becoming a

Christian). Note how strong the warning is. It specifically warns of how much more severe the punishment will be for such people, i.e. as compared to how it will be for unbelievers who were never Christians in the first place.

That has to mean that the writer of the letter to the Hebrews is saying, as the apostle Paul also said above, that a real believer who falls away is in a substantially worse position than someone who has never believed at all. Logically, that must mean that a real believer who falls away will go, in the end, to the Great White Throne judgment for unbelievers and from there to the Lake of Fire.

What else can we possibly conclude? If it did not mean that, then how can it be said that such a person will be treated more severely than one who never knew the truth? We know for a fact that unbelievers are going to the Lake of Fire.

That means that for an apostate believer, (i.e. one who falls away and is unfaithful to Jesus), that somehow, whatever they experience in the Lake of Fire will be more intense than it will be for someone who had never believed. There are, evidently, degrees of punishment, even within the same Lake of Fire.

I don't know how that makes you feel, but it alarms me and increases my fear of the Lord. It makes me want to focus on God and on bearing fruit. I do not want to be classified as a worthless or unproductive servant, especially, given that it has such awesome significance in terms of how we will be judged.

People who fall away after knowing the truth find it very hard ever to repent again

If the previous passage was not enough to make you sit up and think, then consider this one. It indicates that a person who believes and then falls away will also find it very difficult to repent again later. Thus, if we do fall away, it will not be easy to find our way back:

***4**For in the case of those who have once been enlightened and have tasted of the*
Heavenly gift and have been made partakers of the Holy Spirit, ***5**and have tasted*
the good word of God and the powers of the age to come, ***6**and then have fallen*
away, it is impossible to renew them again to repentance, since they again
crucify to themselves the Son of God and put Him to open shame. ***7**For ground*
that drinks the rain which often falls on it and brings forth vegetation useful to
those for whose sake it is also tilled, receives a blessing from God; ***8**but if it yields*
thorns and thistles, it is worthless and close to being cursed, and it ends up being
*burned.***

Hebrews 6:4-8 (NASB)

This passage is clearly speaking of real Christians, not those who have never really believed to begin with. It says they *"have been made partakers of the Holy Spirit"*. How could that be the case if they were never real believers? So, the additional warning given to us is that if we do ever fall away, then we cannot complacently assume that we can be restored by repenting again later. Subsequent repentance may prove to be impossible, or at least very difficult.

Therefore, the moral of all this is that we need to persist, and not to throw away the faith that we have. We must endure whatever trials and difficulties we face and never give up the faith. Then we will be rewarded. But if we do give up our faith and fall away, then we face *"destruction"*. Whatever you believe that means exactly, you will have to agree that it cannot be said to be something positive:

35 Therefore, do not throw away your confidence, which has a great
reward. 36 For you have need of endurance, so that when you have done the will
of God, you may receive what was promised. 37 for yet in a very little while, He
who is coming will come, and will not delay. 38 but my righteous one shall live by
faith; and if He shrinks back, my soul has no pleasure in him. 39 But we are not
of those who shrink back to destruction, but of those who have faith to the
preserving of the soul

Hebrews 10:35-39 (NASB)

That same hardening of our heart and conscience that causes us to fall away also has the effect of making our hearts too leathery and insensitive ever to repent of doing so. We must take very careful note of that and let it affect how we live, so that we resolve to make sure never to fall away. Remember also that in this next passage, God is described as a *consuming fire*, and that is in a letter which is *addressed to Christians, not to unbelievers*:

25 See to it that you do not refuse Him who is speaking For if those did not escape
when they refused him who warned them on earth, much less will we escape
who turn away from Him who warns from Heaven. 26 And His voice shook the
earth then, but now He has promised, saying, "yet once more I will shake not
only the earth, but also the Heaven."

27 This expression, "Yet once more," denotes the removing of those things which
can be shaken, as of created things, so that those things which cannot be shaken
may remain. 28 Therefore, since we receive a kingdom which cannot be shaken,
let us show gratitude, by which we may offer to God an acceptable service with
reverence and awe; 29 for our God is a consuming fire.

Hebrews 12:25-29 (NASB)

A more detailed look at both the assurance and warning passages in the Bible

Each of these two schools of thought, the people who emphasise assurance and those who emphasise warning, tend to focus only on the verses which support their view. They often ignore anything that doesn't suit them. There is something about human nature which causes us to zoom in on what we agree with and to ignore those things which contradict us or which make our position more complicated.

However, I would like to suggest that the right approach is to take seriously *both* the assurance passages and the warning passages. Both are true. They each need to be believed and understood in their proper context and then held, side by side, in a healthy tension. Let's now look at each position again and try to define them more clearly. Let's also look at how they can, and must, be fitted alongside each other simultaneously:

Assurance of salvation

When I first started out as a Christian it was really important to me to find reassurance that I had got eternal life. I wanted to be certain that I wasn't going to lose it due to my own failure to stay the course, or by not being faithful enough to Jesus. I had a deep fear of God's judgment and of going to the Lake of Fire. So, I wanted to be able to *know*, not just to *hope*, that I would never go there. Even the thought of one day going to the Lake of Fire horrified me. It should horrify all of us.

So, to someone like me, the various assurance passages were of great importance. I underlined and memorised them. I also felt that, as a matter of logic, if I had *'eternal'* life now, then how could it come to an end? It seemed to be a contradiction in terms for something which, at the moment, is classed as 'eternal' to be able to come to an end at all, for any reason.

Likewise, if I was already justified, how could I cease to be so? Surely, if the promise of 'eternal'. life meant anything, it seemed to me, logically, that it must be permanent. I also felt it ought not to be dependent on my ongoing faithfulness and avoidance of sin However, I still wondered, what would happen if I did sin in a major way?

What if I was to let Jesus down or even deny Him under pressure? Would I then be lost? Would I cease to be forgiven and justified? If so, then it seemed to me that I would surely be walking on thin ice throughout my whole life, hoping not to let Him down or lose His approval, but always wondering whether I would.

However, even as a new believer, I understood the Gospel well enough to know that that isn't how God operates. I knew that my going to Heaven was not dependent on my complete avoidance of sin, at all times, because that would be impossible anyway.

I knew that if I was justified and forgiven at all, it was because Jesus had died for me, in my place, not because of me constantly avoiding or reducing sin in my life. I could see that such an obligation, if it was true, would make me responsible for my own salvation.

I would be like a hamster on a wheel, always afraid to stop working in case I lost my eternal life. So, the assurance passages really helped me personally. They are in the Bible largely for the benefit of people who are sincere and anxious for reassurance. They are most meaningful to those who have a strong sense of the fear of the Lord. For such people, these assurance passages are a precious source of comfort.

God holds a Christian in the palm of His hand

A good way to look at the assurance passages is to consider yourself to be held in the palm of God's hand. He will never drop you or make any mistake with you. Nor will He ever forsake you or reject you merely because you have let Him down. He knows perfectly well that you will let Him down and that you will inevitably sin. He is totally realistic about you.

So, the real question is not whether God will drop us, but whether we will *choose to throw ourselves out of His hand.* No person will ever be cut off or lose their salvation solely because they let God down or made mistakes or failed Him. If it was based on that, we would all have to be cut off and rejected every single day, because that is how often we fail God or let Him down, at least in my case.

It is not, therefore, based on that. It works the other way round. As we have seen with the 'fruit' passages above, the real question is not whether you have let God down. It is whether you have produced, and are continuing to produce, any genuine, worthwhile fruit for Him. Moving back, therefore, to the image of our being in the palm of God's hand, the point is that if you are a God-fearing, repentant, sincere, person, you would not even want to be presumptuous or complacent.

If so you will not choose to throw yourself out of the palm of God's hand. Neither will you wander off, or show contempt for His forgiveness. On the contrary, you will want to produce fruit for Him. The sort of person who is anxious for reassurance is like that precisely because he will not despise or become complacent about God's mercy and forgiveness. The very fact that it means so much to him, and that he so wants to be reassured, means that he is not likely ever to take it for granted.

Thus for such people, in those circumstances, it is true to say that they do '*have*' eternal life. It is also true to say that no man can snatch them out of God's hand. They are safe and can feel secure. It would be like a refugee who is fleeing from a violent regime. Imagine it is the summer of 1939 and he has crossed the border, from Nazi Germany into France. He is now on a train heading to a port and then a ship to England.

That refugee could ask "*Am I safe now? Will this train definitely take me to the ship and to my new country?*" The answer would be *"Yes, you are secure. This train is definitely going to the coast and you are safe, You can be assured of that."*

What that refugee really means by his question is "*Will anybody make me get off the train against my will, or refuse to let me continue my journey*?" He isn't focusing on whether he himself will *choose* to get off the train. That's not what he is worried about. He fully intends to stay on board.

Thus, for Him, the assurance given is correct and meaningful. That illustration can also help us to understand the warning passages and to realise what kind of people are being addressed and in what circumstances:

The warnings against losing your salvation - the need to persevere

If we extend the train analogy, what would happen if, as time passed, the refugee got more and more relaxed and casual and chose to get off the train? What if he was to get out at a station and wander off to buy a newspaper? What if he just got out to stretch his legs on the platform? Is it possible that the train could set off again without him?

What if he even chose to get off for a more lengthy period and go for a walk and then seek to get back on to a later train? Would there definitely be a later train? Even if there was, would he be able to get onto it? That analogy also has relevance to the assurance passages. So, it would be true to say to that refugee that:

a) the train he is currently on is definitely going to the destination

b) he is guaranteed a seat

c) no fellow passenger can throw him off the train

d) he will not fall out of the train due to any accident.

However, it would also be true, and no contradiction, to say: "But stay on the train and don't seek to get off and get back on a later train. Don't get off at all, even for a moment. Don't take any chances or be complacent. Don't even get out onto the platform at any of the stations along the way, not even for a second, in case you cannot get back on and the train leaves without you."

In other words one could say to him: "*You need to persevere. Stay on the train and don't get off or go anywhere*". The same things can be said about persevering in the Christian life: We must continue to stand and to hold fast and we must never leave the Christian life. Otherwise, we may be judged to have believed in vain:

1Now I make known to you, brethren, the gospel which I preached to you, which also you received, in which also you stand, 2by which also you are saved, if you hold fast the word which I preached to you, unless you believed in vain.
1 Corinthians 15:1-2 (NASB)

The warnings in the train analogy do not contradict the promises or reassurance given beforehand. The two messages fit together perfectly well. A sensible, reasonable person can feel assured of his place on the train and yet still realise his own need to take care to stay on board and not wander off or leave the train. Likewise, we can feel assured that we are going to Heaven when we die but, at the same time, know that we must continue on the Way, hold firm, bear fruit, and not throw away our faith or allow it to go cold.

To put it another way, you could say that your salvation cannot be lost by any kind of accident, or by the actions of any other human being. But you could decide to throw it away yourself, if you were to deny Jesus or to willfully sin against Him, or to stop following Him. Or, you could gradually let it evaporate away by your own indifference, complacency and lack of reverence.

Over time, those casual attitudes turn into neglect, which steadily erodes your faith. You could end up no longer being a disciple, or no longer even a believer at all. However, if that happened, it would be *you* who brought it about, not God, and not other people.

That falling away need not have come from any decisive moment when you deliberately chose to reject Jesus. It could be that your love for Him just ebbed away, bit by bit, over a long period. If so, your faith ends up as a dry, empty shell with no life in it.

That is not something which happens *to* you. It's something you *do yourself*, over a period of time. It's no accident. It's the end result of many small decisions to ignore Jesus Christ or to put Him to one side and to focus instead on the trivial things of this world.

Faith in Jesus Christ can ebb away, just as marriages often do. It happens by a thousand little decisions to neglect rather than cherish, and to focus on something, or someone, else rather than the one we are meant to love. That's how marriages are usually thrown away, by gradual decay, not by any sudden collapse or trauma. It works the same way with faith in God.

So, it is perfectly correct for God to say that you can be *assured* of going to Heaven when you die and that He will never accidentally drop you out of His hand or allow anyone else to snatch you out of His hand. It is also correct, at the same time, for God to *warn* you that *you* must not wander away from Him.

You must not choose to leave the palm of His hand or take yourself away from eternal life. Certain decisions or actions on your part could eventually result in you throwing away your place in Heaven. There is no contradiction in any of that. It isn't even particularly complicated. Any sincere person can quickly grasp it.

The assurance and warning passages are largely aimed at different character types

The assurance passages and the warning passages are generally aimed at different audiences, i.e. different types of person:

a) The *assurance passages* are primarily aimed at the sincere, earnest, anxious, God-fearing, repentant, honest, tender-hearted person. He has no intention of neglecting, despising or throwing away his own salvation. He is only asking for reassurance that it will not be taken away from him by other people or by circumstances.

b) The *warning passages* are generally directed towards those who have the tendency to be glib, complacent, careless, presumptuous, over confident, self-reliant, self-righteous, carnal, insincere, shallow, worldly, etc. God is warning all such people that His mercy is something to be treasured and received with gratitude. It's not to be despised or taken for granted in a presumptuous manner. The Bible therefore tells us that there is a way to throw away our own salvation through our own actions and decisions, but especially by neglect.

When that throwing away occurs it is very rarely ever done in an instant, or as the result of one sin or foolish decision. It is almost always the culmination of a long series of small choices which usually seem insignificant at the time. These many little decisions cause us to move steadily farther and farther away from God.

Each sinful choice or step causes our hearts to get harder and harder, and our love for Him to get colder and colder. Eventually we end up showing indifference to Him. Then we no longer even fear the prospect of falling away, as our mind is focused on other things. It is to such people, and there are many of them in the Church, that the warning passages are mainly directed. However, we are all to take very careful note of them and to be sobered, whatever type of person we may be.

There is a need for a *balanced* understanding of the assurance passages and the warning passages and to *believe both at the same time*

Various writers argue passionately in favour of one or other of these opposing positions, i.e. focusing either 100% on assurance or 100% on warning. Some of them are failing to realise that we actually need to hold both these positions at the same time in a proper balance.

We could summarise that balance between assurance and warning by the following series of statements:

a) We are *held onto* by God's faithfulness. He is holding onto us firmly, with a steady grip. He is reliable and He can be trusted never to abandon or forget us. He will never forsake us. Therefore those of us who feel anxious about whether He is reliable can be reassured. We will never be let down by Him. I am reminded of an occasion when we were out for a walk as a family. We had to cross a very high, very narrow, foot bridge. It had gaps in it so you could see the drop on either side. Our small dog, a Border terrier, was afraid of the bridge and was cowering and trembling as she crossed it. I therefore picked her up and carried her the rest of the way across. As I held her tightly I felt all the tension and fear drain out of her and she relaxed. She had total faith *in me to hold on to her* and never to let her fall over the edge. She trusted me far more than she trusted herself. That is the kind of simple faith or trust that we should have in God.

b) While ever we are sincere, remain in Him, and continue to put our trust in Him, God will never reject us. That is still the case *even when we fail or make mistakes*, as we inevitably shall do. Indeed, no genuine Christian will ever be condemned by God solely for failing or making mistakes, while sincerely trying to serve Him. Even those of us who are failures in the eyes of others may be successes in God's eyes if we are faithfully doing what we can to the best of our ability. God does not judge solely by observable results, as men do. He judges by heart motives. So, being faithful is what really counts, not being visibly successful.

c) We can have a real and meaningful assurance, right now, that when we die we will have eternal life and will not face God's wrath or go to the Great White Throne judgment or the Lake of Fire.

d) But, if we take God for granted, lose respect for Him, cease to honour and love Him and drift away from Him, then it is possible, that our names will be blotted out of the book of life. We will then lose our place in the body of Christ, and lose our salvation.

e) If so, then when we die we would not be counted as part of the Church, but as part of the unbelieving world. We would therefore be judged with the unbelievers at the Great White Throne judgment and go to the Lake of Fire.

f) If so, the judgment upon us would be even more severe than for a person who had never believed. That's because we would have trampled under foot the precious truth of the Gospel and the great sacrifice that Jesus made for us. We would have despised both it and Him.

g) If our name is eventually removed from the book of life and we lose our salvation, it would not really be something that God has done to us. It would be more accurate to say it is something we have done to ourselves. It would be the end result of all our own decisions and choices, probably over many years. In my experience, I have never seen a real Christian fall away or reject Jesus overnight. It is almost always the end product of a steady process of decay and neglect that has been going on for a long time. It is like when a rotten old tree falls over in a sudden strong wind. The inside of that tree had probably been rotting away for a long time, or it would not have fallen over. So, it is all our own fault if we fall away and give up the faith.

The need to accept the assurance passages and the warning passages at the same time

Let us consider another analogy which will, hopefully, make all of this clearer. Imagine a person who, in the 19th century, goes to work for the Christian chocolate manufacturer, George Cadbury. He was amazingly advanced and generous in the way he treated his staff. He provided good pay and working conditions plus all sorts of benefits such as schools, medical clinics and good homes for the staff to live in. He was many decades ahead of his time.

Suppose that on that employee's first day at work the great man himself, George Cadbury, was to say "If you come to work at Cadbury's then you will have a job for life. And, when you are too old or too sick to work any longer, you also have my promise of a cottage for life. Therefore you can continue to live on in your home even when you retire".

If he gave that promise or assurance to an employee it would be entirely valid and meaningful. It is not hollow or false. It really means something. That new member of staff can immediately feel a sense of assurance, even on their first day at the factory. They know that George Cadbury is a godly man whose word can be totally trusted. There is no question of *him* failing to honour *his* promises and deciding, for no reason, to give that job or cottage to someone else.

So, in terms of assurance, that new worker at Cadbury's has that cast-iron promise. He or she can feel reassured by it. That is precisely how we can, and should, feel in relation to God's promises to us. His word is His bond. God can be entirely trusted never to leave us or to let us down. The real question, however, is what if *we* let God down? What if *we leave Him*? What if *we deny Him*?

If we return to our Cadbury analogy, imagine that after a period of time that new worker becomes complacent, ungrateful and hard-hearted and begins to behave badly at the factory. Imagine they are regularly late for work, lazy, unproductive, disrespectful, disobedient, or neglect their duties. Or, imagine that they go further and even steal from the company or intentionally cause damage to company property. What would George Cadbury do then?

He would begin at a very early stage by giving *warnings* about attitude, performance and conduct. He would even be willing to give repeated warnings, escalating in seriousness and intensity. However, nobody would criticise George Cadbury if, eventually, he said "*Your repeated neglect and misconduct, and your indifference to your duties, have made you an unfruitful, unproductive employee. You are not fit to remain in employment here. Therefore I am dismissing you from the company.*"

Wouldn't his eventual response be entirely reasonable and understandable? How could he realistically do otherwise? So. if we neglect God, dishonour Him, persistently disobey Him, and produce no fruit for Him, then what other option does God have, in the end, but to remove us?

If He does so then He is not, breaking His word to us. His assurances were all entirely genuine. They have not been broken or dishonoured. He has been entirely consistent and reasonable, just as with the George Cadbury illustration.

Or, taking the analogy even further, imagine that the worker at Cadbury's chooses, of their own free will, to leave their job and their cottage and to go away to work for some other company. Doesn't that obviously mean that they are no longer an employee of Cadbury's? Of course it does.

In terms of contract law, they have terminated their own contract themselves by their own express words of resignation. It was not something which Mr. Cadbury did. He played no part in it. The employee did it himself, unilaterally, when he wrote the resignation letter.

However such a departure from the company need not necessarily involve any formal or express decision to resign. The employee could just drift away, such that they do not turn up for work, day after day.

Cadbury's would send out letters saying "*Where are you? Please report for work.*" But, eventually the contract of employment would end if the employee failed to return. It could be deemed to be an implied resignation by conduct, i.e. by being persistently absent.

Or, it could even result in an express dismissal for absenteeism. Either way, Cadbury's would have done no wrong at all. The responsibility would be entirely on the part of the ex-employee.

I hope that extended analogy helps you to hold together, in proper balance and tension, these apparently contradictory concepts of assurance and warning. In short, if we become a Christian we work for someone infinitely more faithful, honest, trustworthy, and reliable than George Cadbury. Yet God has every right to make demands of us and to hold us accountable for the degree to which we are faithful to Him and for what fruit we produce, or fail to produce. He has told us very clearly, and repeatedly, what He expects of us.

Therefore, what basis do we have to complain if we are eventually 'dismissed' or removed because we are not faithful to Him and we ignore what He says? Accordingly, it is not enough to adopt only one or other of these two approaches, i.e. assurance *or* warning. Both are true. Both apply to you and to me. They each apply more relevantly to some people than to others. It depends on our heart attitude, i.e. whether we tend to be sincere/tender/anxious types, or casual/self-assured/independent/complacent types.

Do not deny Jesus and He will not deny you. But, if you do deny Jesus, then He will deny you.

The first question is *"Are you saved?"* If you are, then resolve to remain so. Stay firmly rooted in Jesus Christ. Never leave Him and then He will never leave you. Never deny Him and He will never deny you. But, if you do deny Him, then He will deny you. The Bible warns us of that:

32"Therefore everyone who confesses Me before men, I will also confess him before My Father who is in Heaven. 33"But whoever denies Me before men, I will also deny him before My Father who is in Heaven.

Matthew 10:32-33 (NASB)

11It is a trustworthy statement:
For if we died with Him, we will also live with Him;

[12]*If we endure, we will also reign with Him;*
If we deny Him, He also will deny us;
2 Timothy 2:11-12 (NASB)

Consider also this passage from the Old Testament which is addressed to the people of the Southern Kingdom of Judah. Their king at this particular time was Asa, who was a very godly and faithful man. In other words, he was clearly a real believer. Yet this is what one of the prophets was sent to tell him. It was both a promise and a warning:

The Spirit of God came upon Azari'ah the son of Oded, [2] ***and he went out to meet Asa, and said to him, "Hear me, Asa, and all Judah and Benjamin: The Lord is with you, while you are with him. If you seek him, he will be found by you, but if you forsake him, he will forsake you.***
2 Chronicles 15:1-2 (RSV)

Someone might possibly object to this passage on the basis that it is from the Old Testament. However, the point is that the very same warnings are made in the New Testament. In one sense, therefore, I need not include it. However, I do so to underline the fact of the warning and to show that it is how God has always acted. Both now and in the past. In short, it illustrates the position for us very clearly. The question then is whether passages such as those above apply to *believers,* who have already become part of the *Church,* or only to *non-believers.*

In other words, does it mean that even a *real Christian* can 'deny' Jesus? We shall attempt to answer that question in the pages below. However, I would suggest to you that, if I understand the Bible correctly, it is entirely possible for a real Christian to deny Jesus, to turn their back on Him, and thus to lose their salvation and end up in the Lake of Fire.

The importance of fearing God and how the fear of the Lord keeps you alert and faithful

If you fear God and respect Him you will find it is very much easier to continue to honour and follow Him and not to deny Him. The fear of the Lord helps to sustain your faith. It keeps you from slipping into the sin and compromise that would, eventually, lead to you completely ignoring or even denying Jesus. The fear of the Lord is, therefore, helpful to us. It keeps us close to Him and it promotes reverence and holiness.

Therefore if you are wise, you will actively seek to develop the fear of the Lord in yourself. Pray for more of it. Deliberately choose to soften your heart whenever you can. You do that by every little choice you make to honour and obey Him rather than not doing so.

In the end, your eternal fate i.e. whether you stay the course to the very end or fall away, will be decided by the many small decisions you take over the years. Does each choice bring you a little bit closer to Him, or a little bit farther away? Does it soften or harden your heart? Does it honour or dishonour Him? Does it involve being obedient or disobedient? Does it help to produce fruit or does it produce nothing of value?

Ask yourself those questions daily. If you feel you have begun to drift away from God, however slightly or briefly, then put it right straight away by sincere repentance. Keep short accounts with God. Return to Him immediately whenever you wander off into sin or grow cold towards Him. Don't let such times of neglect or coldness be prolonged. Repent quickly. Make that a habit. Then you will never wander far away from Him.

However, if you have no fear of the Lord, or if you are casual or indifferent to things which God considers precious, or if you ignore His Word, then you are in grave danger. Whatever it is that we are becoming, whether good or bad, we have a tendency to become more and more that way. So, you will get more and more concentrated or intense, whichever direction you are going in.

You will become either more and more holy, or more and more carnal. You can't stand still. You have to choose a direction to travel in. So choose to pursue Him and to grow more like Him in every way. Take Him seriously and then you will be secure. However, if you don't, then you are in grave danger. I must warn you of that, most solemnly.

So, I have tried both to reassure you and to warn you at the same time. The Bible does the same. Therefore take all of it seriously, both the promises and the warnings. God will then respond to you in the same way that you respond to Him:

...... for those who honour me I will honour and those who despise Me will be lightly esteemed.

1 Samuel 2:30(b) (NASB)

Rewards at the Judgment Seat of Christ

If we do honour Him, hold fast and persevere, and if we do bear fruit in our lives, then not only will we have assurance of salvation, but we will also be *rewarded* at the Judgment Seat of Christ. See how Paul spoke as he looked back at his life, just before his death, as he waited to be executed. He knew he was saved and would go to Heaven. He also knew, by this stage, that he would be rewarded:

7I have fought the good fight, I have finished the course, I have kept the faith; 8in the future there is laid up for me the crown of righteousness, which

the Lord, the righteous Judge, will award to me on that day; and not only to me, but also to all who have loved His appearing.

2 Timothy 4:7-8 (NASB)

Anxiety about whether you are saved - some further clarification

We have emphasised the need to take seriously both the assurance passages and the warning passages. Let us look now at some of the specific problems and worries that some of us experience. Those who have made a weak or hasty decision to believe in Jesus, or who have not been properly taught about the meaning of repentance or discipleship, begin the Christian life semi-crippled. They can be plagued with doubt as to whether they have really been saved. Even if they have been saved, they often cannot feel any *assurance* about it. Does that apply to you?

Alternatively, if you lack assurance, it could be that the reason you don't feel any assurance of salvation is precisely because you aren't saved. If so, you need to put that right. On the other hand, if you are saved, but just can't ever feel sure of it, then you still need to put it right. Either way, you need to make sure, right now, that you really are a Christian.

It is perfectly valid, if for any reason you feel unsure of your salvation, to pray something like this: "*Lord, I don't know if I am already a Christian, but please help to make sure of it right now by repenting, believing and putting my trust entirely in you*". Then go carefully through all the steps set out in chapter 20, including baptism in water and receiving the Holy Spirit. Do everything the Bible commands us to do.

The part that demons play in either reducing our assurance or increasing our complacency

Often the doubt and fear about whether we are saved is caused, or intensified, by demons whispering into a *real* Christian's mind. They do it deliberately because they want to create extra anxiety and uncertainty. Alternatively, if you are already leaning towards being complacent, the demon will want to increase your complacency and get you to be even more casual. Thus the demon will do the exact opposite.

They will try to *convince false Christians/unbelievers that they are saved*, whereas they try to get *real Christians to doubt their salvation*. They will always try to get you to lean farther in whatever direction you are already leaning. So, if you are an anxious type to begin with, they will get you to be even more anxious. If however you are already a complacent type, they will seek to make you even more complacent.

This deceptive activity by demons is a major problem in both directions. See Books Seven and Nine in this series for more detail on demons and what they do. Are you in the sincere, earnest, tender-hearted group? Do you find you are demoralised by doubts about whether you are really a Christian? Do you feel useless, unworthy and, *"too sinful for God to forgive"* etc?

If so, then take heart. Such thoughts are not your own. Neither are they from God. They are just lies being planted in your mind by a demon. Their aim is to discourage and weaken you by robbing you of your assurance. The demon will whisper those unsettling thoughts to you precisely because he knows you are a tender, sensitive type and that you are likely to accept such lies and be made even more anxious.

God never speaks in those destructive ways or says such negative things. If God wants to tell you that you aren't a real Christian He does it by '*convicting*' you, not by *condemning* or *accusing* you. There's a vital difference. Conviction is healthy and leads you to *repent.* Condemnation is unhealthy and leads you to *despair.* So, ask God to guide you as to whether what you are feeling or hearing is from Him, or from a demon.

If your thoughts about yourself make you feel generally *useless, condemned and worthless*, then you can be sure it is based on demonic whisperings. If so, reject it all and press ahead in your Christian life with even more determination and zeal. If you do that then the demon's trick will have backfired on him. He will have overdone it, as they often do.

If however what you are feeling is a very *specific conviction* that you need to *repent* and stop doing *a particular sin*, then you can be sure that that is God's voice. He never tells you that you are a worthless failure. He says things like: *"What you just said was a lie. Put it right immediately and don't lie again"*. That's the *wholesome and constructive* way in which the Holy Spirit speaks. It is totally unlike what the demons say about you being a worthless, no good failure etc.

The Holy Spirit would never use destructive words like that. Remember that fact next time you feel bombarded by such condemning or disparaging thoughts. The *tone and content* of the words will tell you where they are coming from. Then you will be better able to ignore what the demons say and to hold on to what God is saying.

Is it *arrogant* to feel sure that you're saved and will go to Heaven?

Being sure of your own salvation, i.e. justification, is not arrogance. It would only be arrogant if you thought that it depended on you matching up to a certain standard. That is not what Christianity is about. Justification is not based on our own good deeds, or merit, or anything else that we could boast about. Ironically, it is the genuine believer who confidently puts all his trust in what Jesus did on the cross, rather than on his own merits, who is actually being humble.

Such assurance is the opposite of being arrogant, because we are not puffing ourselves up or relying on ourselves. Neither are we claiming to have any kind of merit. Conversely the man who even hopes that his own deeds might be good enough to '*earn*' him a place in Heaven is both conceited and deluded.

I raise these points because over the years I have met many people who are involved in Roman Catholicism or Islam or cults such as the Mormons or the Jehovah's Witnesses. These groups share one common feature. They do not have any assurance of salvation i.e. that they will go to Heaven. They can only ever *hope* that their behaviour *"might be good enough"*.

That's because they all wrongly believe that salvation is earned by being a "*good person*". Hopefully you will agree with me, by now, that there is no such thing as a good person. Even the very best person is still just a sinner.

Thus, I can feel a genuine assurance that I am forgiven and will go to Heaven when I die. I know that I really have repented of my sins and have turned away from them. I know I have sincerely trusted in Jesus Christ alone, rather than in my own merit or virtue, and that I have been forgiven.

I also know that I am deemed to have all the righteousness of Jesus Christ. That is what justification is all about. I know that all of my sin has been transferred on to Jesus Christ instead of me and that I have His righteousness. I can know those things because I believe the promises that the Bible makes, not because I am good.

In believing those promises, I am not showing any presumption or arrogance, because I am not claiming to have any merit whatsoever. Imagine that I was to put my trust in the Bank of England and to believe that it was and solid and could be trusted. That would not be arrogance on my part, because I am not putting any trust in myself, but rather in the Bank of England.

Likewise, the certainty that I have of my own salvation (justification) is not based on me, but on Jesus Christ Himself and on His faithfulness. In other words, I am trusting that His Word is His bond and that He will never let me down or lie to me. I am not trusting in myself at all.

Only a person who knows that they are forgiven and that they have eternal life can really want to wholeheartedly follow Jesus Christ and serve Him for the rest of their lives. A person who doubts that, or who has no basis for such confidence, is crippled. They are unable to properly follow the Lord Jesus as a disciple, even if they want to.

Let me just clarify this point. When I speak about being a disciple and following the Lord Jesus Christ I do not mean that salvation (justification) is dependent upon you being a good disciple or upon following Him in a sufficiently impressive way. Neither does it depend upon always avoiding sin in your life.

That is not how it works. We follow the Lord Jesus Christ as a disciple and we obey Him, because it is right and proper to do so. It also enables us to grow in holiness or sanctification. However, being an effective or successful disciple is not, and never will be, the *basis* for obtaining justification or forgiveness. As explained earlier we are justified by God's grace and mercy through our faith, not by doing good works for Him.

That also applies to the good works we will do later on, as we learn to be disciples. They are good and worthwhile things to do, and they have a direct bearing on the rewards that we will later receive. They also indicate what our heart is like and whether we are genuine or false. However, they are not, in themselves, what justifies us or what gives us forgiveness or eternal life.

What about people who are complacent?

Although I have said above that there are some people who struggle with doubt and uncertainly, they are much rarer nowadays. When I first became a Christian in 1981 it was common to hear sermons on assurance of salvation. That was because in those days very many more people worried about their eternal destiny and were anxious for reassurance.

That was because when I first became a believer, the men leading churches had grown up in the 1930s – 1960s. They had been brought up with a much more genuine and biblical Gospel. They had been taught as youngsters to fear God and to understand sin and judgment.

Thus when they preached, it frequently brought people under a strong conviction of sin. That caused many of those hearing them to feel a deep concern for their souls and a desire to know for sure that they really were forgiven and saved. However, most of the leaders of the church today grew up in a very different spiritual climate in the 1960's to 1990s.

They never received the same grounding or absorbed the same values or priorities as the previous generation had. In short, many of the current generation of church leaders grew up without ever really knowing the fear of the Lord, even for themselves. Thus they cannot pass on or communicate to others something which they have never even known for themselves.

So, in the early 1980s, the preaching was, on average, very different from what it is today. When I first became a believer, it was fairly common for people, when listening to such godly men preach about sin and judgment, to need reassurance and teaching on how to be sure of their salvation. Today, given that so few leaders ever teach or preach about sin, judgment or Hell, or even mention the fear of the Lord, far fewer people struggle with feeling any lack of assurance.

That is not a good development. Most of us in the West are never even brought to a place of being concerned about our need for salvation to begin with. In fact, there is now the opposite problem, i.e. widespread complacency and apathy. Therefore many congregations feel no need for assurance, because the preaching they hear gives them no conviction of sin, no concern for their souls, and no fear of God.

This applies to many people who are nominal Christians or liberal Christians. They tend to just automatically assume that they will go to Heaven. They give it very little thought, other than to take it completely for granted. You often hear people speak like that at funerals. They will say of the deceased *"He's in a better place now"*. But he may not be! He may be in Hell.

I spoke above about there being people who are saved, but who can never feel assured of salvation. They are now a small minority. So, let us now consider another much larger group, i.e. those who automatically presume they will go to Heaven and feel no anxiety about it. That is not a good thing. This second group is in a far worse situation than the first.

The fact that so many people in the past used to feel anxious and concerned about their own sin and God's judgment was beneficial. It had the effect of causing them to seek for God's forgiveness and to get right with Him. Then they could, in the end, have genuine assurance.

Their concern about their eternal fate led to them taking the necessary steps to deal with their sin and thus to have a basis for genuine assurance. Today, sin and judgment are rarely mentioned in the Western world and good preaching, which brings people to a place of conviction and repentance is rare.

Therefore, it leaves countless people in the worst situation of all. What they really need is to be made *more* anxious, not less. Then they can face up to their need to repent. Instead, what they usually get is false reassurance, for which there is no proper basis. Strong, clear preaching, which produces healthy concern about one's own eternal fate is good and constructive. That is why there is so much of it in the Bible.

Few preachers today are willing to speak frankly and tell it like it is. They fear criticism, or unpopularity, or perhaps have no adequate understanding of the truth themselves. Thus, today, many people are being taught to feel assurance of salvation when they have no proper basis for it.

In other words such people are making glib, quick *"decisions to accept Jesus Christ"*. But they do so without having truly repented or believed, let alone being baptised in water or receiving the Holy Spirit.

They are then misguidedly told to accept that they are *definitely* saved and *never to question it* any further, but, the problem is they may not be saved. If so, that is a very serious matter indeed, because those people are being misled on the most important issue there is.

We end up with many misguided preachers wrongly reassuring and affirming people who are not, in fact, saved at all. This false assurance is preventing them ever getting to the place where they question whether they really are saved, so as to seek genuine assurance. What we all need is the real thing, not fake assurance which has no proper foundation.

The way that even king Solomon let himself down and pursued other gods, despite his great wisdom

You might imagine that making a shipwreck of your life, or even falling away, can only happen to foolish people, not to people like yourself. However, it happened to King Solomon, and he was the wisest man who ever walked the earth, with the exception of Jesus. But Solomon was carnal. He foolishly married many wives.

Even worse, many of them were non-Israelites and unbelievers. Indeed, some of them were even idolaters and worshiped false gods and statues etc. They therefore led Solomon astray and eventually he even cooperated with his wives' idolatry. He probably did it for a quiet life, to avoid arguments with them. The point is that in doing so, he became unfaithful to God:

4For when Solomon was old, his wives turned his heart away after other gods; and his heart was not wholly devoted to the LORD his God, as the heart of David his father had been. 5For Solomon went after Ashtoreth the goddess of the Sidonians and after Milcom the detestable idol of the Ammonites. 6Solomon did

what was evil in the sight of the LORD, and did not follow the LORD fully, as David his father had done.

[7]Then Solomon built a high place for Chemosh the detestable idol of Moab, on the mountain which is east of Jerusalem, and for Molech the detestable idol of the sons of Ammon. [8]Thus also he did for all his foreign wives, who burned incense and sacrificed to their gods.

[9]Now the LORD was angry with Solomon because his heart was turned away from the LORD, the God of Israel, who had appeared to him twice, [10]and had commanded him concerning this thing, that he should not go after other gods; but he did not observe what the LORD had commanded.

1 Kings 11:4-10 (NASB)

If all of that could happen to someone as wise as Solomon, who was way above our league, then it could happen to you. And it could happen to me. The only way for us to avoid such wrong decisions and wrong behaviour is to live faithfully day by day, to fear God, and to stay close to Him.

We do that by regularly repenting, praying for His help, and diligently reading the Bible. NB I should add that it does appear that, in his later years, King Solomon repented of all his folly and wrong deeds. Thus, in the end, it seems that he personally was saved.

Even so, that is no argument for behaving as he did, or for being unfaithful. His eventual repentance was an exception to what most people do, as was that of King Manasseh many years later. It gives us no basis for any complacency. Those two kings, Solomon and Manasseh, both went astray but managed to repent later and find salvation.

However, most of the Kings of Israel and Judah who went astray never came back to God. That is the more usual outcome and that fact needs to sober us. We cannot assume that there is an easy way back, or indeed any way back, if we fall away.

Salvation is a process as well as an event - it means travelling along "the Way"

In some ways, it can be unhelpful and confusing to think of becoming a Christian in terms of passing over a line, in the sense that at one moment you are not a Christian and the next moment you are. There is some truth in that. There has to be such a moment, at some point. Our problem is that, because we are not God, we don't always necessarily know exactly when that point is.

We don't always even know it for ourselves, let alone others. A more helpful and more authentic way to speak of "*becoming a Christian*" or "*getting saved*", is to use the biblical expression for a Christian, namely a follower of "*the Way*".

Look at this series of sample verses (there are others too) where that phrase, "the Way", is used. I have underlined it in each verse. "The Way" is a helpful phrase which has dropped out of the Christian dictionary. That is a shame, because it is a good one.

We ought to use the phrase today. It more accurately conveys what it means to become and remain a Christian. It suggests that you become a person who is on a path, or a road. It also correctly implies that you are someone who is travelling, developing and learning, not someone who has already arrived or finished:

Jesus said to him, "I am <u>the way</u>, and the truth, and the life; no one comes to the Father but through Me

John 14:6 (NASB)

"For the gate is small and <u>the way</u> is narrow that leads to life, and there are few who find it.

Matthew 7:14 (NASB)

[1]Now Saul, still breathing threats and murder against the disciples of the Lord, went to the high priest, [2]and asked for letters from him to the synagogues at Damascus, so that if he found any belonging to <u>the way</u>, both men and women, he might bring them bound to Jerusalem.

Acts 9:1-2 (NASB)

[25]This man had been instructed in <u>the way</u> of the Lord; and being fervent in spirit, he was speaking and teaching accurately the things concerning Jesus, being acquainted only with the baptism of John; [26]and he began to speak out boldly in the synagogue. But when Priscilla and Aquila heard him, they took him aside and explained to him <u>the way</u> of God more accurately.

Acts 18:25-26 (NASB)

But when some were becoming hardened and disobedient, speaking evil of <u>the way</u> before the people, he withdrew from them and took away the disciples, reasoning daily in the school of Tyrannus.

Acts 19:9 (NASB)

About that time there occurred no small disturbance concerning <u>the way</u>.

Acts 19:23 (NASB)

"I persecuted <u>this way</u> to the death, binding and putting both men and women into prisons,

Acts 22:4 (NASB)

It would have been better for them not to have known the way of righteousness, than to have known it and then to turn their backs on the sacred command that was passed on to them.

2 Peter 2:21 (NIV)

To say that we have *"become a follower of the Way"* is, in many ways, more accurate and more helpful than to say we have "*become a Christian"*. It is how the apostles spoke. It implies, correctly, that the Christian life is an *ongoing process* of growth, development and change, rather than an instantaneous transformation. It is very true to say that we are instantly forgiven and justified. However, we are not instantly sanctified or made mature. Neither do we instantly bear fruit. Sanctification matters. It is an essential part of the long, slow process of "*being saved*".

As we saw above, the Bible says that without holiness (which is what the process of sanctification produces in us) we will never see the Lord, i.e. we will not go to Heaven. Apostle Paul also speaks of the ongoing need to be rooted in Jesus Christ, as if we were a plant. He also speaks of the need to be built up or to grow in Him over time:

6Therefore as you have received Christ Jesus the Lord, so walk in Him, 7having been firmly rooted and now being built up in Him and established in your faith, just as you were instructed, and overflowing with gratitude.

Colossians 2:6-7 (NASB)

So, sanctification and growing to maturity as a disciple are crucially important. They are key indicators of the reality or falseness of our position. They show whether or not we truly are continuing on "the Way". Only God knows whether another person is genuine. The rest of us can only go by what we see and hear when considering whether another person really is a Christian.

We can only tell by looking at the 'fruit' of that other person's life and asking: *"Are they rooted in Jesus Christ and growing, or aren't they? Are they producing the fruit of the Spirit or aren't they? Are they changing? Are they becoming more holy in their day to day life or not?"*

That is all you or I can do to tell whether someone else is real. However, those questions are also very important in helping you to see whether you are real yourself. Ask yourself "*What fruit is my own life producing?"*

Can we go to Heaven if we aren't fully sanctified during this life?

Can we go to Heaven if we aren't fully sanctified? The short answer to this is yes, we can. That's because during this life nobody is ever fully sanctified or fully holy. That state of perfection will only come after we die. The Bible does command us to be sanctified and the writer to the Hebrews says that *"without sanctification, no man will see the Lord,"*. However, that does not mean that we must achieve perfection.

Indeed there is no particular level of sanctification that we need to achieve, even at a point lower than perfection. What does it all mean then? What level or standard do we have to achieve? The answer is that there is no such arbitrary level or standard. We simply have to stay *"on the Way"*. We have to continue in the process of being sanctified and pursuing holiness.

Whilst ever we continue on the Way and are still in the process of being sanctified, bit by bit then, despite all our faults and mistakes, we are safe. We are secure because we are *continuing*. We are safe because we have not turned aside, or denied Jesus Christ, or abandoned Him, or betrayed Him, or ceased to follow Him. That is what matters.

Please let me re-emphasise as well, for the avoidance of doubt, that it is entirely possible to be, and to remain, on the Way, i.e. to be a real Christian, while making many ongoing mistakes. Making mistakes and falling into sin does not mean that you are no longer on the Way or that you have ceased to be saved. Far from it. We will all sin and we will all make mistakes and get bogged down at times. The question is whether we are *still continuing to follow Jesus*, despite all our faults and mistakes.

The Lord Jesus doesn't have any *perfect* or *sinless* followers. He doesn't expect to have any and He has never had any. What He does expect, and insist on, is our *faithfulness*. He demands that we do not desert Him or cease to follow Him. There is no question of Him ever deserting us. That is a certainty. We can be assured of that. So, just keep on keeping on - for your whole life.

Never turn away from Him. Never stop pursuing holiness or seeking to know and serve Jesus. Then, whenever you die, or whenever Jesus returns, He will find you faithfully walking along "the Way". He will then reward you for still being on the Way and for the fruit you have produced, even if others have gone ahead of you and have achieved more.

For the avoidance of doubt, sanctification is not what saves us, in the sense of taking away our guilt and giving us eternal life. We are saved in that sense when we are made righteous and forgiven due to being *justified*. That is the moment when we receive all of the righteousness of Jesus.

We can never achieve that kind of righteousness for ourselves by the process of being sanctified. Sanctification and justification are two quite separate concepts.

If you are still unclear as to the difference between them, refer to chapters 10 and 12 again and see also chapter 22.

What if a person dies without having been baptised in water and/or without receiving the Holy Spirit?

What happens if a person has truly started out on "the Way", having truly repented and believed, and then dies before realising the need for water baptism or before receiving the Holy Spirit? My firm belief is that they would go to Heaven. That person would have died while they were "on the Way". The point is that that person did not yet know, and perhaps had no opportunity to learn, the truth about being baptised in water and/or receiving the Holy Spirit.

I once explained the Gospel in hospital to a dying man aged 93. I had never met him before. His name was Stanley. He died ten minutes after I left him. I believe Stanley was saved that day even though he was never baptised in water or baptised in the Holy Spirit. The point is that he had *no opportunity* to do either of those things. But Stanley had set out on the Way, even though his journey was only for ten minutes. That man never had a chance to do anything more than that.

The difference is that you do have the chance to be baptised in water and to seek to receive the Holy Spirit and the gifts of the Holy Spirit. Also the excuse of ignorance about water baptism or baptism in the Holy Spirit or His gifts is not open to you. I do not know what the fate is of a person who ignores or disobeys biblical commands which they do know about. My own feeling is that I would not want to presume on God's mercy by disregarding His known commands.

So, again, it comes back to this - it is an obedience issue. And it is one that I would not want to take any chances on. As the excellent Bible teacher, David Pawson says, "Why would you want to approach Christianity by asking "What's the minimum I have to do to be saved?" " Why would you seek to do only the minimum? Why not ask instead "What does God require of me?" Then, whatever it is, why not do all of it willingly?

Conclusion - making sense of the need to balance the assurance and warning passages

Let us seek to draw the threads together and to make sense of this topic which so many people find confusing. If you read the books written on assurance of salvation and the warnings of the need to persevere, you will see that many authors seem to be unable to hold these concepts in balance. They generally go either to the *'North Pole'* or to the *'South Pole'*. They either adopt and emphasise one, or the other, but rarely both. Yet both are in the Bible. We cannot get away from that fact. So how can we summarise it all?

I would say this - we can be sure of God's faithfulness, but can He be sure of ours? We can have assurance that our salvation will never be lost due to any failure or betrayal on God's part. God will never let us down. But that assurance, which is real, needs to be held in balance alongside an understanding of the fact that people frequently betray or abandon Him. In doing so, they could throw their own salvation away.

Therefore we have every reason to have confidence in Him. We can look forward with assurance to spending eternity with Him. We can and should rejoice at that, and should not be tormented by doubt or anxiety. But, at the same time, we have every reason to think soberly and realistically about our sinful nature and our tendency to be selfish, carnal and rebellious.

That's the way we are. Those tendencies are in us, and if they are not dealt with by the process of sanctification, they will eventually be our undoing. We can bring about our own downfall and be lost eternally if we allow ourselves to drift, and to keep drifting, in the direction that our fleshly, carnal nature wishes to go.

Our sinful nature will never lead us in the right direction. It will never bring us closer to Jesus or make us desire to follow Him. Our flesh will always want the opposite of what Jesus wants. Unless we are determined to die to self, crucify our flesh nature, and live for Jesus Christ, and unless we fear God and realise that He will judge us, then we are likely to drift away.

That is not just a possibility, but a likelihood. If so, then we would be throwing our own salvation away. We would be walking away from the One who died for us and who paid the penalty for us, and throwing all of that back in His face.

We may never do it dramatically or decisively. It probably would not all happen in one day, though I suppose it could. It generally happens over time by the slow process of neglect. It is like tooth decay. There is no single day when the decay happens. Even so, a day is eventually reached where the tooth is so decayed it is beyond treatment and has to be removed. So if, you know that you are a real Christian then rejoice and be assured that God has justified you.

Have confidence *in Him* to finish the job. But, do not have any confidence *in yourself.* Do not presume. Do not take God for granted. Do not neglect or despise Him. Do not stop walking along the Way. Keep going. Keep on learning, studying and growing. Keep on and on putting your old self, your sinful nature, to death. Deny your flesh. Refuse to give it what it craves for. Refuse to be mastered or controlled by it. Choose instead to submit yourself to Jesus Christ and to resist the Devil.

The importance of the fear of the Lord

You will never start to do any of this, or continue doing so, unless you fear the Lord. Therefore ask God to give you a healthy and powerful fear of Him. But don't just leave it to Him. Pursue it for yourself. Read His Word. Learn the Bible. Listen to the voice of the Holy Spirit. Soften your heart. Humble yourself. Be obedient to any of God's commands that you already know about. Then He will open your eyes further and teach you more.

However, if you disobey Him then He will, eventually, leave you on your own to pursue the foolish path you have chosen. Therefore, stay on the narrow path. Do not wander, even for a moment, onto the broad path that leads to destruction. If you do stray onto it, then repent quickly and return, while you still have time, to the narrow path. Let's take seriously what Jesus said on this point:

13"Enter through the narrow gate; for the gate is wide and the way is broad that leads to destruction, and there are many who enter through it. 14"For the gate is small and the way is narrow that leads to life, and there are few who find it.

Matthew 7:13-14 (NASB)

The part God plays in keeping you from falling away

I have spoken of the need to remain faithful and of the part you have to play in that. However, if you are a sincere believer who genuinely wishes to remain faithful to the end, then you are not going to be left to do that all by yourself. God is able, and very willing, to help you to hold on to Him and to enable you to stay faithful:

Now to Him who is able to keep you from stumbling, and to make you stand in the presence of His glory blameless with great joy,

Jude 24 (NIV)

We can take great comfort from this verse and hold it in balance, alongside the many warning passages. It helps to explain how it can be possible to hold firm, despite all our weaknesses and the many temptations we face. It is possible to remain faithful precisely *because He helps us*. He gives us *the grace we need to persist*. It is He who can be trusted to help us to complete the process of becoming a disciple:

And I am sure that he who began a good work in you will bring it to completion at the day of Jesus Christ.

Philippians 1:6 (RSV)

Moreover, the writer of the letter to the Hebrews tells us that we have Jesus, our High Priest, making intercession for us. That means that *He is praying for us* to God the Father. His prayers help us to remain faithful:

24but Jesus, on the other hand, because He continues forever, holds His priesthood permanently. 25Therefore He is able also to save forever those who draw near to God through Him, since He always lives to make intercession for them.

Hebrews 7:24-25 (NASB)

If I thought it all depended on me and on my own faithfulness and perseverance, I would be very alarmed. Thankfully, it doesn't. We can trust Him to help us, if we sincerely ask Him to do so. Sincere people tend to seek His help. Complacent people tend not to. So, even in the light of all the warning passages, I can still rejoice and feel assured of my eventual destination. Despite all my many weaknesses and failings, I know that He is holding onto me and that He is enabling me to hold onto Him.

CHAPTER 22

ASSURANCE AND PERSEVERANCE CONTINUED - THE THREE STAGES OR TENSES OF SALVATION: JUSTIFICATION, THEN SANCTIFICATION, THEN GLORIFICATION

The three stages of salvation - indicating that salvation is more a *process* than an *event*.

We have just spent a lengthy chapter seeking to reconcile what the Bible says about assurance of salvation with the warnings given about the danger of losing our salvation. That would all make more sense if we understood more clearly that salvation is a *process* rather than an *event* and that it takes place in three clearly defined stages. Realising that should make it all much clearer.

Let me therefore go back a stage and explain more fully the three different words which are used for the three stages in the process of salvation. If you understand these three words clearly, and remember the distinctions between them, then you will be better able to understand how the Bible can both reassure us and warn us at the same time.

When the Bible uses the words '*salvation*' or '*saved*' it could be referring to any one of these three stages of salvation. We therefore need to know which of them is being referred to at any given time or in a particular verse.

Stage one of salvation - *"justification"*

Justification takes place in an instant at the very beginning of our Christian life. That is the point at which we are forgiven and born again. At that moment we are reclassified and viewed differently by God. We are suddenly deemed, or considered, to be completely righteous in God's eyes.

It means that in God's eyes, at that instant, all our sin is transferred on to Jesus Christ and all His righteousness is immediately transferred to us. God then chooses to view us as if we were as sinless and righteous as Jesus, even though, in the way we live, we clearly are not.

All of this takes place instantaneously at the moment of our conversion. Justification is not something that we have to work at or develop. It does not depend on our own merit or achievements. It is purely a free gift through God's grace and mercy, based on our sincere faith in the Lord Jesus Christ and on repenting genuinely. Most of the time, when people refer to salvation, they actually mean *justification*. It is the first stage of salvation, which is the basis for forgiveness and for receiving eternal life.

Stage two of salvation - *"sanctification"*

Sanctification means the long, slow process of us actually being made more holy and less sinful *in practice*. It begins at the point when we are justified and forgiven. It then continues until we die. Sanctification is very different from justification. Sanctification means the gradual and difficult process whereby we are *"sandpapered"* by the Holy Spirit over many years.

He does so to remove the sharp edges and corners from our characters and to *change the way that we think, speak and act.* The Holy Spirit will work patiently over decades to clean up our thoughts, language, habits and attitudes. His aim is to reduce our selfishness, pride, dishonesty, thoughtlessness, cruelty etc. It is basically what we mean when we speak of being turned from a new convert into a disciple.

You can't stay a new convert all your life. You must either go forward or fall away. The Holy Spirit is the member of the Trinity who mainly looks after this process of sanctifying you. That is yet another reason why it is so essential for us to receive the Holy Spirit. In other words, the Holy Spirit works on us as a trainer might work with an apprentice gymnast or ballerina to develop them from a raw recruit into a professional.

He has been doing that in my life now since 1981. The job is far from complete. I still have a long way to go to reduce the sinfulness, selfishness and immaturity that I display in my dealings with God and other people. Nevertheless, I can say this: I am further ahead than I was all those years ago.

Another word for this process of sanctification is "*maturing*". It goes on until the day we die. There are many elderly believers in their seventies and eighties who have been walking with the Lord as His disciples for perhaps 60 or 70 years. During that time the Holy Spirit has been "sandpapering" or refining their characters and changing them to be more and more like Jesus.

Some of them have a quality of godliness in their lives which is extraordinary. When an **un**believer becomes old they generally become more cranky, opinionated, unhappy, cantankerous, argumentative, selfish and impatient. However there are some really genuine elderly Christians in their retirement years who are the opposite.

They have been mellowed, refined and matured and have a serenity in their lives. They have such peacefulness, gentleness, self-control and patience that it makes them stand out. They are like works of art that God has been patiently dabbing at with His paint brush for decades. Eventually they reach a place where they remind you of Jesus.

Another way of putting it is that sanctification involves resisting, and refusing to gratify, the desires of our flesh or sinful nature. Instead, we grow in the "fruit of the Spirit". Our sinful nature produces a horrible kind of fruit, but the Holy Spirit produces a very different kind. Let's look first at what our sinful flesh nature produces:

The acts of the flesh

16 So I say, walk by the Spirit, and you will not gratify the desires of the flesh. 17
For the flesh desires what is contrary to the Spirit, and the Spirit what is
contrary to the flesh. They are in conflict with each other, so that you are not to
do whatever you want. 18 But if you are led by the Spirit, you are not under the
law. 19 The acts of the flesh are obvious: sexual immorality, impurity and
debauchery; 20 idolatry and witchcraft; hatred, discord, jealousy, fits of rage,
selfish ambition, dissensions, factions 21 and envy; drunkenness, orgies, and the
like. I warn you, as I did before, that those who live like this will not inherit the
kingdom of God.

Galatians 5:16-21 (NIV)

Let's now look at what the Holy Spirit can produce in us, if we allow Him to do so:

The fruit of the Spirit

22 But the fruit of the Spirit is love, joy, peace, forbearance, kindness, goodness,
faithfulness, 23 gentleness and self-control. Against such things there is no law.
24 Those who belong to Christ Jesus have crucified the flesh with its passions
and desires. 25 Since we live by the Spirit, let us keep in step with the Spirit.

Galatians 5:22-25 (NIV)

We saw above the dreadful things we do when we operate in accordance with our sinful fleshly nature. However, with the help of the Holy Spirit, as we grow in holiness, we can see very different fruit growing out of our lives. The production of that kind of fruit in our characters is what sanctification is really all about.

Remember the series of verses we looked at in the previous chapter about 'fruit'. We saw that God is very concerned indeed to look at the kind of fruit our life is producing. Is it the kind of fruit that comes from a self-centred life devoted to indulging ourselves and gratifying our flesh nature? Or is it the fruit of the Spirit and a steadily increasing number of good works done for God? Do we love others, serve the poor and needy and reach out to those around us who are lost and need the Gospel?

Those things are the kind of fruit which God is looking for. They will demonstrate that we really are genuine Christians. We now see the huge difference between sanctification and justification. Justification takes place in an instant and is not based on effort or achievement. It is based exclusively upon the grace and mercy of God, not on our own merit.

Conversely, sanctification is a process that takes decades and it does partly depend on us. It requires our effort, and a willingness to change. It also involves determination to keep on repenting and to keep on turning away from particular sins, habits and patterns of thinking. It is something that steadily develops as we continue to be disciples of Jesus over the years and decades.

Continuing as a disciple

Our discipleship, i.e. our walk with God, can stop. We can fall away if we are not faithful or if we deny or abandon Jesus. Consider this intriguing verse where the apostle Peter is referred to:

But go, tell his disciples and Peter, 'He is going ahead of you into Galilee. There you will see him, just as he told you.' "

Mark 16:7 (NIV)

I have added the underlining above. Few people notice that Peter is not included among the disciples at that point. It is immediately after the resurrection, and is only a few days since Peter, while afraid for his life, denied three times that he even knew Jesus. This is a controversial point and we can't be dogmatic either way, because the Bible doesn't say anything explicitly.

However, it seems that that denial altered Peter's status. He presumably still believed in God, and probably in Jesus, but was he still saved? Would he have gone to Heaven, if he had died that day? I don't know, but I suspect possibly not. At the very least, he was no longer classified as being Jesus' *disciple*. Had he not repented and come back to Jesus, it seems likely to me that Peter could eventually have ended up like Judas.

Judas went to Hell when he died, despite having been an apostle for three and a half years, (though never a genuine believer). Remember what Jesus had said earlier on this very point. He emphasised the need for us to continue in His Word in order to be classed as being His disciple:

So Jesus was saying to those Jews who had believed Him, "If you continue in My word, then you are truly disciples of Mine;

John 8:31 (NASB)

Following his threefold denial of Jesus, it would seem that Peter was no longer viewed as being a disciple. However, he was restored as a disciple shortly afterwards. This occurred when Jesus asked him three times *'Do you love me?'*

It would seem that Peter then became a disciple again and he recommitted himself to Jesus. From then on, he remained loyal and he never again denied knowing Him. In fact he ended up being executed because of his ministry and his refusal to stop telling people about Jesus.

However, although he was reinstated as a disciple and never again denied or betrayed Jesus, Peter continued to make mistakes, just as we all do. He misjudged situations, made errors and even allowed himself to be intimidated by people. On one occasion apostle Paul had to publicly correct Peter when he made a major error:

11When Peter came to Antioch, I opposed him to his face, because he was clearly in the wrong. 12Before certain men came from James, he used to eat with the Gentiles. But when they arrived, he began to draw back and separate himself from the Gentiles because he was afraid of those who belonged to the circumcision group. 13The other Jews joined him in his hypocrisy, so that by their hypocrisy even Barnabas was led astray. 14When I saw that they were not acting in line with the truth of the gospel, I said to Peter in front of them all, "You are a Jew, yet you live like a Gentile and not like a Jew. How is it, then, that you force Gentiles to follow Jewish customs?

Galatians 2:11-14 (NIV)

What if we make mistakes or have failures?

Peter realised that he was wrong on this point about dealing with Gentiles and that Paul was right. So Peter altered his approach. However, this error by Peter did not cause God to stop viewing Peter as being a disciple. Nor did Peter lose his salvation over it. He was just wrong, as we all are from time to time. That's the difference: denying or turning our back on Jesus can lose us our salvation.

In doing those things we could throw our salvation away. However, merely making mistakes, not knowing things, being wrong, or even *doing* wrong, do not necessarily have that result. These are quite different concepts, with very different outcomes.

We do not lose our forgiveness or even our status as disciples, every time we sin or mess things up or fail. However, we can lose our *future rewards* at the Judgment Seat of Christ if we live unworthily of Jesus or disobey Him.

It may also affect the *role* we are given in the 1000 year reign of Jesus when He returns to the earth. (See Book Four in this series for more details of the Judgment for Christians and of what will occur when Jesus returns to reign on the earth). So, what we do and how we live matters enormously. It will all be dealt with one day when we are judged. Hopefully that will be at the Judgment Seat of Christ. However, if we go so far as to fall away, then it would be dealt with at the Great White Throne. God forbid that that should ever happen to you.

Being a genuine disciple is the means by which we gradually change and learn how to love and obey Jesus. So, being a loyal and committed disciple is the key to becoming sanctified and mature. It is also the key to the rewards we will one day get, or not get, at the Judgment Seat of Christ. If we continue to grow in sanctification we will remain as His followers to the end and stay on "the Way".

If we aren't being sanctified we will eventually drift off, grow cold and fall away. So, sanctification has a major bearing on whether you *continue* as a Christian. You can't just stand still. You must either go forward by being sanctified, or go backwards by not being. There is no other choice and no middle ground.

What happens if we drift away from Jesus and cease to follow Him?

If we go too far in wandering away from Jesus or if we deny Him, despise Him or take Him for granted, then a point may be reached where our name is erased or blotted out of the book of life. I don't know where that specific point is, or when another person has reached it. I know very little about where other people stand with God.

What I do believe is that if a person continues to disregard God and has no fear of Him or respect for Him, such that they go cold and allow their hearts to grow hard and leathery, then they could eventually lose everything. It is not just their reward, that is at stake, but eternal life as well. Remember that the writer to the Hebrews says that without sanctification no one will see the Lord:

Pursue peace with all men, and the sanctification without which no one will see the Lord.

Hebrews 12:14 (NASB)

Look also at what Jesus Himself says in the book of Revelation as He addresses the church at Sardis and urges them to wake up and repent:

'He who overcomes will thus be clothed in white garments; and I will not erase his name from the book of life, and I will confess his name before My Father and before His angels.

Revelation 3:5 (NASB)

Note that in that verse Jesus is speaking to a particular local church. The implication of His words is that if they will not repent and change their ways then He will erase their names from the book of life. They would then be lost. If not, then His statement would be meaningless. Therefore, knowing those facts, we have all the more reason to seek for sanctification so that we can grow continually in holiness.

It is not that we are justified by this process. That has already been done. However, the process of growing in holiness, i.e. being sanctified, is what helps to keep us firmly rooted in Jesus Christ, honouring Him and fearing Him. It has a crucial part to play, as does the fear of the Lord, in keeping us from that complacency that can cause us to throw our own salvation away.

If justification is by faith alone, what about sanctification? Is that by faith alone as well?

Justification certainly is by God's grace, through faith alone. However, sanctification is different. It operates differently and it is achieved differently. Sanctification is, effectively a *'joint venture'* between us and the Holy Spirit. We seek to become sanctified and He helps us to do so. It is not achieved solely by the Holy Spirit and it is not achieved solely by faith either.

It also requires obedience, effort, perseverance, determination, passion and commitment. None of those things are needed in relation to justification. That is given to us freely when we truly repent and believe (trust) in Jesus Christ. So, sanctification requires faith, but it is not achieved by faith alone. It also requires our input. We have to choose wisely, make sacrifices and walk in obedience over many years.

If it did all depend solely upon our faith in Jesus and on what His death on the cross achieved for us, then what would be the purpose of the Judgment Seat of Christ? If *all* that Jesus was to do when we stand before Him as our Judge at the Judgment Seat of Christ was to say *"I view you as having all of my own righteousness imputed to you,"* what would be the basis for Him to praise, rebuke or reward any of us?

We would all surely be equal if it worked that way? We would all simply have His imputed righteousness and nothing more. If so, we'd all be identical. So, that is not the basis for the Judgment Seat of Christ. The confusion comes from mixing up these two entirely separate judgments:

a) **the Great White Throne judgment** - we escape this, i.e. avoid even being present at it, solely on the basis of our having been *justified*. That is because we are deemed to have all of Jesus' righteousness, imputed to us. Thus *real* Christians will not be at that judgment. Its purpose is to punish all those who have sinned and who have never put their trust in Jesus, or have not remained faithful to Him.

b) **the Judgment Seat of Christ** - This is for all genuine Christians. It is intended to evaluate the *fruit* produced by our lives and to see what we *achieved* with the talents and opportunities that we were given (our stewardship). It will involve examining our innermost motives and intentions, as well as looking at our actions. We will all come out with different 'scores' or assessments which are unique to ourselves.

   Those assessments will also be perfectly weighted and discounted to reflect our precise individual circumstances, age, talents, gifts, opportunities, abilities, knowledge, background, etc, plus the nature and extent of the opposition we faced. Only God is clever enough to make a judgment which requires so many factors and variables to be considered. (See Book Four for a fuller discussion of the Judgment Seat of Christ.)

So, though justification is by faith alone, sanctification *is not* by faith alone.

Stage three of salvation - *"glorification"*

This is the final stage of the overall salvation process. As with justification, this also happens in an instant. It occurs after we have died (for most of us). However, those of us who are alive on the earth at the point of the rapture, will be carried up to Heaven without ever having died. But, if we have died prior to the rapture, then our physical bodies will be raised from their graves and we will be transformed and given a new resurrection body.

If, however, we are alive at the point of the rapture (when Jesus comes to take away His Church) then we will still be instantly transformed and given our glorified resurrection bodies, just like those people who have been raised from their graves.

So, every real Christian, whether alive or dead, will then receive a new resurrection body. That resurrection body is eternal and immune from death, illness, injury or decay. Therefore after we have died, (or for some, at the point of the rapture when they are carried up into Heaven whilst still alive) we will be instantly transformed into the glorified condition that we will remain in for eternity. We will then have a perfect resurrection body. It will never grow old, sick or tired and will never die.

But, in addition to that glorified resurrection body, we will also be given a new and perfect *nature.* We will no longer have a sin nature or any tendency to sin at all. At that time (but not before) we will become perfectly sinless, like Jesus. So, this final stage, glorification, needs to be clearly distinguished from both justification and sanctification.

Glorification is an instantaneous event by which we are transformed. It involves not just *"deemed"* or *"imputed"* righteousness. It is *real and actual righteousness.* We will be truly different and will never sin again. Conversely, as we are now, we sin every day even though, if we are Christians, God chooses to view us as if we had all the righteousness of Jesus. However, when we are glorified it will no longer be *"as if"* we were righteous and sinless.

We will *actually be sinless in the way we think, speak and act.* Glorification does not depend on us or on anything we do. It is something that God will do for us miraculously, through His power. It is the final stage of that process of our salvation. It brings to an end the long process of sanctification (sandpapering) that we have discussed above.

Conclusion

So, of these three concepts the first and the last, justification, and glorification, are not dependent on our own efforts. They each happen in an instant. They are both solely dependent upon God. He does it for us, through His grace.

The only part of our salvation that we can contribute to by our own effort is the long process of sanctification while we live on this earth as disciples. Sanctification is not what gives us forgiveness or eternal life, but it is one of the main things that keeps us following Jesus and being faithful to Him.

It may help to think of these three aspects of salvation, i.e. justification, sanctification and glorification, as being the three 'tenses' of salvation. They correspond to the past, present and future tenses of salvation.

So, we can say *"I have been saved "*(justified); *"I am being saved"* (sanctified); and *"I will be saved"* (glorified). All three statements are correct, and the Bible uses the word "saved" in all three of these contexts.

CHAPTER 23

BECOMING A DISCIPLE OF JESUS CHRIST - SOME INTRODUCTORY POINTS

[6] So then, just as you received Christ Jesus as Lord, continue to live your lives in him, [7] rooted and built up in him, strengthened in the faith as you were taught, and overflowing with thankfulness.

Colossians 2:6-7 (NIV)

[34]And He summoned the crowd with His disciples, and said to them, "If anyone wishes to come after Me, he must deny himself, and take up his cross and follow Me. [35]"For whoever wishes to save his life will lose it, but whoever loses his life for My sake and the Gospel's will save it. [36]"For what does it profit a man to gain the whole world, and forfeit his soul? [37]"For what will a man give in exchange for his soul?

Mark 8:34-37 (NASB)

Another neglected and unfashionable aspect of Christianity is the process of becoming a *"disciple"*. Much of modern Western evangelism, (i.e. telling people about the Gospel), consists of little more than inviting you to *"make a decision for Christ"* and to *"invite Jesus Christ into your heart"*. These modern, man-made phrases are not found anywhere in the Bible.

However, having done these things, many people are then immediately urged to regard themselves as Christians, and not to doubt that they are saved. But they may not be. To make it even worse, very often such people are not told that they need to become disciples. They are led to believe that the job is finished at conversion. In fact, it has only just begun. Jesus is calling us to become not just converts, but disciples.

He also wants us to continue as disciples, growing and maturing and bearing fruit until the day we die. A disciple is someone who follows in the footsteps of another person in order to become like them. Therefore a disciple of Jesus is someone who diligently follows Jesus Christ with a view to becoming like Him.

In Old Testament Judaism, Rabbis would travel around Israel and young men would attach themselves to them by literally following them on foot. They would then learn from that Rabbi as he travelled the country teaching and preaching. They would also help the Rabbi and gain knowledge of the Scriptures. They would also learn how to teach and preach, plus many other practical skills, by following, watching and imitating.

God is looking for people who are totally committed

Becoming a real Christian is similar. It must involve a serious and genuine commitment to become a devoted disciple or follower of Jesus Christ, in every part of our lives. We cannot be just a fan or spectator. When we make that decision to follow Jesus we need to do so in the way that He meant us to. Jesus wants us to do far more than simply *agree* with Him or even believe in Him. He also wants us to hand our entire lives over to Him and to follow after Him with total commitment:

When they had brought their boats to land, they left everything and followed Him.

Luke 5:11 (NASB)

For the eyes of the LORD range throughout the earth to strengthen those whose hearts are fully committed to him

2 Chronicles 16:9 (NIV)

That type of commitment is what we need if we are to get mature and become sanctified. And it is largely on the basis of our commitment that we can qualify to be rewarded by Him at the Judgment Seat of Christ. It is also how we stay loyal to Jesus and continue as His disciples. God is looking for men and women that He can rely on and who will, if necessary, stand alone and obey God even when times are hard and dangerous. But such people are very rare:

"I searched for a man among them who would build up the wall and stand in the gap before Me for the land, so that I would not destroy it; but I found no one.

Ezekiel 22:30 (NASB)

I am reminded of a famous quotation from D.L. Moody, a 19th century evangelist concerning the rarity of real commitment and the fact that even the most committed believers are not 100% committed:

"The world has yet to see what God can do with, and for, and through, and in, and by, the man who is fully and wholly consecrated to Him. I will do my utmost to be that man".

(D.L. Moody)

I don't suppose that even D.L. Moody quite managed a 100% score in the end but, judging by the extraordinary fruit that his life produced, he did very well. Why don't you accept that challenge in your life? Resolve to do away with anything that distracts you from your central purpose of obeying and following Jesus Christ as His disciple. Bear as much fruit for Him as you possibly can. Let that become your lifetime goal and your central focus. Keep it always at the forefront of your mind.

We are supposed to be following Jesus

We are meant to learn from Jesus and to seek to become like Him. We are then to do the work that He is doing, by joining in alongside Him. Remember that Jesus Christ is not only our Saviour. He is also our Lord. That means that Jesus has a unique status and authority. He has many titles and is many things all at the same time.

He is Divine. He is the Second Person of the Trinity, the Son of God. He is the Word of God. He is the Messiah of Israel. He is the King of Israel. In addition He is the King of the entire earth. There are very many other titles given to Jesus as well. He is the "Prince of Peace", the "Morning Star", the "Son of David", the "Son of Man" (from Daniel chapter seven), and many others.

It is like where a senior aristocrat and member of the royal family has many different titles and ranks. For example, Prince Charles is the Prince of Wales and at the same time he is the Duke of Cornwall. He has many other aristocratic and military titles as well, such as the Earl of Chester, Duke of Rothesay and the Earl of Carrick. Jesus' many titles show that He has the most immense rank and importance. Because of that we are not only to worship Him, but to follow Him, and obey Him.

You will never understand why you need to be His disciple unless you grasp how extraordinarily powerful and important He is as our Creator, Saviour, King and Judge. These magnificent titles and names that Jesus has show how indescribably important He is. One day, everybody who has ever lived will have to bow down to Him, whether they want to or not. You would be better off to do it now, of your own free choice, rather than be forced to do so later.

We are to regard Jesus as our King because that's what He is

We are meant to treat Jesus Christ as a King. He is entitled to our complete loyalty and faithfulness, in the same way that in medieval times a man would show 'fealty' and allegiance to an earthly king. Jesus is not a democratically elected politician. He is the King as of right. Moreover He is the King of kings, Lord of lords and Name above all names. He has been appointed to that unique position on the basis of merit by God the Father.

There is nobody higher than Him. He also shares the throne of God the Father in Heaven and He rules over the whole universe. Moreover, when He returns to the earth He will be the King of the earth and will sit on King David's throne. We are not discussing a politician that we can vote in and vote out. Jesus is unique and worthy of the utmost respect, reverence and awe.

A more accurate picture of what Jesus is really like

However, for a fuller picture of what Jesus is like, look at these descriptions of Him in the book of Daniel and then in the book of Revelation. These show us a glimpse of Him as He really is. This is how we will one day know Him, when He is seen in His full glory. Once these facts become real to us we will be better able to follow Jesus in the way we should:

13 "In my vision at night I looked, and there before me was one like a son of
man, coming with the clouds of Heaven. He approached the Ancient of Days
and was led into his presence. 14 He was given authority, glory and sovereign
power; all peoples, nations and men of every language worshiped him. His dominion is an everlasting dominion that will not pass away, and his kingdom is one that will never be destroyed.

Daniel 7:13-14(NIV)

11 I saw Heaven standing open and there before me was a white horse, whose
rider is called Faithful and True. With justice he judges and makes war. 12 His
eyes are like blazing fire, and on his head are many crowns. He has a name
written on him that no one knows but he himself. 13 He is dressed in a robe dipped
in blood, and his name is the Word of God. 14 The armies of Heaven were
following him, riding on white horses and dressed in fine linen, white and clean.
15 Out of his mouth comes a sharp sword with which to strike down the nations.
"He will rule them with an iron sceptre." He treads the winepress of the fury of
the wrath of God Almighty. 16 On his robe and on his thigh he has this name
written KING OF KINGS AND LORD OF LORDS.

Revelation 19:11-16 (NIV)

However, now let us go to the other end of the spectrum and consider this quite different description of Jesus Christ. This next passage reveals how far He humbled Himself when He came to the earth for the first time as a man. He put aside all of His glory and majesty. Instead, He went to the very lowest depths in order to save us. It was that willingness on His part to humble Himself that led to God exalting Him to the very highest place:

5 Your attitude should be the same as that of Christ Jesus:
6 Who, being in very nature God,
did not consider equality with God something to be grasped,
7 but made himself nothing,
taking the very nature of a servant,
being made in human likeness.
8 And being found in appearance as a man,
he humbled himself
and became obedient to death—
even death on a cross!

[9]Therefore God exalted him to the highest place
and gave him the name that is above every name,
[10]that at the name of Jesus every knee should bow,
in Heaven and on earth and under the earth,
[11]and every tongue confess that Jesus Christ is Lord,
to the glory of God the Father.

Philippians 2:5-11 (NIV)

Jesus Christ commands us to spend the rest of our lives following Him, doing His will, and serving Him with complete loyalty. That is a huge privilege, with many benefits, but it is also a duty. He wants us to lay aside every other competing aim or goal and put Him first above everything else:

[24]Then Jesus said to His disciples, "If anyone wishes to come after Me, he must
deny himself, and take up his cross and follow Me. [25]"For whoever wishes to
save his life will lose it; but whoever loses his life for My sake will find it. [26]"For
what will it profit a man if he gains the whole world and forfeits his soul? Or what will a man give in exchange for his soul?

Matthew 16:24-26 (NASB)

[3]By this we know that we have come to know Him, if we keep His
commandments. [4]The one who says, "I have come to know Him," and does not
keep His commandments, is a liar, and the truth is not in him; [5]but whoever
keeps His word, in him the love of God has truly been perfected. By this we know
that we are in Him: [6]the one who says he abides in Him ought himself to walk
in the same manner as He walked.

1 John 2:3-6 (NASB)

But your hearts must be fully committed to the LORD our God, to live by his decrees and obey his commands, as at this time."

1 Kings 8:61 (NIV)

So, being a disciple means putting Him above our family, job, children, wife, country, money and possessions. He must take first place and He must be Lord of your life. He does not put that to you as a suggestion. It is an emphatic command, which He is fully entitled to make. That is what discipleship is really about. It means beginning to see Him as He truly is and to follow Him with total devotion in a way that reflects who He is.

This is a far cry from what much of modern Western Christianity is about. Most of it is dismally lukewarm and half-hearted. There is little or no concept of Jesus Christ being our King. If we are not wholehearted about obeying Jesus, then we will inevitably end up doing wrong and displeasing Him. That is how it works. If we set our hearts to obey and follow Jesus we will grow. If not, we will degenerate:

He did evil because he had not set his heart on seeking the LORD.
2 Chronicles 12:14 (NIV)

People often say words to the effect of *"By all means practice your religion, but don't take it too seriously"*. It has become a cultural expectation in Britain that people should keep quiet and be "*moderate*" and private about their faith and not go over the top about it or to discuss it openly. We are expected to keep our relationship with Jesus strictly to ourselves, as if He was something to be ashamed of. Above all, we are frowned upon if we get excited about Him. These are pressures which British culture puts on us. But that attitude is not what Jesus wants. He wants us to be passionate about Him and totally loyal.

We must not be ashamed of the Name of Jesus

Also, have you noticed that it is the name of Jesus specifically which unbelievers do not like. Even Christians feel squeamish about using the name of Jesus in front of others. People will fairly happily say the word "God", but not "Jesus". That is a cultural pressure, but we must refuse to be hemmed in by it. We must resolve to speak His name without embarrassment or shame, whoever we are with, or wherever we are.

In Great Britain it is culturally acceptable to show passion about a football team, but not about following Jesus. That may be our culture, but it's still wrong. We need to disobey the pressures of our culture and obey Jesus instead. Let Ezra be your model. Make it your aim to learn God's Word with dedication and to put it into practice in your life:

For Ezra had devoted himself to the study and observance of the Law of the LORD, and to teaching its decrees and laws in Israel.
Ezra 7:10 (NIV)

The cost of being a genuine disciple - trouble, hardship, persecution and suffering

Let us look now at a long list of passages from the Bible where Jesus, Paul, Peter and John talk frankly about the committed and faithful way in which Jesus wants us to follow Him. We need to be willing to endure hardship, abuse, persecution and suffering for the sake of His name. Consider how different this type of commitment is from the limp and passive way in which most churches now operate in the West:

11"Blessed are you when people insult you, persecute you and falsely say all
kinds of evil against you because of me. 12Rejoice and be glad, because great is

your reward in Heaven, for in the same way they persecuted the prophets who were before you.

Matthew 5:11-12 (NIV)

"No one can serve two masters. Either he will hate the one and love the other, or he will be devoted to the one and despise the other. You cannot serve both God and Money.

Matthew 6:24(NIV)

"Then you will be handed over to be persecuted and put to death, and you will be hated by all nations because of me.

Matthew 24: 9 (NIV)

[7]But whatever was to my profit I now consider loss for the sake of Christ. [8]What is more, I consider everything a loss compared to the surpassing greatness of knowing Christ Jesus my Lord, for whose sake I have lost all things. I consider them rubbish, that I may gain Christ

Philippians 3:7-8 (NIV)

[12]In fact, everyone who wants to live a godly life in Christ Jesus will be persecuted, [13]while evil men and impostors will go from bad to worse, deceiving and being deceived.

2 Timothy 3:12-13 (NIV)

For indeed when we were with you, we kept telling you in advance that we were going to suffer affliction; and so it came to pass, as you know.

1 Thessalonians 3:4 (NASB)

[12]Dear friends, do not be surprised at the painful trial you are suffering, as though something strange were happening to you. [13]But rejoice that you participate in the sufferings of Christ, so that you may be overjoyed when his glory is revealed. [14]If you are insulted because of the name of Christ, you are blessed, for the Spirit of glory and of God rests on you.

1 Peter 4:12-14 (NIV)

This final verse is spoken by Jesus Himself to the lukewarm, half-hearted church at Laodicea:

[15]I know your deeds, that you are neither cold nor hot. I wish you were either one or the other! [16]So, because you are lukewarm—neither hot nor cold—I am about to spit you out of my mouth.

Revelation 3:15-16 (NIV)

I have included a long list of passages about the hardships and cost of discipleship. I could actually have put in many more verses. I included so many because I wanted to demonstrate, beyond all doubt, that this is a consistent biblical theme. I am not exaggerating or taking anything out of context.

We need to therefore follow and obey Jesus with all our heart, not passively or with limits or conditions. This will lead us into suffering, persecution, and maybe even death, for Him and for the sake of His Name. Even so, we must not be ashamed of Him or keep Him hidden out of view.

We must be openly identified with Jesus, even if it costs us. We are bound to attract ridicule, abuse and persecution if we openly follow Him in the way we should. But He commands us to do so, and it is worth it. Therefore, be willing to swim in the opposite direction from the people around you.

Be willing to give up your ambitions, your independence and your comforts to follow Him and be His disciple. You will be hated, insulted and persecuted. But you will also gain from it and you will be rewarded for it eternally. Look at this inspiring comment made by a man called Jim Elliot, who was urging people to give their whole lives to God's service:

"He is no fool who gives what he cannot keep to gain what he cannot lose" - Jim Elliot,

The martyred American missionary, Jim Elliot, was killed at the age of 28 by the Auca Indians in South America to whom he brought the Gospel. He was obedient and he paid the ultimate price. So have millions of other martyrs over the centuries, and especially in our own century.

Indeed, more Christians are having to die for their faith today than ever before. When Jesus spoke of picking up your cross daily and following Him He meant that the decision to become His disciple was potentially a life or death issue. It may well mean giving up your life, quite literally.

That is happening now to Christians all over the world, especially in Islamic countries. At the very least, it means the loss of comfort, privileges and the rulership of our own lives. That's what real discipleship means. There is no other way. The only question is whether you are willing to pay that price. If you are not, and you want a "nicer," more moderate Christianity, which does not involve such intense commitment, then how can you say you are His disciple?

You would be your own disciple, following your own path. We will never be able to face the ultimate test and be willing to be martyred for Jesus if we have not first learned how to pass the hundreds of little tests that we face along the way.

If we can't cope with being criticised or laughed at for His sake, then how can we realistically expect to face death for Him? Likewise, if we can't sacrifice our time or our money for His sake, how can we expect to pass the test of martyrdom?

Therefore we must learn how to be faithful, and how to show courage and endurance. We do so by passing all the small, seemingly insignificant tests along the way. That's why they matter so much. They are your chance to train and to get ready for the big test that may, one day, come to you if you follow Jesus. That's one reason why it makes sense to be thankful when we are persecuted. Opposition strengthens us and gets us ready to face those bigger tests.

Being a committed and diligent disciple has a huge bearing on how we will fare at the Judgment Seat of Christ. It will determine whether Jesus greets us there with approval and rewards, or with rebuke and disapproval. I want His approval and reward very much indeed. I want God to help me now to be willing to pay whatever price is needed in order to please Him, honour Him and be true to Him:

[24]Do you not know that in a race all the runners run, but only one gets the prize? Run in such a way as to get the prize. [25]Everyone who competes in the games goes into strict training. They do it to get a crown that will not last; but we do it to get a crown that will last forever. [26]Therefore I do not run like a man running aimlessly; I do not fight like a man beating the air. [27]No, I beat my body and make it my slave so that after I have preached to others, I myself will not be disqualified for the prize.

1 Corinthians 9:24-27 (NIV)

This final chapter is meant to be a brief introduction to the concept of discipleship, i.e. what it is, what it can involve and why it matters. I will develop these themes much more fully in the remaining books in the Real Christianity series. They are all about different aspects of how you can seek to grow in Christian maturity, overcome obstacles and become an effective disciple.

If you have genuinely repented and believed in Jesus, then that is what makes you into a Christian. However, you shouldn't just stop there. You have to grow and go forward or else you will inevitably go backwards, or *"backslide"*. You can't stand still as a Christian. It's impossible. Moreover, if standing still is all that you want, then it raises serious questions about your motives and the genuineness of your belief in Jesus in the first place.

How can you say that you believe Jesus is Lord, but not want Him to be the Lord of your life or to follow, obey, and stand up for Him? At the very least, if you don't want to pay the price and face the pressure and opposition that comes from following Jesus, then it calls into question whether you truly believe in Him and in what He says.

Seize every opportunity that God offers you to serve Him and to grow. The following books in this series are intended to help you to see many of the pitfalls and hazards we will face in our life as a disciple. I aim to show how we can best avoid such problems, become more alert, discerning and wise, and learn how to be an 'overcomer'.

God wants you to win the battles you are going to face and to become a successful, productive, faithful disciple of Jesus Christ. He wants you to bear a lot of fruit so that He can reward you. Conversely, the Devil wants you to fail, to be ineffective, and to bear little or no fruit.

How well you do in each of those battles in your life is largely down to you. It will be decided by the approach you choose to take, the decisions you make and the habits you develop in the years ahead. So, don't even consider stopping at the point of becoming a new convert. Go on and gladly accept everything God has to offer you. Take your place as an active follower of Jesus. Aim to make a difference in the world and, one day, to hear Him say to you:

"Well done, good and faithful servant".

Real Christianity Book 2

Growing in the character of a disciple

Sean Kehoe

Book 2 in the Real Christianity series looks at what happens next, after we become a Christian, and at how we can grow into mature disciples. That involves an ongoing process of change, whereby we are meant to become more and more like Jesus Christ in our character, attitudes and conduct. Another word for this process is 'sanctification', such that we develop lives of obedience, self-sacrifice, humility and discipline. Indeed, the very word 'disciple' has the same root meaning as discipline, because it involves following and obeying Jesus in our daily lives, even when it is very hard to do so. Christian character cannot be formed overnight. It is a fruit which has to be grown and which takes years, or even decades, to develop. This book introduces you to some of the key things that are needed to bring about that growth, but it is very honest about how costly and difficult it is going to be.

The book also looks at four much neglected subjects which are vital if we are to become effective disciples. These are thankfulness, faithfulness, truthfulness and forgiving others. Forgiveness, in particular, is a severely misunderstood subject. The book therefore spends time explaining what forgiveness doesn't mean, and doesn't involve, as well as what it does. That is needed because many people have such a garbled, inaccurate definition of it that they find forgiving others impossible. A proper grasp of all these issues will give you a much stronger start in the Christian life. However, even if you began many years ago, they will now help you to progress farther and faster as a disciple.

All of the books in this series, plus audio MP3s, can be ordered online from **www.realchristianity.com**.

Real Christianity **Book 3**

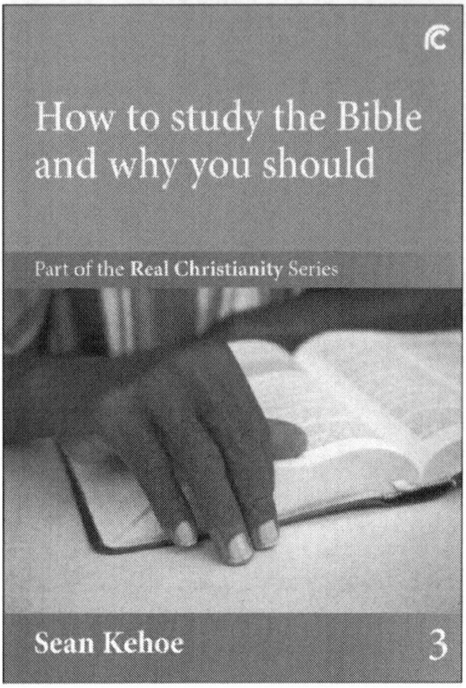

How to study the Bible and why you should

Sean Kehoe

Book 3 in the Real Christianity series explains how to study the Bible more effectively. Even in Evangelical and Pentecostal churches, which were once known for their devotion to God's Word, the Bible is now widely neglected, misunderstood and even ignored. To read the Bible properly does require some skill but, more importantly, that you approach it diligently and with the right heart attitude and method. Many of us find it difficult because nobody has shown us how. Even worse, some have been taught wrong ways, which then handicap them. This book looks at the right way to interpret the Bible, known as the 'golden rule'. That is to take the Bible literally unless the words used, or the context, plainly indicate that we should do otherwise, such as where a figure of speech is used.

It also looks at the main errors in people's thinking, which undermine faith and promote unbelief, namely 'scepticism', 'liberalism' and 'allegorism' or the 'allegorical approach'. The author has a very high view of Scripture and would urge you to take it literally and seriously, with a determination to understand it, act upon it, and be changed by it. The Bible is utterly unique. It is God's Word to us. No equivalent book has ever been, or ever will be, written. The author also advises on Bible translations, recommending those which take a literal 'word for word' approach, rather than 'dynamic equivalence', or even paraphrasing, which often take liberties with God's Word. He is convinced that every determined person, provided they can read and write, is able to gain a balanced understanding of the whole Bible for themselves, whoever they are, and regardless of ability or education

All of the books in this series, plus audio MP3s, can be ordered online from **www.realchristianity.com.**

Real Christianity Book 4

The Judgment Seat of Christ

Sean Kehoe

Book 4 in the Real Christianity series looks closely at a subject which most churches ignore and which is, therefore, very little known or understood. It is the judgment which awaits Christians, at the 'Judgment Seat of Christ'. On that momentous day our whole lives, from conversion onwards, will be evaluated in a face to face meeting with Jesus Christ Himself. He will either reward and congratulate us, or rebuke us and leave us empty handed. N.B. This is not to be confused with the Great White Throne judgment, for the unsaved, at which they will be condemned. One would imagine that this hugely important issue would be taught thoroughly and be a regular topic of conversation. Yet it is rarely even mentioned in most churches.

The author explains what it is and why it matters. In particular, he focuses on what each of us can do now to improve Jesus' assessment of us and to increase the rewards, and praise, which He gives us on that Day. The author also looks very closely at the criteria for this judgment, and identifies at least 30 different issues on which we will be assessed. If we address these things now, while we have time to change, we can alter the outcome of that judgment. We are meant to see life as a test, and to be motivated by the prospect of rewards. Indeed, that is why Jesus Himself told us about them and urged us to seek for them. So, contrary to what many imagine, we are actually supposed to seek for rewards, and also for a high place in Jesus' Millennial Kingdom and in the eternal state thereafter.

All of the books in this series, plus audio MP3s, can be ordered online from **www.realchristianity.com**.

Real Christianity **Book 5**

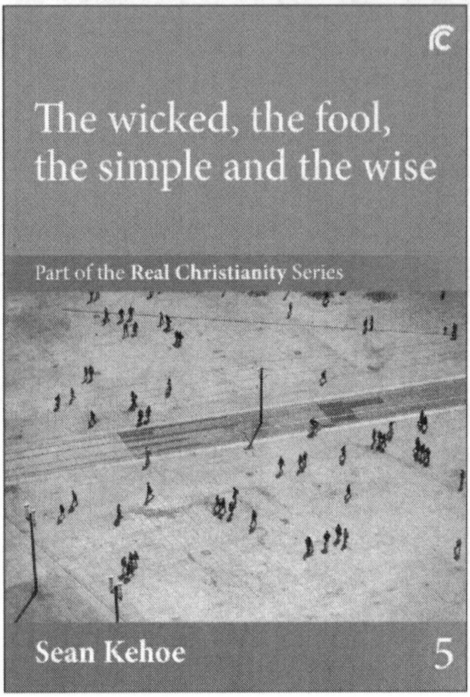

The wicked, the fool, the simple and the wise

Sean Kehoe

Book 5 in the Real Christianity series looks at the four broad character types in the Bible - the wicked, the fool, the simple (or naïve) and the wise. God says a lot about all of these, and urges us to become wise. Yet, we hear very little about it in most churches. If people think about this at all, they tend to take it for granted that they are wise. But that is a problem, because God thinks very few people are wise, even within churches, and that most Christians are actually simple, or naïve. So, the author's first task is a delicate one. It is to convince you that you probably aren't wise. Then he seeks to explain why you should seek to become wise and how that can be achieved, by diligent study of the whole Bible and by spending time with those who are wise, or at least wiser than you.

He also emphasises that wisdom is available to everyone, not just the academically clever or educated. Indeed, they are often the most foolish of all. If you doubt that the pursuit of wisdom is crucial, look at the first eight chapters of Proverbs, in which God makes that same point over and over again. He does so because most of us aren't wise, but desperately need to become so. Admittedly, ceasing to be naïve, or foolish, will require a lot of time, effort, diligent study and a willingness to be brutally honest with ourselves. However, it is truly worth all of that effort. More importantly, it is what God commands us to do, which ought to settle it.

All of the books in this series, plus audio MP3s, can be ordered online from **www.realchristianity.com**.

NOTES

NOTES

NOTES

NOTES

NOTES

NOTES

NOTES

NOTES